NCO Guide

NCO Guide
5th Edition

Revised by
1SG Frank Cox, USA (Ret.)

The *NCO Guide* was preceded by
The Noncom's Guide, written by
LTC Charles O. Kates, USA (Ret.)

STACKPOLE
BOOKS

Copyright © 1995 by Stackpole Books

Published by
STACKPOLE BOOKS
5067 Ritter Road
Mechanicsburg, PA 17055

All photographs courtesy the U.S. Army.
Cover design by Mark B. Olszewski with Tina Marie Hill.
Color photographs of medals by Ken Smith.

5th Edition
Printed in U.S.A.
10   9   8   7   6   5   4   3   2

Library of Congress Cataloging-in-Publication Data

Cox, Frank, 1954–
    NCO Guide.—5th ed. / revised by Frank Cox.
        p.   cm.
    "The NCO guide was preceded by the Noncom's guide, written by LTC
Charles O. Kates, USA (Ret.)."
    Includes index.
    ISBN 0-8117-2563-4 (alk. paper)
    1. United States.   Army—Non-commissioned officer's handbooks.
I. Title.
U123.C68   1995
355.3'38'0973—dc20   95–15388
                                                                                    CIP

In memory of
all who have fallen while serving the nation

THE NCO CREED

No one is more professional than I. I am a Noncommisioned Officer, a leader of soldiers. As a Noncommissioned Officer, I realize that I am a member of a time-honored corps, which is known as "The Backbone of the Army."

I am proud of the Corps of Noncommissioned Officers and will at all times conduct myself so as to bring credit upon the Corps, the Military Service, and my country regardless of the situation in which I find myself. I will not use my grade or position to attain pleasure, profit, or personal safety.

Competence is my watchword. My two basic responsibilities will always be uppermost in my mind—accomplishment of my mission and the welfare of my soldiers. I will strive to remain tactically and technically proficient. I am aware of my role as a Noncommissioned Officer. I will fulfill my responsibilities inherent in that role. All soldiers are entitled to outstanding leadership; I will provide that leadership. I know my soldiers and I will always place their needs above my own. I will communicate consistently with my soldiers and never leave them uninformed. I will be fair and impartial when recommending both rewards and punishment. Officers of my unit will have maximum time to accomplish their duties; they will not have to accomplish mine. I will earn their respect and confidence as well as that of my soldiers. I will be loyal to those with whom I serve, seniors, peers, and subordinates alike. I will exercise initiative by taking appropriate action in the absence of orders. I will not compromise my integrity, nor my moral courage. I will not forget, nor will I allow my comrades to forget, that we are professionals, Noncommissioned Officers, leaders!

Contents

Preface

Consciously or subconsciously, NCOs know that service in the downsized Army equates to a need to remain fully informed about military requirements and trends, as well as individual and unit responsibilities. Fewer soldiers, higher technology, changing threats, mission diversity, deadlier battlefields, tighter standards, higher educational requirements—the related matters go on ad infinitum. How does a hard-charging junior or senior NCO stay ahead of, sort, and use a deluge of information about the many different facets of service?

Informed NCOs become so by using time productively. Among their efforts they read Army regulations, field manuals, military journals, and other official literature to hone their professional edge. They visit libraries and research military and related information products. Army Continuing Education System statistics show that annually thousands spend time studying college texts or using alternative educational resources to pursue career-enhancing college degrees.

The informed also read and use *NCO Guide*. This paperback tool is an educational resource and ready reference to key Army subjects. It draws from education, experience, training, and hundreds of public information sources. The guide begins with discussion of how and why the Army continues to change and ends with how to make the most of a transition from service to civilian life. As a desktop reference, it serves the reader when fellow soldiers have questions about pay, benefits, entitlements, personal appearance, uniforms, insignia, assignments, and personal and professional problems. Readers are also informed about the developmental aspects of soldiering and about fitness, education, promotion, and dozens of other necessary topics. Where it falls short, the guide extends itself through referrals to official and other commercial publications that may contain late-breaking updates.

NCO Guide may be read by opportunistic careerists, but they are not its intended market. It is aimed at dedicated professionals—the corporals, sergeants, first sergeants, and sergeants major who will turn to it when they need self-help guidance or information that will benefit fellow soldiers. The guide is also intended for the general public, so that civilians may better relate to and understand noncommissioned service and the mechanics of developing, maintaining, and sustaining strong defenders of the Constitution.

The fifth edition has been fully revised and expanded to include topics NCOs must understand. It contains new or updated information about the following: leadership counseling, battle-focused training, the Army safety program, personnel and property accountability, master fitness principles, weight control, the Army Physical Fitness Test, the NCO Education System and civilian education, professional reading and writing and multimedia, life insurance, and medical and dental insurance. It also addresses sensitive contemporary issues such as professional ethics, AIDS, discrimination, sexual harassment, and homosexuality.

Readers will also find sections about the military justice system, including military discipline, command authority and soldier rights, nonjudicial punishment, the *Manual for Courts-Martial*, and its Uniform Code of Military Justice. On the flip side, information about awards and decorations is also included. Enclosed are full-color photographs of military awards, including the Medal of Honor, which was posthumously awarded in mid-1994 to two brave senior NCOs, MSG Gary Gordon and SFC Randall Shughart, who were killed in action during Operation Ranger in Somalia.

This edition of *NCO Guide* has reformed content and improved relevancy. Material carried from the fourth to the fifth edition received brevity edits, and all new material was tightly composed and edited to contain less mundane detail, flow more logically, and be more readable and indispensable. It is also more practical and less vulnerable to problems associated with information that changes prior to publication or while in print.

I have expanded my personal copy of *NCO Guide* with marginal notes and have increased its utility by adding plastic index tabs and self-stick notes. I encourage similar treatment of your copy, so that you too may quickly turn to the chapter, section, and subsection entries you need to better understand the profession of the NCO corps.

Frank Cox
1SG, USA (Retired)

Acknowledgments

I am grateful to the following for information or photographs: the staff of *Defense Issues;* Training and Doctrine Command for NCO Education System material; Army and Air Force Exchange Service; the staff of *NCO Journal;* Army Research Institute; the staff of the *Army Veterans Education Guide;* Army Training Support Center; Association of the United States Army; Office of the Chief of Public Affairs staff for *Sergeant's Business;* Defense Finance and Accounting Service—Indianapolis; Department of Education for *The Student Guide;* Department of Veterans Affairs; Defense Activity for Nontraditional Education Support; Army Family Advocacy Program; Army Community Services; Dependent Dental Plan * DELTA; print media staff of the American Forces Information Service; the staff of *Army* magazine; Enlisted Records and Evaluation Center; ROTC Cadet Command; Center for Military History; and Army Career and Alumni Program.

I also thank the following: Non Commissioned Officers Association; Total Army Personnel Command; U.S. Army Sergeants Major Academy; U.S. Army Fitness School; Civilian Health and Medical Program of the Uniformed Services; Center for Army Lessons Learned; the staff of the Army News Service; the Friends of Ernie Pyle; the staff of *SOLDIERS* magazine; Army Continuing Education Services; the staff of Times Publishing Company, especially for *Army Times;* Office, Deputy Chief of Staff for Operations; Army Safety Center; Army Family Liaison Office; Walter Reed Army Medical Center; the staff of *Countermeasure;* Community Family Support Center; staff of *Inside the Turret;* staff of *The Retired Officer;* Judge Advocate General's Corps; 1st Cavalry Division; 6th Cavalry Brigade (Air Combat); Commemoration Committee, DOD 50th Anniversary of World War II; DOD Still Media Records Center; staff of *Field Artillery Professional Bulletin;* III Corps and Fort Hood; Army Armor Center and Fort Knox; Army Community and Family Support Center; Army Infantry Center and Fort Benning; Army Natick RD&E Center; Army Parachute Team; Special Operations Command; and Army Test and Evaluation Command.

I am indebted to my editor, Ann Wagoner, for her professional support and guidance during production of *NCO Guide, 5th Edition.* And I thank my wife, Kelly, for her understanding and for making me take needed breaks and encouraging me through the daily hours of composition, editing, and revising.

1

America's Army

THE ARMY IS CHANGING, SERGEANT

Army Chief of Staff GEN Gordon R. Sullivan identified the new strategy of America's Army in the lead article of the Association of the U.S. Army's 1993–94 *Green Book:*

> To be ready today and tomorrow, despite reduced resources and force structure, requires real growth as an institution. The Army must make its own paradigm shift. We must make an intellectual commitment to exploit, to push out boldly—in short, to grow as soldiers and as an institution. It's not enough to be trained and ready. We must make the smart changes that add up to an Army trained and ready for [the year] 2023 and beyond.

Paradigm Shift is a book published in 1993 about using new and emerging information technologies to reinvent business organizations and position them for success in a fiercely competitive global marketplace. General Sullivan's use of paradigm shift as a complex military term has parallel meaning; it refers to the Army leadership's new strategy of increasing soldiers', weapons', and supporting systems' capabilities by equipping them with the latest information, communications, intelligence, and other "smart," or automation-oriented, technologies.

The strategy also requires the Army to undergo basic changes in the way it operates and is organized to fight and conduct other missions. Like the mythical Phoenix, the real strategy has risen from what could have been the ashes of a modern Army war-fighting doctrine. It transcends the negative, restrictive aspects of factors including unavoidable budgetary constraints totaling billions of dollars, personnel reductions in the hundreds of thousands, and existing and emerging regional threats.

Just as sergeants must understand a commander's intent in paragraph 3 of an operation order, so must all soldiers know the senior general's intent when he uses the term *paradigm shift*. In the AUSA *Green Book* article Sullivan put it this way: "Our commitment to be trained and ready for today and tomorrow represents exactly the kind of dramatic leap forward—the shift of paradigm—that will enable us to grow an Army ready for the 21st century."

Secretary of Defense William J. Perry is in large part behind the paradigm shift, according to an article by Robert Holzer and Stephen C. LeSueur in the June 6, 1994, issue of *Army Times*. The article leads with the following eye-opener: "Pentagon officials are anticipating a *military revolution* [emphasis added] that will change the nature of modern warfare as significantly as armored vehicles and aircraft carriers changed warfare more than 50 years ago." Holzer and LeSueur attribute the change to modern technologies, including precision-guided munitions, sophisticated communications systems, and improved intelligence data, and to associated needs for new concepts of operations and new kinds of organizations, perhaps including the "2K" and "10K" units discussed later in this chapter.

A formal Revolution in Military Affairs initiative was established by the Secretary of Defense in January 1994, according to the *Army Times* article, "to focus the U.S. military on developing the concepts for future warfare that many officials believe are crucial to continued American preeminence in global affairs."

Sergeant Major of the Army Richard A. Kidd penned an article in the AUSA *Green Book* titled "Soldiering When Less Is More" that describes how soldiers fit into the world's best Army as it adjusts to the so-called paradigm shift. He said soldiers "understand the rationale for a smaller Army based on a reduced threat and for shifting and relocating forces to handle a new national strategy. But what soldiers and their families are sometimes confused by is, 'How is it that as we're getting smaller, we're finding ourselves deploying more often and doing more with less?' and 'Why does it appear that the American public is so willing to allow a quality force that has proven itself in peace and in combat to be dismantled, possibly affecting its highly acclaimed effectiveness?'"

Doing More with Less

Answers to these questions are plentiful in *Challenges and Opportunities*, the fiscal year 1995 Army posture statement. The 103-page document, jointly authored by Secretary of the Army Togo D. West and General Sullivan, makes it clear that a properly managed and focused Army can and will do more with less. The posture statement also indirectly shows that citizens, industries, and the government of the United States are firmly behind Army efforts to ensure military vitality well into the future.

Military personnel, factory and assembly line workers, general and subcontractors, educators, government officials, business and industry leaders and their employees—millions of Americans contribute in various ways to funding, manning, equipping, training, maintaining, and sustaining the Army for the national defense. Concerning sufficient funding, declining budgets will continue to represent the Army's toughest challenge. Personnel reductions also present a significant obstacle. West and Sullivan said personnel reductions are occurring across the entire Army. Between 1989 and 1999, the Army will pare almost one third of its workforce, totaling 614,000 people.

Personnel reductions initially were viewed far and wide as a disadvantage but have become part of the paradigm shift—and an advantage. West and Sullivan said, "In some ways, America's 21st Century Army will be as different from the Army of Desert Storm as [GEN George C.] Marshall's World War II Army was different from [GEN Ulysses S.] Grant's Army of the Potomac. New ways of viewing the world, new missions, new ways to accomplish those missions, new technologies, and new ways of doing business are all part of a deliberate transformation that is fundamentally changing every aspect of the Army."

According to West and Sullivan, transformation efforts are aimed at creation of a *power-projection* Army, a strategically and operationally flexible force capable of rapidly deploying from the continental United States to protect and defend American interests anywhere in the world. The leaders also explained how the Army will continue to serve as the world's premier fighting force. "The incorporation of information technologies onto existing and future Army systems, [such as] the Apache Longbow attack helicopter, reflects a fundamental shift in the Army's modernization strategy," they said. "In December 1992, the first M1A2 Abrams Main Battle Tank rolled off the production line in Lima, Ohio. Improvements incorporated into the tank were unlike any before, focusing exclusively upon embedding advanced information technologies instead of improving the tank's armor, mobility, or gun."

Third Wave Warfare
West and Sullivan continued, "Production of the first M1A2 tank, along with acceptance of the first Apache Longbow in Mesa, Arizona, during August 1993, represent entry of the U.S. Army into what authors Alvin and Heidi Toffler have labeled 'Third Wave Warfare.' Incorporation of information technologies into existing and future Army systems reflects a fundamental shift in the Army's modernization strategy and portends development of digitized formations that will be able to capitalize upon advanced information technologies to overmatch any potential 21st Century adversary."

Items such as mounted and handheld global positioning devices, small-dish satellite communications equipment, over-horizon target acquisition gear, and more advanced technologies are being put into the hands of more soldiers and bolted to more of the Army's existing and planned weaponry and supporting systems. The goal is to enable smaller, smarter, better controlled and informed, more lethal U.S. warriors to rapidly defeat larger, less sophisticated enemy forces anywhere, anytime, under any conditions.

In his book *Preparing for the Twenty-First Century*, best-selling author and economist Paul M. Kennedy said the United States would, economically speaking, "muddle" into the 21st century. But he also said, "In the traditional domain of 'hard' or military-based power, the United States is unequaled by any other nation, including Russia and China."

The United States must remain unequaled in an unbalanced world because its armed forces are undergoing revolutionary changes during unstable times. LTC Tom Slear described the purpose of the changes in his article published in the March 1994 issue of *SOLDIERS* magazine:

> The days of the large standing Army that could overwhelm adversaries by sheer numbers ended in the 1980s as the Warsaw Pact's military power went limp. In the future, according to Army planners, land forces will have to be mobile, lethal, versatile, and lean. The standard will be quick insertions and decisive victories using high-tech systems and carefully tailored active, Reserve, and National Guard forces. A tough mission, no doubt, but strategic planning and the hardware improvements of the last few years have provided a jump start.
>
> When it comes to fighting and winning a major regional conflict, no one is in our league, according to one informed senior officer. The Army demonstrated during Operation Desert Storm that we own the battlefield,

day and night. That ownership can be slippery. The half-lives of present-day innovations are measured in one or two years. Standing still amounts to conceding defeat.

Owning the night in the next century won't be enough. To win the next battle, the Army will have to get to a trouble spot quickly with a sustainable fighting force. It will have to dominate the information war, acting promptly on incoming data to strike targets deep in enemy territory with a new generation of indirect fire weapons. And commanders at all levels will have to maneuver quickly and decisively, leaving an enemy with no option but in timed and feeble counterattacks.

ARMY ROLES, MISSIONS, AND FUNCTIONS
According to the American Forces Information Service (AFIS), the roles, missions, and functions of the military are defined as follows: *Roles* are the broad and enduring purposes for which the services were established by Congress in law; *missions* are the tasks assigned by the president or Secretary of Defense to combatant commanders in chief (CinC); and *functions* are specific responsibilities assigned by the president or Secretary of Defense to enable the services to fulfill their legally established roles. An AFIS *Defense Issues* publication summed up roles, missions, and functions as follows: "Simply stated, the primary function of the services is to provide forces organized, trained, and equipped to perform a role—to be employed by a CinC in the accomplishment of a mission."

Hundreds of thousands of soldiers are involved in vital roles, missions, and functions on a daily basis. Several thousand support counterdrug operations in Central and South America. More than one thousand Special Operations Forces members operate in dozens of countries. One hundred twenty-five thousand soldiers are stationed in Korea, Japan, Europe, Panama, and elsewhere. Many thousands more are busy providing security assistance to foreign allies, training for combat, doing medical research, providing disaster relief, and meeting other needs.

According to AFIS, soldiers are busier than ever in a rapidly changing world. Four factors drive change in the U.S. military: the end of the Cold War; budgetary constraints; the 1986 Goldwater-Nichols Act (which mandates periodic changes in roles, missions, and functions, as necessary); and new regional crises, such as those in Somalia, Bosnia, and Haiti.

The four factors affect how the military is structured, trained, and employed, according to the Chairman of the Joint Chiefs of Staff, GEN John M. Shalikashvili. The Army's new regional focus, combined with major troop reductions overseas, puts enormous emphasis on strategic mobility. Airlift and sealift mobility improvements being made today will enable deployment of an Army light division and a heavy brigade to any crisis area in about two weeks, and two heavy divisions in about a month.

Spearhead units move faster. Elements of the Joint Rapid Deployment Task Force (JRDTF) remain ready to deploy to trouble spots in less than one day. In the 82nd Airborne Division, for example, units on Division Ready Force (DRF) One status must be prepared to stage for deployment on Air Force aircraft in less time than it takes to view a feature film about combat. Follow-on units that are on DRF Two and DRF Three status deploy sequentially behind the DRF One force. Other JRDTF units operate likewise and can quickly begin to "flesh out" an area of operations in about 24 hours. The light and heavy divisions and separate brigades referred to above would be part of this process; they would flow into action behind the rapid deployment forces.

An alternative way to deploy massive firepower to overseas hot spots was studied by the Army Training and Doctrine Command (TRADOC) in an option called Early Entry Lethality and Survivability Battle Lab (EELS). EELS would allow the Army to take specific numbers of weapon systems and highly trained soldiers from front-line divisions and put them as needed in 2,000-man and 10,000-man units. These "2K" and "10K" early-entry units would be small enough to be easily transported yet powerful enough to meet a variety of missions, ranging from peacekeeping to fighting on their own until reinforcements arrive.

A detailed review of the roles, missions, and functions of the armed forces was undertaken to ensure the new regional strategy and military force structures were aligned. It is an understatement to say that accomplishing an alignment of force structure with strategy is not easy. It has been tough on high-level officials like Perry, West, and Sullivan, and at least equally hard on subordinate commanders, NCOs, and rank-and-file soldiers who feel the impact of the changes and adjust to them. Still, the effort is worth making because the objective is to maintain and improve combat readiness even as the government reduces the military's size and the cost of maintaining it. NCOs play a vital role in the effort, as illustrated in chapter 2.

Soldiers of the 101st Airborne Division (Air Assault) participate in an urban warfare exercise in Saudi Arabia during Operation Desert Shield.

NEW THREATS

The AUSA Institute of Land Warfare published a 1993 *Background Brief* titled "The Nature of the Global Threat and Relevance to Army Missions" that looks at troubled areas on Earth and the impact they have on the Army. The brief, still very relevant today, was prepared by retired COL James B. Motley, Ph.D., an AUSA Institute of Land Warfare Fellow. The remainder of this section is an edited, condensed, and supplemented version of his educated and researched view of the world.

Threats to U.S. interests and world leadership during the balance of the century range from regional ethnic and cultural conflicts to drug trafficking, the proliferation of conventional military weaponry, high-technology weaponry in the hands of potential adversaries, and weapons of mass destruction. More than 20 nations have or are acquiring weapons of mass destruction that include nuclear, chemical, and biological weapons and related delivery systems. Many of these arsenals are or will be in the hands of unstable and unreliable governments. Several nations with space-launch capabilities could modify those launches to acquire targets in the United States.

Regional instabilities will warrant continuous monitoring. U.S. military forces will have to remain at a high state of combat readiness and be able to react rapidly to keep local crises from escalating. Joint and combined operations will be the norm, with the ground elements playing the major role of providing the decisive blows to destroy enemy capabilities, to keep adversaries apart, or to intervene to save a nation from other man-made and environmental calamities.

U.S. national military strategy and the Army's strategic role have been affected profoundly by global changes. Rather than deterring the massive military might of a hostile global superpower, America's Army now faces new challenges. While emphasizing and supporting multinational operations under the auspices of international bodies such as the United Nations, the United States must retain the capability to act unilaterally when and where U.S. interests dictate. This strategy is, in many ways, more complex than the containment strategy of the Cold War.

The Former Soviet Union. With the disintegration of the former Soviet Union, internal crises prevail and the possibility of large-scale civil disorder exists within the republics of the former Soviet empire. Russia and some of the other republics still have the capability to strike the United States with weapons of mass destruction. Thousands of nuclear weapons remain in Belarus, Kazakhstan, Russia, and Ukraine. Because many of the nations that have or are acquiring weapons of mass destruction are led by megalomaniacs, strongmen of proven inhumanity, or weak, unstable, or illegitimate governments, the potential for proliferation of these weapons is an issue of major U.S. concern.

Europe and the Balkans. A lasting peace settlement in Bosnia may require a guarantee by the United States and its allies. Scenarios for possible U.S. and allied intervention in Bosnia include using ground troops to deter attacks on ethnic Albanians in Kosovo province.

In July 1994, elements of U.S. Army Europe were stationed in Macedonia to deter Serbian aggression and prevent a widening of the war. *Army Times* reported in March 1994 that the "U.S. military is involved in four contingencies in Europe that put U.S. troops in harm's way. They are Operation Provide Comfort (based in Turkey to aid Iraqi Kurds), Operation Provide Promise (which air drops humanitarian aid to Bosnians), Operation Sharp Guard (a maritime embargo of Serbia), and Operation Deny Flight (ordered to keep Serbian aircraft from attacking Muslim targets).

Asia and the Pacific. Potential for instability and conflict in Asia and the Pacific remains. North Korea's leadership, militarized society, and quest for nuclear weapons are also of major concern. Hostilities along the Indo-Pakistani border could trigger a ballistic missile exchange once development programs under way in both countries are complete. The potential for violent instability in evolving democracies such as the Philippines could present new challenges to U.S. interests. China's economic reforms have not been matched by political freedoms; the selling of Chinese weapons to other countries is a matter of concern to China's neighbors and to the United States.

The United States continues to face the threat of nuclear-armed missiles from China. Military equipment China is acquiring from Russia and other countries may upset the balance of power in Asia by the year 2000. Today, China continues to threaten to use military force to recover Taiwan and claims the entire South China Sea, including many shipping routes that carry oil from the Middle East to Japan.

The fact that China has the capability to attack U.S. territory, forces, and interests cannot be taken lightly. The Chinese have developed a small force of nuclear-tipped ICBMs, some of which are aimed at the United States, and a small force of intermediate-range ballistic missiles, many of which could be targeted against U.S. forces and allies in Asia.

The U.S. trade deficit with Japan is at record levels and placing increasing pressure on both countries. An additional problem is finding, in the post–Cold War era, the right security role for the Japanese in a way that will not reawaken fears elsewhere in Asia.

There is serious concern about the status of North Korea's nuclear efforts. These concerns extend beyond the Korean peninsula. If North Korea acquires nuclear weapons, the probability for stability in northeast Asia becomes questionable. With nuclear weapons, North Korea could put these weapons and the technology that produced them into the international marketplace. North Korea has sold Scud missiles to several Middle East countries and a modified Scud, with greater range, to Iran and Syria.

In an *Army Times* special report in the spring of 1994, GEN Gary Luck, commander of U.S. Forces in Korea, said that even without nuclear weapons, North Korea is a formidable military foe. North Korea has more conventional weapons and more soldiers than South Korea and the U.S. Forces command combined.

South Asia. U.S. interests in maintaining stability in Pakistan, a country with 110 million people (42 percent of the U.S. population), centers around one overriding factor—its potential nuclear capability. Pakistan reportedly has the components and know-how to assemble at least one nuclear bomb. With India also believed to have a nuclear weapons capability, South Asia is an area where potential nuclear rivals confront each other. Thus, there is reason for U.S. concern.

Indications are that the collapse of communism in the former Soviet Union has caught up with the Communist Party of the Philippines and its armed wing, the New People's Army (NPA). Notwithstanding a growing internal rift over strategy and ideology, and a strength that has declined to fewer than 12,000, the NPA is larger than any other communist guerrilla force in the world (except, perhaps, the Khmer Rouge in Cambodia) and still presents a threat to the government of the Philippines.

The Middle East and Africa. This region is least affected by positive global changes in the international security environment. The end of superpower competition has removed a major source of instability in Africa, but the lasting effects of political repression and economic mismanagement will be worsened by the continuing spread of HIV-AIDS and ecological devastation. Africa's problems—poverty and unchecked population growth—increasingly will compete with other regional concerns for international attention. The politics and conflict associated with food shortages in Somalia and chronic drought in Ethiopia are but two examples. Sudan is most likely to be the next Somalia. Civil wars elsewhere in Africa require careful attention.

Algeria has almost completed building a nuclear reactor bought from China. The secrecy of the purchase and Algeria's failure to accede to the nuclear Nonproliferation Treaty are reasons for concern. Libya has produced and stockpiled as many as 100 tons of chemical agents, continues to shop throughout the world for an alternative source of longer-range missiles, and continues its support for a variety of terrorist or insurgent groups worldwide.

In Somalia, a country with virtually no government, no civil institutions, and no law and order, the military aspect of the U.S.–led humanitarian relief effort, Operation Restore Hope, progressed fairly smoothly, except for the 30 U.S. servicemembers who were killed, and nearly 200 injured. But after U.S. military forces were withdrawn, rehabilitation of a country that lacks the most basic building blocks of a modern civil society was virtually reversed. In the March 13, 1994, issue of *The Indianapolis Star*, an Associated Press report by Susanne M. Schafer described how JCS Chairman GEN Shalikashvili stood by soldiers departing from Somalia. In her report, Schafer said Shalikashvili chose "to emphasize for those soldiers returning home that they should remember their part in eradicating the horrific scenes of stick-thin Somalis clamoring for bits of food—not the sad scene of a lifeless U.S. soldier being dragged through the streets by hostile mobs."

Syria is attempting to acquire from China and North Korea, as well as from Western firms, an improved chemical and biological capability and continues to provide support and safe havens to groups that engage in international terrorism.

Persian Gulf Region. In the oil-rich Persian Gulf, struggle for influence continues among Iraq, Iran, and Saudi Arabia. (According to *Army Times*, the Persian Gulf region will supply 40 percent of the world's oil by the year 2000.) Operation Desert Storm temporarily deflated Iraq's ambitions, but Saddam Hussein's defiant actions could lead to further U.S. and coalition military operations against Iraq.

Iraq's Saddam Hussein's next military challenge could be more audacious than those conducted to date. He could, for example, launch a ground attack against the Kurds in the north or the Shiites in the south. U.S. and allied air power would probably be unable to stop these attacks; if this was the case, ground troops would be required. Saddam Hussein has adopted a long-term strategy of driving a wedge between the U.S.–led coalition that carried out Operation Desert Storm and the overextended United Nations.

Iran has made no secret of its ambitions to reemerge as a preeminent regional power as it spends $2 billion a year to buy conventional weapons, mainly from Russia and China; builds a nuclear, chemical, biological weapons arsenal; and develops its naval forces. Years after the end of its eight-year war with Iraq in 1988, Iran continues to rebuild its armed forces, the strongest in the Persian Gulf region. With the ability to put 500,000 men in the field and the capability to counter Iraqi air power, Iran is placing its priority on acquiring strategic weapons, nuclear reactors, surface-to-surface missiles, and light bombers. Iran is also seeking nuclear power plants.

With the sale of two submarines, Russia has helped Iran gain a naval edge in the Persian Gulf. These submarines can cruise in the deep waters just outside the Strait of Hormuz and threaten the large volume of oil traffic using the narrow straits. To counter this threat, several Gulf countries are ordering new submarines and surface submarine-hunter vessels, thus further intensifying the arms race in the volatile Persian Gulf region.

More serious is the war of subversion that Iran is waging throughout the moderate Arab world. In Egypt, Islamic terrorists are randomly killing foreign tourists in an attempt to stop Egypt from gaining foreign currency. In Lebanon, Hezbollah (Iran's Lebanese subsidiary) remains the only independent militia in the country. In North Africa, Iran is supporting Islamic fundamentalists trying to bring down moderate regimes in Algeria and Tunisia. And Iran has become a predominant influence in Sudan, the largest country in Africa.

Latin America. A major problem in Latin America continues to be drug trafficking, which corrupts local governments, subverts judicial processes, and distorts economies. Nowhere is this more evident than in Peru, where U.S. antidrug and military assistance is being provided on a limited basis. The country has been under the intimidation and threat of the Shining Path guerrilla organization for many years. It and other guerrilla groups are closely linked with the thriving drug trade operatives who finance their operations. Guerrilla acts of terrorism are increasing, and carrying the fight to rebels and drug-producing organizations is increasingly difficult.

Guerrilla warfare perpetrated by factions of the National Liberation Army (ELN) and Revolutionary Armed Forces of Colombia (FARC), along with massive drug production, undermines the political evolution of Colombia. U.S. military support of the Colombian armed forces in their war against the drug lords continues.

Cuba is a matter of concern. Experts agree that Fidel Castro's time in power is limited. A military coup could spark a civil war, as could a sudden popular uprising, or Castro's death could set off a power struggle. Any of these scenarios could generate a refugee flood to the United States much larger than the Haiti situation.

As of July 1994, thousands of Haitians were desperate to escape one of the hemisphere's poorest and most repressive countries and were building boats and planning voyages to Florida. Estimates on the exodus of Haitians range from 15,000 to 180,000 people. Such an influx will severely tax the infrastructure of South Florida, where ongoing post–Hurricane Andrew efforts to reconstruct areas and feed and house thousands continue.

Future Trends. In the emerging global security environment described above, regional crises, war, and challenges to U.S. vital interests will continue to be very real possibilities. In the aftermath of Operation Desert Storm, regional military forces recognized the importance of acquiring modern weapons. The pursuit of high-tech weapons and the expansion of native production capabilities are likely to be the focus of regional acquisition efforts for the remainder of the 1990s and beyond. In a world that is more lethally armed, more unstable, and more uncertain, America's Army must continue to be well trained and maintain an overwhelming modernization advantage to dominate potential adversaries. The smaller the Army becomes, the more modern and technologically overmatching it must be.

Violent nationalism and the tendency of groups or nations to resort to terrorism, drug-related violence, insurgency, and internal repression and external aggression demonstrate how dangerous the world remains. These factors pose an explosive mix of social, demographic, and military trends that could present a serious challenge to U.S. interests requiring decisive military action.

The global arms bazaar is another trend that is making the world more dangerous. According to one knowledgeable Pentagon source, it is a robust and deadly free market, leading to spiraling arms purchases in heavily armed, unstable regions of the world. Technological change has a significant impact on Army systems modernization plans. Countries with the necessary military infrastructure and economic resources will move toward smaller, high-tech, more lethal forces, and can do so in a very short period of time. Poorer countries have the capability to field some advanced systems in limited, specialized areas such as precision-guided munitions or sophisticated air defense systems. Those unable to get or include high technologies will retain large conventional land forces for internal security purposes.

Of grave concern is the proliferation of nuclear weapons and the means to deliver them. It is estimated that by the year 2000, at least fifteen developing nations will have the ability to build ballistic missiles and eight either have or almost have nuclear capabilities. Thirty countries will have chemical weapons and ten will be able to deploy biological weapons as well. A possibility exists that some countries may use mass-destruction weapons in regional confrontations, thus threatening U.S. interests abroad.

U.S. security is best guaranteed by a clear-eyed assessment of the global challenges. The Army is continually studying the development of trends, assessing threat technologies, monitoring regional flash points, and analyzing intentions and capabilities of nations or groups with goals opposed to U.S. interests. Because of the emerging nature of the global security environment, threats to U.S. interests can arise suddenly, particularly in regional crises. The Army must be adaptable and remain versatile, deployable, lethal, and expansible. Soldiers must continuously hone their skills to be ready to deter or defeat threats wherever they originate.

CURRENT AFFAIRS
The issues soldiers are concerned about on a daily basis would fill thick volumes—pay, duty, uniform costs, chow, charge of quarters or staff duty, the media's coverage of the military, women in combat (or male attitudes toward them), homosexuals, the quality of training, leadership, supervision, field training exercises, the weather, separation hardships, marital discord, blisters and other ailments, orders, directives, verbal instructions. It would be easy for a weak NCO to get caught up in the complaining, and perhaps to participate in it. But, given the nature of the paradigm shift and global security environment described above, soldiers have much more important business to attend to in the Army.

NCOs with a more realistic view of service know the following:
- Pay will go up with time in service, fluctuating annual pay hikes, and promotions.
- Duties must be done.
- The annual clothing allowance can be used to offset uniform price hikes.
- Chow will be good at times, bad at others.
- CQ and staff duty come with the uniform.
- The media get paid to get the story and will do so even when endangering themselves and the subjects of their coverage—even in the middle of the night on an assault beach in Somalia.
- Professional female soldiers are as good as professional male soldiers and are being provided increasing opportunity in the Army.
- Homosexual policy training is being conducted Armywide to help soldiers deal with the Clinton Administration's drive to integrate gays and lesbians into the military.
- Soldiers will get from combat training what they put into it.
- Most leaders and supervisors do a fine job; those who do not get ostracized in today's Army.
- Field training is critical to combat readiness.
- The weather will change.
- Separation from loved ones occurs in many occupational sectors of American society and must be dealt with in a sensitive manner by the chain of command.
- Marital discord can be resolved through reconciliation, counseling, or divorce.
- Blisters require bandages.
- All soldiers get orders, even the most senior general officers.

As the Army wrestles with fundamental changes in the way it operates and is organized, an array of disconcerting issues face soldiers and the NCOs who lead and train them. In a mid-June 1993 issue of *Army Times,* eight pages were devoted to a series of articles that still apply today. The articles, led by one titled "Blue Mood Rising," addressed numerous negative issues that impact on morale and soldiers' perceptions of their service. In the lead story, author Tom Philpott said, "[Soldiers] throughout the armed forces have begun to feel that what they do, what they sacrifice to serve, is neither understood nor appreciated by their commander in chief, Congress, or, perhaps, the nation."

Perhaps. But selfless service calls for personal sacrifice and dedication to duty, regardless of the circumstances. Soldiers get paid to serve the nation. If elements of the nation seem less than caring, well, that's just how it is—so don't sweat it. Besides, according to annual national polls, the military is the highest-rated institution in the nation. And in the Army family, plenty of good people do care and go about their business because it must be done. Hard-charging NCOs know that, as Sergeant Major of the Army Richard Kidd put it, "Soldiers must stay in their lane"—meaning this: Leave other people's business to them. Concentrate on your own job; do what must be done to be the best at what you get paid to do.

This is good advice from the top enlisted soldier. Sergeants and their soldiers have enough to concern themselves with on a daily basis. Job tasks, fitness, appearance, good order and discipline, meeting the standards of service, upholding their sworn or affirmed oath to defend the Constitution and obey the orders of superior officers—these are some of the unchanging principle requirements of soldiering in a changing Army, in a dangerous world.

2

The Role of the NCO

The backbone of the Army is the noncommissioned [officer.]
     —Rudyard Kipling, *The 'Eathen*, 1896

NCO CORPS HISTORY
Why Study Military History
In the winter of 1992, *NCO Journal* published a short article by CSM Wade P. Hampton, who at the time was command sergeant major of the 11th Air Defense Artillery Brigade. The article addresses why soldiers should study military history and is based on a speech Hampton gave to a Primary Leadership Development Course (PLDC) class at Fort Bliss, Texas. This is an excerpt:

> In the winter of 1778, GEN George Washington led his Army into its winter encampment, what we now call Valley Forge. His Army had been in the field for three years, training for three years, and led by officers for three years. This Army was not fit, had never won a campaign, was not proud, was poorly led, poorly disciplined, and defeated.
>
> That winter, Washington did several things to improve his Army, but the most important thing was to allow Baron [Frederick] von Steuben to form an NCO corps. During the harsh winter, that corps established discipline and training and provided sound leadership to soldiers. The corps—the first American NCOs—allowed Washington to march out of Valley Forge with some of the finest light infantry units in the world.
>
> For most NCOs, there is a tendency to equate the study of military history as something that is an exclusive concern of officers. But I want to tell you how and why NCOs should study history. Learning from your mistakes can be painful. Learning from others' is painless and easy. History gives us a way of looking at how people in other days accomplished their missions. When reading about von Steuben's model company, you are struck by the similarities of his approach and today's Army. He taught an elite group a unique method of fighting. These soldiers passed those lessons to others. The victory at Yorktown, which won our independence, can be said to have been earned on the drill fields at Valley Forge.
>
> The most important part of the study of history is applying lessons learned. This helps us avoid mistakes and precludes trying things that have

not been proven by our experiences. For example: Maintenance of personal equipment and weapons has always been an NCO's job. But what can happen when this task is forgotten or ignored? Read about Task Force Smith in 1950 and you'll find the answer. Let us start now to preserve the past so that it will enhance our performance and guide us into the future.

History and Military Leadership

In a 1989 book titled *The Story of the Noncommissioned Officer Corps*, Arnold G. Fisch, Jr., and Robert K. Wright, Jr., compiled the story of how, beginning in 1775, NCOs came to be recognized as the "backbone of the Army." The book, published by the U.S. Army Center of Military History (CMH) in Washington, D.C., emphasizes NCOs' traditional roles in training and their development as leaders. In it, former Army Chief of Staff GEN Carl E. Vuono and former Sergeant Major of the Army Julius W. Gates identified the book as "a significant contribution . . . [that] honors the dedicated service and achievements of countless thousands of NCOs over the past two hundred years. From their early roles as file closers, quartermaster sergeants, and musicians, NCOs have evolved into leaders of our soldiers, as their first-line trainers, as standard bearers in our units, and as leaders who instill discipline in the force."

The CMH book includes the evolution and development of the NCO corps since 1775, and it has portraits of NCOs in action. It views NCO leadership responsibilities and addresses them through extracted documents, including Baron von Steuben's historic *Regulations for the Order and Discipline of the Troops of the United States*, published in 1789. The book also presents an evolution of NCO rank insignia and a gallery of noncommissioned heroes.

Here is an extract from *The Story of the Noncommissioned Officer Corps* about such heroes:

> Entering the fort made the ranger sergeant feel uneasy—too much saluting, too many people scurrying around acting important. Ever since this latest struggle against the French and their Indian allies had started in earnest, things had been this way. For the first time in anyone's memory British regulars had been sent across the ocean in large numbers, bringing a whole array of notions that had turned fighting upside down. Suddenly, officers everywhere were making an infernal racket and worrying about how you looked, not how well you could shoot. They even dressed wrong. Their red coats and shiny buttons stood out clearly in the bright summer sun, but that was hardly something that you wanted when you were trying to sneak up on an enemy outpost!
>
> Although the scene at the fort always reminded him of an anthill after someone had kicked it over, he sighed and motioned to the private with him to proceed. They had a mission to carry out. Major Rogers had told him to deliver a message personally to the general, and it was best not to dawdle. Pausing only to ask directions to headquarters from the British sergeant (he was easy to spot—the one with the axe on a stick, called a halberd) at the gate, the two New Englanders set about their task. Although the private was young enough to be impressed by the fort, the sergeant had been in action for four years, and he wasn't about to let anyone forget that he wore the elite green uniform of a ranger.

The pride that he felt in his unit went hand in hand with the efficient arrangement of his weapons, uniform, and equipment. From his clean and well-maintained musket and hatchet to his leggings and moccasins, the sergeant projected an image of someone completely at home in the virgin forests that covered the frontiers of the North American colonies. Moving silently through the woods around Lake Champlain was second nature to this man—a fact that Major Rogers had noticed and rewarded, first by hand-picking and then by promoting him. Leading a small patrol and acting as the army's eyes and ears carried a high degree of risk and the burden of making split-second decisions that could mean life or death for the soldiers serving under him, but that was what the sergeant wanted to do, and it was what he did best.

Army Chief of Staff GEN Gordon R. Sullivan stressed history's importance to major commanders in the spring 1993 issue of *Army History*, a professional bulletin published by the CMH for the development of Army historians. Sullivan said:

> In the continuing reshaping of the Army we have to make hard decisions concerning manpower. I am concerned that pressure to reduce staffing is causing commanders to place their command historians and museum curators at risk. Recently revised, the above referenced regulations [AR 5-3, *Installation Management and Organization*; and AR 870-5, *Military History*] specify history as a separate staff office on the commander's staff and expand its responsibilities. Often a one-person office and lacking visibility among the staff, the historian is frequently first to be nominated for reduction or elimination in times of limited resources. Museum staffs are similarly small, vulnerable targets when cuts are being considered. My view is that we can neither restructure the Army correctly nor record the resulting changes objectively without the contributions we must get from these experts on the Army's past.
>
> Military history must play a key role in current and future decision-making. History's long-term worth to the Army is inestimable, and your command historian should be one of your most productive and valued staff officers, providing information, perspective, and insights not available from any other source. Consequently, I request that you . . . use your historian to his or her fullest capability. Likewise, your museums contain irreplaceable relics of the Army's heritage which must be preserved for future generations of soldiers.

You can bet that general officers throughout the Army got the chief's message. If history means that much to the Chief of Staff of the Army and to senior commanders throughout the Army, shouldn't it matter to you?

History has been recorded in many ways during the U.S. military's existence. During World War II, for example, history was witnessed and reported to the nation realistically, poignantly, sincerely, eloquently, and compassionately by the revered war correspondent Ernest T. "Ernie" Pyle, who covered the war in Europe and the Pacific and was killed by a sniper's bullet. Announcing the tragic news of Pyle's death to the nation in April 1945, President Harry S. Truman said, "No man in this war has so well told the story of the American fighting man as the American fighting man wanted it told. He deserves the gratitude of all his countrymen."

Pyle is very much a beloved part of the Army's history. A small civilian museum dedicated to his memory is open to the public from May through October at the Ernie Pyle State Historic Site in Dana, Indiana.

Official museums operate throughout the Army and benefit thousands of soldier-scholars every year. At Fort Bliss, Texas, soldiers can visit the NCO Museum. At Fort Knox, Kentucky, you can visit the Patton Museum of Cavalry and Armor. At Fort Bragg, North Carolina, the 82nd Airborne Division Museum is chock-full of paratrooper and glider infantry history. Soldiers interested in the history of women in the Army can visit the WAC (Women's Army Corps) Museum at Fort McClellan, Alabama. The Finance Museum is located at Fort Benjamin Harrison, Indiana, the "Home of the Army Dollar." Visitors to the Pentagon should visit a small alcove called the Hall of Heroes to read the names of the nation's Medal of Honor recipients. Virtually all major installations and many minor ones have some kind of history facility—all are worth visiting.

RESPONSIBILITIES
Although commissioned and noncommissioned officer responsibilities may be shared, the tasks necessary to accomplish them should not be. NCO responsibilities are divided into twelve broad categories:

1. Individual training of soldiers in MOSs and in basic soldiering skills.
   • Train soldiers to fight, win, and live.
   • Teach soldiers the history and traditions of the Army, military courtesy, personal hygiene, appearance standards, and drill and ceremonies.

A drill sergeant instructs a recruit in the handling of a grenade.

2. Personal and professional development of soldiers.

- Recommend that good soldiers attend service school specialist or career-development courses as needed and as appropriate.
- Fix responsibility. Give soldiers tasks they can do based on their abilities, experience, and know-how. Train soldiers to take on increasingly difficult or complex tasks.
- Train soldiers to replace you, just as you trained to replace your superiors.
- Hold soldiers responsible for their actions.
- Ensure that required publications are available and convenient.
- Help soldiers cope with personal problems. Until the problem is resolved, you have a soldier with a problem in your unit, so it is your problem, too.
- Counsel soldiers on their strengths and weaknesses; build on strengths and help them strive to overcome weaknesses.
- Recommend promotions and awards through the NCO support channel.
- Do not promise promotions and awards.
- Develop an ability to deal with personal and professional development.

3. Accountability for the squad, the section, or the team.

- Know what each soldier in the unit that you lead is doing during duty hours (and off-duty hours as well when a problem spreads from off duty to on duty).
- Know where your soldiers live and how to contact them.
- Know why a soldier is going on sick call or other appointments, how he or she is treated, and what is wrong.
- Use the unit to accomplish as many missions as possible, *but never volunteer troops for missions to make yourself look good in the eyes of superiors*. Know your team's limitations.
- Know the readiness status or operating condition of unit weapons, vehicles, and other equipment.

4. Military appearance, physical conditioning, and training.

- Make corrections when you see something wrong *wherever* you may be and to *whomever* is concerned. Be polite and diplomatic.
- Supervise the physical fitness training and development of your soldiers, in accordance with FM 21-20, *Physical Fitness Training*, and AR 350-15, *The Army Physical Fitness Program*.
- Ensure that you and your soldiers meet the Army's weight and body fat standards in accordance with AR 600-9, The Army Weight Control Program.

5. Physical and mental well-being of the soldier and his or her family.

- Know your soldiers' family situations and help them if they have problems.
- Make sure your soldiers know what services and benefits they and their families are entitled to. Your personnel service NCO can provide this information.

6. Supervision, control, motivation, and discipline of subordinates.

- Counsel soldiers and maintain counseling records.
- Support subordinate NCOs when you have any. Similarly, when they are wrong, tell them so, *but do it privately*.
- Teach your soldiers about the Uniform Code of Military Justice.
- Recommend commendations and passes.
- Recommend bars to reenlistment or elimination actions if appropriate. Weeding out the bad soldiers will encourage good soldiers to stay.
- Conduct corrective training when required.

- Keep soldiers informed—do not let them be surprised by details, field training exercises, inspections, or other events.

7. Communication between the individual soldier and the organization.
- Use, and insist that soldiers use, the chain of command and support channels.
- Listen and act on soldiers' suggestions and complaints, but be able to distinguish between belly-aching and real concerns.
- Support and explain reasons for current policies.
- Try to develop a feeling of loyalty and pride in your team and unit.
- Do not complain to, or in the presence of, your soldiers.

8. Plan and conduct day-to-day unit operations.
- Provide input to the training NCO for individual skill training.
- Conduct team training.
- Supervise events as required by training schedules.

9. Maintain established standards of performance.
- Explain clearly what you expect from soldiers.
- Conduct special training to correct weaknesses.
- Train soldiers to standards set by soldiers' manuals and other literature.
- Provide up-to-date information for appropriate levels of self-development tests.
- Be professional.

10. Maintenance, serviceability, accountability, and readiness.
- Inspect soldiers' equipment often. Use the manual or approved checklist. Hold soldiers responsible for repairs and losses.
- Learn how to use and maintain equipment soldiers use. Be among the first to operate new equipment, whether tanks or word processors.
- Enforce maintenance and supply system procedures.
- Encourage economy and deal with soldiers who abuse equipment.
- Keep up-to-date component lists and conduct inventories. Know what is on hand and turn in excess or unserviceable equipment.

11. Appearance and condition of unit billets, facilities, and work areas.
- Inspect often and supervise maintenance.
- Conduct fire and safety inspections and drills.
- Set and enforce cleanliness standards.
- Eat in the mess hall and observe mess operations.

12. Advise on, support, and implement policy established by the chain of command.

THE CHAIN OF COMMAND

The importance of the chain of command to success is nothing new in military affairs. How well any social institution works depends upon how effectively orders and information are passed from top to bottom and back. The role of the NCO in making the chain work is vital.

The chain is defined as the succession of commanding officers from a superior to a subordinate through which command is exercised. There is only one chain of command in the Army, but it is reinforced by the NCO support channel. Both are communication channels used to pass information up and down. Neither is a one-way street, nor are the two entirely separate. In order for the chain of command to work, the NCO support channel must be operating.

The NCO Support Channel
The NCO Support Channel begins with the command sergeant major and ends with the lowest-ranking NCO. In addition to passing information, this channel is used for issuing orders and getting jobs done. The channel leaves the commander free to plan, make decisions, and program future training and operations.

The command sergeant major is the senior enlisted advisor to the commander, and although he is not in the chain of command, he knows what instructions are being issued through it, and this helps him supervise the NCO support channel.

The NCO support channel is a formal entity, directive in nature. But regardless of where information or tasks begin, the officer counterpart in the chain of command at that level must be kept informed to prevent duplication and conflict.

Command is not normally delegated to enlisted soldiers, although any unit that is temporarily without officers may actually be commanded by an enlisted person, as sometimes happens in platoons or platoon-sized units.

Sergeant Major of the Army
The sergeant major of the Army is the senior sergeant major grade of rank and designates the senior enlisted position of the Army. The individual who occupies this office serves as the senior enlisted advisor and consultant to the Chief of Staff of the Army in the following areas: problems affecting enlisted personnel and solutions to these problems; professional education, growth, and advancement of NCOs; and morale training, pay, promotions, and other matters concerning enlisted personnel.

Command Sergeant Major
The command sergeant major (CSM) is the senior NCO of the command at battalion level or higher. He or she executes policies and standards pertaining to performance, training, appearance, and conduct. The CSM provides advice and initiates recommendations to the commander and staff in matters pertaining to enlisted personnel. Activities of the local NCO channel emanate from the CSM. This channel functions orally through the command sergeant major or first sergeant and normally does not involve written instructions; however, either method may be used, and both are considered directive in nature.

First Sergeant
The position of the first sergeant is similar to that of the command sergeant major in importance, responsibility, and prestige. The first sergeant is in direct and daily contact with sizable numbers of enlisted personnel, requiring of him or her outstanding leadership and professional competence. The first sergeant is the senior in companies, batteries, and troops. Normally, company commanders use the NCO support channel to conduct many routine activities, particularly in garrison. The first sergeant conducts company administration and operations as directed by the company commander.

Platoon Sergeant
The platoon sergeant is a key person in the command structure of the Army. It is normal for platoon sergeants to become commanders during the absence or disability of commissioned officers of the platoon. When the platoon leader is present, the platoon sergeant is a key assistant and advisor.

Section, Squad, and Team Leaders

Section, squad, and team leaders are responsible for the personal appearance and cleanliness of their soldiers, for property accountability and maintenance, for the whereabouts of their soldiers at all times, and for the ability to perform the primary mission at all times.

THE NCO AND THE OFFICER

The essence of the officer/NCO relationship is best expressed in an old Army story:

> An old major, a veteran of long service and some hard campaigns, was giving some officer candidates a practical exercise in how to lead troops. The problem involved putting up a flagpole. To do it, he had provided a sergeant and a detail of three privates with tools. But it was up to the officer candidates to figure out the best way to do the job.
>
> They pondered the situation carefully. Several false starts were made; solutions were advanced and tried but failed because nobody seemed to be in charge; each candidate thought only he knew the right way and competed loudly with the others to be heard.
>
> Finally, the old major stepped in and with a gesture silenced the babble. "Gentlemen," said he, "allow me to demonstrate how a good officer would do this job." He turned to the sergeant and said, "Sergeant, please have the men put up the flagpole." Nothing more was said and in a few minutes the pole was up.

The good officer knows that the good NCO gets the job done. The good NCO knows that the good officer will let him do it.

PRECEDENCE AND RELATIVE RANK

The determination of rank and precedence among enlisted personnel is sometimes not as critical as it is among officers (especially when deciding who will command), but it is necessary to resort to some system on those occasions when determining among two or more individuals of equal rank which one will be responsible for functions within the enlisted support channel.

Among enlisted personnel of the same grade of rank in active military service, including retired personnel on active duty, precedence or relative rank is determined as follows:

1. By date or rank.
2. When dates of rank are the same, by length of active service in the Army.
3. When 1 and 2 above are the same, by length of total active service.
4. When the foregoing tests are not sufficient, by age.

ENLISTED INSIGNIA OF THE
UNITED STATES ARMED FORCES

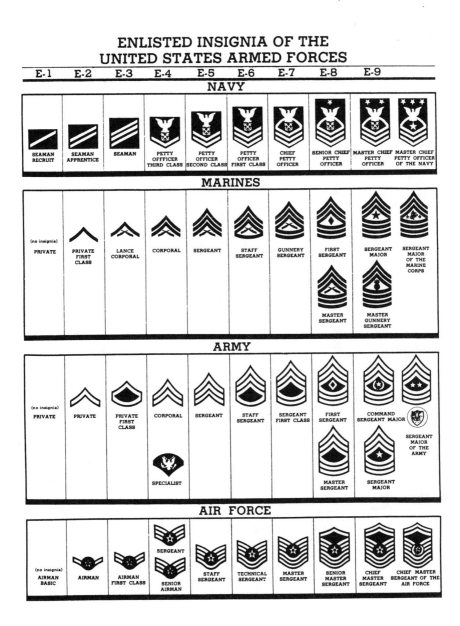

Courtesy Armed Forces Staff College, AFSC 1. (Note: Air Force Insignia and the Sergeant Major of the Army insignia have been redesigned.)

OFFICER INSIGNIA OF THE UNITED STATES ARMED FORCES

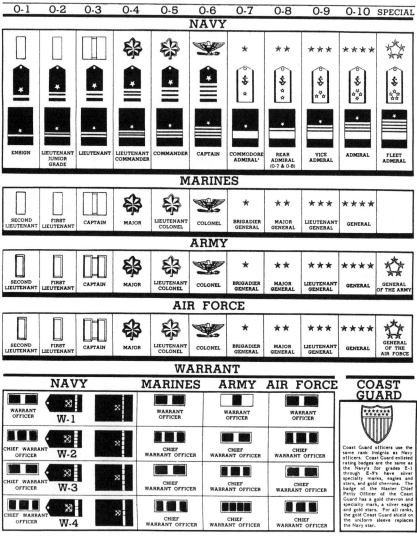

Courtesy Armed Forces Staff College, AFSC 1.

A squad leader, center left, discusses plans with his soldiers.

LEADERSHIP

Regardless of where, when, under what circumstances, or by whom it is used, leadership boils down to getting soldiers to willfully carry out orders and accomplish the mission. The more expert the leader, the more likely soldiers are to follow.

NCOs must be able to motivate and inspire soldiers to carry out missions for the greater good of the Army. Good leaders come by leadership attributes through a never-ending process of self-study, education, training, and experience. Although many principles of leadership exist, the ability to lead by example has stood the test of time and rigors of battle.

Leadership Competencies

The nine leadership competencies NCOs should possess are communications, supervision, teaching and counseling, soldier-team development, technical and tactical proficiency, decision making, planning, management technology, and professional ethics.

A good leader continues to seek self-improvement, strengthens personal attributes, and knows soldiers and the unit.

Technical and tactical knowledge are important to leadership. Be proficient with your weapon and all other items of unit equipment. Develop technical and tactical skills and knowledge through practice and study.

Seek responsibility and take responsibility for your actions. Pay attention to what is going on, figure out what needs to be done, and take responsibility for doing it.

Make sound and timely decisions. Problem solving, decision making, and planning are all part of a leader's responsibilities. Identify the problem, analyze and develop courses of action, make a plan, decide on a course of action, implement your plan, and assess it. Implementing your plan will task your abilities to communicate, coordinate, supervise, and evaluate your plan. This seven-step problem-solving process is described in FM 22-100, *Military Leadership*.

Know your soldiers and look out for their well-being. Show you care. Make the needs of the people in your unit coincide with unit tasks and missions. Reward individual and team behavior that is supportive. Develop morale by alleviating causes of personal concern so that your soldiers can concentrate on their jobs. Ensure that your soldiers are properly cared for and have proper equipment and tools to do their work.

Keep your soldiers informed. Your ability to communicate can make the difference between success and failure. Be available. Discuss upcoming training and other missions with soldiers. Get feedback from your soldiers. Make sure short-range and long-range training plans are available to your soldiers to help them plan for personal situations.

Develop a sense of responsibility in your subordinates. Challenge them—especially those who exhibit potential to handle more responsibilities. Delegate. Do not be afraid of losing some power or authority. By delegating, you actually increase the power of your unit because you give subordinates a chance to think and carry out their plans and thus increase their motivation and your means of accomplishing your mission.

Ensure that subordinates understand tasks and have good supervision. Eliminate psychological and physical barriers that sometimes inhibit good communication.

Train your soldiers as a team. Army success depends on team cohesiveness. Cohesion demands mutual respect, trust, confidence, and understanding among soldiers. Cohesion and discipline go hand in hand.

Employ soldiers and your unit according to capabilities. Develop capabilities through individual and unit training under your leadership and guidance. Be aware of fatigue and the draining effects of fear. Train soldiers to meet unit standards. If you have the desire, you can become increasingly efficient as a leader.

Discipline
AR 600-20 defines discipline as a function of command. Leaders must see that all military personnel present a neat and soldierly appearance and take action when conduct is prejudicial to good order and military discipline.

An NCO present at a scene of disorder must act promptly to restore order. One initial action should be to call for the military police.

In public, you may request the civilian police to take an offender into custody when no military police are available. Make on-the-spot corrections of uniform or courtesy violations wherever possible, and never refer matters to an individual's commander that should be handled by the NCO support chain.

NCOs are authorized to—and must, when they have knowledge of any quarrel, fray, or disorder among persons subject to military law—take action to quell these disorders and apprehend the participants. In order to fulfill your duty, you may have to risk physical injury, so proceed with judgment and tact, but *take action*.

You must exercise your military authority with promptness, firmness, courtesy, and justice. One of your most effective nonpunitive disciplinary measures is extra training or instruction.

Training or instruction given to an individual to correct deficiencies not only must be directly related to the deficiency observed but also oriented to improving performance.

Leadership Performance Indicators

Performance indicators (PI) are used with leadership competencies and supporting skills, knowledge, and attitudes (SKA). For example, the leadership competency involving communications requires the following:

- (SKA) Be a good listener. Associated PI are to provide feedback on what was briefed; display knowledge of information by properly implementing the commander's intent; be able to back brief information received; respond to subordinate's input.
- (SKA) Clearly communicate your intent. Associated PI are that a majority of your subordinates understand the information and understand the action necessary to accomplish the mission.

The following apply to making decisions:

- (SKA) Implement a plan. PI include that subordinates are able to describe what actions must be taken to accomplish the mission.
- (SKA) Use and expect good judgment. PI is that leaders use all available information when making a decision.

And so it goes. Each of the nine leadership competencies has associated skills, knowledge, and attitudes, as well as performance indicators that will inform or show you that your soldiers are performing to standard.

Leading Soldiers into the 21st Century

Look to Training Circular (TC) 22-6, *The Army NCO Guide*, and FM 22-100, *Military Leadership*, to determine what it takes to lead soldiers into the next century—it requires many of the same things it takes to lead them today. Determine what your organization expects of you, who your immediate leader is and what he or she expects of you, and the level of competence and the strengths and weaknesses of your subordinates. Identify the key people outside of your unit whose willing support you need to accomplish the mission.

Demonstrate tactical and technical competence; that is, know your business. Teach your subordinates. Be a good listener. Treat your soldiers with dignity and respect. Stress the basics, including courage, candor, confidence, and commitment. Set the example through selfless service, and abide by Army values. And set and enforce standards.

AR 600-100, *Army Leadership*, states why leadership is extremely important today, and will be tomorrow:

> In an era when technological advantages have narrowed, and access to information of all kinds is relatively limitless, the most effective and efficient way for the Army to maintain its competitive edge is by enhancing the effectiveness of people and organizations. Good leadership can facilitate

this goal. Whether preparing for war, fighting a war, or supporting a war, leadership skills, knowledge, and attitudes must be consistent with the warfighting doctrine of the U.S. Army.

Solving Your Soldiers' Problems

No pay due, marital strife, substance abuse, failure to comprehend or to comply, inability, a medical condition, weight control, failing or a low score on the Army Physical Fitness Test, nonpayment of just debts, spouse or child abuse, poor self-management skills—the kinds of problems soldiers can encounter go on and on. Small problems often are easily resolved without assistance. The bigger ones, and those that are perceived as big ones, may call for the skills of an effective NCO counselor.

Recognizing Soldiers with Problems

Some soldiers will come to you, explain their problem, and seek your guidance or assistance. Others will not. Those that do not may be hard to spot—unless you know what to look for during daily contact. Watch for signs when you speak with or observe your soldiers.

If a soldier who is normally on time to work begins to show up late, he or she might be losing sleep for any number of innocent reasons. Sleep loss can also be caused by partying late into the night, or because of substance abuse. Observe the soldier's appearance. Is it neat? Does he or she look disheveled? Do you smell alcohol on the soldier's breath? If married, is the soldier getting along well with his or her spouse? Does the soldier have teenage children who stay out late, and does the soldier wait up?

Something is wrong when a soldier who usually has a good attitude and behaves properly suddenly develops an improper attitude or exhibits irrational behavior. Does the soldier's supervisor treat him or her fairly? Is some factor external to the Army the cause of the problem? Has the soldier been paid? Is the soldier lashing out or venting because emotional release is needed?

The only effective way to identify and deal with the myriad problems that crop up in Army units is to stay tuned in to your soldiers. Show that you care and are accessible. Relate to them. Get to know them.

Also get to know FM 22-101, *Leadership Counseling*. It covers the concept and fundamentals of counseling—of dealing with problems as well as counseling to praise—and uses dialogue to illustrate directive, nondirective, and combined counseling methods.

The directive, or autocratic, approach is counselor-centered, meaning the counselor talks and the soldier listens. Using this method, you state the problem to the soldier, identify its causes, and list available options. This I-talk-you-listen method may be appropriate if a soldier's problem-solving skills are limited or if the soldier is immature or insecure and needs guidance. The directive approach has three disadvantages: It can cause resentment because it may question a soldier's ability. It may address symptoms and not the problem. And the decision-making responsibility is up to you; the soldier may later blame you because he or she does not feel responsible for the solution to the problem.

The nondirective, or democratic, approach involves the soldier in the counseling. It is usually more relaxed and focuses on self-discovery. The role of the counselor is to help the soldier become self-reliant, to talk his or her way toward the problem's resolution. You must be an effective listener and know when to interject your thoughts or redirect a soldier who digresses from or avoids the subject.

In the combined approach, the leader uses parts of the directive and nondirective methods. It is the most frequently used counseling method. The combined approach assumes that the soldier must eventually be responsible for planning and decision making. The soldier will take charge of solving the problem but may need some help along the way.

Before counseling a soldier, you should tell him or her that you intend to do so, and give a place, date, and time for the session. The place may be dictated by the circumstances. If the soldier is the problem, your office would be appropriate. If the soldier has a problem, you may want to counsel away from the office, perhaps at the post club, or at a nearby gym or other facility. Determine beforehand whether the counseling will be personal or professional in nature. Be sure to follow up with the soldier, and report your effort and its results to your supervisor. Counseling is an important part of soldier team development (FM 22-102).

TRAINING

Training in all its phases must be intensive . . . it must be intelligently directed so that every individual, including the last private in the ranks, can understand the reasons for the exertions he [or she] is called upon to make.
—Dwight D. Eisenhower
General of the Army

Battle-Focused Training

Effective training is the Army's number one priority during peacetime. Training management is the process used by Army leaders to identify training requirements and then plan, resource, execute, and evaluate training. *Battle focus* is the process of deriving peacetime training requirements from wartime missions. According to TC 25-30, *A Leader's Guide to Company Training Meetings*, a battle focus allows commanders to achieve a successful training program by purposely narrowing the focus of the unit's training efforts to a reduced number of vital tasks that are essential to wartime mission accomplishment.

According to *NCO Journal*, battle-focused training has been a part of the Army's training philosophy for some time now, yet many NCOs still do not understand the concept. The central idea is to first develop a unit's Mission Essential Task List (METL, pronounced "mettle") and then develop from it critical individual and collective tasks for training.

The two key documents NCOs must read to understand battle- focused training and the METL development process are FM 25-100, *Training the Force*, and FM 25-101, *Battle Focused Training*. It is important to read the brief FM 25-100 first, because it defines terms that are essential to understanding concepts in the detailed FM 25-101.

FM 25-101 is crucial. Its five chapters cover a training overview, the METL development process, planning, execution, and assessment. It also includes the following must-know information:
• Six leadership responsibilities (train the trainer, train the combined arms team, centralize training planning, decentralize execution, establish effective communications, and demand that standards are met).

- Nine principles of training (train as a combined arms and services team, train as you fight, use appropriate doctrine, use performance-oriented training, train to challenge, train to sustain proficiency, use multiechelon training, train to maintain, make commanders the primary trainers).
- Seven steps of the training management cycle (get the wartime mission, establish the METL, prepare a training assessment, prepare long- and short-range planning calendars and the near-term training schedule, execute training, evaluate training, conduct a unit assessment).
- Seven Battlefield Operating Systems (intelligence, maneuver, fire support, mobility and survivability, air defense, combat service support, and command and control).
- Four forms of execution guidance (prepare yourself, prepare resources, prepare support personnel, prepare the soldiers).
- Three forms of training presentation (lecture, conference, and demonstration).
- Five fundamentals on the battlefield (shoot, move, communicate, sustain, secure).
- Three phases of leader development (reception and integration, basic skills development, and advanced development and sustainment).

NCOs can get and stay "battle focused" by following guidance published in the Fall 1993 issue of NCO Journal:
- Read, study, and often refer to FM 25-100 and FM 25-101 until you understand and apply battle-focused training concepts.
- Know and use your unit's and next higher unit's training guidance. See your unit training NCO for information.
- Know your unit's mission and what individual and collective tasks support the wartime mission. Consult your chain of command to learn all you can, including your unit's classified ground deployment plan—if you have the appropriate security clearance and a need to know.
- Know your job, all technical and tactical aspects of it.
- Apply the nine principles of training listed in FM 25-101.
- Realize that you are part of and must train as a combined arms and services team.
- Train as you would fight. Using the crawl-walk-run training philosophy and get to and maintain competence at the "run" level. Ensure your soldiers can perform all critical tasks to standard under the toughest, most realistic peacetime training conditions so that they will operate effectively on the battlefield.
- Use appropriate Army doctrine. Ask officers in your unit to help you locate information about Force XXI, and apply it to appropriate leadership doctrine including FMs 22-100, 22-101, 22-102, 22-103, 25-100 and 25-101.
- Use performance-oriented training—and participate in it.
- Train to challenge your soldiers, to sustain proficiency, and to maintain a fighting edge.
- Use multiechelon training techniques so that all ranks involved in training benefit at appropriate skill levels.
- Remember that your commander is the primary trainer and relies on you to understand and comply with his or her training guidance.
- Know and use available training resources, such as those available at the local training and audio-visual support center, or at the unit's supporting supply room or next higher level logistics operation (S-4, for example).

• Get familiar with upcoming requirements on yearly and quarterly training schedules.

• Make time to analyze your unit's weekly training schedules to determine what should have been done better, what needs to be done now, and what must be done to stay combat ready.

• Observe your soldiers during training and assess their weaknesses, deficiencies that could get them killed and jeopardize the mission in combat. Use chapter 5 of FM 25-101 to conduct your evaluations.

• Conduct after-action reviews (AARs) after each training event to determine what went wrong and why, what went right and why, and how performance can be improved—and then apply lessons learned in the AAR during additional training.

• Work as a team with your officers.

Performance-Oriented versus Conventional Training
It is necessary to understand the differences between performance-oriented training and conventional training:

Performance-Oriented Training	*Conventional Training*
Uses short demonstrations and "learning by doing."	Uses lectures to instruct.
Makes the soldier active and centers training on him.	Places the instructor in the central active role.
Digests content into a set of high-priority skills that are important to learn in the allotted training time.	Selects content in relation to what the instructor can cover in allotted time.
Sets standards all soldiers must meet; when soldiers do not meet them, they practice until they can.	Uses grades to rate what the soldier has learned.

The Purpose of Performance-Oriented Training
Performance training prepares soldiers, teams, and units for job performance. The question "Does this training really prepare my soldiers to do their jobs?" should become your guide as you prepare for performance training. For any given skill, a properly structured and formulated training objective is both the training and the test. This approach can be described like this:

TRAINING OBJECTIVE = TRAINING + TEST + EVALUATION

A properly constructed training objective consists of three elements: task to be performed, conditions of performance, and a training standard. Stated differently, the training objective answers three questions: *What skill do I want my soldiers to acquire? Under what conditions do I wish my soldiers to demonstrate that skill? How well do I expect these soldiers to perform?*

To learn best, your soldiers must:
• Realize the needs for training.
• Understand what is expected.

- Have an opportunity to practice what was learned.
- Get reinforcement that they are learning.
- Progress through training in a logical sequence.
- Be willing to learn.

An airborne soldier in ground exercise.

Preparing and Conducting Individual Training

Specific training guidance should consist of the commander's training objectives, who will receive the training, the dates and times the training is to occur, where the training will take place, and the reasons why the commander decided the training is necessary.

Your expertise in the subject, bearing, appearance, manner, and desire to help your soldiers learn are vital motivation factors. You must take part in the training to ensure that standards are met. Use fast learners to help slower ones. Make sure soldiers can execute the fundamentals. Conduct a post-training evaluation to determine training effectiveness and efficiency.

Pay close attention to the contents of soldier's manuals, which specify the standards. The objective of performance training is not simply to enable your soldiers to get a "GO," but to ensure survival under real conditions.

Training of the individual soldier is the basis for the collective training of squads, sections, platoons, and companies. As stated early in this chapter, Field Manuals 25-100 and 25-101 detail the essential components of the training process.

As the soldier's manual is to individual performance-oriented training, the Army Training and Evaluation Program (ARTEP) is to collective training. Each ARTEP consists of a series of training and evaluation outlines. Each outline specifies for a particular element the following information:

- Unit the outline applies to.
- Mission to perform.
- General conditions under which the unit will perform.
- Training standards for evaluating performance.
- Collective training objectives, guidance for estimating support necessary to conduct evaluations, and tips to trainers and evaluators.

Individual Training and Evaluation Program (ITEP)

AR 350-37 states that the ITEP is in place throughout the Army to "formalize the role of individual evaluation in units and organizations. Individual training follows a specific process for each MOS, unit, and item of equipment. Following training, an evaluation is conducted to determine training effectiveness by measuring performance against a soldier's manual and Army Training and Evaluation Program (ARTEP)."

The two primary methods used to evaluate individual skill proficiency are Common Task Testing (CTT) and the commander's evaluation. CTT is a hands-on test used to evaluate proficiency on common tasks, such as "React to Indirect Fire." Commander's evaluations are local tests or assessments of proficiency on critical MOS tasks.

Training in Units

AR 350-41, *Training in Units*, prescribes Army policy for training doctrine. It outlines essential training functions accomplished in units and complements FM 25-100 and FM 25-101. The regulation explains training requirements and strategy that relate directly to battle-focused training and the METL development process. It provides training guidance and lists training distractors to avoid. Among other chapters, chapter 6 addresses leader development. It also covers Army policy about the following: soldier training courses; physical fitness; weapons qualification; nuclear, chemical, biological (NBC) training; the Combat Lifesaver program; Code of Conduct; survival, evasion, resistance, and escape (SEER) training; law of war training; and moderniza-tion training. Appendix B of AR 350-41 lists required common military training (CMT) subjects to be taught in all Army units and schools.

Common Leader Combat Skills

The skills NCOs need to ensure that their soldiers can fight, win, and survive in com-bat vary from unit to unit, but certain proficiencies, known as Common Leader Com-bat Skills (CLCS), run throughout the Army. Army NCO Education System courses, discussed in Chapter 4, teach CLCS skills, including the following: occupy assembly area, break contact, conduct fire and movement, react to indirect fire, react to air attack, consolidate and reorganize, conduct continuous operations, move (traveling, traveling overwatch, and bounding overwatch formations), apply troop leading proce-dures, operate in NBC environment, defend, react to ambush, and disengage. All of these skills are addressed in FM 7-8, The Infantry Platoon and Squad (Infantry, Air-borne, Air Assault, Ranger).

SAFETY

> *It's never good to see somebody die, but it's worse when it didn't have to happen.*
> —CWO 5 David Spurgeon
> Army Safety Center Investigator

The Army Safety Program

Senior NCOs at the U.S. Army Sergeants Major Academy (USASMA) agree that the preservation of personnel and material resources is critical to maintaining a unit's combat readiness. In its Advanced NCO Course safety lesson guide, USASMA stresses how every NCO is responsible for ensuring that unsafe acts or unsafe condi-tions are recognized and steps taken to correct them. By doing this, a unit's ability to operate at maximum combat efficiency will be maintained.

The Army Safety Program includes goals, objectives, policies, and responsibili-ties. Its safety goals are to reduce and keep to a minimum accidental manpower and monetary losses and provide a safe and healthful environment. Objectives include the following: injury prevention, damage control, accident prevention, regulatory compli-ance, and liability reduction. Policies of the safety program support the Army mission, make accident prevention a command responsibility, and use available resources on hazards that pose the most immediate threat to safety. Program safety responsibilities are as follows:

- Know and comply with safety policies, regulations, and standard operating proce-dures (SOP).
- Conduct inspections to ensure compliance with safety procedures.
- Train your soldiers to avoid unsafe acts and conditions.
- Identify hazards before accidents occur.
- Ensure that soldiers have the ability to safely perform a stated task.
- Provide proper tools and safety equipment.

- Correct unsafe acts and conditions.
- Report unsafe acts and conditions that cannot be corrected.
- Conduct safety meetings.

How many times have you started a mission and considered safety as your prime intention? Probably not often. Safety is a by-product of every successful or completed mission and must receive the highest regard. As a supervisor, it is extremely important to be aware not only of potential hazards that affect you but also of conditions that may affect those working under your authority.

NCO Safety Program

At the U.S. Army First Sergeant Course, students preparing to assume key roles in companies and batteries throughout the Army get a safety pitch from the academy commandant. The commandant lays out an entire program in 30 minutes that he expects students to teach to their units. Here is the program.

Safety should be a METL task. All leaders in a unit should do and update safety assessments. Safety guidance should be published and posted in plain view. Units should organize for safety. Leaders should develop long-, short-, and near-term safety education programs. Safety should be part of every quarterly training briefing (attended by the commander and first sergeant). Develop a safety feedback system to remain informed about real and potential hazards. Put safety first when executing missions. Include safety aspects of training in every after-action review. Reward safety excellence, and punish negligence.

The commandant included these safety principles: Leaders are responsible; protect every soldier's life; safety takes precedence over fairness; safety is a battle-focused concept; safety and performance complement each other; and everyone is a safety officer.

With 10 minutes remaining in his program, the commandant also said that privates and specialists are the soldiers most often killed in accidents. Privately owned vehicles (POVs) cause the most deaths, with alcohol being a prime contributor, along with not wearing seat belts and speeding. He said that most safety briefings are CYA (cover your a--) in nature, and that soldiers think they are immortal, that "It won't happen to me." Soldiers need to be trained to watch out for the other guy and think and act defensively.

The commandant also included 30 seconds worth of shock training in his program. He showed a film that was gruesome and then said, "Shock training like this will get you by for a weekend, but it won't make soldiers act safely over the long term." Take a look at FM 43-5, *Unit Maintenance Operations,* and AR 385-10, *The Army Safety Program.*

If you or somebody else in your unit is in an accident, you will need to complete DA Form 285, *U.S. Army Accident Report.* If you must complete the report, you can refer to the educational instruction package for the report, available from the U.S. Army Safety Center, ATTN: CSSC-S, Fort Rucker, AL 36362-5363. Or call DSN 558-3842, or commercial (205) 255-3842.

POV SAFETY CHECKLIST

This checklist is designed to assist NCOs in briefing and checking personnel before departure for PCS, TDY, or holiday leave.

Date of Inspection: _____

Rank/Name: _____   Unit: _____
Destination: _____   Estimated miles: _____
Departure date: _____   Return date: _____
Anticipated weather conditions: _____

1. Is the vehicle in safe operating condition?   Status
        Check coolant and radiator hoses   _____
        Check oil level

2. Check these items carefully:
        a. Headlights   _____
        b. Turn signals and brake lights   _____
        c. Emergency flashers   _____
        d. Spare tire and jack equipment   _____
        e. Tires—bald/cracking   _____
        f. Windshield wipers—worn/torn   _____
        g. Windshield cracks   _____
        h. Muffler   _____
            1. Loud noise   _____
            2. Hanging low to ground or loose   _____
            3. Exhaust odors inside vehicle   _____
        i. Seat belt operation
        j. Brakes
            1. Emergency brake
            2. Foot brake

3. Check these items to ensure:
        a. Valid operator's license   _____
        b. Valid license plate registration   _____
        c. Valid proof of insurance   _____
        d. First-aid kit   _____
        e. Safety emergency triangle or flares   _____

                                            NCO Inspector   _____
                                            Signature   _____
                                            Date   _____
                                            Title   _____

PERSONNEL AND PROPERTY ACCOUNTABILITY

No NCO can function without some knowledge of Army administration. As you rise in rank, your ability to understand and perform administrative tasks becomes more and more important.

Most situations that arise in the administration of an Army unit are covered somewhere in Army regulations or other publications. Knowing where to look for guidance is almost as important as knowing the answers. Some soldiers can memorize large portions of pertinent regulations, and they amaze everyone by quoting up-to-date information on a variety of subjects. Most soldiers, however, must be content to stumble through various indexes when searching for information. There is nothing wrong with this approach. The following resources are essential for the NCO administrator.

AR 310-1, *Publications, Blank Forms, and Printing Management.*

AR 310-2, *Identification and Distribution of DA Publications and Issue of Publications.*

DA Pam 25-50, *Consolidated Index of Forms and Publications.*

DA Pam 310-23, *Index and Descriptions of Army Training Devices.*

DA Pam 310-13, *Posting and Filing Publications.*

AR 310-25, *Dictionary of U.S. Army Terms.*

AR 310-50, *Authorized Abbreviations and Brevity Codes. Manual for Courts-Martial,* 1984 (includes UCMJ).

JCS Pub 1, *DOD Dictionary of Military and Associated Terms.*

Each MOS has a corresponding set of basic reference publications. The effective NCO will know them and what is in them. The series above is basic to every good publications library. In addition, the learning resource center and the MOS library are valuable sources for these and other publications.

DUTY ROSTERS

AR 220-45, *Duty Rosters,* clearly states the rules for preparing and maintaining DA Form 6, the duty roster. These rules are logical and easy to understand. Yet accurately putting them into practice requires meticulous attention to detail.

Duty rosters are kept to record the duty performed by each person in an organization. Commanders are authorized to establish procedures that best suit the unit, but they must comply with AR 220-45, the longest off duty, the first on, and impartiality in assignment of duties to individuals.

The "From" date on the roster is always the date immediately following the "To" date on a previous roster and is entered at the time the new roster is prepared. The "To" date is always the date of the last detail made from the roster and is entered when the roster is closed. Intermediate dates are entered as details are made, and no date will be entered for any day that the detail was not made.

Duty rosters contain only the names of those personnel required to perform the duty involved. When a new roster is prepared, all names are entered *alphabetically by rank,* beginning with the highest-ranking person and using the appropriate grade of rank. Subsequent names are added to the bottom of the roster. Frequently, rosters are published in advance and when absences of personnel already assigned duty occur, they often occur at the last moment. Many commanders allow personnel to substitute for one another on various details, and in some units, individuals make extra money by selling their services as substitutes. In such cases, the person who maintains the

DUTY ROSTER

NATURE OF DUTY	ORGANIZATION	FROM (Date)	TO (Date)
Charge of Quarters	Co A, 3d Infantry	14 Feb	

GRADE	NAME	Day → (February 14–28 / March 1–5 …)
SFC	Bierce	8 9 10 11 1 2 12 13 3 4 14 5 6 7
SFC	Le Faneau *(7)*	10 11 12 13 3 4 14 5 1 2 6 7 3 4 5 6 7
SSG	Dunsany *(3)*	7 8 9 10 11 1 /// A A A 2 12 13 14 1 4 5
SSG	Harthorne *(4)*	9 10 11 12 2 3 13 14 4 D 5 6 1 2 3 4 5 7 8
SSG	Lovecraft	3 4 5 6 7 7 8 8 9 10 9 11 13 14 1 2
SSG	O'Neill *(1)*	A A A 9 10 11 12 14 13 1 2 3 1 2
SSG	Yteaina	11 12 13 14 12 13 1 14 1 2 3 4 5 6 7 8 2 3
SGT	Arnold	1 2 3 4 5 6 6 7 7 8 9 10 11 12 13 14 0
SGT	Bolce *(8)*	1 2 3 4 6 7 5 6 7 8 9 10 11 1 2 3 4
SGT	Couperin	12 13 14 1 2 3 4 1 2 5 6 7 8 9 10 11 12 13
SGT	Falstaff	2 3 4 5 7 8 6 7 8 9 10 11 12 13 4 1
SGT	Percy *(10)*	13 14 1 10 11 12 4 5 13 14 6 7 8 A A 1
SGT	Woolsey	4 5 6 7 10 8 9 10 11 12 13 2 3 1 2 14
CPL	Boswell *(11)*	3 4 5 6 8 9 7 8 9 10 11 1 2
CPL	Johnson *(7)*	14 1 2 14 3 4 1 5 6 2 3 7 8 9 10 11
CPL	Pope	6 7 8 9 5 6 10 11 7 8 12 13 9 1 2 3 4 10 11
CPL	Spenser *(2)*	A A A 6 9 7 8 1 2 12 13 14 15 13 14
SSG	Fairleigh *(5)*	8 9 10 11 12 13 9 10 11 12 3 4 13 14 15 13 14
CPL	Queen *(6)*	1 2 3 1 2

This is a consolidated duty roster. Therefore, 18, 19, 22, 25 and 26 February and 4 and 5 March are holidays.

The following remarks go on the back of the roster:

(1) Sick in quarters
(2) 72 hour Pass (soldier of the month)
(3) Leave 21-24 Feb
(5) Assigned and joined
(6) Relieved as company clerk
(7) Excused-detailed as company clerk
(8) AWOL
(9) PCS
(10) Leave 2-9 Mar
(11) Dead

SEE REMARKS ON REVERSE.

DA FORM 6, 1 JUL 74   PREVIOUS EDITIONS OF THIS FORM WILL BE USED UNTIL EXHAUSTED.

For use of this form, see AR 220-45, the proponent agency is The US Army Adjutant General Center duty roster must be notified of any changes, and recovery of any promised compensation is strictly up to the individuals concerned.

Details of *units* are made the same as they are for individuals, in turn according to one roster. However, commanders are authorized to use other methods, providing that equity is maintained.

The diagonal lines in the right corner of any block indicate duty on that date.

The numbers in parentheses immediately following a person's name refer to a corresponding explanatory remark on the reverse of the roster. A remark *must* be made to explain the reason an individual's name is added or deleted from a roster, but the authority responsible for the preparation and maintenance of the roster determines the necessity of using an explanatory remark each time an individual is not available.

A number is used with the abbreviation "A" in the column for 14 February to indicate the last number charged, as shown on the accompanying duty roster.

The duty roster should be available at all times for inspection by commanders, supervisors, and personnel concerned. If you are charged with the responsibility for maintaining a duty roster, do not feel that your integrity is being impugned when a soldier subject to detail according to the roster asks to see it.

Publish your rosters as far in advance as possible to give all concerned fair warning as to when they are coming up for duty. Be consistent when you publish your rosters. If you post the detail announcements on Monday, always post them on Mondays. Smart soldiers will always contact the person responsible for the duty roster when making plans, so never discourage personnel from doing this. Thinking ahead benefits everyone.

MILITARY PROPERTY

Everyone in the Army is accountable and responsible for government property; the amount of property a soldier is responsible for generally increases in value as he or she advances in rank. Safeguarding government property requires basically lots of good old-fashioned common sense.

Classes of Supply

Supplies are items necessary to equip, maintain, and operate a military command, including food, clothing, arms, ammunition, fuel, materials, and machinery of all kinds. Supplies are divided into 10 categories called classes and into lettered subclasses known as material designators (A through T).* For example, Class I C supplies are combat rations.

Class I—Subsistence, including health and welfare items. Subclassifications include inflight rations, refrigerated subsistence, nonrefrigerated subsistence, and combat rations.

Class II—Clothing, individual equipment, tentage, organization tool sets and tool kits, hand tools, administrative and housekeeping supplies, and equipment. Subclassifications include weapons, power generators, and textiles.

---

* For a detailed discussion of supply, see Edwards, *Combat Service Support Guide*, 2nd edition (Stackpole Books, 1993).

DOD CLASSES OF SUPPLY

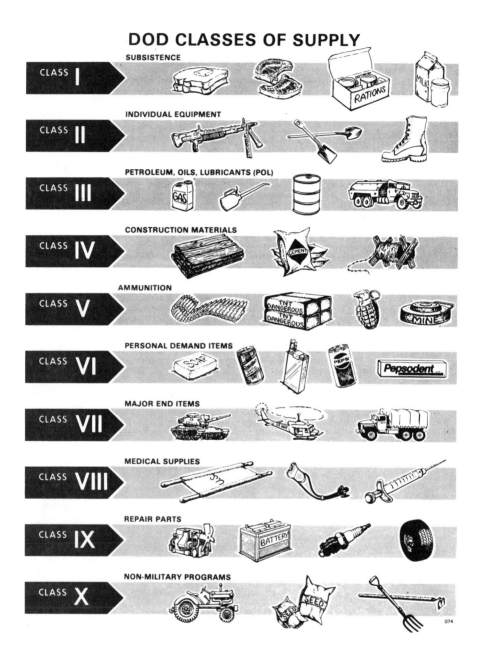

CLASS I — SUBSISTENCE

CLASS II — INDIVIDUAL EQUIPMENT

CLASS III — PETROLEUM, OILS, LUBRICANTS (POL)

CLASS IV — CONSTRUCTION MATERIALS

CLASS V — AMMUNITION

CLASS VI — PERSONAL DEMAND ITEMS

CLASS VII — MAJOR END ITEMS

CLASS VIII — MEDICAL SUPPLIES

CLASS IX — REPAIR PARTS

CLASS X — NON-MILITARY PROGRAMS

Courtesy Armed Forces Staff College, AFSC 1.

Class III—Petroleum, oils, and lubricants.

Class IV—Construction materials.

Class V—Ammunition, including chemical, biological, radiological, and special weapons.

Class VI—Personal demand items, including beer and liquor ("Class VI store" items).

Class VII—Major end items, such as tanks and helicopters. Subclassifications include bridging and fire-fighting equipment, administrative and tactical vehicles, missiles, weapons, and special weapons.

Class VIII—Medical materials.

Class IX—Repair parts and components.

Class X—Material to support nonmilitary programs, such as agricultural and economic development.

Basic Principles

All persons entrusted with government property are responsible for its custody, care, and safekeeping. No commander or supervisor can assign a soldier a duty that would prevent exercising the proper care and custody of property. When you assume accountability for remotely located property, keep records to show the location of the items and the persons charged with safekeeping.

Army property will *not* be used for private purpose, sold, given as a gift, lent, exchanged, or otherwise disposed of unless authorized by law. Giving or accepting an issue, document, hand receipt, or any form of receipt to cover articles that are missing, or appear to be missing, is prohibited.

Units accumulate varying types and amounts of equipment and supplies that are not reflected on the property books, for swapping purposes: If A Company has an extra buffing machine but no lawn mower while B Company needs a buffer but its lawn mower is excess property, sergeants are supposed to get together and make the appropriate trade so that A Company's grass gets cut and B Company's barracks floors shine like glass.

Accounting for Property

Property falls into three distinct categories:

- *Nonexpendable*. Property not consumed in use that retains its original identity during the period of use. Includes all serial-numbered items, such as weapons, vehicles, office machines, and so on. Nonexpendable property requires formal accountability throughout its life. A continuous chain of receipts is required if these items pass between different persons.
- *Expendable*. Office supplies, cleaning materials, and other supplies that are consumed upon issue. Expendable property does not require formal accountability except for some sensitive categories, such as drugs.
- *Durable*. Certain kinds of hand tools. Tools must be issued on a hand receipt.

Responsibilities

Responsibility for property results from possession or the command or supervision of others who have possession of Army property. This responsibility may be assigned by appropriate authority in writing or orally.

Supervisors have the responsibility to ensure the safety and care of property issued to or used by their subordinates. Supervisors are also responsible for maintaining the proper atmosphere that leads to supply discipline among subordinates.

Direct responsibility is a formal assignment of property responsibility to a person within the supply chain who has the property within his or her custody but not necessarily in his possession. Accountable officers have direct responsibility unless it has been specifically assigned to another person. An accountable officer maintains formal records that show the balance, conditions, and location of all property assigned to a property account. Enlisted personnel who are sergeants or higher rank, when appointed by proper authority, may serve as accountable officers.

Responsibilities of Hand-Receipt Holders

Signing a hand-receipt, including signing for clothing and equipment, is probably the most familiar aspect of the supply system to most soldiers. It carries with it definite responsibilities; you must follow these simple rules:

• Inventory equipment and supplies receipted to you.

• Have property for which you have signed on hand or accounted for by a receipt, turn-in, or some other type of authorized credit document.

• Prevent loss, damage, or destruction of property under your control.

• When you turn an item in, get a receipt for it.

• Report loss or theft to your superior.

• When you transfer, be sure all property is turned in or passed into the custody of your replacement or whoever succeeds you in custody of the property. You will not be allowed to clear the installation until you have accounted for all the property for which you are responsible.

• Report to your supervisor any circumstances that make the proper security of property or equipment impossible. Failure to do so can result in your being charged for any loss or damage because you knew the facts and did not report them.

Statements of Charges and Reports of Survey

Statements of Charges (DD Form 362) and *Reports of Survey* (DA Form 4697) are unpleasant methods the Army has of getting its money back from soldiers who have been careless or negligent in their duty as property custodians.

A *Statement of Charges* is prepared in the following situations:

• Liability for loss, damage, or destruction of property is admitted.

• The charge does not exceed the monthly basic pay of the person being charged.

• Individuals do not offer cash payment to make good the lost, damaged, or destroyed property. (All military personnel and civilian employees of the Department of the Army who voluntarily admit liability may offer to replace the property through cash purchase.) If the charges levied by a *Statement of Charges* exceed two thirds of an individual's monthly basic pay, the unit commander will attach a letter requesting that the charges be prorated over a two-month period or longer.

A *Report of Survey* is required to account for lost, damaged, or destroyed property, when it is known that negligence or misconduct is suspected and liability is not admitted. In addition, a *Report of Survey* is prepared in the following situations:

• A sensitive item is lost or destroyed.

• It is directed by higher authority.

- Property loss is discovered as a result of change of accountability inventory.
- The value of the damages or shortages in occupied government quarters exceeds the responsible person's monthly basic pay.
- A person admits liability, and the loss, damage, or destruction exceeds the individual's monthly basic pay.
- A soldier refuses to admit liability and does not offer repayment.

Senior NCOs may be appointed survey officers. Such investigations are painstakingly thorough. The survey officer is charged with finding out the facts. He or she, based on the facts of the investigation, must recommend whether or not to fix liability upon the subjects.

If you are ever the subject of a *Report of Survey*, remember these guidelines:
- Keep calm, tell the truth, and cooperate with the survey officer.
- The survey officer has a job to do; do not take it personally.
- If the survey officer finds you liable, he or she must show you the report and explain your right to legal counsel and to appeal the recommendation if approved.
- If you appeal, get legal counsel; consult an Army lawyer even if you don't appeal.
- You may request remission of indebtedness or an extension of the collection period if the report is approved.
- Many *Reports of Survey* do not recommend pecuniary liability. If you have taken every reasonable precaution to protect the property in your possession, and you can prove it, you should have nothing to fear. If responsibility is fixed on you and the report is approved, then take your medicine.

Enforcement of Supply Discipline

Various disciplinary and administrative measures are available to a commander to enforce supply discipline and reduce the incidence of lost, damaged, or destroyed government property. When property is lost, damaged, or destroyed by a subordinate, the usual reaction is to reach for AR 735-5 and initiate a report of survey. This action may be appropriate or, in some cases, required.

Military discipline goes hand in hand with supply discipline. Commanders have the following administrative tools available in connection with the report of survey.
- An oral reprimand. In more serious cases, a formal letter of admonition or reprimand may be used and, when appropriate, filed in the soldier's Official Military Personnel File.
- Noting a soldier's inefficiency or negligence in his or her NCOER.
- Article 15 or court-martial in cases of misconduct or neglect resulting in damaged or lost military property.

A *Report of Survey* is not a form of punishment nor a deterrent. Nonjudicial punishment, however, is both. Its use in conjunction with a *Report of Survey* may be indicated, depending upon circumstances. Even when no liability is found, the facts may warrant command action. There is little doubt that strong measures should be taken against a supply sergeant whose stocks are found $10,000 short because of his or her misconduct or neglect. But similar action also would be appropriate against supervisors if investigation revealed inadequate supervision, such as if required inventories had never been made or verified.

3

Fitness

Before the gates of Excellence the high gods have placed sweat.
—Hesiod, 8th century B.C.

PHYSICAL FITNESS TRAINING

According to FM 21-20, *Physical Fitness Training*, a good fitness program can reduce the number of soldiers on profile and sick call, invigorate training, and enhance productivity and mental alertness. A good PT program also promotes team cohesion and combat survivability. It will improve soldiers' combat readiness. Chapter 1 of FM 21-20 states:

> A soldier's level of physical fitness has a direct impact on his [or her] combat readiness. The many battles in which American troops have fought underscore the important role physical fitness plays on the battlefield. The renewed nationwide interest in fitness has been accompanied by many research studies on the effects of regular participation in sound physical fitness programs. The overwhelming conclusion is that such programs enhance a person's quality of life, improve productivity, and bring about positive physical and mental changes. Not only are physically fit soldiers essential to the Army, they are also more likely to have enjoyable, productive lives.

Soldiers in many Army units are required to take part in daily PT. Students attending NCO Education System (NCOES) courses are required to do PT five times per week, except when in the field overnight, in compliance with Training and Doctrine Command (TRADOC) Regulation 351-17, *NCO Training in TRADOC NCO Academies*. Students are required to lead fitness training on a rotational basis and are evaluated by NCO academy small-group leaders on their ability to plan and conduct the training. Upon arrival at any NCOES course—Primary Leadership Development Course, Basic NCO Course, Advanced NCO Course, or Sergeants Major Course—students must have passed the APFT within the previous six months.

Soldiers attending NCOES courses and those on the job or in training elsewhere in the Army should know that an effective PT program includes the following:

• *The five components of fitness—cardiorespiratory (CR) endurance, muscular strength, muscular endurance, flexibility, and body composition.* CR endurance is the efficiency with which the body delivers oxygen and nutrients needed for muscle activity and transports waste products from the cells. Muscular strength is the greatest amount of force a muscle or muscle group can exert in a single effort. Muscular endurance is the ability of a muscle or muscle group to perform repeated movements with less than maximum force for extended periods of time. Flexibility is the ability to move the joints or any group of joints through an entire, normal range of motion. Body composition is the amount of body fat a soldier has in comparison to total body mass.

- *The seven principles of exercise (PROVRBS, pronounced "proverbs")—progression, regularity, overload, variety, recovery, balance, and specificity.* Progression means the intensity or duration of exercise must gradually increase to improve fitness. Regularity means that, to get a training effect, a person must exercise often, at least three times a week; and it means getting adequate rest and sleep, and maintaining a proper diet. Overload means the workload of each exercise session must exceed the normal demands placed on the body in order to achieve a training effect. Variety means providing different activities in the PT program to reduce boredom and increase motivation and progress. Recovery means following hard training days with easier days; it also means exercising alternate muscle groups every other day. Balance means including activities that address the five components of fitness. Specificity means gearing the program toward specific goals, emphasizing running, for example, for soldiers who need to improve their running ability.

- *The four FITT principles—frequency, intensity, time, and type.* Frequency means doing PT at least three, preferably five, times a week. Intensity of CR workouts must be at the proper training heart rate (THR), depending on current fitness level. The THR is most accurately calculated as follows: (1) Subtract your age from the number 220 to determine your maximum heart rate (MHR); (2) take your resting pulse (while completely relaxed) for 30 seconds and multiply the number of pulses by 2 to determine your resting heart rate (RHR); (3) determine your heart rate reserve (HRR) by subtracting the RHR from the MHR; (4) calculate your THR based on 60 to 90 percent of your HRR by multiplying the percentage (that is, .6, .7, .8, or .9) by the HRR, then adding the result to your RHR to determine your THR—that is, the number of beats per minute of your heart you must maintain during aerobic exercise to achieve a training effect (and burn fat).

Muscular strength and muscular endurance workout intensity refers to the percentage of maximum resistance used for a given exercise and is expressed as "repetition maximum." Basically, for strength training you would exercise close to your one-repetition maximum but with fewer repetitions per set (heavy weight, few repetitions, several sets); for endurance training you would exercise well below your one-repetition maximum with many repetitions per set (light weight, many repetitions, several sets).

The time component of the FITT principles means at least 20 to 30 continuous minutes of intense exercise must be used to improve CR endurance. For muscular strength and endurance, exercise time equates to the number of repetitions done. FM 21-20 states that, for moderately fit soldiers, 8 to 12 repetitions with enough resistance to cause muscle failure improves both endurance and strength.

The last FITT principle, type, refers to the kind of exercise performed. The basic rule is that, to improve performance, you must practice the particular exercise, activity, or skill you want or need to improve. For example, to be good at push-ups you must do push-ups; no other exercise will improve push-up performance as effectively.

- *The three phases of fitness—preparatory, conditioning, and maintenance.* The preparatory phase, for poorly conditioned soldiers, helps the CR and muscular systems get used to exercise. The conditioning phase includes progressively more strenuous activities aimed at reaching the desired fitness level. The maintenance phase sustains a high fitness level achieved in the conditioning phase. The starting phase for individuals and units will vary depending on individual or average age, fitness level, and previous fitness activity. Using individual and average unit APFT scores as a fitness assessment tool will help you determine the phase of your soldiers and unit.
- *The three types of PT programs—unit, individual, and special populations.* Unit programs must support unit Mission Essential Task List requirements. Fitness trainers can develop unit programs by following the principles found in chapter 1 of FM 21-20. Individual programs, which may be needed in certain units, such as major command staffs, hospitals, recruiting offices, and the Reserve Officer Training Corps, will be successful if unit leaders develop environments that encourage and motivate soldiers to accept individual responsibility for their own fitness. Special population programs vary according to individual needs. Examples: A soldier who failed the APFT because of a poor run time may need a program that focuses on CR endurance; a soldier who is overweight and who is on a medical profile against running may be put on a swimming, bicycling, or walking program to improve CR endurance; a pregnant soldier (who by regulation is exempt from the APFT) may continue to exercise on her own.
- *The three kinds of evaluation standards—Initial Entry Training (IET), One Station Unit Training and Advanced Individual Training (OSUT and AIT), and the Army standard.* The IET standard means entry-level soldiers must score at least 50 percent on each of the three events of the APFT to pass the test. The OSUT and AIT standard requires soldiers in these statuses to achieve at least 60 percent on each of the events of the APFT to pass. The Army standard is 60 percent as well, but certain elite and task-organized units (airborne, Ranger, Special Forces, "Task Force XXI") may conduct evaluations based on higher standards.
- *The four kinds of flexibility—static, passive, neuromuscular facilitation (PNF), and ballistic.* Good stretching techniques improve flexibility. Static stretching involves the gradual lengthening of muscles and tendons as a body part moves around a joint, and is safe and effective. Using the static method, the soldier assumes each stretching position slowly until he or she feels tension, and holds it for 10 or more seconds. Passive stretching requires the use of a partner or equipment such as a towel, pole, or rubber tubing. PNF stretching requires the soldier to perform a series of intense contractions and relaxations using a partner or equipment, and develops an ability to stretch through a greater range of motion. Ballistic stretching includes bouncing or bobbing to attain a greater range of motion, and stretch and should be avoided because it can cause injury.
- *The five responsibilities of leadership—develop confidence, aggressiveness, alertness, teamwork, and a competitive spirit.* FM 21-20 states: "Effective leadership is critical to the success of a good physical training program. Leaders must understand and practice the new Army doctrine of physical fitness. They must be visible and active participants in PT programs. In short, leaders must lead PT! Their example will emphasize the importance of physical fitness training and will highlight it as a key element of the unit's training mission."
- *The two kinds of PT formations—extended rectangular and circle.* The extended rectangular formation is used when conducting by-the-numbers PT that includes

push-ups, sit-ups, and similar cadence-oriented exercises. The circular formation is more appropriate for guerrilla and grass drills, and routines involving running.

• *The roles of the five personnel who administer the APFT—the officer or NCO in charge, event supervisors, demonstrators, scorers, and support personnel.* The soldier in charge ensures that the APFT is properly administered; gets all necessary equipment and supplies; arranges and lays out the test area (if necessary); trains the event supervisors, scorers, and demonstrators (using Training Videotape 21-191); ensures events are explained, demonstrated, and scored; and reports results to superiors. Event supervisors administer test events; ensure necessary equipment is on hand; read test instructions and have events demonstrated; supervise scoring; and rule on questions and scoring errors or disputes. Scorers supervise the testing soldiers' performance; enforce test standards; count aloud the repetitions performed on the push-up and sit-up events; and record raw scores on DA Form 705, *APFT Scorecard.* Support personnel handle safety and crowd control.

THE ARMY PHYSICAL FITNESS TEST

Soldiers taking the APFT are encouraged to make a maximum effort and to pass and excel. The test is administered at least every six months, normally in the spring and fall. Described in detail in chapter 14 of FM 21-20, the APFT includes timed push-ups, sit-ups, and a two-mile run (or alternate aerobic event in certain circumstances). The push-up event measures the endurance of the chest, shoulder, and triceps muscles. The sit-up event measures the endurance of the abdominal and hip-flexor muscles. The two-mile run or alternate aerobic event measures CR and leg muscle endurance. Instructions for each APFT event in FM 21-20 must be read verbatim before each is administered.

Members of the special populations mentioned earlier in this chapter may be unable to take some or all of the APFT events for medical or other authorized or unavoidable reasons. In order to get credit for the APFT, however, the two-mile run or an alternate aerobic event must be taken and passed. Alternate aerobic events include the 800-yard swim, 6.2-mile bicycle ride (in one gear), and 2.5-mile walk. Like the run, the alternate events must be completed unassisted in a prescribed amount of time relative to age and gender. Unlike the run, the alternates are not scored; test-takers get credit for either passing or failing the event. Soldiers who fail any or all of the events must retake the entire test. In case of test failure, commanders may allow soldiers to retake the test as soon as the soldiers and commander feel they are ready. Soldiers without a medical profile will be retested not later than three months following the initial APFT failure.

Soldiers in the ranks of sergeant through command sergeant major know that APFT entries are recorded on DA Form 2166-7, the *NCO Evaluation Report* (NCOER). NCOER raters enter "pass," "fail," or "profile" on part IVc of the NCOER. According to AR 623-205, *Enlisted Evaluation Reporting System,* these entries reflect the NCO's status on the date of the most recent APFT administered by the unit within the 12-month period prior to the last rated day of supervision. The regulation states that "APFT numerical scores will be entered as bullet comments to justify 'Excellence' or 'Needs Improvement' ratings based solely on the APFT." Raters must explain an APFT entry of "fail" or "profile."

In compliance with Army retention policy, soldiers who have six months or more time in service who fail two consecutive record APFTs must be processed for

Soldiers complete the running requirement of the Army Physical Fitness Test.

separation for unsatisfactory performance under chapter 13 of AR 635-200, *Enlisted Personnel*. Receipt of a "Chapter 13" for fitness failure indicates that the soldier is unqualified for further service because he or she will not develop sufficiently to participate in further training or become a satisfactory soldier. It also means failures would likely continue to recur, and the ability of the soldier to perform duties effectively in the future, including potential for advancement or leadership, is unlikely. Entry-level soldiers, those with less than six months' time in service, who repeatedly fail diagnostic and record APFTs may be separated under chapter 11 of the *Enlisted Personnel* regulation. A "Chapter 11" covers inability, lack of reasonable effort, or failure to adapt to the military environment.

On the other hand, soldiers who excel on the APFT may earn the Army Physical Fitness Badge. Fit soldiers also receive verbal commendations and other accolades, are retained in service and selected for advanced military schooling, and can be promoted provided they meet other service-selection criteria, including presenting a sharp military appearance—which requires weight control.

WEIGHT CONTROL

AR 600-9, *The Army Weight Control Program*, states that each soldier (commissioned, warrant, or enlisted) is responsible for meeting service weight control standards. To help soldiers meet their responsibility, height and weight screening tables are published in the weight control regulation. The regulation's proponent agency, the Office of the Deputy Chief of Staff for Personnel (ODCSPER), recommends that soldiers strive to remain at least 5 percent below their individual screening table weight maximum. NCO supervisors should ensure that they and their soldiers practice weight control by individually attaining and maintaining an acceptable weight and body composition through self-motivation or involvement in an official weight control program.

For some, the ODCSPER guidance is easy to follow. Others have a real problem. Whether compliance is easy or not often depends on a number of factors, including the individual's body type—ectomorph (thin), mesomorph (medium to well proportioned), or endomorph (soft, heavier). Each of the body types can meet the standards, and each can fail to comply and exceed the maximum body fat allowable for gender, age, height, and weight. An ectomorph in poor shape who eats a high-fat diet may carry much excess body fat. Conversely, an endomorph on a well-balanced diet including high fiber and who exercises regularly may carry little body fat. AR 600-9 states that the stringent Department of Defense body fat goal is 20 percent for males, 26 percent for females. Army body fat standards are as follows:

Age Group:	17–20	Age Group:	21–27
Male (% body fat):	20	Male (% body fat):	22
Female (% body fat):	28	Female (% body fat):	30
Age Group:	28–39	Age Group:	40 & older
Male (% body fat):	24	Male (% body fat):	26
Female (% body fat):	32	Female (% body fat):	34

Commanders and NCO supervisors must monitor all soldiers under their control to ensure that the soldiers maintain proper weight, body composition (the proportion of lean body mass, including muscle, bone, and essential organ tissue, to body fat), and personal appearance. Soldiers should be coached to select their personal weight goal within or below the 5 percent zone and strive to maintain that weight through adjustment of lifestyle and fitness routines. If a soldier consistently exceeds the personal weight goal, he or she should seek the assistance of master fitness trainers for advice in proper exercise and fitness and health-care personnel for a proper dietary program. Soldiers exceeding the screening table weight or identified by the commander or supervisor for a special evaluation will have determination made of body fat, using the measuring tape–body circumference method.

WEIGHT FOR HEIGHT TABLE (SCREENING TABLE WEIGHT)

Height (in inches)	Male Age				Female Age			
	17–20	21–27	28–39	49+	17–20	21–27	28–39	40+
58	—	—	—	—	109	112	115	119
59	—	—	—	—	113	116	119	123
60	132	136	139	141	116	120	123	127
61	136	140	144	146	120	124	127	131
62	141	144	148	150	125	129	132	137
63	145	149	153	155	129	133	137	141
64	150	154	158	160	133	137	141	145
65	155	159	163	165	137	141	145	149
66	160	163	168	170	141	146	150	154
67	165	169	174	176	145	149	154	159
68	170	174	179	181	150	154	159	164
69	175	179	184	186	154	158	163	168
70	180	185	189	192	159	163	168	173
71	185	189	194	197	163	167	172	177
72	190	195	200	203	167	172	177	183
73	195	200	205	208	172	177	182	188
74	201	206	211	214	178	183	189	194
75	206	212	217	220	183	188	194	200
76	212	217	223	226	189	194	200	206
77	218	223	229	232	193	199	205	211
78	223	229	235	238	198	205	210	216
79	229	235	241	244	203	209	215	222
80	234	240	247	250	208	214	220	227

Note: For screening purposes, body fat composition is to be determined in accordance with appendix B, AR 600-9.

When males are tape tested they must have the abdomen and neck measured; females have the hips, forearm, neck, and wrist measured. All measurements are taken three times and must be to within one quarter of an inch of one another to be considered valid. Valid measurements are recorded on DA Forms 5500-R (males) and 5501-R (females), *Body Fat Content Worksheet*. Recorded measurements are then converted to prescribed body site factors, using site factor tables in AR 600-9. If carefully measured and correctly calculated, the result will fairly accurately show a soldier's body fat percentage. The tape test is not difficult to learn to administer. The male test takes about five minutes, and the female test takes a little longer because more body sites are measured and calculated.

To help soldiers fight fat, NCO supervisors must provide educational and other motivational programs to encourage personnel to attain and maintain proper weight and body fat standards. Programs must include nutrition education sessions conducted by qualified health care personnel, as well as exercise programs. Commanders must enforce body fat standards and monitor, measure, and if necessary, place individuals into the Army Weight Control Program, then continue to monitor individuals in compliance with AR 600-9. Soldiers entered into the program will not be allowed to reenlist or extend their enlistment, will be considered nonpromotable, and will not be assigned to command positions (e.g., squad leader, platoon sergeant, first sergeant, command sergeant major).

Further, overweight soldiers will be denied attendance at professional military or civilian schooling. AR 351-1, *Individual Military Education and Training*, states that personnel who do not meet body fat standards are not authorized to attend professional military schooling. All soldiers scheduled attendance at schooling will be screened prior to departing their home station or losing command. Their height and weight will be recorded on their temporary duty orders, DD Form 1610, or on their permanent-change-of-station (PCS) packet. Soldiers exceeding established screening weight will not be allowed to depart their command until the commander has determined they meet the standards.

School commandants will take the following action upon determining that a student has arrived for a professional military school exceeding established body fat composition standards. Soldiers arriving at any Department of the Army (DA) board select school or those who PCS to a professional military school who do not meet body fat standards will be processed for disenrollment and removed from the DA board select list. Personnel arriving at professional military schools (other than DA board select or PCS schools) who do not meet body fat composition standards will be denied enrollment and reassigned in accordance with AR 600-9.

Actions to initiate mandatory bars to reenlistment or initiation of separation proceedings for soldiers who are eliminated for cause from NCOES courses will be in accordance with AR 601-280, *Army Reenlistment Program,* and AR 635-200, *Enlisted Personnel*. Additionally, soldiers who by AR 600-9's definition are considered as weight control failures will be processed for separation from the Army.

Soldiers who are entered into the weight control program and then successfully meet their body fat reduction goal will be removed from the program but monitored for a year. Failure to meet the standards at any time during the monitoring period will result in initiation of separation action.

Evelyn Harris, a reporter for the American Forces Information Service in Alexandria, Virginia, wrote an article published in *SOLDIERS* magazine entitled "Fighting Fat." Harris said that soldiers who consider themselves too fat—or who come close to qualifying for the Army Weight Control Program—should look at modifying their lifestyles and eating habits for life. Soldiers interested in an improved diet may seek guidance in appendix C of AR 600-9, "Nutrition Guide to the Weight Control Program."

According to the guide, proper nutrition and regular exercise are necessary to help you lose weight and improve your state of fitness. It says, "Invest in yourself." Here is how:

- Make a decision to lose weight and shape up.
- Get motivated.
- Develop a strategy (diet, exercise routine, lifestyle changes).
- Carry out this strategy and enjoy the payoff—a healthy appearance, an improved self-image, a sense of accomplishment, and a feeling of pride.

In her article, Harris quoted LTC Hannah Henley, a dietician at Walter Reed Army Medical Center in Washington, D.C.: "If a person is only slightly overweight, say 10 pounds, I'm likely to suggest starting with a regular exercise program. This helps ensure that the number of calories you burn equals the number you take in." Sticking to a balanced, low-fat diet is also recommended. Harris added, "Studies show the average American man eats 2,360 to 2,640 calories per day. The average women eats between 1,640 and 1,800. Reducing calories taken in leaves fewer calories for the body to burn to lose weight. Army Master Fitness Training Course material states that a healthy man can safely take in as few as 1,500 calories per day, and a healthy woman can consume as few as 1,200."

Harris recommended that to look and feel healthy as you work to cut or maintain your weight, follow the U.S. Department of Agriculture's dietary guidelines:

- Reduce salt and keep total fat intake below 30 percent of daily calories.
- Eat five servings daily from the vegetable and fruit groups and lots of complex carbohydrates.
- Choose leaner meats, fish, and lower-fat dairy products for protein and calcium.

Vegetables, fruits, and complex carbohydrates, such as whole-grain breads, are "secret weapons" for anyone trying to maintain a healthy diet, according to Harris. They are filling and satisfying because they are high in fiber, but they are generally lower in calories. Henley, the dietician, added that a gram of fat contains nine calories, whether saturated or not. A gram of carbohydrate or protein contains four calories.

TOTAL FITNESS 2000

The goal of the Army's Total Fitness 2000 (TF2000) Program is to maximize the Army's readiness, its ability to deploy, and job performance, according to Dr. Louis F. Tomasi, chief research physiologist and instructor, U.S. Army Physical Fitness School. TF2000 will also improve the state of individual fitness and encourage the development and practice of healthy lifestyles. In an article published in the *NCO Journal*, Tomasi said TF2000 involves aspects of the Army Health Promotion Program, including fitness education and training, nutrition, physical health, substance abuse education, and mental health.

TF2000 fitness education is being provided to initial entry training, NCO Education System, and Army Physical Fitness School students. It is also offered to family members, Army civilians, and retirees. TF2000 physical fitness training includes unit physical training (PT) programs, individual PT (covering weight control, diet, exercise, and sports), special population PT (for soldiers on medical profiles, who are pregnant or overweight, APFT failures, or medically unscreened soldiers who are over 40).

TF2000's nutrition component includes an education program; dining facility, commissary, club system, post exchange, and concession involvement; and recommendations for food choices when dining out. The physical health aspect of TF2000 covers weight control, blood pressure, cholesterol (which should be 200 or below), and dental health. The substance abuse aspect covers tobacco and chemical dependency cessation. Its mental health aspect covers stress management and suicide prevention.

Tomasi said implementation of TF2000 is not difficult. Many policies and functional aspects are in existing regulations. Program policies may be found in AR 600-63, *Army Health Promotion Program*, and in AR 350-41, *Training in Units*. AR 350-41 now includes the contents of the old AR 350-15, *Army Physical Fitness Program*, in chapter 9. To find out more about TF2000, consult your unit master fitness trainer or chain of command.

MASTER FITNESS TRAINERS

Qualified soldiers throughout the Army serve as master fitness trainers (MFTs), a title they earn in one of the Army's most physically and mentally stimulating offerings, the Master Fitness Course. Soldiers who attended the month-long MFT course prior to Army drawdown budget cuts, as well as those who attend the current two-week (86-academic-hour) version of the course, come away prepared to address the following as unit fitness advisors:

- Army fitness literature.
- Muscle physiology.
- Muscular strength and endurance.
- The human oxygen transport system.
- Exercise physiology.
- Cardiovascular disease risk.
- Army Weight Control Program.
- Weight control and diet.
- Physiological differences (men/women).
- Athletic shoe selection.
- Unit assessment.
- How to "sell" a fitness program.
- Anatomy of human motion.
- CPR training.
- Flexibility.
- Circuit training.
- Nutrition and physical performance.
- Administration of the APFT.
- Body composition.
- Unit and individual program development.
- Training injuries.
- Environmental considerations.
- Special populations.
- Reserve Component unit considerations.

Course topics are aimed at fitness program development, PT, exercise science, health and wellness, and fitness administration and evaluation. The U.S. Army Physical Fitness School (PFS) sponsors the MFT Course. To do so, the PFS deploys mobile training teams (MTTs) to conduct on-site training for hundreds of soldiers in the United States and abroad each year. The course is two weeks long and tailored to be academically and physically challenging. It covers all the topics listed above and contains scientific theory material that requires good reading comprehension. Enlisted graduates receive the P5 additional skill identifier (ASI), Master Fitness Trainer. Total cost to bring a fitness school MFT to an installation is about $10,000. That expense will train 50 to 70 students.

Student allocations in the course should be focused toward leadership positions. NCOs selected for the course should be in the grade of sergeant and above. Installations that present Advanced NCO Course (ANCOC) instruction should note that ANCOC small-group leaders have priority for attendance. Students should have a general-technical (GT) score of 107 or higher to better assure success. Again, and according to the MFT Course fact sheet, there is a high correlation between reading ability and success in the course.

All students are administered an APFT at the start of the course and must score at least 240 to be enrolled. Instructors strictly enforce APFT standards. Medical profiles that limit individual participation in physical training will not be accepted.

To assist your commander in bringing the MFT Course to your installation, draft a memorandum for Commandant, U.S. Army Physical Fitness School, ATTN: ATZB-PF-O, Fort Benning, GA 31905-5000. The subject is "Request for Master Fitness Training (MFT) Course." State the need or reason for the MFT course at your installation. For example, your installation has not received the course in the past two fiscal years, or perhaps, your installation has a projected shortage of qualified MFTs assigned. Give primary and alternate dates for the request. State that you understand all requirements and agree to fully support and fund a mobile training team to conduct training at your installation. Provide a point of contact who will be there when the course is taught, and provide telephone numbers. The memo must be signed by a brigade-level or higher commander.

4

Military Education

Although there have been NCO schools in the Army well back into the 1800s, there has never been a system as all-embracing as [the Noncommissioned Officer Education System], a network of instruction which has helped make the corps the envy of other world armies.

—L. James Binder
Editor in chief, *Army* magazine

In the March 29, 1994, issue of *Army Times*, staff writer Bernard Adelsberger quoted the U.S. Army Sergeants Major Academy Commandant, COL Frederick Van Horn, as saying, "You can build a tank in a couple of weeks, but building a leader is a longer process. Growing a noncommissioned officer from sergeant to sergeant major by way of a school system, by way of self-development, by way of assignments and experience, is a 20-year process."

Indeed it is. And all along the way, NCOs are expected to meet service standards, remain motivated, do their best, train and lead subordinates, and support superiors and one another. NCOs who try every day to measure up and who want to excel should know that the melding of the NCO Development Program and the NCO Education System cannot be separated, and that tomorrow's Army will expect even more of its NCO corps.

THE NONCOMMISSIONED OFFICER DEVELOPMENT PROGRAM (NCODP)

The NCODP is a leadership tool designed to be used at the battalion or equivalent level, equally applicable to TDA (table of distribution and allowances, which are nonfighting) and TOE (table of organization and equipment, which are fighting or supporting) units. NCO professional development training is structured to the needs of the unit NCOs as assessed by the unit commander. Soldiers who demonstrate the potential for or are performing duty in leadership positions participate in the NCODP, although separate classes may be conducted for senior NCOs.

The NCODP has the following objectives:
* Strengthen the leadership development of the first-line NCO supervisor.
* Assist and provide guidance in the continuing development of NCOs.
* Increase the confidence of the NCO as a leader.

- Realize the full potential of the NCO support channel for the chain of command.
- Improve unit effectiveness.

Although the Enlisted Personnel Management System and the Noncommissioned Officer Education System provide a valuable foundation for the development of NCOs, the NCODP builds upon their contributions because only through the practical application of skills in the unit can soldiers achieve their goal of becoming truly professional.

Unit commanders develop NCODPs that are responsive to the needs of their unit and the aspirations and development of their junior leaders. Time and resources are provided for the conduct of professional training, including formal periods of instruction and counseling of NCOs. The unit commander ensures that there is clear identification of those tasks that are noncommissioned officer business and that there is a clear and distinct NCO support channel that complements the supervisory chain of command.

NCODP training is implemented at the lowest level feasible, which may be company, troop, battery, or separate detachment. Unit programs complement formal training presented at military and civilian institutions. Professional training includes instructions applicable to soldiers of all career management fields, as well as those specific NCO responsibilities outlined in FM 22-600-20. Portions of the NCODP may be formalized into periods of unit development training. Topics selected are attuned to the geography, mission, and needs of the unit, and supplement professional training gained from daily, routine operations.

Appendix B, "Suggested Topics for NCO Training Program," of AR 350-17, *Noncommissioned Officer Development Program (NCODP)*, contains a partial list of references that may be used to conduct NCODP.

THE NONCOMMISSIONED OFFICER EDUCATION SYSTEM (NCOES)

The NCOES is an integrated system of resident training—service school and NCO academy, supervised on-the-job training, self-study, and on-the-job experience—that provides job-related training for NCOs throughout their careers. The NCOES is designed to provide progressive, continuous training from the primary through the senior level.

NCOES sustains the Army with trained leaders and technicians. It is an integral part of the Enlisted Personnel Management System (EPMS). The NCOES applies to all enlisted personnel of all components of the Army. The EPMS, which the NCOES supports, is characterized by five skill levels representing progressively higher levels of performance capability, experience, and grade. Five levels of training have been established in support of these skill levels. Completion of initial entry training provides the soldier the foundation of professional and technical knowledge needed to perform at the first duty station; combined with subsequent individual training in the unit, the soldier qualifies at skill level 1. The next four levels of training (primary, basic, advanced, and senior) are taught through the NCOES.

Graduation from the appropriate level of NCOES formal schooling is a prerequisite for promotion. Full linkage of NCOES to promotions ensures that NCOs acquire the appropriate skills, knowledge, and attributes needed to assume the duties and responsibilities of the next higher grade, according to the Total Army Personnel

ENLISTED TRAINING SYSTEM

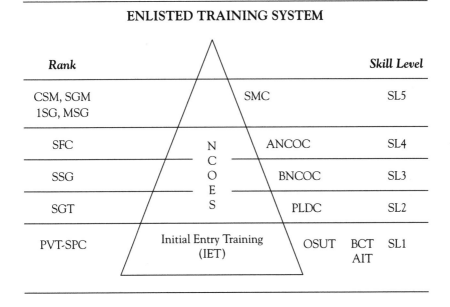

Rank		Skill Level
CSM, SGM 1SG, MSG	SMC	SL5
SFC	ANCOC	SL4
SSG	BNCOC	SL3
SGT	PLDC	SL2
PVT-SPC	Initial Entry Training (IET) OSUT BCT AIT	SL1

Command. Linkage aligns NCO professional and leader development with the Army philosophy of "select, train, promote, utilize." In 1989, graduation from the Primary Leadership Development Course (PLDC) became a prerequisite for promotion to sergeant. Corporals and specialists who meet the cut-off score for promotion to sergeant but have not graduated from PLDC will have their promotions held up until the first day of the month following graduation.

In 1992, graduation from the Basic NCO Course (BNCOC) became a prerequisite for promotion to staff sergeant. A soldier must be a PLDC graduate to be boarded and must be a BNCOC graduate to be promoted to staff sergeant. Sergeants who meet the promotion cut-off score but who have not graduated from BNCOC will not be promoted until the first day of the month following graduation. Additionally, soldiers who fail BNCOC will not be eligible for promotion based on meeting a cut-off score prior to failure.

In 1993, graduation from the Advanced NCO Course (ANCOC) became a prerequisite for promotion to sergeant first class. Soldiers must be BNCOC graduates to be eligible for promotion consideration and must be ANCOC graduates to receive permanent promotion to sergeant first class. Conditional promotion applies to soldiers whose sequence numbers have been reached for promotion to sergeant first class but have not yet attended or completed ANCOC. These soldiers will be promoted conditionally pending successful completion of ANCOC. ANCOC is also a prerequisite for promotion consideration to master sergeant.

Also in 1993, graduation from the U.S. Army Sergeants Major Course (USASMC) became a prerequisite for promotion to sergeant major and appointment to command sergeant major. Conditional promotion applies to soldiers whose sequence numbers have been reached for promotion to sergeant major but who have not yet attended or completed the USASMC.

The NCOES section of the Total Army Personnel Command (PersCom) has informed commanders at every level that NCOES training receives high priority and that soldiers must attend school when scheduled. NCOES linkage to promotion is related directly to training the force (FM 25-100), leader development (FM 22-100), and readiness. According to PersCom, maintaining a strong, competent, and highly motivated NCO corps is every leader's responsibility, and promotion linkage ensures training the right soldier at the right time for the next level of leadership.

Command sergeants major, in concert with Army selection boards, ensure that soldiers who need NCOES training receive it. Soldiers who are not otherwise qualified will not be sent for training merely to fill a quota. In the past, the Army's NCO academies were plagued by soldiers who did not want or deserve to be there.

Although PersCom schedules soldiers for resident training (other than for the First Sergeant Course), local selection authority governs attendance at PLDC. Soldiers are selected for PLDC based on a battalion-level (or equivalent) Order of Merit List. To be eligible, a soldier must have trained on 70 percent of all MSO tasks in his individual soldier's job book within the past six months, must have passed the Army Physical Fitness Test within the past six months, must meet the weight standards, must be eligible for reenlistment, and must be recommended by his unit commander.

Noncommissioned Officer Academies (NCOA)

The mission of NCO academies is to provide NCOES training to qualified soldiers, train them in the fundamentals of leadership, prepare them to train subordinates, offer them increased educational opportunities, prepare them to work in all kinds of environments, instill increased self-confidence and a sense of responsibility, and provide selected personnel with specific critical MOS training.

To ensure that soldiers are provided equal opportunity to attend NCOES courses, the NCOA network has been divided into geographic training regions. If certain NCOES training is not available within a region, that region's student population may receive its training at the nearest NCOA that offers the training. Appendix D, AR 351-1, lists the NCOA regions.

NCOA courses do not award an MOS, an additional skill identifier, or a higher skill level. Leadership courses offered in academies emphasize training management and leadership skills that focus on senior and subordinate relationships, needs of the soldier, discipline, counseling, and techniques of soldier motivation. NCOAs ensure that students maintain high standards of military courtesy, conduct, and fitness. The level of discipline maintained by NCOAs should not, however, interfere with the learning environment, and treatment of students is designed to reflect favorably on the image of the Army and the objective of the NCOAs.

Overweight soldiers who report at any of the four NCOES courses are tape-tested by instructors (small-group leaders) to determine body fat content. If they are over the limit for their age, gender, and height, they are denied enrollment and sent home.

Soldiers who show up exceeding their body fat standard cost small-group leaders time away from their classes and cost the Army round-trip tickets and other expenses.

When an overweight soldier returns to his or her unit, that individual will soon receive bad news. The soldier's first general officer in the chain of command will already have been informed, via a memorandum from the academy commandant, that the soldier failed to maintain the standard. Subsequently, the soldier will be barred from reenlistment or be separated if he or she fails to make satisfactory progress in the weight control program.

Primary Leadership Development Course
The PLDC emphasizes to specialists and corporals how to lead and train and the duties, responsibilities, and authority of the NCO. It is a four-week course conducted at NCOAs in CONUS and overseas and is open to soldiers who have not previously attended a primary-level leadership course. Successful completion of PLDC is required for promotion to sergeant.

Basic NCO Course
The BNCOC provides a hard-hitting squad leader, section leader, tank commander, and weapons and equipment NCO who can lead soldiers in combat. The length of the course varies according to MOS. BNCOC is conducted at NCOAs. First priority goes to soldiers selected for promotion to staff sergeant and to staff sergeants who have not previously attended. BNCOC is mandatory for promotion to staff sergeant.

Advanced NCO Course
ANCOC stresses common core and MOS-related tasks, with emphasis on technical and advanced leadership skills and knowledge of military subjects required to train and lead other soldiers at the platoon or comparable level. Course lengths vary with MOS requirements. ANCOCs are presented in regional NCOAs. Selection is by DA selection board, and the program is centrally managed by PersCom. The sergeant first class section board evaluates personnel for attendance. Successful completion of this course is required for promotion to sergeant first class.

U.S. Army Sergeants Major Course
This nine-month course is the capstone of the NCOES. USASMC prepares master sergeants and first sergeants for troop and staff assignments throughout the defense establishment. Being selected to attend the USASMC is a great honor and a big step forward in an NCO's career because it paves the way for eventual selection for staff or command sergeant major.

The course's objectives are to prepare students to assist in the solution of command problems; to improve senior NCO capability to develop and maintain discipline; to instruct students in tactical, administrative, and training operations; to update them on contemporary Army problems; to improve their communication skills; to develop intellectual depth and analytical ability; to increase their understanding of military management practices; to sustain physical conditioning and appearance standards; and to prepare students to develop and conduct physical fitness training themselves.

The USASMC is held at the U.S. Army Sergeants Major Academy, Fort Bliss, Texas. Because senior NCOs selected for attendance at the USASMC must move to Fort Bliss, then move elsewhere to assume duties as a sergeant major, preparation is a key element, especially for married soldiers.

Selection is based on records, potential value to the Army, and ability to absorb and profit from the course. All personnel eligible for selection are considered available to attend. Soldiers selected who are later determined to be unavailable will be deferred for attendance to the next class following the end of their unavailable status.

Students are notified by PersCom annually and, once elected, must submit acceptance statements within 30 days of release of the selection list for primary selectees or activation of the alternate list.

Once a soldier has been selected, he or she may not decline. Soldiers eligible for selection who do not want to attend must submit a statement of declination through command channels to PersCom. Approved declinations become a permanent part of the soldier's official military personnel file. Soldiers declining will not be reconsidered for future USASMC attendance.

Authorized NCOES Codes

The following letters and digits must be entered on soldiers' Personnel Qualification Record (PQR) so that PersCom career managers may make accurate decisions. Soldiers are individually responsible for periodically reviewing their PQR to ensure that the codes are current and correct. If a soldier's NCOES code is incorrect, he or she must take action immediately through the local personnel service center to make a correction.

- A—Sergeants Major Academy graduate (resident or nonresident program).
- F—Sergeants Major Academy selectee (resident or nonresident program).
- C—Sergeants Major Academy nongraduate (resident or nonresident program).
- D—Sergeants Major Academy declinee (resident or nonresident program).
- S—Advanced NCO Course graduate.
- T—Advanced NCO Course selectee.
- M—Advanced NCO Course nongraduate.
- W—Basic NCO Course graduate.
- 2—Primary NCO Course graduate.
- 0—Has not completed any NCOES course.

References

AR 351-1, *Individual Military Education and Training*
AR 614-200, *Selection of Enlisted Soldiers for Training and Assignment*
AR 600-200, *Enlisted Personnel Management System*
DA Pam 351-4, *Army Formal Schools Catalog*

Dismissal from Courses

Students may be removed from NCOES courses by the school commandant before course completion for disciplinary reasons, lack of motivation, academic deficiencies, or other valid reasons, such as illness or injury. Failure of a student to maintain established academic, physical fitness, conduct, and weight control standards at any time during a course is cause for elimination. Failure to maintain standards may constitute an infraction of the UCMJ or may indicate a lack of motivation or aptitude.

Students whose actions during training constitute a probable violation of the UCMJ may be suspended, dismissed, or reported to a commander exercising court-martial jurisdiction. Students who show a probable lack of motivation will be counseled.

If disenrollment is determined to be appropriate and is adequately documented, the student is notified in writing of the proposed action, the basis for the action, and the consequences of disenrollment. The student has the right to appeal but must submit any appeal within two days after receipt of written notification. Appeals are reviewed by a disinterested command sergeant major.

Soldiers eliminated from the 1SG Course and the USASMC are not eligible for reentry. Those eliminated academically from other NCOES courses will not be eligible for further NCOES training for a period of six months.

According to the Office of the Deputy Chief of Staff for Personnel, NCOs eliminated for cause from an NCOES course face a mandatory bar to reenlistment or separation proceedings. "For cause" can mean for lack of discipline or motivation, or for other problems, like insubordination or alcohol abuse.

Soldiers dismissed from NCOES courses receive negative academic reports that go into their personnel records, scarce travel funds are needlessly depleted, and more-qualified soldiers are denied the chance to attend courses.

FUNCTIONAL COURSES
Unlike NCO academy courses, functional courses are not generally mandatory—but they are quite important to day-to-day activities and mission-critical operations. Specifically identified senior NCOs, such as first sergeant, battle staff, operations, and intelligence position selectees either must or should attend the associated functional course. Additionally, NCOs who currently serve in one of these positions should voluntarily seek enrollment in the associated functional course. Functional courses are both career enhancing and beneficial from a professional viewpoint. The better armed you are with the skills, knowledge, and attitudes you may derive from such courses, the better prepared you will be on the job.

Sound off! Soldiers march to class.

First Sergeant Course

This course stresses training in the most critical tasks in the duty position of first sergeant. The course curriculum includes instruction in physical training and appearance, unit administration, logistics, security, field operations, discipline, esprit de corps, personnel actions, communications, and problem solving. No priority is given to MOS or unit status in the selection of students. All first-time first sergeants must attend. The major commands select about 90 percent of each class, and PersCom selects the other 10 percent. PersCom's selectees attend the course in a TDY en route status, generally to an overseas duty position. Candidates for this five-week course must meet the physical fitness and weight standards.

Battle Staff NCO Course

This six-week course is taught at the USASMA and for NCOs assigned to key tactical staff positions—S-1 or G-1 (battalion or division personnel and administration), S-2 or G-2 (intelligence), S-3 or G-3 (operations and training), S-4 or G-4 (logistics). Students learn about the various staff positions in an academically demanding environment.

Operations and Intelligence Course

This course trains senior NCOs (sergeants first class through sergeants major) for either operations or intelligence sergeant duties at the battalion or higher level. Student quotas are managed similarly to the first sergeant course quotas. The major commands receive allocations. Selectees attend on either TDY or TDY en route to another assignment status.

Army Correspondence Course Program

A variety of exportable training courses specific to CMF and MOS are available through this program. Courses are designed for your professional development and include individual subcourses on specific topics developed by respective proponent schools. You may enroll in this program as an individual student or via the group enrollment program. Group enrollment allows an NCO to use these courses to supplement individual training. It provides professionally designed training for the NCO supervisor and awards promotion points for those who successfully complete each subcourse.

Army Training Extension Course (TEC)

This self-paced training medium is for individuals and groups. The training is oriented toward common skills and critical MOS tasks. Proponent schools develop TECs and soldiers in the MOS validate them. Generally, soldiers use TECs in groups as part of unit training or individually for self-study. These courses are usually distributed to unit learning centers, but you can requisition individual lessons. TECs are designed in various formats—printed, audiovisual, audio, and job performance aids. Printed lessons are, however, the most predominant medium.

Additional Qualification Training Courses

Soldiers may apply for a number of additional qualification training courses. (Soldiers are sometimes directed to take certain language training in connection with special assignments.)

Special Forces Training. Soldiers who meet the prerequisites and who volunteer for Special Forces training must be airborne qualified and must attend and successfully complete the three-week-long Special Forces Selection and Assessment Course. Students are in a "TDY and return" status during the course. Those who pass will be scheduled to attend the Special Forces Qualification Course. Soldiers who attend the qualification course must complete a common phase, a MOS-specific phase, and a final phase that combines and tests what was learned in the first two phases. Depending on the MOS (weapons, engineering, communications, medical, intelligence), the qualification course can take a year to complete. Language training may also be required. Soldiers who pass the course join the ranks of professionals who serve in U.S. Army Special Operations Command assignments around the world.

Ranger Training. This voluntary training conducted by the U.S. Army Infantry School, Fort Benning, Georgia, is designed to develop leadership skills and provide a knowledge of Ranger operations involving direct combat with the enemy. Enlisted graduates receive a special qualification identifier ("V") for their MOS code. Ranger training is available on a voluntary basis for eligible male personnel. Applications should be submitted according to the instructions contained in AR 614-200.

Airborne Training. This voluntary functional training conducted by the U.S. Army Infantry School, Fort Benning, Georgia, is designed to qualify volunteers in the use of the parachute as a means of deployment and, through mental and physical training, to develop leadership, self-confidence, and aggressive spirit. Graduates receive an additional skill identifier ("P"). Airborne training is available on a voluntary basis for enlisted personnel on assignment to airborne units. Eligible personnel volunteering for airborne training should submit applications according to the instructions contained in AR 614-200.

Air Assault Course. Obstacle courses, physical training, aircraft safety, Pathfinder operations, combat assaults, slingloading operations, rappelling from UH-60 Blackhawk helicopters, 12-mile road marches with rucksack and rifle—this 10-day course is packed with challenge. To attend, soldiers must receive permission from their commander, pass the APFT (in the 17- to 21-year-old age group), and obtain funding.

Language Training. The Defense Language Program is designed to provide personnel minimum essential professional linguistic skills to meet specific Army requirements. Basic language training is provided through the Defense Language Institute, Presidio of Monterey, California. Training requires full-time attendance. Nonresident training is conducted in education centers, units, or established language training facilities using approved materials. Details of the management of the program are set forth in AR 350-20, AT 611-6, and AR 621-5. An additional skill identifier ("L") is usually awarded to graduates of the program.

Equal Opportunity Training. The Defense Equal Opportunity Management Institute at Patrick Air Force Base, Florida, conducts the 16-week training program. Selected officers and qualified enlisted volunteers are provided the skills and knowledge needed to assist the commander in increasing unit effectiveness and efficiency through improved racial harmony and equal opportunity. Enlisted personnel who successfully complete the training are awarded the appropriate additional special skill identifiers. Details on eligibility and application for this training may be obtained from your local Equal Opportunity NCO.

Noncommissioned Officer Logistics Program (NCOLP) Training. NCOLP training is conducted at the U.S. Army Quartermaster School, Fort Lee, Virginia. Its purpose is to provide program members a broad overview of logistics operations. Graduates are qualified for assignment to key logistic management positions that require technical knowledge of two or more logistics functions. NCOLP training is available for enlisted personnel who possess the special qualification identifier "K," indicating NCOLP membership. Procedures for application are contained in AR 614-200.

5

Civilian Education

ARMY CONTINUING EDUCATION SYSTEM (ACES)

Your *Army Continuing Education System Record*, DA Form 669, can serve a very important purpose during your military career—or it can collect dust. Maintained at your local Army Education Center, it contains information used by education counselors to document your pursuit of higher education. Semester after semester throughout your career, you should (whenever the mission allows) contribute course completion slips to your record. Consider that you would be making regular deposits to an intellectual savings account that would grow with enormous interest—the kind Army promotion boards and civilian employers will have for you as your educational value increases.

You should invest in yourself. The Army does, and benefits in the process. The Army Continuing Education System (ACES) mission is, in part, to improve the combat readiness of the Army by planning, researching, and implementing educational programs and services to support the professional and personal development of quality soldiers and their adult family members, according to AR 621-5. In support of the mission, ACES supports five goals, three of which apply to soldiers, as follows:

- Develop confident, competent leaders.
- Support the enlistment, retention, and transition of soldiers.
- Provide self-development opportunities for soldiers.

The ACES meets its mission goals by providing quality educational programs and services throughout the Army. Education and training mutually support and enhance the combat readiness of the Army and are key elements in the NCO Development Program. ACES programs and services are designed to expand soldiers' skills, knowledge, and attitudes. Programs and services discussed later in this chapter contribute to the three pillars of leader development: institutional training, operational assignments, and self-development. Self-development, supported by ACES, is a planned, progressive, sequential program that leaders use to enhance and sustain the nine leadership competencies discussed in chapter 2.

Under the guidelines of AR 621-5, NCOs and the soldiers they lead should meet the following educational objectives:

• Master academic skills needed to perform duties of their primary MOS and meet prerequisites for the NCO Education System.

• In cases of exception to the enlistment rule regarding having a high school diploma, earn a high school diploma or equivalent before completing a first enlistment.

• Earn a college degree, license, or professional certificate in a MOS-related discipline, as recommended in DA Pamphlet 600-25, *The NCO Professional Development Guide*.

Army Education Center Counselors

Counselors are wonderful people who are critical to the success of the ACES mission. They help soldiers establish realistic education goals and continue to provide counseling through attainment of the goals. They also help soldiers get maximum benefit from limited tuition assistance and other resources. Soldiers who are new to an installation are required by AR 621-5 to receive education counseling within the first 30 days of their arrival, and then receive follow-up counseling as needed.

Soldiers should not need a regulatory push to receive counseling, however; they should virtually run to get the valuable advice and assistance counselors provide. Counselors help with school selection, application procedures that can be lengthy and complex, prerequisite assessments, and obtaining financial aid. When they cannot help locate financial aid for formal courses of instruction, counselors can recommend free alternative methods of obtaining educational credit. (See "DANTES," "CLEP," and "GRE" later in this chapter.) But soldiers must take the first step and call the local Army Education Center, make an appointment, and speak with a counselor.

High School Completion Program (HSCP)

The HSCP is an off-duty program that provides soldiers and adult family members the opportunity to earn a high school diploma or equivalency certificate. Tuition assistance (TA) is authorized for soldiers up to 100 percent of the tuition costs of courses, subject to the following: ACES will pay TA only to accredited institutions and will not pay fees covering such items as books, matriculation, graduation, and parking.

Montgomery GI Bill enrollees must complete a high school completion program or earn an equivalent certification during their first enlistment. The HSCP is open to all non–high school graduates.

Functional Academic Skills Training (FAST)

The FAST Program, formerly called Basic Skills Education Program (BSEP), provides instruction in academic competencies necessary for job proficiency and preparation for advanced training. FAST, available at Army Learning Centers (ALCs), helps improve soldiers' job performance and helps them meet reenlistment eligibility and MOS classification requirements.

Because this program is self-paced using instructional material (software at ALCs that are computer-equipped), FAST is available during duty and off-duty hours. FAST covers reading, writing, arithmetic, and other subjects soldiers must comprehend to excel in service.

NCO DEVELOPMENT TIMELINE

This timeline represents promotion, training, and assignment opportunities as a "generic" soldier progresses from initial entry through command sergeant major. It can aid individuals in seeing where they stand and where they are going, and may assist leaders in counseling and advising their subordinates on professional development.

| | EDUCATION AND TRAINING | | Promotion | EXPERIENCE | |
YOS	Civil	NCOES	Potential	Assignments MOS and CMF	Other
0	Complete HS or GED or begin college		4–6 months	PVT	
1			6–12 months	PFC	
2	HS graduate desirable	PLDC	12–26 months	SP4-CPL	
3			18 months–		
4			5 years	SGT	
5	Complete work on college	BNCOC			Recruiter
6	associate's degree				Drill SGT
7		ANCOC	5–8 years	SSG	
8					
9					
10	Continue or complete work on college				Sr. Drill SGT SGT
11	bachelor's degree		9–13 years		RC Advisor
12				SFC and PSG	ROTC Cadre
13					Recruiter
14					
15	Continue or complete work on college	SMC			
16	bachelor's degree				
17			14–18 years		RC Advisor
18			estimated	1SG and MSG	ROTC Cadre
19					
20	Complete work on college				
21	bachelor's degree				
22			18–22 years		ROTC Cadre
23			estimated	SGM and CSM	RC Advisor
24					
25					
26					
27					
28					
29					
30					

Service Members Opportunity Colleges Army Degrees Programs (SOCAD)
Under the Service Members Opportunity Colleges (SOC), there are degree and certification programs wherein a soldier is normally awarded a degree or certificate for an academic or technical course of study. The programs were developed to provide common curricula in disciplines related to Army MOSs.

The SOC is a network of schools across the country and overseas that have recognized and responded to soldiers' expectations for postsecondary education. They must have liberal entrance requirements, allow soldiers to complete courses through nontraditional modes, provide academic advisement, offer maximum credit for experiences obtained in service, have residence requirements that are adaptable to the special needs of soldiers, have a transfer policy that recognizes traditional and nontraditional learning obtained at other schools, promote the SOC, and provide educational support to servicemembers. Under SOCAD, the college must limit the residence requirement and offer a flexible curriculum.

COLLEGE AND UNIVERSITY DEGREE PROGRAMS
Thousands of degree programs are available to soldiers—too many to list here. But you may use dedicated resources to find out more information about obtaining an associate in arts or science degree, bachelor of arts or science degree, or master of arts or science degree. Some resources, such as the annual *Army Veterans Education Guide*, also include preaddressed postcards to schools that value soldier-students. The guide is published by School Guide Publications, 210 North Avenue, New Rochelle, NY 10801. A recent edition of the guide contained brief articles with the following information:
- What to look for in a college.
- How to use your educational benefits.
- How to select a college major.
- What to understand about SOC.

The guide may be obtained through your local Army Education Center. It routinely includes a directory of some 60 institutions that are interested in receiving applications from military personnel. Most of the institutions include preaddressed business reply postcards you may use to write for more information and application forms.

If you want to take college courses but are concerned about your ability to comprehend course material, use DA Pamphlet 351-20, the *Army Correspondence Course Program Catalog*. It is filled with offerings that will teach you the basics of many subjects. For example, suppose you want to earn an electrical engineering degree. You could contact your local education center to request to take the basic electricity course listed in the pamphlet. The course is open to "any student who meets the basic qualifications for correspondence study." After successfully completing 17 sequential electricity subcourses, you should be fully prepared to enroll in a college course that deals with the subject of electricity. Apply this method to other subjects and you will see the value of "boning up" through correspondence studies.

In one of its annual supplements, *Army Times* devoted an entire section to education. The 1994 edition of the *Handbook for Military Families* covered study opportunities, college aid, commissioning programs, graduate programs, and senior NCO schooling. The education section of the handbook began, "Education benefits are one of the biggest draws of military service. Yet many service members don't know what benefits are available, or how to use them."

In the November 15, 1993, issue of *Army Times* is a 16-page education insert that, among other advice, offers these tidbits: "Become an informed consumer; visit your base education center; follow your degree plan." And in yet another *Army Times* issue an article entitled "Getting Ahead: A Matter of Degree" states the following: "ACES has 168 education centers at Army posts worldwide and administers college courses at most posts . . . [and more] than 100 colleges and universities are represented on posts throughout the United States and overseas."

It is easy to research education opportunities. It takes effort to pursue them.

While serving as a drill sergeant in 1992 and 1993, SFC Rebecca Marcum used what little free time she had to pursue a college degree in business. Unable to complete the degree while "on the trail" as a drill sergeant, she nevertheless continued to work toward it and completed her program after she was transferred to the Defense Equal Opportunity Institute in Florida. Marcum, proudly wearing her graduation cap and gown, appeared displaying her Indiana Wesleyan University bachelor of science degree on the cover of the winter 1993–94 issue of *NCO Journal*. Many NCOs overcome adversity and earn college degrees.

Army Education Center counselors can help you complete DD Form 295, *Application for the Evaluation of Learning Experiences during Military Service*. The completed form is used to inform institutions, agencies, and employers about in-service educational achievements. Schools use the form to determine how many and what kinds of college credits to award to soldiers based on military education, training, and experience. Your pursuit of a degree should include completing and forwarding DD Form 295 to the college or university of your choice.

If you are working on an undergraduate (associate's or bachelor's) degree, you should know about independent ways to earn credit through the following programs: Defense Activity for Nontraditional Education Support (DANTES), including the College Level Examination Program (CLEP) and Defense Subject Standardized Tests (DSST); the American College Testing Proficiency Examination Program (ACT/PEP); Graduate Record Examination (GRE); and the Annenberg Project and Center for Public Broadcasting (AP/CPB).

The DANTES, CLEP, DSST, ACT/PEP, GRE, and AP/CPB offerings all require independent study. Many subject packets include texts, workbooks, and audio or video tapes that are used in conjunction with the paper materials. Most of the for-credit tests offered by these programs and agencies are worth three or four semester hours of credit each. The GRE, which includes a general exam and subject exams, is worth much more. The GRE sociology examination, for example, is worth 30 semester hours of undergraduate credit, 15 lower division (100 and 200 level), and 15 upper division (300 and 400 level).

If you are interested in earning a master's degree, get a copy of *Graduate School and You*, a guide for prospective graduate students. It is available from the Council of Graduate Schools, One Dupont Circle, N.W., Suite 430, Washington, DC 20036-1173. The guide describes in general terms the graduate school environment and the purpose of graduate-level education, "concentrated study in one area." It describes the two major kinds and levels of graduate degrees, professional and research, master's and doctoral, respectively. And the guide discusses career options, choosing a school, and the application process (which some would describe as a complex, lengthy ordeal). The guide also includes a valuable timetable for applying to graduate school.

NCOs who want to seriously research a degree program or school should delve into the five-volume *Colleges and Universities Blue Book*, which is available at most well-stocked public libraries and should be on hand at your post education center. The *Blue Book* lists all accredited colleges and universities in the United States. It gives succinct descriptions of schools (with complete addresses), entrance requirements, costs per year, and the collegiate and community environments, and includes state maps.

No matter what career path you are on in the Army, as an NCO, it is up to you to make the most of it. Find a school and program that interests you and applies to your profession within the Army (or is related to it), visit an education center, see a counselor, get an educational assessment, coordinate with the school of your choice and get evaluated for credit by the school, get enrolled in class and pursue nontraditional offerings, and earn a degree—or two or three. And as you progress, consider what the German Nazi leader, Martin Bormann, had to say about education: "Education is a danger. . . . At best an education which produces useful coolies for us is admissible. Every educated person is a future enemy." Bormann's ghost can count on educated U.S. NCOs understanding and enforcing the values and ideals of educated, free people when confronted with future regional bullies, tyrants, and oppressors.

College Programs and Locations

Before a PCS move, it is beneficial for a soldier pursuing a degree to know the availability of schooling at the new site. Many colleges offer courses on post, at least on a limited basis. If an institution is close to an installation, it will sometimes elect to offer certain popular courses on base but will require students enrolling in smaller or more specialized courses to attend classes on campus.

Education centers at major posts sometimes serve similar installations in the nearby region. High school and college preparatory course work is available at nearly all Army installations.

Skill Recognition Programs

The Skill Recognition Programs provide ways to get recognition within the civilian sector for skills learned in service. This recognition can come in the following forms:

- *Credit for military experience*. The American Council on Education evaluates Army service school courses and recommends the number of semester hours of credit that civilian schools may award based on a soldier's military training and experience. Examples include vocational, lower-level baccalaureate and associate's degree, upper-level baccalaureate, and graduate-level credits. These recommendations are published in the *Guide to the Evaluation of Educational Experiences in the Armed Services (ACE Guide)*.

- *Army apprenticeship*. This program provides participants documentation of apprentice skills acquired while in the Army that is understood by civilian industry. It improves the performance and motivation of soldiers, provides a recruiting incentive for MOSs that are related to skills with apprenticeships, and improves the supervisor-soldier relationship.

NCO LEADER SELF-DEVELOPMENT CAREER MAP

TITLE OF CAREER MANAGEMENT FIELD: FINANCE/ACCOUNTING

CMF NUMBER: 71 (MOS 73C, D, Z)

THE FOLLOWING ARE ONLY RECOMMENDATIONS. It may not be feasible to complete all recommended courses since assignments may preclude off-duty education. Alternate methods of achieving CMF course recommendations are possible (examinations, correspondence courses, and ACE-recommended credits). See an education counselor for assistance in completing recommended courses/goal.

OPERATIONAL LEADER DEVELOPMENT

RANK, SKILL LEVELS & DUTY ASSIGNMENTS	PVT PFC SPC/CPL SKILL LEVEL 10	SGT SKILL LEVEL 20	SSG SKILL LEVEL 30	SFC SKILL LEVEL 40	MSG	SGM/CSM
	TEAM LEADER →	RECRUITER/RETENTION /DRILL SERGEANT	OPS/INTEL SERGEANT	FIRST SERGEANT →		CSM (D)
		SQUAD LEADER →	PLATOON SERGEANT →			

INSTITUTIONAL LEADER DEVELOPMENT

INSTITUTIONAL TRAINING	RCT AIT	PLDC	BNCOC	ANCOC	SERGEANTS MAJOR COURSE
				RECOMMENDED BATTLE STAFF NCO AGR ISG COURSES	

LEADER SELF-DEVELOPMENT

RECOMMENDED NCODP-RELATED COURSES

PRIOR TO PLDC:
1. English Composition
2. Basic Mathematics
3. Computer Literacy
4. Reading

Recommended Reading Standard: 10
Achieve Writing Standard *

PRIOR TO BNCOC:
1. Communication Skills
2. Personnel Supervision
3. Behavioral Science

Recommended Reading Standard: 10
Achieve Writing Standard *

PRIOR TO ANCOC:
1. Principles of Management
2. Organizational Behavior
3. Information Mgt Systems
4. Technical Writing

Recommended Reading Standard: 10
Achieve Writing Standard *

PRIOR TO SMC:
1. Research Techniques (Statistics)
2. Human Resource Management
3. World Geography

Recommended Reading Standard: 12
Achieve Writing Standard *

RECOMMENDED CMF-RELATED COURSES AND ACTIVITIES

Skill Level 10
1. Intro to Business
2. Accounting
3. Keyboarding
4. Communications
5. ACCP: Finance Spec Crs;
   Military Accounting Crs

Skill Level 20
1. Algebra
2. Principles of Management
3. Computer Operations
4. Computer Hardware
5. ACCP: Programming & Budgeting Spec Crs; Intro to Disbursing Operations; Basic Level Technical/Sustainment Course

Skill Level 30
1. Speech
2. Algebra
3. Problem Solving
4. Human Relations
5. Decision Making
6. Information Systems
7. ACCP: Adv Level Tech/Sustainment Course

Skill Level 40
1. Applied Management
2. Planning
3. Organizing
4. Stress Tolerance
5. Interpersonal Skills

Skill Level 50
1. Public Relations
2. Business Communications
3. Organizational Effectiveness

RECOMMENDED CMF-RELATED CERTIFICATION OR DEGREE GOAL

AA/AS IN: Accounting, Finance, Management, Economics, Marketing, Mathematics, Banking, Communications, Banking, Communications, Public Administration, Statistics, Business, Data Processing, Payroll, Public Budgeting, Personnel Admin, Info Systems, Bookkeeping, Computer Science, Mgt Info Systems BY THE 10th YEAR OF SERVICE.

BA/BS IN: Accounting, Finance, Management, Economics, Marketing, Mathematics, Banking, Communications, Finance, Management, Economics, Business, Data Processing, Payroll, Public Budgeting, Personnel Admin, Information Systems, Bookkeeping, Computer Science, Management Information Systems BY THE 16th YEAR OF SERVICE.

NOTE * See DA Pam 600-67. The Army Writing Standard is writing that can be understood in a single, rapid reading, and is generally free of errors in grammar, mechanics, and usage.

APPROVED BY: Commandant, U.S. Army Finance School

DATE: 4 October 1991

LEGEND
ACCP – Army Correspondence Course Program
CYBIS – Network Computer Instruction (Where Available)
LC – Course found in Learning Center

Career maps, like this one for finance and accounting soldiers, are aids designed to illustrate MOS career tracks. Notice the CMF-related education goals.

Occupations with apprenticeships are those that are learned through experience and on-the-job training and are supplemented by related technical instruction. They involve manual, mechanical, or technological skills and knowledge requiring a minimum of 2,000 hours of work experience plus related instruction. They do not fall into the categories of selling, management, clerical, or professional skills requiring advanced knowledge and academic degrees. These occupations are identified in Department of Labor pamphlets and appendix I, AR 621-5.

Enrollment is open to soldiers who perform satisfactorily on the job and possess an MOS (primary or secondary) that relates to the program and that has been registered with the Bureau of Apprenticeship Training. Also eligible are soldiers who possess a qualifying MOS in which they were initially registered but are no longer serving because of priorities and mission requirements.

• *Certification.* Some Army MOSs correspond to civilian occupations that require licensing or certification as a prerequisite for employment in certain states or business (truck mechanics, for instance, who may have to pass such tests as the National Institute for Automotive Service Excellence). Certification requirements and agencies are listed in Army apprenticeship or industry recognition pamphlets in the AR 621 series.

Involvement in these programs is voluntary but can foster professional development. It will not, however, result in duty assignments that are made solely to assist soldiers in fulfilling skill recognition program requirements.

Normally, certification or licensing through civilian agencies, if desired, will be done at the individual's expense. Exceptions occur when certification automatically follows successful completion of a course for which tuition assistance is authorized.

Army training programs will not be altered to meet civilian standards for skill recognition programs, but in some instances, civilian agencies, as a prerequisite to registration, certification, or formal recognition, might require additional non-mission-related training or experience before recognizing a soldier as fully qualified. When this is necessary, the soldier must acquire the additional training and experience through local trade or vocational schools, or by other means.

Programs stress individual initiative. An individual cannot be enrolled in more than one occupational skill area within an apprenticeship program at any one time. The soldier may, however, change to another occupational area or program as many times as desired, provided prerequisites are met.

Education Services Support

Education services support consists of counseling; participation in programs such as the Montgomery GI Bill, the Veterans Educational Assistance Program (VEAP), and the Servicemen's Opportunity Colleges Program; tuition assistance; VA educational benefits; Defense Activity for Nontraditional Education Support (DANTES); the Skill Recognition Program; and a range of local educational opportunities available through Army education offices.

DANTES independent study and examination program services are available to all eligible active-duty soldiers. One important aspect of the DANTES is the College Level Examination Program (CLEP), which also enables students to earn credit by examination. The examinations measure knowledge of the basic concepts and applications involved in courses that have the same or similar titles. They are divided into two types: general examinations and subject examinations.

The general examination measures college-level achievement in five basic areas of the liberal arts: English composition, social sciences and history, natural sciences, humanities, and mathematics. Test material covers the first year of college, often referred to as the general or liberal education requirement.

Subject examinations measure achievement in specific college courses and are worth course credit. Examples of test titles include Introduction to Business Management, General Psychology, Western Civilization, and American Literature.

Each civilian education institution has its own evaluating criteria for using CLEP test scores to determine credit. You should have official transcripts forwarded to the registrar of the college or university at which you desire to receive credit (some institutions require that a minimum number of semester hours of classwork be completed before CLEP credit will be accepted). Another type of subject test that, like CLEP, substitutes for college classroom work is the DANTES Subject Standardized Tests.

THE GI BILL

Valuable education benefits offered under the GI Bill are available today for would-be college graduates and for those soldiers who wish to pursue certain kinds of training. Originally named the Servicemen's Readjustment Act of 1944, which was signed into law by President Franklin D. Roosevelt on June 22 of that year, the GI Bill—now called the Montgomery GI Bill after its latest champion, Congressman G. V. "Sonny" Montgomery—takes the form of the following: the Montgomery Active Duty GI Bill, the Montgomery Selected Reserve GI Bill, and the Noncontributory GI Bill. The Post-Vietnam Veterans Educational Assistance Program (VEAP) is also covered by the GI Bill. A wide range and various levels of benefits, valued at hundreds of dollars a month for up to 36 months, are available to soldiers. You are urged to take full advantage of the benefits to which you are entitled.

The Active Duty GI Bill

The Active Duty GI Bill (chapter 30, U.S. Code) provides up to 36 months of benefits. Soldiers covered by Category I of this program are those who first entered active duty after June 30, 1985, and who contributed a nonrefundable $100 a month for the first 12 months of service. Active-duty members may begin using their benefits after completing two years of service. Members of the National Guard who are in the Active Guard and Reserve Program also are covered by this contributory program, but they must have entered service after November 29, 1989, and must not have previously served on active duty.

Soldiers with remaining benefits under the Vietnam Era GI Bill (chapter 34, USC) are entitled to benefits through an automatic conversion to Category II of the Montgomery Active Duty GI Bill. A Vietnam-era soldier who never used his or her benefits is today entitled to 36 months of entitlements under the Montgomery program. Vietnam-era soldiers do not have to contribute to the program to receive benefits, including an additional allowance paid for dependents. Soldiers in Category II—thousands of whom are senior NCOs today—can verify their benefits by contacting the local or regional DVA office.

NCOs supervising soldiers who declined to take part in the contributory Active Duty GI Bill program or who may be affected by the drawdown should inform their soldiers that they may be covered under Category III of the Active Duty GI Bill.

Effective February 3, 1991, the law was amended to allow members who originally declined to participate, or who were not eligible to participate, the opportunity to contribute and participate before involuntary separation from the Army. On October 23, 1992, the law was further expanded to allow the same opportunity to those soldiers who voluntarily separated from service under the Special Separation Benefit and Voluntary Separation Incentive programs. Members in Category III earn one month's benefit for each month of active-duty service, up to 36 months.

The Selected Reserve GI Bill

The Montgomery Selected Reserve GI Bill (chapter 106, USC) is available to members of the Army Reserve and the Army National Guard. It applies to members who entered Selected Reserve status after June 30, 1985. To receive up to 36 months of entitlements under this program, members must have a six-year commitment that began after September 30, 1990. Members must also have completed Initial Active Duty for Training, be high school graduates or have equivalent certificates, and serve in an active Reserve or National Guard unit and remain in good standing. With few exceptions, benefits under this program expire 10 years from the date of eligibility for the program or on the day the member leaves the Selected Reserve.

The Veterans Educational Assistance Program

The VEAP (chapter 32, USC) is a program in which a soldier makes contributions from his or her military pay, which are matched on a $2 for $1 basis by the U.S. government. This program is for soldiers who entered service between January 1, 1977, and June 30, 1985, who opened a VEAP account before April 1, 1987, and who contributed from $25 to $2,700 (refundable), and completed their first period of obligated service. Benefit entitlement is 1 to 36 months, depending upon the number of monthly contributions.

Monetary Value of the GI Bill

As indicated above, the monetary value of the benefit program you qualify for will depend on various factors, including the date you entered the military, your status in the military, how long you have been or were in service, and the character of a previous discharge or separation. Also, if you are in a contributory program, the amount of money the government will contribute depends on how much you contribute, up to a maximum matching contributory amount.

In-service benefits are worth less, monetarily, then postservice benefits and normally cover only tuition and fees. But here is a kicker: Under current federal law, if you receive a college or university assistantship, fellowship, or grant that pays or offsets part or all of your tuition and fees or research expenses, you may still be entitled to receipt of education benefits—*meaning monthly entitlements received from the DVA are yours to keep.*

Entitlement retention applies to serving, separated, and retired soldiers who compete for and receive school assistantships and the like—and who can work at the school a specified, normally at least 20, hours a week. For example, in 1994, a retired first sergeant was awarded a graduate school assistantship valued at more than $10,000 that covered his tuition and fees, and because he is married and has three children, he is still entitled to receive from the DVA $692 a month as an entitlement while he attends school. He uses the entitlement to offset family living expenses.

Another soldier, a logistics sergeant, is using in-service-level DVA entitlements and Army tuition assistance to pay tuition and fees associated with a bachelor's degree in business. The amount is hundreds of dollars less a month than what the first sergeant above is entitled to receive, but the sergeant is completing his degree program while on active duty, with financial help from the DVA and the Army.

Various rules and certain service- or usage-oriented restrictions cover the programs and situations described above. Visit your Army Education Center or local DVA office, obtain counseling, and get the most recently published copies of the following:

• Depart of Veterans Affairs (DVA) Pamphlet 27-82-2, *A Summary of DVA Benefits*.
• DVA Pamphlet 22-90-2, *Summary of Educational Benefits*.
• DVA Pamphlet 22-90-1, *Avoiding VA Education Overpayments*.

When you decide to apply for benefits, first make sure the education or training program you choose is approved by the DVA, then complete and submit DVA Form 22-1990 at least two months prior to the beginning of the program. If you choose to use some of your benefits while in service, your commander and local education assistance officer must sign the form. Depending on your personal situation, you also may need to provide a copy of your marriage license, divorce decrees from any previous marriages, and children's birth certificates. Provide these documents, if they apply, because the level of your education benefits may be increased according to the number of legal dependents.

Except for the Selected Reserve program, education benefits expire 10 years from the date of your last discharge or release from active duty. The DVA can extend the ten-year period by the amount of time you were prevented from training during the period because of a certified disability, or being held by a foreign government power. Certain other extensions apply as well and are covered in DVA Pamphlet 22-90-2.

You may use GI Bill benefits for the following purposes:
• To seek an associate's, bachelor's, master's, professional, or doctoral degree at a college or university.
• To participate in a cooperative training program.
• To participate in an *accredited* independent study program leading to a college degree.
• To take courses leading to a certificate or diploma from a business, technical, or vocational school.
• To work and train in an apprenticeship or job-training program offered by a company or union.
• To take a correspondence course.
• To participate in a program abroad that leads to a college degree.
• To take remedial, deficiency, and refresher courses, under certain circumstances.
• To receive tutorial assistance for a deficiency (such as in math), if you attend school at least half time.
• To participate in the DVA work-study program, provided you attend school or train three-quarters or full-time.

Soldiers with private pilot licenses are entitled to benefits leading to more advanced flying certification. This program has been extended indefinitely.

You may be entitled to benefits under more than one education program, or you may be eligible for vocational rehabilitation if you have a service-connected disability. In either case, you are strongly encouraged to discuss your education plans with a local DVA counselor. If local counselors are unavailable, contact DVA regional offices. Regional offices maintain jurisdiction over benefit claims. DVA Regional Office locations and areas they serve are as follows:

- P.O. Box 4616, Buffalo, NY 14240-4616 (Connecticut, Delaware, Maine, Massachusetts, New Hampshire, New Jersey, New York, Ohio, Pennsylvania, Rhode Island, Vermont, West Virginia).
- P.O. 54346, Atlanta, GA 30308-0346 (Alabama, Arkansas, District of Columbia, Florida, Georgia, Louisiana, Maryland, Mississippi, North Carolina, Puerto Rico, South Carolina, Tennessee, Virginia, foreign schools).
- P.O. Box 66830, Saint Louis, MO 66136-6830 (Colorado, Illinois, Indiana, Iowa, Kansas, Kentucky, Michigan, Minnesota, Missouri, Montana, Nebraska, North Dakota, South Dakota, Wisconsin, Wyoming).
- P.O. Box 8888, Muskogee, OK 74402-8888 (Alaska, Arizona, California, Hawaii, Idaho, New Mexico, Nevada, Oklahoma, Oregon, the Philippines, Texas, Utah, Washington).

DVA toll-free telephone service is available in all 50 states, Puerto Rico, and the U.S. Virgin Islands. Call (800) 827-1000.

Other Financial Aid

The U.S. Department of Education (DOE), in *The Student Guide* for 1994 and 1995, will inform you and your family members about federal student aid programs and how to apply for them. Its advice is to contact the financial aid administrator at the school you, your spouse, or your children are interested in and ask about the total cost of education. Ask the state higher education agencies about state aid. Check the local library for state and private financial aid information. Check with companies, foundations, religious organizations, fraternities or sororities, and civic organizations such as the American Legion. Also ask about aid through professional associations.

The Student Guide is free and may be available at the local Army Education Office. If it is not, write to the Federal Student Aid Information Center (FSAIC), P.O. Box 84, Washington, DC 20044. If answers to questions about federal student aid are needed right away, call the FSAIC toll-free at (800) 433-3243 between 9 A.M. and 5:30 P.M. eastern time, Monday through Friday. If you have a family member who is hearing impaired, he or she may call the FSAIC's TDD (telecommunications device for the deaf) at (800) 730-8913.

Undergraduates may receive grants, work-study aid, and educational loans through the DOE. Graduate students may receive loans and federal work-study assistance, but not grants, through the DOE. Graduate students seeking grant money may research through *Grants for Graduate Students*, published by Peterson's Guides, and similar publications.

A Final Thought on Education

Buy bonds. Series EE savings bonds—the same ones hawked during annual Army Savings Bond campaigns—may be entirely tax free when used for education. If you have children, and considering the rising cost of education, purchasing bonds on a regular basis is a smart way to invest in their future and protect your financial security. For example, assuming an annual interest rate of 6 percent (the current minimum rate), putting just $50 a month into bonds for a 1-year-old child who will begin college at age 18 will yield $17,356. Investing $100 a month will yield $34,712. If you are an NCO with an older child, one who is 12 and who will begin college in 6 years, putting $50 a month into bonds will provide $4,227; $100 a month will yield $8,454—minimum!

If you are a young NCO, say a sergeant with five or six years in service, you may purchase bonds for yourself, hold them five years or so, then use them to augment other financial aid you will apply toward a bachelor's or master's degree. An extra $5,000 or so in tax-free funding would be nice, wouldn't it?

Beginning with Series EE bonds purchased in 1990, the interest earned can be excluded from federal income tax if you pay tuition and fees at colleges, universities, and qualified technical schools during the same year the bonds are cashed. The exclusion applies to the educational expenses of yourself, your spouse, and any other dependent, according to the Savings Bonds Public Affairs Office in Washington, D.C. Some restrictions apply. Contact your unit savings bond coordinator for more information.

6

Self-Development

Everyone has room to improve. Every soldier in your pay grade is competing for that same promotion you desire. The farther you go up the ladder, the more you must compete for the next higher position. You must realize that you have control over how competitive you are. . . . Study one area, one task, once a week. It may take an hour or two away from your free time, but you will find the rewards will be worth it.

—CSM (Ret.) Walter J. Jackson in *Soldier's Study Guide*

MOS KNOWLEDGE

The Army does reward selfless, dedicated, confident, competent service. NCO Evaluation Report (NCOER) writers know they can justifiably recommend favorable actions for rated NCOs who meet Army service standards. NCOs who excel render strong indicators of their current abilities and future utility.

If you are among the best in your MOS at your skill level, your intellectual and professional potential will be viewed favorably by NCOER senior raters and other influential soldiers. It may help promotion, school, and training selection boards identify and select you to be among the NCOs who will lead the Army into the 21st century.

In the best-selling book *In Search of Excellence*, authors Thomas J. Peters and Robert H. Waterman, Jr., were discussing excellence in terms of quality production when they made this point: "[A] friend at American Express reminds us, 'If you don't shoot for one hundred percent, you are tolerating mistakes.' You'll get what you ask for." In the potentially life and death context of military service, NCOs cannot afford to make mistakes.

Airborne, air assault, infantry, armor, artillery, air defense, security, expeditionary force, humanitarian assistance, disaster relief, peacekeeping, peacemaking, Special Operations—mistakes made (or tolerated) on these and other missions can result in dire consequences. Giving less than 100 percent to your professional self-development can result in substandard job performance and career stagnation, or worse, mission failure at a critical time and place. Your knowledge in your occupational specialty, whatever it is, is important. If your MOS knowledge did not matter, the Army would drop your MOS from among the several hundred listed in AR 611-201, *Enlisted Career Management Fields and Military Occupational Specialties*.

But valuing NCOs only for their MOS knowledge is like appreciating a utility helicopter only because it can fly. Just as cargo capacity and speed are important characteristics of the helicopter, leadership ability and training management skills are valuable attributes of the NCO. Leadership and training management skill, as well as MOS knowledge, become more important as NCOs are utilized in positions of greater authority and responsibility.

To acquire knowledge, study your MOS-specific soldier's manual. Study FMs 22-100, *Military Leadership*; 22-101, *Leadership Counseling*; and 22-102, *Soldier Team Development* to prepare for leadership. Training management questions come from FM 25-101, *Battle Focused Training*. To better comprehend FM 25-101, first read FM 25-100, *Training the Force*. FM 25-100 is brief and to the point in its explanations of some key terms and concepts you will encounter in detail in FM 25-101. All of these references should be in your possession. Contact your unit publications clerk to order any you don't have.

LEADERSHIP KNOWLEDGE
To excel as a leader, crack open FM 22-100 and find the following:
- *Four leadership requirements*—lead in peace to be ready for war; develop individual leaders; develop leadership teams; and decentralize.
- *Two leadership modes*—direct (junior level) and indirect (senior level).
- *Three parts of FM 22-100*—(1) doctrine and principles of leadership from squad to battalion level; (2) historical lessons regarding "Be, Know, Do" fundamentals; (3) effects of continuous operations, weather, terrain, and high technology.
- *Four factors of leadership*—the led, the leader, the situation, and communications.
- *Eleven principles of leadership*—know yourself and seek improvement; be tactically and technically proficient; seek and take responsibility for your actions; make sound and timely decisions; set the example; know your soldiers and care for them; keep your soldiers informed; develop a sense of responsibility in your soldiers; ensure tasks are understood, supervised, and accomplished; develop teamwork; and employ your unit within its capabilities.
- *Nine leadership competencies*—communications, supervision, teaching and counseling, soldier team development, tactical and technical proficiency, decision making, planning, use of available systems, professional ethics.
- *Four parts of the Professional Army Ethic*—loyalty, duty, selfless service, integrity.
- *Five things you must know as a leader*—the standards, yourself, human nature, your job, your unit.
- *Three things you provide as a leader*—purpose, motivation, direction.
- *Two kinds of stress*—physical (cold, heat, injury, disease) and mental (fear, conflict, pressure).
- *Three leadership styles*—directing, participating, delegating.
- *Two types of authority*—command and general military.
- *Two kinds of performance considered during leadership assessment*—yours and your subordinates'.

FM 22-100 will also teach you about the battlefield challenge, the demands it will place on you, subordinates under your control, and superiors who must control you. Part two of the field manual looks at past battles; how leaders accomplished their missions, inspired soldiers, and faced stress; and what factors led to victory. Part two also addresses how leaders prepared themselves and their soldiers for combat.

The leadership manual also defines the Army's purpose—to protect the nation and its values—and it describes beliefs, values, and norms. Beliefs are assumptions we make, convictions we hold as true, and very deep seated feelings. Soldier values are courage, candor, competence, and commitment, all of which influence decision-making behavior. And norms are social rules and laws of our society, as well as group beliefs and values that are formal (based on laws) and informal (unwritten rules or group codes). Understanding beliefs, values, and norms will enable you to develop as an NCO leader; they will shape your character by identifying to you your inner strengths and weaknesses.

You should uphold the Professional Army Ethic described in FM 22-100. Be a good role model, develop your subordinates ethically, and avoid ethical dilemmas. To do so, determine the nature of dilemmas you encounter, analyze them, choose and execute courses of action that serve the unit, Army, and nation. You also must be familiar with the following:

- Laws, orders, regulations.
- Basic national values.
- Traditional Army values.
- Unit values.
- Your values.
- Institutional pressures.

To provide purpose, motivation, and direction, as described by the manual, keep your soldiers informed, set goals, plan ahead, make informed decisions when time permits (otherwise, quickly decide based on education and experience), supervise tasks, evaluate performance, train your soldiers, coach them, counsel them, be ethical, build a team, reward good effort and accomplishment, and correct or recommend punishment for offenders.

To be an effective leader, you must also understand fatigue, both battle fatigue and the common everyday variety that can set in on the job. Fatigue impacts performance.

Continuous operations cause fatigue (see FM 22-9). Leaders must also know that conditions such as inclement weather can affect performance and planning requirements. In foul weather or under other adverse conditions, fatigued soldiers participating in continuous operations need strong leadership. Tired soldiers operating under adverse conditions who also encounter disrupted communications due to enemy electronic warfare activities will present tough leadership challenges. Add nuclear, biological, and chemical (NBC) threats or hazards and—well, you can understand the importance of effective leadership.

As a leader, the NCO must build cohesion, develop confidence, train the unit, develop a high level of physical fitness and a winning attitude. Read FM 22-100.

Leadership Counseling
This is straight out of FM 22-101:

To be an effective counselor, a leader must understand *be*, *know*, and *do* attributes. FM 22-100 describes these attributes in detail. Briefly, what a leader must *be* is described by the professional Army ethic and professional character traits. What he or she must *know* includes technical and tactical information, people, and the situation. What he [or she] must *do* is provide leadership that directs, implements, and motivates.

Counseling is the basic responsibility of every leader and an important part of taking care of the troops. [Counseling] recognizes and encourages good performance. Its principal objectives are developing the soldier, improving well-being, and resolving problems. Military experience points out the need for leaders at all levels in the Army to counsel effectively.

FM 22-101 is packed with useful guidance and is a companion of FM 22-100. Military counseling is a principle tool of leadership. As NCOs read FM 22-101, they will encounter many suggestions and a single order, on page 8, which in big, bold words states: *"It is an absolute requirement that leaders regularly counsel their soldiers. The leader who neglects to counsel his subordinates is negligent in his [or her] performance of duty."*

Pretty strong words—and for good reason. Effective leadership is the Army's key to success in training and combat. Leaders must counsel regularly to be effective. Counseling can range from a few words of praise or guidance to long, structured sessions. Effective leadership counseling may also help valuable soldiers decide to stay in the Army.

In order to be an effective counselor, you must possess effective leadership skills and demonstrate your competence to soldiers. Soldiers watch leaders very closely. Your competence will help establish and maintain their faith in you. They will trust you, listen to you, and willingly follow your guidance.

Use the opportunity provided by attentiveness to suggest information that fits the circumstance. In other words, tell the soldier what to do when you know he or she is listening. You can suggest alternatives, persuade, urge, advise, direct, punish, and reward using directive, nondirective, or combined approaches to counseling.

When you counsel a member of the opposite sex, ask the person whether he or she would mind if another person of his or her gender were present during counseling. You must show that you care—avoid violating the soldier's confidence—but maintain a professional distance. To avoid an allegation of harassment or other wrongdoing, you may decide it is in your and the soldier's best interest to have a third party present. Use your judgment, but err on the cautious side.

The Directive Approach. The directive approach to counseling is often suited to "I talk, you listen" situations in which the counselor must correct a soldier who is the problem. The directive approach is commonly used when making on-the-spot corrections. You give advice, offer solutions, and tell the soldier what must be done. This approach may also be used to praise on the spot as well.

The directive approach is simple, quick, and provides immediate solutions. But it has shortcomings. Your dominant influence may cause resentment because the soldier may feel that you are taking the ability to solve the problem away from him or her. The approach may address only symptoms of the real problem. And decisions are made by the leader, not the soldier, so the soldier may later blame the leader if the solution did not fix the problem. Sometimes, regardless of its shortcomings, you must use the directive approach to counsel an unresponsive soldier who will not connect bad behavior or conduct with the consequences.

The Nondirective Approach. NCOs using the nondirective approach to counseling will find it is more relaxed and focused on self-discovery. The counselor leads the soldier to find the solution. The soldier can verbalize and work out solutions through personal insight, judgment, and realization of the facts. The counseled soldier must understand, however, that he or she must be willing to openly discuss the subject and must take responsibility for the solution.

Often, a soldier will come to you with a problem, a concern, or perhaps a good idea. This is the time, if it is convenient, to use the nondirective approach. If it is not a convenient time, you should set a better time and appropriate place. During counseling, avoid offering solutions; let the soldier work it out, if possible. Certainly, you must guide the conversation to keep it focused on the subject, but make the soldier realize that the session is on his or her time. This way, the soldier may be less inclined to become defensive or to feel guilty.

Try to establish rapport. Display sincere interest. Give the soldier an opportunity to state the problem. Don't interrupt. Ask leading, open-ended questions to clarify the nature and scope of the problem. Let the soldier respond. Listen for responses that indicate the soldier is approaching a resolution. Approve the soldier's solution if it is honest and may work.

If you are unable to help the soldier, refer him or her to someone who can, such as the local chaplain, finance officer, legal officer, or whomever else is appropriate. If time permits, go with the soldier. Briefly tell the official about the problem, then depart. After the soldier returns to your control, follow up to ensure the problem has been, is, or will be resolved. Keep superiors informed about the situation, your actions, the soldier's actions, and the resolution.

The Combined Approach. Using the combined approach, you apply parts of the directive and nondirective approaches to adjust your counseling style as the conversation tone and the requirements of your role as counselor change. You can adapt to emphasize what is best for the soldier.

This approach assumes that the soldier will eventually take charge of solving the problem but just needs some help along the way. Use the ethical decision-making process (FM 22-100) and related problem-solving process (FM 22-101) to help guide the soldier. If you work from directive to nondirective, listen for information that defines the problem and allow the soldier an opportunity to suggest his or her own solutions. You may add your own suggestions as well. But remember, the counseling goal is to get the soldier to "own" or resolve the problem.

Chapter 2 of FM 22-101 goes into more detail about the counseling approaches and uses stories to make more points, some of which are that the directive approach is the quickest method but does not encourage maturity; the combined approach is moderately quick but may take too much time in some situations; and the nondirective approach encourages maturity but takes considerable time and requires the greatest counseling skill. The directive approach is also good for immature or insecure soldiers, while the combined and nondirective methods encourage open communication. And the directive and combined approaches give the counselor an opportunity to use his or her experience, while the nondirective approach develops personal responsibility. All three methods require you to listen, observe, and respond appropriately.

Reception, integration, performance, personal, discipline, growth, and guidance counseling are also covered in FM 22-101. Which counseling approach to use will depend on the circumstances and how well you know the soldier and his or her duties.

Appendix A of FM 22-101 is especially valuable. It covers effective communication, how to be an active listener and keep the dialogue moving, what to interpret from silence at various points during counseling, and how to respond under friendly and hostile circumstances. It also covers questioning techniques. Appendix C lists and describes military community support agencies you may refer your soldiers to when needed. NCO supervisors may use the lesson outlines in appendix F to support counseling training for subordinate leaders.

A towed howitzer crew conducts a fire mission.

Soldier Team Development

Ways to determine whether you serve in an excellent unit are uncovered in appendix B of FM 22-102. A spirit of "us" and "we," rather than "I" and "me," fills the ranks. Unit members look out for and take care of one another. The unit has developed its own workable ways of accomplishing missions to standard, rather than relying heavily on being guided by outsiders and regulatory material. The excellent unit has a steady high-performance rhythm, and members have effective stress and pressure coping skills. The unit has high standards, ethical values, and its own way of expressing how well it is performing. Members will voluntarily work however hard and long is necessary based on unit operational needs.

Appendix B also lists excellent-unit soldier qualities, the relationship between soldiers and their gear and soldiers and the unit—they "live, eat, sleep, breathe, and fight" about *The Unit*. As you study FM 22-102, notice how the manual equates a military unit to a family unit. It says, "Each [element] is a tightly knit family where soldiers know one another intimately—their likes and dislikes, their faults and strengths, their beliefs and ideas. . . . [The] effectiveness of battalions and higher military units depends on the formation of these 'families' in the smallest groups." It is the same in business, as emphasized by the previously mentioned book, *In Search of Excellence*.

Clearly there are major differences between business enterprises and the military, but excellent civilian and military organizations share common attributes such as the "us" and "we" outlook. And team building is a key task of the leaders in many sectors of our society.

Building strong soldier teams is critical in the Army. Readiness is the goal.

An outnumbered and overpowered team can achieve its mission goal when it has a strong desire—the spirit—to do so. Spirited soldiers believe in their cause. Your leadership should nurture a winning spirit; it is critical to building a cohesive team. You should build cohesion in numerous other ways as well. Respect your soldiers and help them develop physically, socially, emotionally, and spiritually. Doing so will give them the stamina necessary for sustained performance under stress, and will teach them to mature, work together, and face danger with hope and purpose. Signs of self-discipline, initiative, effective judgment, and confidence will be positive indicators of your effort.

Values. You must teach and stress to your soldiers the values of the professional Army ethic—loyalty, duty, selfless service, and integrity. Your role is not to change their long-held personal values. We are all different. But impress upon them the importance of professional values. Development of the four basic soldierly values is vital as well. Develop their *candor*, which is honesty and faithfulness to the truth. Teach them to be *competent*; their working knowledge and ability contribute directly to mission success. Develop in them a sense of the mental and moral strength—*courage*—it will take to enable them to retain control and continue the mission when they are in harm's way. And make them understand that *commitment* to unit accomplishment takes priority over personal wishes, wants, and perhaps needs.

Do a mental assessment of your soldiers' willingness and ability to work as a cohesive unit. Listen, observe, and monitor. In each new situation, you must reassess and correct to retain and build teamwork. Practice verbal and nonverbal communication. Encourage development of your unit's "vocabulary"—short-cut words and terms—to communicate complex messages. *Ensure they always comply with the commander's intent.*

Teach your soldiers to use the chain of command so that decisions are made at the right level. Give them their own planning and decision-making responsibilities as well so that they know the mission and operate within the commander's guidance. FM 22-102 states, too, that combat teamwork requires training so that soldiers think on their feet and communicate effectively.

Every new soldier in your unit will go through a formation stage, the process of checking out other soldiers and his or her leaders. As trust develops, the soldier will participate more actively in unit missions. You must help by answering a new soldier's questions about your team, its work, and the soldier's personal concerns. Develop the soldier's strengths into unit strengths.

Put the new soldier to work as soon as possible. Afterward, watch for signs that he or she is trying to exert independence. The soldier will be trying to find his or her range and limits as a unit member. You will know this is happening when you begin to feel resistance to your leadership. Share with the soldier your thoughts and feelings about the unit and ask him or her to do likewise, to teach the soldier to pass information back and forth. This will help break down a communication barrier before it can form. You want the soldier to depend on you and others on the team, and vice versa, to build cohesion.

Constantly guide your developing team. Retain control. Listen. Establish lines of authority and develop individual and team (squad, section, platoon, battery, company, troop) goals. Focus your team on training to standard.

Training is paramount. Treat each job, task, or detail your unit must perform as a training opportunity. Use mission opportunities to motivate and challenge soldiers. FM 22-102 states that the following principles will aid in developing cohesion:

- Train as a unit.
- Train for the wartime mission.
- Acknowledge accomplishment.
- Evaluate training events.

Training in combat is different. Time will be critical. Soldiers' lives will be at stake. The field manual and experienced combat infantry veterans emphasize that the NCO leader must use every available opportunity to sharpen survival skills. In combat, you must teach your soldiers to know the enemy, what the threat is, and how to respond to hostile activity. Training is conducted during real operations, which causes extreme stress, so you must help your soldiers use coping skills. (Turn to FM 26-2, *Management of Stress in Army Operations*, for more information.) Realistic training during peacetime and the ways you demonstrate your ability on the battlefield will contribute to your soldiers' self-confidence.

On a battlefield, you must ensure that your soldiers remain informed. "The soldier wants to know all he can about his situation," states FM 22-102. Keep the news flowing as regularly as the situation permits. Do not speculate or allow rumors to grow. The unit's supporting Army Public Affairs team or detachment, American Forces Radio and Television services, and the chain of command will all be able to provide bits and pieces of accurate information. As you are informed, and especially when the bits and pieces form a complete picture of some sort, pass along the news as quickly and as objectively as possible. Avoid distractions, however; keep your soldiers focused on their mission.

Suppress fearful behavior because it can spread.

Teamwork provides results on and off the battlefield. You will be the key to sustaining cohesion among your soldiers. Focus on teamwork, training, and weapons and gear maintenance. Do everything within your power to ensure timely supply of needed items and learn the supply system.

Appendix A of FM 22-102 is a tool you may use to assess the current level of cohesion among your soldiers. Use it to determine what kind of leader you are and whether your unit is oriented properly toward values, standards, mission goals, training, and combat development. Study *Soldier Team Development*.

TRAINING MANAGEMENT KNOWLEDGE

To do well as a training manager you must read FM 25-101 cover to cover. Read it entirely through one time. Then read it again, slowly, chapter by chapter. Use a highlighter. Mark key words, terms, and concepts. Get to know the training management cycle, beginning on page 1-11 of the manual. When studying with your peers, discuss battle-focused training at length.

A tip to First Sergeant Course selectees: Learn the training management cycle well; you will be expected to understand and explain it. Regarding all senior NCOs, the commandant of the U.S. Army Sergeants Major Academy in 1993 called them "*accelerators* who are involved in all aspects of the training management cycle. You are the commander's conscience, ensuring that battle focus is maintained as training management-oriented orders, directives, policies, procedures, and peculiarities are scheduled and accomplished. Remember that 'feedback is the breakfast of champions' [according to *The One Minute Manager*]. You also need to know how local level training meetings, training briefings, and after-action reviews are conducted. Emphasize standards. Make sure everyone in your unit understands what battle tasks are. Train trainers to allow no double standards in training."

NCO Journal made this eye-opening point about the relationship between NCO leaders and the requirement to understand battle-focused training: "There are no exceptions for not being trained or to train in the battle focus concept. Leaders can't simply ignore this process and hope they get by without it. Ignoring it in peacetime will cost lives in war. NCOs who ignore it will fail." Absorb FM 25-101. (*Battle Focused Training*, FM 25-101, is discussed in chapter 2.)

7

Personal Enrichment

Control of units is dependent upon effective communication. Faulty communication causes most unit problems. It leads to confusion and can cause a good plan to fail. . . . Failure to communicate effectively while solving problems and while executing plans is one of the greatest obstacles to success in training and in battle. A leader's communication skills can either help or hinder in the use of all his or her other skills. —U.S. Army Sergeants Major Academy

PROFESSIONAL READING, WRITING, AND MULTIMEDIA

Reading *NCO Guide* shows that you are interested in receiving helpful information about professional matters. Reading is a vital personal literacy ability you must use to stay informed and keep your soldiers informed, and to manage your career and help your soldiers learn to manage theirs. Writing ability is critical for similar reasons. And increasingly, computer literacy matters because it enables NCOs to receive and transmit text and supporting communications across vast electronic networks.

Senior enlisted soldiers, especially, should be endowed with reading, writing, and related computing skills. This chapter, therefore, contains significant content directed toward enhancement of effective communications skills, knowledge, and attitudes.

Also included is information about two professional associations that communicate daily with government and industry on soldiers' behalf. Officials of the Non Commissioned Officers Association and the Association of the United States Army read a lot and respond in writing and in person when they believe they must to represent the interests of soldiers and their families. When they write, it is often to Congress, the White House, and other key federal agencies. High-level officials of both associations know the value of effective communication.

NCOs who have completed *The Army Writing Program* (AR 600-70) know why text communications may or may not be clearly understood by intended readers. The ability to read, rapidly understand, and respond in writing to memorandums, letters, reports, and other documents hinges on a command of comprehension, grammar, vocabulary, and related skills. To write clearly and efficiently you must organize your thoughts, put them in order of precedence, and front-load the most important message you want the reader to get. Soldiers who have trouble reading and writing may seek help through counselors in the Army Continuing Education System (ACES, covered in chapter 5). ACES counselors can also recommend computer-aided instruction courses to help you develop or advance computer literacy skills.

NCOES Contribution to Literacy

Largely due to formal training provided by NCO Education System (NCOES) small-group leaders, many thousands of NCOES graduates know that BLUF ("Bluff")—Bottom Line Up Front—means putting the intended meaning of their writing in the first sentences and paragraph. Add the BLUF technique to your writing style; it will pay off.

Senior NCOs must routinely read inches-high piles of official documents that flow through local mail distribution systems. Some intended meanings get through to the busy readers, but too many remain buried because of poor writing skills. Readers in leadership and supervisory positions who are fortunate enough receive BLUF-polished material from subordinates should commend the effort.

The Army standard is Bottom Line Up Front, according to AR 600-70 and guidance in the following: TRADOC Pamphlet 350-5, *Effective Staff Writing;* DA Pamphlet 600-67, *Effective Writing for Army Leaders;* and Adjutant General Memorandum 361-3, "Principles of Writing."

Probably no Active Component NCOs today were in service when *Improve Your Writing,* DA Pamphlet 1-10, was published January 1, 1959. Yet the writing guide, an ancestor of AR 600-70, is still valid. It states: "Much Army writing is stilted, verbose, and hard to understand. It wastes manpower by wasting the time of writers and readers. . . . The people who write well should be openly commended; those who need help should get it. . . . Today's style is characterized by a clear purpose [BLUF], clearly and simply expressed. . . . There is a strong preference for short words, short sentences, and short paragraphs." The pamphlet was widely distributed to military writers of that earlier era by former Army Chief of Staff GEN Maxwell D. Taylor.

Write and Read to Succeed

Some NCOs in key positions still do not write clearly. Their basic written English defects involve sentence structure, grammar, punctuation, mechanics, usage, tense, and relational agreement—which, along with *gobbledygook,* contribute to reader anxiety.

Gobbledygook, which fills official writing, is avoidable content that detracts from communication. Examples include but are not limited to unnecessary confusion, overdone illustrations and explanations (complexity), buzzwords (jargon), militarese (educationese, computerese, academicese, bureaucratese, legalese, medicalese), prolixity (wordiness), obfuscation (vagueness), digression (getting off the point), and—here is a big one—redundancy; in other words, repetition; that is, overamplification; or you might say, a single point made several times, several ways, as this one is, repeatedly, over and over, again and again, until the reader feels lectured rather than informed.

Acronym abuse is another error, as the following *Government Computer News* paragraph will illustrate to a vulnerable reader:

> IEEE in 1990 prescribed the set of APIs known as Posix 1003.1, or Posix.1. In 1993, NIST's FIPS 151-2 defined a "profile" or subset of Posix.1, containing what NIST and others consider the key elements. But to be truly open, systems must concern themselves with larger questions than just the APIs.

In fairness to the technology-centered newspaper, acronyms in the example (IEEE, API, NIST, FIPS) were explained earlier in the article. Government information and communications officials who are the newspaper's intended readers understand computer industry language. Its editors know their readership's acronym range and limits—and so should you. Do not confuse intended readers by using unfamiliar acronyms. First explain terms, then use acronyms, sparingly.

Also, avoid gobbledygook and use English writing references to make your communication technically sound. Otherwise, capable readers will have to mentally negotiate content obstacles until they find your main idea and supporting points.

Institution of a mandatory writing test for MOS proponent school faculty and NCO academy cadre would address and reduce the problem readers encounter in academic material. School and NCO academy commandants who attend high-level professional meetings and conferences about noncommissioned education matters can recommend a writing assessment or test.

It may bruise professional pride to admit it, but some NCOs who write school lesson plans or academy lesson guides struggle to write clearly—and fail—and contribute indirectly to Advanced Individual Training and NCOES attrition. Deficient readers are most affected by defective writing. Writing defects and reading deficiencies result in missed and misunderstood communications, which result in undesirable consequences.

In October 1993, Sergeant Major of the Army Richard A. Kidd was consulted for an *Army Times* article about soldiers' reading ability. Staff writer Sean D. Naylor reported that Kidd favored instituting NCO reading tests "as a first step toward making certain reading levels mandatory for NCOs as they rise through the ranks." Kidd's proposed "first step" has been taken. Soldiers attending primary, basic, and advanced NCOES courses must read at the 10th-grade level. Sergeants Major Course (SMC) students must read at the 12th-grade level.

Many well-educated NCOs read and write far beyond the minimum levels. Nevertheless, in a more recent *Army Times* article, staff writer Bernard Adelsberger reported, "Most [SMC] academic failures can be traced to low reading and English language comprehension skills."

Students who get recommended for an academic drop too often face the consequence as a result of documented reading deficiency. In such cases, failed technical and common core exams as well as poorly coordinated, led, or supported training events can be attributed to substandard reading ability. Reading-associated failures occurring in NCOES courses matter both statistically and professionally. Related failure statistics equate to fewer trained NCOs in the field. Professionally, NCOs must read to lead.

As often as NCOs must read to succeed in school and on the job, it seems, they must likewise write to accomplish the following common endeavors:

* Meet an academic requirement.
* Request fiscal and other support.
* Commend, appreciate, and admonish.
* Apply for training and schooling.
* Support a command directive.
* Update a promotion board president.

- Render or appeal a report of survey.
- Counsel a soldier.
- Correspond with a peer.
- Evaluate and rate a subordinate.
- Advise a superior.
- Share professional knowledge.
- Record training observations.
- Inform or request information.
- Give a military briefing.
- Provide MOS training guidance.
- Submit a trip report.
- Produce local or broader doctrine.
- Draft administrative or command policy.
- Describe task procedures.

Fiction and Nonfiction

Other necessary and enriching purposes are served by reading and writing. Perhaps you have a favorite author whose fiction sweeps you away from the realities of Army life. Having time to enjoy the entertainment of a good novel is a luxury. Nonfiction, on the other hand, serves more to inform and educate than to entertain. You should read nonfiction to develop your intellect, enhance your potential, and benefit your soldiers. The more you know, the more your soldiers can know, and the more your unit and the Army can grow.

So what to read? By whom? And what to write? To whom?

It's your choice—so long as it is primarily nonfiction, and what you read and write contributes to your military career potential, education goals, personal avocations such as sports and health, and other beneficial pursuits.

It is OK to read and write fiction occasionally, but focus most of your energy on nonfiction. One exception to the guidance is based on income made as a part-time novelist or short-story writer. Another goes to your right to enjoy your free time.

Personal Reference Library

Whatever your literary pursuits, you need basic reference books to be an adept communicator. Put *Websters Ninth New Collegiate Dictionary* in your personal reference library. It is highly recommended. So is *Army Dictionary and Desk Reference*, by CPT Tim Zurick, U.S. Army Reserve (Stackpole Books). *The Synonym Finder*, by J. I. Rodale, and *Roget's Thesaurus in Dictionary Form* will enable (*endow, equip, outfit, arm*) you with the ability to find the exact word to fit the context (*meaning, relationship, subject, theme, topic*) of your thoughts. You will also find *Instant Synonyms and Antonyms* (Career Publishing, Inc.) to be useful when comparing and contrasting people, places, and things.

Books such as *English Simplified* (Harper Collins); *Hodge's Harbrace College Handbook* (Harcourt, Brace, Jovanovich); and *The Little English Handbook* (Harper Collins) are recommended writing tutors. If you write for publication, pick up a copy of the *Associated Press Stylebook and Libel Manual*. The "AP Stylebook" is used by Army Public Affairs journalists who produce Army News Service items, *SOLDIERS* magazine, Army newspaper articles, and other official Command Information Program material. You may also want to invest in more detailed style manuals such as *Words into Type*

(Prentice Hall, Inc.); and *The Chicago Manual of Style* (The University of Chicago Press).

Vocabulary books are plentiful, and vocabulary flash card sets such as *The English Vocabulary Cards* will be useful and educational. Slip five or ten cards a day into your uniform pocket, study them, and seek *appropriate* ways to use them in conversation and writing. Two 1,000-word English language sets are available from Visual Education Association, 581 West Leffel Lane, P.O. Box 1666, Springfield, OH 45501. Outside Ohio call (800) 243-7070. With a vocabulary builder at hand you can look up words such as *harbinger*, which is what literacy is to success, and *precursor*, which is what this sentence is relative to the next.

If you intend to sell your writing, see the additional references listed in the Writing for Profit subsection below.

Other Recommended Publications

Recommended reading comes from chapter 2, The Role of the NCO, which covers NCO corps history and references an Army Center of Military History book, *The Story of the Noncommissioned Officer*, which is available through the Government Printing Office (GPO). Write to Superintendent of Documents, U.S. Government Printing Office, Washington, DC 20402. Also recommended is *Guardians of the Republic: A History of the Noncommissioned Officer Corps of the U.S. Army* (Ballantine Books).

Freelance writer Jessica Johns, in a January 1993 *Army Times* article, said military librarians and historians recommend the following:

• *The Harper Encyclopedia of Military History: From 3500 B.C. to the Present* (Harper Collins).

• *The World Factbook* (Brassey's). Information in this annual book is provided by the Central Intelligence Agency. A computer software version of the *Factbook* is available from Reasonable Solutions Software, 1121 Disk Drive, Medford, OR 97501-6639.

• *American Military History* (U.S. Army Center of Military History), available through the GPO.

Check at your post library to locate these three books, as prices ranging from $28 to $50 can be avoided with a library card.

Other recommended history and historical figure books include *The Civil War*, by renowned author Shelby Foote; *No Name on the Bullet*, a biography of Audie Murphy, by Don Graham; *Ernie's War*, the best of Ernie Pyle's World War II dispatches, edited by David Nichols; and *Inside the Green Berets*, by COL (Ret.) Charles M. Simpson, III (Presidio Press).

Chapter 6 covers the importance of first reading the primary field manuals about leadership, counseling, and training management. After the required reading, discover how to more effectively manage things and lead people by reading *In Search of Excellence*, by Thomas J. Peters and Robert H. Waterman, Jr. The authors also explain why military metaphors—taking military viewpoints toward business productivity and service—have not applied to "excellent company" strategy for years.

You may also benefit by reading *Small Unit Leadership*, by COL (Ret.) Dandridge M. Malone (Presidio). This Vietnam veteran of the battle of Firebase 25 will give you examples of how to spur soldiers to do their jobs. He sees leadership in terms of tasks, conditions, and standards.

Stackpole Books, *NCO Guide*'s publisher, offers more than 100 other titles of interest to the military reader. If you study strategy, for example, you will enjoy the 16 Osprey Campaign series books distributed by the publisher.

As often as it has been mentioned in this guide, you should by now know that *Army Times* is an excellent, highly recommended source of military news, features, and other information. Follow stories and columns that interest you as they are published in multiple issues of the newspaper, fill a scrapbook, reap a deeper understanding of your interests and concerns—and keep your soldiers informed.

SOLDIERS, the official monthly magazine of the Army, is also a recommended source of feature information about unit activities and Army people. Clip and save from it and your local command newspaper, which will inform as well.

Professional associations, including the Non Commissioned Officers Association (NCOA) and the Association of the United States Army (AUSA), publish *NCOA Journal* and *AUSA News*, respectively. The AUSA also mails its monthly *Army* magazine to members. More on these associations will follow in respective sections below.

You should read, clip, and save material from *NCO Journal*, which is published by the U.S. Army Sergeants Major Academy.

Trade magazines and Army professional journals that apply to your MOS should be read to keep up with trends, changes, and other matters related to your specialty. Combat arms soldiers may read *Infantry*, *Armor*, and *Field Artillery Professional Bulletin*. Other combat arms, combat support, and combat service support publications are available as well, including *Combat Service Support Guide*, a Stackpole Books publication by MAJ John E. Edwards. Check with your first sergeant or command sergeant major for other recommendations.

If you are stationed overseas, read *The Stars and Stripes*, which is published in several editions to provide daily news, sports, features, columns, and other information to soldiers and their families. Soldiers at remote locations, such as the NATO Missile Firing Range on the Greek island of Crete, receive an edition of *The Stars and Stripes* that is delayed but still valuable. Daily offerings from *USA Today*, *The Wall Street Journal*, and certain other major newspapers serve soldier-readers who are stationed at major installations abroad.

NCOs should read military and civilian publications with various liberal, independent, and conservative biases to better understand the dangerous, unstable world described in chapter 1. To understand more about the economic world, read *Preparing for the Twenty-First Century*, by Paul Kennedy, and *The Work of Nations*, written by Robert B. Reich when he was a faculty member of Harvard's John F. Kennedy School of Government. Do not shy away from loftier subject matter. Just as you "train to challenge," you must "read to challenge." Find out why high technology is changing the world and how technology has revolutionized the work place. Read *Turning the Tables*, by Dan Burstein, and *Paradigm Shift*, by Don Tapscott and Art Caston.

Other Recommended Topics

As a professional soldier, you should also seek information about how the world population explosion is affecting U.S. vital interests. The Clinton administration favors policies that aim to slow Third World population growth. Developing nations, on the other hand, press hard to convince industrialized nations, primarily the United States, to reduce consumer appetites for products made from dwindling world resources.

Read about ecology and the environment. The Army, backing the nation, strongly supports sound ecological and environmental practices. Learn how certain nations of the world destroy whole habitats and nonrenewable natural resources to produce goods and compete in global export markets, in some cases because this produces their sole income. Countless oxygen-producing trees hundreds of years old are clear-cut and exported for their commercial value. Some developing nations burn entire forests to uncover fertile soil, which is exhausted in a few growing or grazing seasons. The global impact is alarming—even to some of the coldest political regimes.

If you wonder why the cost of quality seafood keeps going up, discover the growing international concern about the high-tech rape of the world's commercial fishing holes in the Atlantic, Pacific, and elsewhere. Poor nations that depend on the world's oceans for food are especially vulnerable to the devastation.

Famine and mass starvation in certain African countries result in catastrophes, and soldiers must deploy, as they did to Somalia, to escort and defend international aid operations. Political unrest and old ethnic or racial hatreds are also worth understanding. Surely, more than one soldier among the 200 who deployed to secure Rwanda's Kigali airport in July 1994 had questions about their mission.

These subjects do matter and should concern you. Stay informed. Read. Your knowledge will help if a concerned soldier says, "Why do we have to go?" If it is you who gets asked, and you have kept current, you will be prepared to answer. Reading and keeping your soldiers informed will improve morale and readiness.

Academic and Job-Related Writing Resources

An NCO pursuing a college degree must research assignments before writing term and research papers or a thesis. *Writing Research Papers,* by James D. Lester, and more recent research books cover topic development, library work, note-taking techniques, writing, formatting, and reference citation requirements and procedures. A good research-writing book will cover two dominant scholastic writing styles—MLA (Modern Language Association) and APA (American Psychological Association)—and will help you to critically analyze, argue, or explain your assignment.

To organize your thoughts and quickly write effective Army correspondence, get a copy of *Guide to Effective Military Writing* by William A. McIntosh (Stackpole Books) at your local post exchange or military clothing sales store. Compare it with AR 600-70.

Writing for Profit

You may need to add a few other books to your personal reference library to make money selling your writing. Recommendations for general or technical subjects include the following:

- *The Writer's Legal Companion*, by Brad Bunnin and Peter Beren (Addison Wesley Publishing Co., Inc.).
- *Technical Writer's Freelancing Guide,* by Peter Kent (Sterling Publishing Co., Inc.).
- *The Tech Writing Game*, by Janet Van Wicklen (Facts on File, Inc.).
- *How to Start and Run a Writing and Editing Business*, by Herman Holtz (John Wiley and Sons, Inc.).
- *Writer's Encyclopedia*, edited by Kirk Polking (Writer's Digest Books).

If you do write fiction, consider adding to your library the Elements of Fiction series from Writer's Digest Books. Included are *Manuscript Submission* by Scott Edelstein, *Plot* by Ansen Dibell, *Characters & Viewpoint* by Orson Scott Card, *Dialog* by Lewis Turco, and *Theme & Strategy* by Ronald B. Tobias. Other Writer's Digest Books references include *Creating Characters: How to Build Story People* by Dwight V. Swain and *The Writer's Digest Handbook of Short Story Writing*.

Regulations about For-Profit Writing

Before you try to make a buck selling your writing, consult AR 600-50, *Standards of Conduct*, and the *Department of Defense Ethics Guidelines*. Visit your local ethics counselor at the Judge Advocate General's Office to discuss your topic, research methods, data resources, commercial intention, and proposed business relationship with your publisher. Let the counselor be your guide. If you get the nod to proceed, then go for it. If the counselor recommends that you not publish, then discuss alternatives—switching, for example, from nonfiction to autobiographical fiction—but do not twist sound guidance into an illegal framework, based on a profit motive. Put the Professional Army Ethic first.

If you are on active duty, do not allow a publisher to print your official rank before your name on a cover or to use your rank to solicit for sales, because doing so is a conflict of interest in most for-profit cases; it could make potential customers believe that, contrary to federal law, the government endorses your work. See AR 600-50, page 8, paragraph 2-5b.

Now the good news. AR 600-50, page 8, paragraph 2-6e(1-3) states:

> [Department of the Army (DA)] personnel are encouraged to engage in teaching, lecturing, and writing. . . . However, DA personnel will not, either with or without compensation, engage in activities that are dependent on information obtained as a result of their Government employment, except when the information does not focus specifically on the agency's responsibilities, policies, and programs, and—(1) the information has been published and is generally available to the public; or (2) the information would be made available to the public under the FOIA [Freedom of Information Act], 5 USC 552; or (3) it will be made generally available to the public and the appropriate commander gives written authorization for the use of nonpublic information on the basis that the use is in the public interest.

AR 600-50 and the overriding DOD ethics guidelines, which are similar, give potential enlisted soldier-authors a lot of leeway. Officers in procurement and acquisition positions have much more restrictive guidance to follow. Just remember, however, that certain restrictions apply, some of which will depend on your subject matter and your own position. Further, and it should go without saying, do not disclose classified information. Again, you are strongly encouraged to visit your local ethics counselor before selling a manuscript.

Writing for Professional Development

Your professional development should be shared. As you learn, share your knowledge by writing about it. Submit material to the following:

- *NCO Journal.* The editor is always on the hunt for good material. Here are the guidelines: Keep the reader in mind; address the subject to a wide audience; write conversationally; keep it simple and short (four double-spaced pages fill a magazine page); and include photos or other illustrations. The editor also wants letters from NCOs who agree or disagree with what they read in the journal, or who have a better idea about aspects of NCO business. Book reviews are also welcomed. Include the title, author, publisher, date published, price, whether it is hard or soft bound, and number of pages. For more information, contact the editor and ask for a reprint of "Wanted: Writers." The address is *NCO Journal*, ATTN: Editor, USASMA, Fort Bliss, TX 79918.
- The AUSA Institute of Land Warfare (ILW). The ILW wants to hear from you. Request a copy of "Manuscripts Wanted" from the institute at 2425 Wilson Boulevard, Arlington, VA 22201, or call (800) 336-4570. The AUSA needs land warfare papers, essays, and books. You may also submit material to *Army* magazine at the same address. Write and ask for a copy of the magazine's style requirements.
- Center for Army Lessons Learned (CALL). If you have learned a valuable professional lesson, relate it in writing to the CALL. Send material to Commander, Combined Arms Command, ATTN: ATZL-CTL, Fort Leavenworth, KS 66027-7000. Lessons shared help drive doctrinal and force structure improvements.

Literacy On-Line

Do you compute? According to survey findings of the Army Times Publishing Company, nine out of every ten active-duty members use some kind of computer in the work place. That statistic represents 90 percent of the largest U.S. workforce, according to the Associated Press (AP). More and more members are using computers at home as well. A recent AP chart published in the *Indianapolis Star* projected that 60 percent of all U.S. households will have a personal computer (PC) by the year 2000. Today, according to the *Star* report, nearly four out of every ten households have a PC, whereas in 1990 only one in four households had a PC.

If you are among the growing majority in the Army who use a PC at work or home, or both, you may check spelling and grammar with word-processing programs such as MicroSoft Word and WordPerfect. If your word processor does not have built-in spelling or grammar checkers, you may buy add-on programs. You can also purchase educational software to develop your typing and writing skills.

With your home computer, you may also electronically subscribe to on-line services such as Military City Online (MCO), offered jointly by Army Times Publishing Company and America Online. MCO made its debut in March 1994 and enables subscribers to read at home, via modem connection, the latest news and service-related information *Army Times* has to offer. MCO also provides electronic bulletin boards and live-discussion capabilities. It is the military's version of other registered on-line subscription services such as CompuServe, Prodigy, Dow Jones News Retrieval Service, Delphi, and America Online.

One particular on-line service should be of interest to NCOs: the U.S. Army Sergeants Major Academy (USASMA) NCOES Training Bulletin Board System (BBS), which is in place to enhance communications between USASMA Training Course Development Division officials and supported units in the Active and Reserve Components. To call the BBS operator, dial DSN 978-8621. To connect via modem, dial 978-8277. To send a facsimile, dial 978-8469. To leave a voice message, call DSN 978-8814 or commercial (915) 568-8814.

If you want to take an "on-ramp" (electronically connect) to the "Information Superhighway" (National Information Infrastructure), you can use selected on-line services as electronic gateways to access a global network of networks called the Internet. But remember, telecommunicating at its root involves *communicating*. Your goal should be to ensure that your intended reader gets the message. If you do compute and want to telecommunicate on the Internet, you may find a plethora of books on the subject, including *The Internet Companion: A Beginner's Guide to Global Networking*, by Tracy LaQuey, with Jeanne C. Ryer. These authors will tell you what the Internet is, how it works, and how to use it to communicate with people and find information.

Army Times gave a good reason for electronically connecting to the world. "Soon," wrote staff writer Margaret Roth in November 1993, "almost anyone with a personal computer, a modem and [communications] software will be able to log on to a defense computer network and receive the *Early Bird*, which will appear on the screen just as it does on paper."

Savvy noncommissioned readers know the value of reading the *Early Bird*. It contains up to 50 selected late-news extracts a day from major U.S. and foreign English-language newspapers. Articles cover military news and other topics of interest to the nation or, specifically, to Army brass and supporting officers who represent the Army to businesses, industries, and Congress. Reading the *Early Bird* will give you an edge on current events.

PROFESSIONAL ASSOCIATIONS
The Non Commissioned Officers Association (NCOA)
The NCOA is a federally chartered, nonprofit, fraternal association founded in 1960. Its purpose is to accomplish the following:
- Uphold and defend the Constitution and support a strong national defense with a focus on military personnel issues.
- Promote health, prosperity, and scholarship among its members and their families through legislative and benevolent programs.
- Improve benefits for soldiers, veterans, and their families and survivors.
- Help soldiers, veterans, and their families and survivors in filing benefit claims.

Through its office near the Pentagon, NCOA actively lobbies Congress, the White House, the Department of Veterans Affairs, the military services, and other federal agencies to fulfill its goals. The association also supervises the following: major nonpartisan voter registration drives in the United States and abroad; a nationwide network of coordinators who monitor state and local administrative and legislative activities affecting NCOA members; a nationwide outreach program for hospitalized veterans; and fellowship and intern programs for undergraduate college students.

The NCOA is a leader in advocating improvements in benefits for enlisted soldiers. The association's director of marketing, Sandra Powell, said, "NCOA was instrumental in the development of the Montgomery GI Bill, creating severance pay for enlisted soldiers, providing equity in hazardous duty pay, and fair unemployment compensation for former soldiers." Powell said NCOA's five registered lobbyists submit testimony to Congress an average of 35 times a year and maintain liaison with other federal agencies to ensure laws are implemented and policies developed with equity for enlisted military personnel and veterans.

Annual membership for NCOs is $20. The association offers many member benefits including the Certified Merchants Program and The Buying Network, which provide substantial discounts on commercial products and services. Members may also receive NCOA Journal and may qualify for the competitive NCOA Visa Card. Members with families may purchase CHAMPUS Aid, a health insurance supplement offered through Academy Insurance Group, Inc. The association also offers a motor club that provides roadside assistance and towing. Additionally, property and casualty insurance is offered, and each member receives free accidental death and dismemberment insurance.

For more information, write to Non Commissioned Officers Association, ATTN: Membership Processing, P.O. Box 105636, Atlanta, GA 30348-5636, or call (800) 662-2620.

The Association of the U.S. Army (AUSA)

The AUSA is a private, nonprofit organization established in 1950. It supports Active and Reserve Component members, Army civilians, retirees, and Army families. Its goals are as follows:

- People support for those in the Army.
- Industry support of the Army.
- Public education about the Army.
- Professionalism within the Army.

AUSA's legislative affairs office stays on top of issues that affect soldiers during and after service. The association pushes for pay equity, adequate military housing, cost-of-living allowances, and standard subsistence allowances for all personnel, as well as the following:

- Full reimbursement of expenses for official travel and changes of station.
- Quality medical and dental care.
- Community morale, welfare, and recreation activities at fair costs.
- An upgraded retirement system.

Regular membership costs $25 a year. Among its membership benefits are opportunities to participate in chapter activities and discount product and service programs. AUSA also offers MasterCare, a CHAMPUS supplement that provides short-term health insurance, long-term care, hospital income protection, and accidental death and dismemberment coverage. LifePlan is the association's group term life insurance program; Vision One Eyecare is its discount eyewear program, available at Sears, Montgomery Ward, and J. C. Penney optical shops. AUSA also offers discount car rental and lodging programs, and has its own Visa card.

Members in the rank of sergeant and above receive AUSA News and Army magazine. Corporals who elect to pay a discounted $22 a year for membership will receive both the newspaper and the magazine. Corporals and other soldiers whose pay grades are E-4 and below may opt to join for $10 a year, but the reduced fee does not include Army magazine.

For more information, call (800) 336-4570 or write Association of the United States Army, 2425 Wilson Blvd., Arlington, VA 22201.

8

Professional Respect

COURTESY

Military courtesy is respect shown to superiors by subordinates and mutual respect demonstrated between senior and subordinate personnel. It is basic to military discipline and founded upon respect for and loyalty to properly constituted authority.

Saluting

The hand salute is a formal sign of courtesy between soldiers. It is both recognition of rank and authority and a greeting exchanged between members of a unique professional organization with special rules and codes of conduct. Precisely whom to salute is defined in AR 600-25, *Salutes, Honors, and Visits of Courtesy*. But the best rule to follow when saluting is "When in doubt, whip it out." The salute is a recognized form of greeting, and no soldier should feel embarrassment because he or she may have saluted someone who is not strictly entitled to it by AR 600-25.

All soldiers in uniform are required to salute when they meet and recognize persons entitled to the salute. Salutes are exchanged between officers (commissioned and warrant) and enlisted personnel. Salutes are exchanged with personnel of the Army, Navy, Air Force, Marine Corps, and Coast Guard entitled to the salute. It is customary to salute officers of friendly foreign nations as well.

Civilians may be saluted by persons in uniform when appropriate, but the uniform hat or cap should not be raised as a form of salutation. Salutes are not required if either the senior or subordinate or both are in civilian attire.

Soldiers under arms give the salute prescribed for the weapon with which they are armed. The practice of saluting others in official vehicles is appropriate and should be observed. Salutes are not required to be given by or to personnel who are driving or riding in privately owned vehicles except by gate guards.

When military personnel are driving moving vehicles, they should not initiate a salute. Salutes are not required in public areas, such as theaters, outdoor athletic facilities, or other situations when the act would be inappropriate or impractical.

Accompanying the hand salute with an appropriate greeting, such as "Good morning, sir," or "Good morning, ma'am," is proper. Personnel do not salute indoors except when reporting to a superior officer.

The salute is given when the person approaching or being approached is recognized as being authorized a salute, usually at six paces. The officer is obliged to return the salute. *Never turn and go another direction to avoid saluting someone.*

If a superior remains in your area but does not engage in conversation, he is saluted only once, upon the initial greeting; should a superior engage you in conversation, however, then you must salute when he finishes talking to you and departs.

Always salute with precision and enthusiasm. Never salute with anything in your hands or mouth. Never duck your head when you salute, but always keep your chin up and your back straight. Give a greeting clearly, in a normal tone of voice. You should not greet people in the same tone of voice you use when shouting out commands on the drill field.

You do not have to salute when you are in any of the following situations:

- A prisoner.
- Marching; the officer or NCO in charge salutes for everyone.
- Indoors, except when reporting or on guard duty.
- Carrying articles or occupied so that saluting would be awkward.
- It is inappropriate to do so, such as when assisting a superior who is injured.
- In ranks; the officer or NCO in charge will salute for the whole formation.
- Engaged in athletics or sports.
- In places of public assembly or conveyance.
- Maneuvering against a hostile force or participating in field training.

"Outdoors" may actually be indoors, such as in buildings used for drill halls, gymnasiums, and other roofed structures commonly used for drilling and exercising. Theater marquees and covered walkways open on both sides are considered outdoors, and it is appropriate to salute when underneath them.

Saluting in Vehicles. Vehicle drivers salute only when the vehicle is stopped and the engine is off. When troops are riding in a vehicle, the senior member salutes for the group.

Saluting in Groups. Individuals in formations never salute except at the command *present arms*. The officer or NCO in charge does the saluting for the entire group. If the troops are not at *attention* when it becomes necessary to salute a senior, the person in charge calls them to *attention* before saluting.

A soldier in formation, not standing at *attention*, comes to the position of *attention* when spoken to by a senior.

When a group not in formation is approached by a superior, the first person seeing him or her calls *attention*, and all come to *attention* and salute, unless they are at work or engaged in organized athletics.

Saluting on Guard. In garrison, guards armed with a rifle halt and face toward the music (when the national anthem or "To the Color" is played), person, or colors to be saluted and present arms. When challenging, the first salute is given when the officer has been recognized and advanced.

A sentinel armed with a pistol gives the hand salute, except when challenging, and then the weapon is held at the *raise pistol* position and kept there until the challenged party departs.

If the officer to whom a sentinel may be talking salutes a senior, the sentinel also salutes. Wherever he is posted, indoors or outdoors, a guard or a sentinel salutes all officers, except when saluting would endanger the officers or interfere with duty performance.

Reporting. If you are reporting to your company commander, you must salute and formally report. If you are told to report to a senior officer on the staff and discuss the details of a paper with him, whether you salute depends on the protocol considered acceptable on the particular staff and the frequency with which you visit.

When reporting to a commander, a salute is always given at the report and again when dismissed. When reporting indoors and without arms, first remove your hat and then knock on the commander's door. When given permission to enter, advance to within two paces from the commander's desk, halt, salute, and make your report: "Sir [or Ma'am], Sergeant Onagainoffagain reporting as directed." Hold the salute until it is returned. After stating your business, salute again, and exit the room.

When reporting while under arms, never remove your hat. If carrying a rifle, enter with the weapon at the trail and give the rifle salute at *order arms*. Otherwise, give the hand salute. Outdoors, a solder may approach an officer with the weapon at either *trail* or *right shoulder arms* and execute the rifle salute at *order* or *right shoulder arms*.

Forms of Address

The title "sir" or "ma'am" should be used on all occasions when addressing an officer or a civilian. For a detailed discussion on the use of these titles, see the section dealing with etiquette in this chapter.

Privates and privates first class are addressed as "private." Corporals and specialists are called "corporal" and "specialist" respectively. Sergeants through the rank of master sergeant are referred to as "sergeant," except first sergeants, who are called "first sergeant." Likewise, sergeants major and command sergeants major (including the Sergeant Major of the Army) are called "sergeant major."

FLAGS

The flag of the United States, the national color, and the national standard are not dipped by way of salute or compliment. An exception to this is the rule followed by naval vessels when, upon receiving a salute of this type from a vessel registered by a nation formally recognized by the United States, the compliment must be returned.

The organizational color or standard may be dipped in salute in all military ceremonies while the U.S. national anthem, "To the Color," or a foreign national anthem is being played, and when giving honors to the organizational commander or an individual of higher grade, including a foreign dignitary of higher grade, but not otherwise.

The U.S. Army flag is considered an organizational color and is also dipped when the U.S. national anthem, "To the Color," or a foreign national anthem is being played. It is also dipped when giving honors to the Chief of Staff of the U.S. Army, his direct representative, or an individual of higher grade, including a foreign dignitary of equivalent or higher grade, but in no other case.

Flag is a general descriptive term for a cloth device with a distinguishing color or design that has a special meaning or serves as a signal. The flag of the United States, the white flag of truce, and weather flags are examples.

In the military service, the *color* is a flag of a dismounted unit; an *ensign* is a national flag; a *pennant* is a small triangular flag usually flown for identification of a unit; a *standard* is a flag of a mounted unit; and a *guidon* is a swallow-tailed flag carried by Army units for identification, especially in drills and ceremonies.

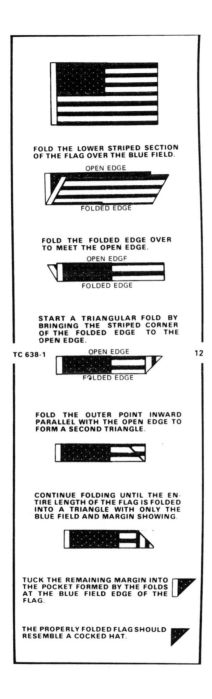

FOLD THE LOWER STRIPED SECTION OF THE FLAG OVER THE BLUE FIELD.

FOLD THE FOLDED EDGE OVER TO MEET THE OPEN EDGE.

START A TRIANGULAR FOLD BY BRINGING THE STRIPED CORNER OF THE FOLDED EDGE TO THE OPEN EDGE.

FOLD THE OUTER POINT INWARD PARALLEL WITH THE OPEN EDGE TO FORM A SECOND TRIANGLE.

CONTINUE FOLDING UNTIL THE EN-TIRE LENGTH OF THE FLAG IS FOLDED INTO A TRIANGLE WITH ONLY THE BLUE FIELD AND MARGIN SHOWING.

TUCK THE REMAINING MARGIN INTO THE POCKET FORMED BY THE FOLDS AT THE BLUE FIELD EDGE OF THE FLAG.

THE PROPERLY FOLDED FLAG SHOULD RESEMBLE A COCKED HAT.

When folding the U.S. flag, it is important to fold it in the traditional manner as shown.

The Flag of the United States

The flag of the United States is displayed at all Army installations. It represents the Union—the 50 stars on a field of blue. The field is always to the left of the observer because it is the "field of honor."

The flag should never be used as part of a costume or dress, or on a vehicle or float unless it is attached to a staff, nor should it be displayed as drapery. Bunting—strips of cloth in the colors of the flag—is used for draping and decoration. No lettering or any other kind of object should ever be placed on the flag, and its use in advertising is discouraged.

Soiled, torn, or weathered flags should be burned, privately.

On Army installations, three different sizes of U.S. flags are flown.

• *Post flag.* Flown in fair weather, except on those occasions when the garrison flag is prescribed. Its dimensions are 19 feet fly by 10 feet hoist.

• *Garrison flag.* Flown on holidays and important occasions. Its dimensions are 38 feet fly by 20 feet hoist.

• *Storm flag.* Flown in lieu of the post flag in inclement weather. It is also used to drape caskets at a military funeral. Its dimensions are $9\,^{1}/_{4}$ feet fly by 5 feet hoist.

When the U.S. flag and flags of other nations are flown from staffs, the U.S. flag is always displayed at the right end of the line. It is hoisted first and lowered last. In a group of flags consisting of state, society, or city flags, the U.S. flag should be placed in the center of the arrangement at the highest point.

In an auditorium or on a platform, if the U.S. flag is displayed on the platform or the stage, it is to the speaker's right. If not displayed on the stage or platform, the U.S. flag is placed on the right of the audience. The other flags are displayed on the side opposite the national flag. If the flag is displayed against the wall behind the speaker, it is above and behind the speaker's stand.

Whenever displayed with another flag in a crossed staff arrangement against the wall, the U.S. flag is placed to the right (the observer's left), and its staff is placed in front of the staff of the other flag.

Flag Detail

Generally, a flag detail consists of one NCIOC, two halyard pullers, and two to eight flag handlers. The purpose of the handlers is to ensure correct folding and unfolding of the flag and to ensure that it does not touch the ground. Two handlers are needed when raising or lowering the storm flag, six handlers for the post flag, and eight handlers for the garrison flag.

Members of the flag detail are equipped according to local standing operating procedure and letter of instructions.

During the ceremony, the NCOIC subtly gives necessary commands or directives to ensure proper performance by the flag detail. On windy days, the NCOIC may assist the flag handlers in securing or folding the flag.

ETIQUETTE

Etiquette is the set of rules or forms for manners and ceremonies established as acceptable or required in professional or official life. As a professional NCO, you must know these rules as they pertain to official social events. Guidance set forth in this section and courtesy go hand in hand, and if you take courtesy to others as your guiding principle, no matter what the situation, you can never go wrong.

Proper Speech

You should make every effort to develop and maintain good speech habits. As an NCO, you must be able to express yourself clearly and effectively.

Good speech begins with a good vocabulary and an understanding of grammar and pronunciation. Constantly misusing and mispronouncing words in front of your soldiers will undermine your authority and cause you to lose their respect. A good speaker is listened to and understood. Being able to converse in an interesting, intelligent, and entertaining manner is a social asset that will reflect favorably upon you. Never discuss your personal or business affairs at social gatherings. Never gossip, criticize others, boast, or engage in arguments. Maintain a broad interest in current events, movies, television, and so on, so that you may contribute to the conversation intelligently when such topics arise.

Telephone Etiquette

It is essential that proper telephone courtesy be observed at all times.

When answering the phone, identify your unit or office first and then give your rank and name. Do not shout into the telephone or speak as if you were giving a command on the drill field. Speak clearly, in your normal tone of voice. If you are the first sergeant of Alpha Company, do not simply bellow your rank into the telephone, but give the caller the same courtesy you demand of your troops when they answer the telephone.

Pay attention to the caller's rank, title, and name, and use them, wherever appropriate, during the conversation. If the person being called is not in, offer to take a message or refer the caller to another party who may be able to help. Listen patiently and politely. Speak distinctly and with confidence.

When calling someone else, give your rank and name first. If you should get discourteous or bewildered people on the other end of the line, bear with them. It does no good for you to lose your patience. And try not to tie up the telephone with long-winded personal conversations.

Should you dial a wrong number, *never* just hang up without saying anything. The proper procedure is to excuse yourself for the interruption and then check the number you have dialed. Never ask, "What number is this?" but say "Have I reached 979-9383?"

Never let a telephone ring and ring because you happen to be talking to someone on another line. No military telephone should be left unattended during duty hours, and if one rings more than five times without being answered, someone is remiss. If a phone is not answered by the fourth ring, pick it up yourself. Normally, NCOs do not "take calls" for lower-ranking personnel, but if put in this circumstance, do it gracefully and without complaint. If there is a problem keeping your receptionist or a clerk in the office, deal with the subordinate; don't take it out on the caller.

Tobacco Use

The Department of Defense discourages smoking. In the Army, nonsmoking offices and work places are now the rule. Smoking must be confined to designated areas. For soldiers, the risks of smoking in a tactical environment are enormous. One smoker could place his entire unit in jeopardy.

During off-duty hours, it is your choice to smoke or not, but if you do, you are responsible for being careful and considerate of those who do not. Observe No Smoking signs, and never be insulted if a person asks you not to smoke in his or her presence. Never smoke in an automobile if nonsmokers are present. Do not smoke at ceremonies such as military reviews or funerals, and do not smoke while wearing gloves.

If you are not sure whether it is appropriate to light up, ask permission. Never smoke when going through a reception line, and never carry a lighted cigarette with you into the dining room or onto the dance floor. If ashtrays are provided and your hosts smoke during dinner, then you may smoke.

Tobacco smoke is very distasteful to many people; it permeates hair and clothing and is carried home. Generally, the smoking of pipes or cigars is not appropriate at official affairs unless permission is granted first. It is discourteous to talk to someone with a pipe or cigar in your mouth.

As for snuff or "chew," this habit is totally inappropriate in any social setting.

Etiquette in the Work Place

Good manners are never out of place. Never sit with your feet on your desk. Never sit at your desk reading non-job-related materials. The worst impression you can give a visitor is to be seen reading a novel with your feet propped up on the desk.

When a superior who is not your immediate supervisor enters your work area, you are obliged to stand. And when someone comes to see you, on business or just calling, you should stand and greet that person. If you cannot stand—for example, if you are on the telephone—indicate by a nod of the head or a gesture with a free hand that the visitor should be seated. Never keep a person standing unless he or she is to be disciplined.

If coffee or tea is available, offer your visitor some. This may not always be appropriate, as when an NCO from another staff section drops by to deliver a report, but if the person is a friend or well known to you, make the offer a standard part of your greeting.

Never lean or sit on another person's desk. If the person you are visiting is thoughtless enough not to offer you a seat, remain standing.

You should consider that a visit in person takes precedence over a telephone call. If you happen to be on the telephone when a visitor arrives, finish your conversation quickly and call the other party back later.

It is best not to eat where you work. It is undignified for an NCO to eat at his or her desk. Give yourself a break. Find a few minutes to step outside your work area, find a quiet spot, and eat your lunch there.

Be tolerant. At work certain people just do not get along, generally for the most frivolous reasons. Over a period of time, minor problems can turn into animosity. Set the example. If you encounter someone you dislike, suppress your intolerance. Allowing other people to annoy you is evidence of your own lack of self-discipline.

CUSTOMS

The customs of the service make up the unwritten "common law" of the Army. Customs are rich in tradition, and knowing what they are and observing them should be second nature.

Of course, times are changing. Today, hardly anyone remembers the ancient taboos against soldiers carrying packages or pushing baby carriages while in uniform. But customs that are still accepted should be observed, and the soldier who flouts them should be taken aside and vigorously counseled about maintaining tradition and esprit in the Army.

Following are some customs observed today:
- If you are male, do not carry an umbrella while in uniform. AR 670-1 does not authorize an umbrella as part of the male uniform.
- Never sit on another soldier's bed or bunk in the barracks without permission.
- *Never* criticize a subordinate NCO in front of his or her troops.
- *Never* criticize the Army in front of civilians.
- Never accept gifts from subordinates.
- Never go over the heads of superiors.
- Never "pull rank" on another NCO (this action shows poor leadership).
- Never offer excuses.
- Act upon the commander's "desires" or "suggestions" as if they were orders (which they are, really, but politely phrased).
- *Never* "wear" a superior's rank by saying something like, "The colonel wants this done right away," when in fact the colonel has said no such thing.
- *Never* turn and walk the other way to avoid giving the hand salute.
- *Never* run indoors to avoid standing Reveille or Retreat.
- With the exception of on-the-spot corrections or military courtesy and discipline breaches, never give orders to another NCO's troops.
- Never appear in uniform while under the influence of alcohol.
- If you are a man, always show deference to women and children.

Remember these two responses to questions or orders from your superiors, and you will never go wrong: "I don't know sir, but I'll find out," and "I'll do it or have it done."

Bugle Calls
These signals to the troops are transmitted on the bugle. Traditionally, Army bugle calls have been divided into four major categories.
- Alarm ("Fire," "To Horse").
- Formation ("Adjutant's Call," "Assembly").
- Service ("Church Call," "Fatigue," "First Sergeant's Call," "Mess Call," "Officer's Call," "Recall," "Retreat," "Reveille," "School Call," "Sick Call," "Taps," "Tattoo," "To the Color").
- Warning ("Boots and Saddles," "Drill Call," "First Call," "Guard Call," "Stable Call," "To Quarters").

Bugle calls help order the activities of soldiers throughout the day. At most installations, the few calls that are used are played from recordings on a public address system, although a live bugler is sometimes used to sound Retreat and Reveille.

Following are brief explanations of some of the more common calls, with traditional lyrics that solders have created to accompany the music:

First Call. This call is actually the first bugle call of the day, given as a warning that Reveille is to take place within a few minutes.

Mess Call. In former days, this call was affectionately dubbed "Soupy."

> Soup—y, soup—y, soup,
>   Without a single bean,
> Pork—y, pork—y, pork
>   Without a streak of lean;
> Coffee, coffee, coffee,
>   Without a bit of cream!
>   (or: The weakest ever seen!)

The tune has also been sung with these words: "Come and get your chow! Come and get it now!"

Reveille. The word *reveille* is originally from the Latin *evigilare,* to watch or to wake. The custom of sounding some sort of call to signify the beginning of the day is very ancient. The British adopted the practice from the French and were calling it "revelly" as early as 1644.

Of course, "First Call" is actually the initial bugle call of the Army day, and if you are still in bed when Reveille is sounded, you are late. But Reveille has come into our vocabulary as the word for the bugle call that signifies to awake.

The traditional words to the call are:

> I can't get 'em up, I can't get 'em up,
>   I can't get 'em up in the morning;
> I can't get 'em up, I can't get 'em up,
>   I can't get 'em up at all;
> Corp'rals worse than the privates,
> Sergeants worse than the corporals,
> Lieutenants worse than the sergeants,
> And capt'ns the worst of all.

Taps. This call is the last bugle call of the military day. "Taps" is also traditionally played at military funerals. Originally, the U.S. Army used the French *"L'Extinction des feux"* ("Lights Out") to end the day. The music for "Taps" was written by BG Daniel Butterfield in July 1862 at Harrison's Landing, Virginia, when he was a member of the Army of the Potomac during the Peninsular campaign of the Civil War.

In 1932, the French adopted "Taps" for use in their own army.

Both the *American Heritage Dictionary of the English Language* and *Webster's New World Dictionary of the American Language* suggest the term comes from the "tap" of the drum, which was once used to signal "Tattoo."

Following are three versions of the words sometimes sung to accompany the music of this call:

I	II	III
Fades the light,	When your last	Day is done
And afar	Day is past,	Gone the sun
Goeth day,	From afar	From the lake
Cometh night;	Some bright star	From the hills
And a star	O'er your grave	From the sky;
Leadeth all,	Watch will keep	All is well
Speedeth all	While you sleep	Safely rest;
To their rest.	With the brave.	God is nigh.

Tattoo. This call is usually played at or very near 2100 hours, and it signifies that lights should be off within 15 minutes. It is the longest bugle call in the U.S. Army— 28 bars. The first 8 bars are from the French *"L'Extinction des feux"* and the following 20 bars are a British Army infantry tattoo.

Originally, this word appeared in English as *tap toe* or *tap-too*. The *Oxford English Dictionary*'s earliest source is from 1644 and reads: "If anyone shall bee found tiplinge or drinkinge . . . after . . . the Tap-too beates, hee shall pay 2s 6d." The commonly accepted origin of the military version is from the practice in 17th-century armies of provost marshals' visiting the civilian inns and taverns at night, informing the proprietors when it was time for the troops to return to garrison. Eventually, that custom gave way to a party of drummers parading around a garrison at the same time each night, beating a signal to inform soldiers it was time for them to return to quarters. The first beat of the drum as the musicians fell in was known as "first post," the final beat as "last post." "Last post" is sometimes used today as another name for a military obituary.

To the Color. This call is the bugle call played immediately after Retreat. The first note of "To the Color" signals that the flag is to be lowered. While this call is being sounded, military personnel in uniform give the appropriate salute. On many posts, the interval between the end of Retreat and the beginning of "To the Color" is used to fire a salute cannon. This call was adopted by the U.S. Army in 1835, replacing the cavalry "To the Standard."

CASUALTY ASSISTANCE AND HONORING THE DEAD
Chances are that at some point in your military career you will be detailed to act as a casualty notifier, Survivor Assistance Officer (SAO), or body escort. You will find the experience one of the most difficult and trying duties you will ever face. If you perform these duties well, you will receive a deep sense of personal satisfaction from knowing you have helped someone in distress.

Notification of Next of Kin
As a casualty notifier, you represent the Secretary of the Army. You are expected to be courteous, helpful, and sympathetic. Your presence should soften the blow, if possible, and show the Army's concern.

Department of the Army policy is to make personal notification of the next of kin of all deceased and missing soldiers. The deceased soldier's desires for notification of next of kin listed on DD Form 93 (*Record of Emergency Data*) will be followed.

Paragraph 5-4, AR 600-8-1, prescribes that enlisted personnel in the senior grades may be used as notifiers providing an officer is not available and the grade of the enlisted person used is equal to or higher than that of the deceased.

If the person to be notified is not fluent in English, a qualified interpreter should accompany you. The linguist should interpret only what is spoken between you and the next of kin. Contact your installation personnel officer in cases that require a linguist.

Be prepared for an adverse reaction on the part of the person being notified. If you know beforehand that the next of kin has a medical problem, consult the family doctor. If one cannot be identified, consult any physician in the area where notification is to be made. If you feel it is best, get the doctor to go with you when you make notification. Army Medical Corps doctors cannot accompany you on these calls, although they may be consulted if they have been treating the person being notified.

Just in case, be sure to have with you the telephone numbers for a local hospital, ambulance service, and fire department rescue squad.

If the person being notified does suffer medically as a result of the news, you must keep your casualty commander notified. Additionally, all personal notifications must be confirmed promptly by commercial telegram. These details are set forth in Department of the Army Pamphlet 608-33, *Casualty Assistance Handbook*.

Be careful to observe the following basic guidelines:

- Present the best possible military appearance.
- Make your visit promptly after receiving casualty information, but only during the hours from 0600 to 2200, unless otherwise directed.
- Be natural in speech, manner, and method of delivery. What you say is of the utmost importance.
- If the next of kin is alone at the time of your visit, offer to call someone or ask a neighbor to step in.
- You may inform the next of kin that survivor's assistance will be rendered, but do not specify date or time on which such a visit will be made.
- Advise the next of kin that a confirmation of your visit will be sent by telegram.
- In cases of death, if the remains have been recovered, tell the next of kin that a message on the disposition of the remains will be coming. If the remains have not been recovered, tell the next of kin how memorial services are conducted (see AR 600-8-1).
- If the next of kin are not at home when you visit, make an effort to locate them, using neighbors or local authorities, as necessary. Be most discreet so as not to compromise the purpose of your visit, especially if you deal with friends or neighbors. Should the next of kin be on vacation and too far away for you to carry out your visit, redirect action at once by telephone through the casualty reporting chain of command.
- Once you begin notification action, you must continue to completion.
- You may inform the primary next of kin that personal notification will be made to the secondary next of kin if required. When notifying the secondary kin, you may inform that the primary kin have already been notified.
- Inform the next of kin that a letter from the soldier's commander will give more complete details (see Chapter 6, AR 600-8-1).

Be careful to observe the following prohibitions:

- DO NOT notify by telephone.
- DO NOT call for an appointment before making the visit.
- DO NOT hold notes or a prepared speech in your hand when approaching the residence of the next of kin.
- DO NOT disclose the purpose of your visit or the contents of your message except to the next of kin.
- DO NOT leave word with neighbors or others to have the next of kin contact you, should you find them away from home.
- DO NOT speak hurriedly.
- DO NOT pass on any gory or embarrassing details.
- DO NOT use military jargon when speaking with the next of kin.
- DO NOT touch the next of kin unless there is extreme shock or fainting.
- DO NOT discuss entitlements. Advise that the SAO will be in touch.

- DO NOT discuss disposition of remains or personal effects.
- DO NOT inform the secondary kin that they will receive an SAO visit.
- DO NOT commit either your organization or the Department of the Army to carrying out any action or obtaining any information by a given time.
- DO NOT, under ANY circumstances, "fortify" yourself with alcohol or any other substance before making the visit.

Survivor Assistance

As a survivor assistance officer, you are charged by the Secretary of the Army to render assistance necessary to settle the personal affairs of a deceased soldier. Keep the thoughts and feelings of the next of kin uppermost in your mind at all times. Above all, be *prepared*. Nothing can reflect more adversely upon you than to demonstrate ignorance or indecision when dealing with the next of kin. Should you be asked questions for which you do not know the answers, remain cool and assure the next of kin that you will get the answers. A thorough study of the references given to you by your local casualty office should ensure that you are not caught unprepared for any contingency.

Your point of contact as an SAO is the local casualty section. You may receive assistance from the staff judge advocate, surgeon, provost marshal, public affairs officer, and finance, housing, and transportation officers. You are expected to make contacts with these officers, as required, without referral by the casualty section.

The Casualty Branch of your local Adjutant General Office should furnish you a complete packet relating to your duties as notifier/SAO at the time you receive a case for action. This packet should contain details pertaining to the services available to you locally to assist you in the completion of your duties. The details should include a telephone directory of services available to you locally as well as most of the information sources listed below.

Reference Materials for SAO
DOD Military Pay and Allowances Entitlements Manual.
AR 37-104-3, *Military Pay and Allowances Procedures: Joint Uniform Military Pay System (JUMPS—Army).*
AR 40-121, *Uniformed Services Health Care Benefits Program.*
AR 600-8-1, *Army Casualty and Memorial Affairs and Line of Duty Investigations.*
AR 600-25, *Salutes, Honors, and Visits of Courtesy.*
AR 608-2, *Servicemen's Group Life Insurance (SGLI); Veterans Group Life Insurance (VGLI).*
AR 608-50, *Legal Assistance.*
AR 640-3, *Personnel Records and Identification of Individuals, Identification Cards, Tags, and Badges.*
AR 672-5-1, *Military Awards.*
DA Pam 55-2, *Personal Property Shipping Information; It's Your Move.*

Body Escort Detail

Body escort detail is an extremely important duty. Soldiers selected to act as escort represent the Army and the United States. The escort's mission is to see that the remains of the deceased reach the final destination chosen by the next of kin and that they are treated with honor, respect, and dignity during transport.

Maintaining a correct state of personal appearance is of primary importance. The uniform for this duty is the Army green uniform. Neatness and cleanliness of your person are a part of the respect shown for the dead.

You will receive a package containing papers necessary to your assignment, including VA Form 40-1330 (*Application for Headstone or Marker*) and DD Form 1375 (*Request for Payment of Funeral and/or Interment Expenses*). You will also receive a Statement of Condition of Remains (a locally reproduced form) and the deceased's death certificate, which you should give to the funeral director when you arrive at your destination.

You are responsible for the remains from the time you sign for them to the time you obtain a receipt for them from the funeral director at your destination. The statement of the condition of the remains serves as your receipt.

When remains are to be transported in a casket, they may be sent by air or by rail, although the latter is used less often than air transportation. But regardless of how the remains are being shipped, you should be at the terminal well before the time of departure. Determine at that time where you should go to make sure that the casket has arrived. Examine the casket and check the label at the head of the casket that shows the deceased's name and social security number. Sign your name on the label to show that you have checked it. Be sure that no cargo is placed on the casket.

When the casket is placed in the cargo compartment of the airplane, it is moved in a feet-first position. On the aircraft, the body should be placed in a head-first position, with the head toward the nose of the aircraft. The airplane employees should be reminded of this. In a railcar, the remains are placed feet-first.

Salute the casket while it is being loaded on the carrier.

When traveling by airplane, tell the flight attendant that you are escorting a deceased person and wish to be the first to leave after landing. When the casket is being moved, you should accompany it to ensure proper handling and to make sure that the remains do not become separated from you.

If any emergency or unavoidable delay occurs, notify the receiving funeral home by telephone. Also call the mortuary officer at the shipping installation. You may call this officer collect. Be sure to include the new arrival time and flight number of the airplane.

When you reach your destination, go immediately to watch the casket being unloaded. As soon as the remains arrive in the terminal, drape the flag over the casket with the blue-starred field above the left shoulder of the deceased. The remainder of the flag should be draped evenly over the casket. Secure the flag on the shipping case with the elastic flag band. If the casket was shipped by rail, remove the baggage tag and turn it in at the baggage room.

The funeral director will meet you at the terminal. The remains will be loaded into a hearse for transfer to the funeral home. The casket should be moved feet-first. *Salute the remains before the door of the hearse is closed.*

Cremated remains are shipped in an urn placed inside a shipping box that you hand-carry and keep in your possession at all times. You will also carry along the flag, folded and in a plastic case; you do not place or drape the flag on the shipping box.

When you arrive at your destination, remove the urn from the shipping box. During the interment service, the flag may be taken out of its case, folded to resemble a cocked hat, and placed in front of the urn. At the end of the service, it is put back into its case and presented to the next of kin.

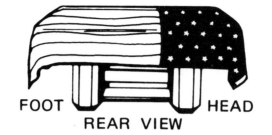

FOOT   HEAD

REAR VIEW

CENTER THE FLAG ON THE CASKET SO THAT THE BLUE FIELD IS AT THE HEAD AND OVER THE LEFT SHOULDER OF THE DECEASED.

HEAD   FOOT

CLOSED CASKET OR SHIPPING CASE.

When escorting cremated remains, you will obtain from the funeral director a receipt for the remains instead of a statement on the condition of the remains.

In all other aspects, the details of escort duty for cremated remains are the same as for escorting a body in a casket.

Ordinarily, the family of the deceased will not be present at the terminal when you arrive, and your first contact with them will not occur until you have reached the funeral home. But should they be present at the terminal, be sure to introduce yourself to them at that time. Should there be an SAO present, be sure to make yourself known. He or she may be of great help to you if you should need assistance.

You should accompany the funeral director in the hearse. Use this opportunity to find out all you can about the next of kin and the other relatives of the deceased whom you will meet at the funeral home. Try to find out their attitude and any other facts that will help to make your assignment easier.

When you arrive at the funeral home, salute the casket as it is being unloaded.

Once at the funeral home, you and the funeral director will fold the flag that has been draped over the casket. The funeral director will inspect the casket to see that it has not been damaged during shipment. If the remains are to be viewed, he also opens the casket for inspection. You are responsible for inspecting the uniform and decorations of the deceased. If the casket is to be closed, arrange the flag as you did at the terminal. If it is to be half or fully open, use the methods shown in the accompanying illustration.

When you and the funeral director have completed these steps, he will prepare the statement of the condition of the remains and sign it. You are responsible for returning the statement to the supervisor of mortuary operations at the installation that prepared the remains. You will also give the funeral director the certificate of death, which will have been included in your packet.

If there is an SAO present, he or she will handle all matters pertaining to insurance, back pay, casualty information, awards, military funeral arrangements, and such. If an SAO is not present, offer the family your assistance and sympathy, but remain quiet, tactful, and dignified. Offer to remain for the funeral services. If the family wants you to stay, you are required to do so.

If burial is to be made in a private cemetery, show the family VA Form 40-1330 and DD Form 1375. If the remains are consigned to a funeral director before interment in a government or national cemetery, show the family DD Form 1375. Explain to the next of kin that the forms should be filled in as soon as possible and mailed to the military activity listed on the form.

When you have completed your assignment, you are to return to your duty station. After your return, you are required to submit a short report in letter form concerning your escort duty. Be sure to include any problems you encountered during your escort duty and how they were resolved.

9

Evaluation and Management Systems

NCO EVALUATION REPORTING SYSTEM

Since January 1988, the Army has used an annual evaluation report that emphasizes Army values, NCO responsibilities, and counseling duties. The report focuses on the NCO's skills; Army-required attributes; and current and potential performance. This two-form system is used to evaluate all NCOs. DA Form 2166-7, *NCO Evaluation Report*, is used to evaluate personnel in the ranks of sergeant through command sergeant major. DA Form 2166-71, *NCO Counseling Checklist/Record*, is used in conjunction with face-to-face counseling for all NCOs. AR 623-205, *NCOER System*, provides detailed information. The system is aimed at strengthening the ability of the NCO corps to meet professional challenges. It enables the best NCOs to serve in positions of increasing responsibilities because it provides boards and other EPMS decision-making agencies with more accurate information.

Performance Counseling/Checklist

Performance counseling informs soldiers face to face about their jobs and expected performance standards. It also provides performance feedback. The goal of this part of the system is to help NCOs to be successful and to meet applicable standards. Although past performance must be acknowledged, the best counseling looks ahead to the future and what can be improved.

Counseling at the end of a rating period is ineffective because no time remains to improve performance; therefore, under this system, counseling takes place within 30 days of each rating period and at least quarterly thereafter. The first session tells the rated NCO what is expected, and the quarterly sessions (for active-duty NCOs) tell what he or she has done well and what could be done better. After initial counseling, ARNG and USAR soldiers are counseled semiannually.

The NCO Counseling Checklist/Record is designed to be used with the NCOER as the only counseling support document. It includes the information needed to assist you in preparing and conducting a counseling session. It also provides a section to record counseling results. After a counseling session, the rater maintains the checklist until the next session or the end of the rating period. The counseling form includes reference material related to counseling, Army values, and NCO responsibilities. Read it before counseling anyone.

NCO COUNSELING CHECKLIST/RECORD

For use of this form, see AR 623-205; the proponent agency MILPERCEN

NAME OF RATED NCO	RANK	DUTY POSITION	UNIT

PURPOSE: The primary purpose of counseling is to improve performance and to professionally develop the rated NCO. The best counseling is always looking forward. It does not dwell on the past and on what was done, rather on the future and what can be done better. Counseling at the end of the rating period is too late since there is no time to improve before evaluation.

RULES:
1. Face-to-face performance counseling is mandatory for all Noncommissioned Officers.
2. This form is for use along with a working copy of the NCO-ER for conducting NCO performance counseling and recording counseling content and dates. Its use is mandatory for counseling all NCOs, CPL thru SFC/PSG, and is optional for counseling other senior NCOs.
3. Active Component. Initial counseling must be conducted within the first 30 days of each rating period, and at least quarterly thereafter. Reserve Components. (ARNG, USAR). Counseling must be conducted at least semiannually. There is no mandatory counseling at the end of the rating period.

CHECKLIST – FIRST COUNSELING SESSION AT THE BEGINNING OF THE RATING PERIOD

PREPARATION
1. Schedule counseling session, notify rated NCO.
2. Get copy of last duty description used for rated NCO's duty position, a blank copy of the NCO-ER, and the names of the new rating chain.
3. Update duty description (see page 2).
4. Fill out rating chain and duty description on working copy of NCO-ER. Parts II and III.
5. Read each of the values/responsibilities in Part IV of NCO-ER and the expanded definitions and examples on page 3 and 4 of this form.
6. Think how each value and responsibility in Part IV of NCO-ER applies to the rated NCO and his/her duty position.
Note: Leadership and training may be more difficult to apply than the other values/responsibilities when the rated NCO has no subordinates. Leadership is simply influencing others in the accomplishment of the mission and that can include peers and superiors. It also can be applied directly to additional duties and other areas of Army community life. Individual training is the responsibility of all NCOs whether or not there are subordinates. Every NCO knows something that can be taught to others and should be involved in some way in a training program.
7. Decide what you consider necessary for success (a meets standards rating) for each value/responsibility. Use the examples listed on pages 3 and 4 of this form as a guide in developing your own standards for success. Some may apply exactly, but you may have to change them or develop new ones that apply to your situation. Be specific so the rated NCO will know what is expected.
8. Make notes in blank spaces in Part IV of NCO-ER to help when counseling.
9. Review counseling tips in FM 22-101.

COUNSELING
1. Make sure rated NCO knows rating chain.
2. Show rated NCO the draft duty description on your working copy of the NCO-ER. Explain all parts. If rated NCO performed in position before, ask for any ideas to make duty description better.
3. Discuss the meaning of each value/responsibility in Part IV of NCO-ER. Use the trigger words on the NCO-ER, and the expanded definitions on pages 3 and 4 of this form to help.
4. Explain how each value/responsibility applies to the specific duty position by showing or telling your standards for success (a meets standards rating). Use examples on pages 3 and 4 of this form as a start point. Be specific so the rated NCO really knows what's expected.
5. When possible, give specific examples of excellence that could apply. This gives the rated NCO something special to strive for, Remember that only a few achieve real excellence and that real excellence always includes specific results and often includes accomplishments of subordinates.
6. Give rated NCO opportunity to ask questions and make suggestions.

AFTER COUNSELING
1. Record rated NCO's name and counseling date on this form.
2. Write key points made in counseling session on this form.
3. Show key points to rated NCO and get his initials.
4. Save NCO-ER with this checklist for next counseling session.

CHECKLIST – LATER COUNSELING SESSIONS DURING THE RATING PERIOD

PREPARATION
1. Schedule counseling session, notify rated NCO, and tell him/her to come prepared to discuss what has been accomplished in each value/responsibility area.
2. Look at working copy of NCO-ER you used during last counseling session.
3. Read and update duty description. Especially note the area of special emphasis; the priorities may have changed.
4. Read again, each of the values/responsibilities in Part IV of NCO-ER and the expanded definitions and examples on pages 3 and 4 of this form; then think again, about your standards for success.
5. Look over the notes you wrote down on page 2 of this form about the last counseling session.

6. Think about what the rated NCO has done so far during this rating period (specifically, observed action, demonstrated behavior, and results).
7. For each value/responsibility area, answer three questions: First, what has happened in response to any discussion you had during the last counseling session? Second, what has been done well?; and Third, what could be done better?
8. Make notes in blank spaces in Part IV of NCO-ER to help focus when counseling. (Use new NCO-ER if old one is full from last counseling session).
9. Review counseling tips in FM 22-101.

DA FORM 2166-7-1, AUG 87

COUNSELING

1. Go over each part of the duty description with rated NCO. Discuss any changes, especially to the area of special emphasis.

2. Tell rated NCO how he/she is doing. Use your success standards as a guide for the discussion (the examples on pages 3 and 4 may help). First, for each value/responsibility, talk about what has happened in response to any discussion you had during the last counseling session (remember, observed action, demonstrated behavior and results). Second, talk about what was done well. Third, talk about how to do better. The goal is to get all NCOs to be successful and meet standards.

3. When possible, give examples of excellence that could apply. This gives the rated NCO something to strive for, REMEMBER, EXCELLENCE IS SPECIAL, ONLY A FEW ACHIEVE IT! Excellence includes results and often involves subordinates.

4. Ask rated NCO for ideas, examples and opinions on what has been done so far and what can be done better. (This step can be done first or last).

AFTER COUNSELING

1. Record counseling date on this form.

2. Write key points made in counseling session on this form.

3. Show key points to rated NCO and get his initials.

4. Save NCO-ER with this checklist for next counseling session. (Notes should make record NCO-ER preparation easy at end of rating period).

COUNSELING RECORD

DATE OF COUNSELING	RATED NCO's INITIALS	KEY POINTS MADE
INITIAL		
LATER		
LATER		
LATER		

DUTY DESCRIPTION (PART III of NCO-ER)

The duty description is essential to performance counseling and evaluation. It is used during the first counseling session to tell rated NCO what the duties are and what needs to be emphasized. It may change somewhat during the rating period. It is used at the end of the rating period to record what was important about the duties.

The five elements of the duty description:

1 & 2. Principal Duty Title and Duty MOS Code. Enter principal duty title and DMOS that most accurately reflects actual duties performed.

3. Daily Duties and Scope. This portion should address the most important routine duties and responsibilities. Ideally, this should include number of people supervised, equipment, facilities, and dollars involved and any other routine duties and responsibilities critical to mission accomplishment.

4. Area of Special Emphasis. This portion is most likely to change somewhat during the rating period. For the first counseling session, it includes those items that require top priority effort at least for the first part of the upcoming rating period. At the end of the rating period, it should include the most important items that applied at any time during the rating period (examples are preparation for REFORGER deployment, combined arms drills training for FTX, preparation for NTC rotation, revision of battalion maintenance SOP, training for tank table qualification, ITEP and company AMTP readiness, related tasks cross-training, reserve components annual training support (AT) and SIDPERS acceptance rate).

5. Appointed Duties. This portion should include those duties that are appointed and are not normally associated with the duty description.

DA FORM 2166-7-1, AUG 87   2

NCO Counseling Checklist/Record (continued).

VALUES/NCO RESPONSIBILITIES (PART IV of NCO-ER)

VALUES: Values are what soldiers, as a profession, judge to be right. They are the moral, ethical, and professional attributes of character. They are the heart and soul of a great Army. Part IVa of the NCO-ER includes some of the most important values. These are: Putting the welfare of the nation, the assigned mission and teamwork before individual interests; Exhibiting absolute honesty and courage to stand up for what is right; Developing a sense of obligation and support between those who are led, those who lead, and those who serve alongside; Maintaining high standards of personal conduct on and off duty; And finally, demonstrating obedience, total adherence to the spirit and letter of a lawful order, discipline, and ability to overcome fear despite difficulty or danger.

Examples of standards for "YES" ratings:

- Put the Army, the mission and subordinates first before own personal interest.

- Meet challenges without compromising integrity.

- Personal conduct, both on and off duty, reflects favorably on NCO corps.

- Obey lawful orders and do what is right without orders.

- Choose the hard right over the easy wrong.

- Exhibit pride in unit, be a team player.

- Demonstrate respect for all soldiers regardless of race, creed, color, sex, or national origin.

COMPETENCE: The knowledge, skills and abilities necessary to be expert in the current duty assignment and to perform adequately in other assignments within the MOS when required. Competence is both technical and tactical and includes reading, writing, speaking and basic mathematics. It also includes sound judgment, ability to weigh alternatives, form objective opinions and make good decisions. Closely allied with competence is the constant desire to be better, to listen and learn more and to do each task completely to the best of one's ability. Learn, grow, set standards, and achieve them, create and innovate, take prudent risks, never settle for less than best. Committed to excellence.

Examples of standards for "Success/Meets Standards" rating:

- Master the knowledge, skills and abilities required for performance in your duty position.
- Meet PMOS SQT standards for your grade.
- Accomplish completely and promptly those tasks assigned or required by duty position.
- Constantly seek ways to learn, grow and improve.

Examples of "Excellence":

- Picked as SSG to be a platoon sergeant over twelve other SSGs.
- Maintained SIDPERS rating of 98% for six months.
- Scored 94% on last SQT.
- Selected best truck master in annual battalion competition.
- Designated Installation Drill Sergeant of Quarter.
- Exceeded recruiting objectives two consecutive quarters.
- Awarded Expert Infantryman Badge (EIB).

PHYSICAL FITNESS AND MILITARY BEARING: Physical fitness is the physical and mental ability to accomplish the mission – combat readiness. Total fitness includes weight control, diet and nutrition, smoking cessation, control of substance abuse, stress management, and physical training. It covers strength, endurance, stamina, flexibility, speed, agility, coordination and balance. NCOs are responsible for their own physical fitness and that of their subordinates. Military Bearing consists of posture, dress, overall appearance, and manner of physical movement. Bearing also includes an outward display of inner-feelings, fears, and overall confidence and enthusiasm. An inherent NCO responsibility is concern with the military bearing of the individual soldier, to include on-the-spot corrections.

Examples of standards for "Success/Meets Standards" rating:

- Maintain weight within Army limits for age and sex.
- Obtain passing score in APFT and participate in a regular exercise program.
- Maintain personal appearance and exhibit enthusiasm to the point of setting an example for junior enlisted soldiers.
- Monitor and encourage improvement in the physical and military bearing of subordinates.

Examples of "Excellence":

- Received Physical Fitness Badge for 292 score on APFT.
- Selected soldier of the month/quarter/year.
- Three of the last four soldiers of the month were from his/her platoon.
- As Master Fitness Trainer, established battalion physical fitness program.
- His entire squad was commended for scoring above 270 on APFT.

DA FORM 2166-7-1, AUG 87

NCO Counseling Checklist/Record (continued).

LEADERSHIP: Influencing others to accomplish the mission. It consists of applying leadership attributes (Beliefs, Values, Ethics, Character, Knowledge, and Skills). It includes setting tough, but achievable standards and demanding that they be met; Caring deeply and sincerely for subordinates and their families and welcoming the opportunity to serve them; Conducting counseling; Setting the example by word and act/deed; Can be summarized by BE (Committed to the professional Army ethic and professional traits); KNOW (The factors of leadership, yourself, human nature, your job, and your unit); DO (Provide direction, implement, and motivate). Instill the spirit to achieve and win: Inspire and develop excellence. A soldier cared for today, leads tomorrow.

Examples of standards for "Success/Meets Standards" rating:

- Motivate subordinates to perform to the best of their ability as individuals and together as a disciplined cohesive team to accomplish the mission.
- Demonstrate that you care deeply and sincerely for soldiers and welcome the opportunity to serve them.
- Instill the spirit to achieve and win; Inspire and develop excellence through counseling.
- Set the example: BE, KNOW, DO.

Examples of "Excellence":

- Motivated entire squad to qualify expert with M-16.
- Won last three platoon quad inspections.
- Selected for membership in Sergeant Morales Club.
- Inspired mechanics to maintain operational readiness rating of 95% for two consecutive quarters.
- Led his squad through map orienteering course to win the battalion competition.
- Counseled two marginal soldiers ultimately selected for promotion.

TRAINING: Preparing individuals, units and combined arms teams for duty performance; The teaching of skills and knowledge. NCOs contribute to team training, are often responsible for unit training (Squads, Crews, Sections), but individual training is the most important, exclusive responsibility of the NCO Corps. Quality training bonds units: Leads directly to good discipline; Concentrates on wartime missions; Is tough and demanding without being reckless; Is performance oriented; Sticks to Army doctrine to standardize what is taught to fight, survive, and win, as small units when AirLand battle actions dictate. "Good training means learning from mistakes and allowing plenty of room for professional growth. Sharing knowledge and experience is the greatest legacy one can leave subordinates."

Examples of standards for "Success/Meets Standards" rating:

- Make sure soldiers-
  a. Can do identified common tasks.
  b. Are prepared for SQT and Commander's Evaluation.
  c. Develop and practice skills for duty position.
  d. Train as a squad/crew/section.
- Identify and recommend subordinates for professional development courses.
- Participate in unit training program.
- Share knowledge and experience with subordinates.

Examples of "Excellence":

- Taught five common tasks resulting in 100% GO on Annual CTT for all soldiers in directorate.
- Trained best howitzer section of the year in battalion.
- Coached subordinates to win consecutive soldier of month competitions.
- Established company Expert Field Medical Badge program resulting in 85% of all eligible soldiers receiving EFMB.
- Distinguished 1 tank and qualified 3 tanks in platoon on first run of tank table VIII.
- Trained platoon to fire honor battery during annual service practice.

RESPONSIBILITY AND ACCOUNTABILITY: The proper care, maintenance, use, handling, and conservation of personnel, equipment, supplies, property, and funds. Maintenance of weapons, vehicles, equipment, conservation of supplies, and funds is a special NCO responsibility because of its links to the success of all missions, especially those on the battlefield. It includes inspecting soldier's equipment often, using manual or checklist; Holding soldiers responsible for repairs and losses; Learning how to use and maintain all the equipment soldiers use; Being among the first to operate new equipment; Keeping up-to-date component lists; Setting aside time for inventories; and Knowing the readiness status of weapons, vehicles, and other equipment. It includes knowing where each soldier is during duty hours; Why he is going on sick call, where he lives, and his family situation; It involves reducing accidental manpower and monetary losses by providing a safe and healthful environment; It includes creating a climate which encourages young soldiers to learn and grow, and, to report serious problems without fear of repercussions. Also, NCOs must accept responsibility for their own actions and for those of their subordinates.

Examples of standards for "Success/Meets Standards" rating:

- Make sure your weapons, equipment, and vehicles are serviceable, maintained and ready for accomplishing the mission.
- Stop waste of supplies and limited funds.
- Be aware of those things that impact on soldier readiness e.g., family affairs, SQT, CTT, PQR, special duty, medical conditions, etc.
- Be responsible for your actions and those of your subordinates.

Examples of "Excellence":

- His emphasis on safety resulted in four tractor trailer drivers logging 10,000 miles accident free.
- Received commendation from CG for organizing post special olympics program.
- Won the installation award for Quarters of the Month.
- His constant instruction on maintenance resulted in six of eight mechanics earning master mechanic badges.
- Commended for no APCs on deadline report for six months.
- His learn and grow climate resulted in best platoon ARTEP results in the battalion.

NCO Counseling Checklist/Record (continued).

Types of NCOERs
Only the following reports, authorized by AR 623-205, are submitted.

Annual Reports. Annual reports are submitted 12 months after the ending month of the last report. If 12 months have elapsed since the ending month of the last report, but the required 3-month minimum rating period or rater qualification criteria have not been met, the annual report period is extended until the minimum requirements are satisfied. Annual reports should not be signed before the first day of the month following the ending month.

Change-of-Rater Reports. Providing minimum rater qualifications are met and *no other reports have been submitted* in the preceding three months, change-of-rater reports are rendered when there has been a normal change of the designated rater, the individual has been on extended TDY, the rater has left the Army, or the rater is relieved or incapacitated. Change-of-rater reports may be signed at any time during the closing or following month of the report.

Complete-the-Record Reports. At the option of the rater, a complete-the-record report may be submitted on a soldier who is to be considered by a DA centralized board for promotion, school, or CSM selection provided the soldier is in the zone of consideration, has been in the current duty assignment under the same rater for at least three months, and has not had a previous report for the current duty assignment.

Relief-for-Cause Reports. Relief-for-cause is the early release of a soldier from a specific duty or assignment, directed by superior authority, and based on a decision that the soldier has failed in his or her duty performance through inefficiency or misconduct. The reasons for relief must be clearly explained by the rating official in his narrative portion of DA Form 2166-7, along with a statement that the soldier concerned has been informed of the reasons for the relief. When the relief is directed by someone not on the designated rating chain, that official describes the reasons for the relief in an enclosure to the report. The minimum rating period for these kinds of reports is normally 30 days, but a general officer in the chain of command (or the general court-martial convening authority) may waive this requirement and authorize the relief report to be written in clear-cut cases of misconduct. Relief-for-cause reports are signed at any time during the closing or following month of the report.

Restrictions
A number of restrictions apply to the type of material that may be included in an efficiency report:
•   The zeal with which a soldier performs duty as a member of a court-martial counsel for an accused, or an Equal Opportunity NCO cannot be referred to in an efficiency report.
•   No reference may be made to unproved derogatory information in a report. This prohibition prevents allegations from being included in reports and excludes information that would be unjustly prejudicial.
•   Although incidents caused by alcohol or drug abuse may be taken into account by rating officials, a soldier's participation in the Alcohol and Drug Abuse Prevention and Central Program (ADAPCP) is not normally mentioned. Although paragraph 2-13, AR 623-205, authorizes raters to mention a soldier's voluntary entry into the ADAPCP and successful rehabilitation "as a factor to the rated soldier's credit," this kind of information should not be included in a report unless previous reports cited problems arising from substance abuse.

NCO EVALUATION REPORT

For use of this form, see AR 623-205; the proponent agency is DCSPER

SEE PRIVACY ACT STATEMENT IN AR 623-205, APPENDIX E.

PART I - ADMINISTRATIVE DATA

a. NAME *(Last, First, Middle Initial)*		b. SSN		c. RANK		d. DATE OF RANK	e. PMOSC

f. UNIT, ORG., STATION, ZIP CODE OR APO, MAJOR COMMAND | g. REASON FOR SUBMISSION

h. PERIOD COVERED			i. RATED MONTHS	j. NON-RATED CODES	k. NO. OF ENCL	l. RATED NCO COPY *(Check one and Date)*		m. PSC Initials	n. CMD CODE	o. PSC CODE
FROM	THRU					1. Given to NCO	Date			
YY	MM	YY MM				2. Forwarded to NCO				

PART II - AUTHENTICATION

a. NAME OF RATER *(Last, First, Middle Initial)*	SSN	SIGNATURE

RANK, PMOSC/BRANCH, ORGANIZATION, DUTY ASSIGNMENT		DATE

b. NAME OF SENIOR RATER *(Last, First, Middle Initial)*	SSN	SIGNATURE

RANK, PMOSC/BRANCH, ORGANIZATION, DUTY ASSIGNMENT		DATE

c. RATED NCO: I understand my signature does not constitute agreement or disagreement with the evaluations of the rater and senior rater. Part I, height/weight and APFT entries are verified. I have seen this report completed through Part V. I am aware of the appeals process (AR 623-205).	SIGNATURE	DATE

d. NAME OF REVIEWER *(Last, First, Middle Initial)*	SSN	SIGNATURE

RANK, PMOSC/BRANCH, ORGANIZATION, DUTY ASSIGNMENT		DATE

e. ☐ CONCUR WITH RATER AND SENIOR RATER EVALUATIONS   ☐ NONCONCUR WITH RATER AND/OR SENIOR RATER EVAL *(See attached comments)*

PART III - DUTY DESCRIPTION (Rater)

a. PRINCIPAL DUTY TITLE	b. DUTY MOSC

c. DAILY DUTIES AND SCOPE *(To include, as appropriate, people, equipment, facilities and dollars)*

d. AREAS OF SPECIAL EMPHASIS

e. APPOINTED DUTIES

f. Counseling dates from checklist/record	INITIAL	LATER	LATER	LATER

PART IV - VALUES/NCO RESPONSIBILITIES (Rater)

a. Complete each question. *(Comments are mandatory for "No" entries; optional for "Yes" entries.)*

			YES	NO
V **A** **L** **U** **E** **S** **PERSONAL** Commitment Competence Candor Courage **ARMY ETHIC** Loyalty Duty Selfless Service Integrity	1. Places dedication and commitment to the goals and missions of the Army and nation above personal welfare.	1		
	2. Is committed to and shows a sense of pride in the unit - works as a member of the team.	2		
	3. Is disciplined and obedient to the spirit and letter of a lawful order.	3		
	4. Is honest and truthful in word and deed.	4		
	5. Maintains high standards of personal conduct on and off duty.	5		
	6. Has the courage of convictions and the ability to overcome fear - stands up for and does, what's right.	6		
	7. Supports EO/EEO	7		
	Bullet comments			

DA FORM 2166-7, SEP 87   REPLACES DA FORM 2166-6, OCT 81, WHICH IS OBSOLETE

RATED NCO'S NAME (Last, First, Middle Initial)	SSN	THRU DATE

PART IV (Rater) · VALUES/NCO RESPONSIBILITIES	Specific Bullet examples of "EXCELLENCE" or "NEEDS IMPROVEMENT" are mandatory. Specific Bullet examples of "SUCCESS" are optional.

b. COMPETENCE

- o Duty proficiency; MOS competency
- o Technical & tactical; knowledge, skills, and abilities
- o Sound judgment
- o Seeking self-improvement; always learning
- o Accomplishing tasks to the fullest capacity; committed to excellence

EXCELLENCE (Exceeds std)	SUCCESS (Meets std)	NEEDS IMPROVEMENT (Some) (Much)
☐	☐	☐ ☐

c. PHYSICAL FITNESS & MILITARY BEARING

APFT ____ HEIGHT/WEIGHT ____

- o Mental and physical toughness
- o Endurance and stamina to go the distance
- o Displaying confidence and enthusiasm; looks like a soldier

EXCELLENCE (Exceeds std)	SUCCESS (Meets std)	NEEDS IMPROVEMENT (Some) (Much)
☐	☐	☐ ☐

d. LEADERSHIP

- o Mission first
- o Genuine concern for soldiers
- o Instilling the spirit to achieve and win
- o Setting the example; Be, Know, Do

EXCELLENCE (Exceeds std)	SUCCESS (Meets std)	NEEDS IMPROVEMENT (Some) (Much)
☐	☐	☐ ☐

e. TRAINING

- o Individual and team
- o Mission focused; performance oriented
- o Teaching soldiers how; common tasks, duty-related skills
- o Sharing knowledge and experience to fight, survive and win

EXCELLENCE (Exceeds std)	SUCCESS (Meets std)	NEEDS IMPROVEMENT (Some) (Much)
☐	☐	☐ ☐

f. RESPONSIBILITY & ACCOUNTABILITY

- o Care and maintenance of equip./facilities
- o Soldier and equipment safety
- o Conservation of supplies and funds
- o Encouraging soldiers to learn and grow
- o Responsible for good, bad, right & wrong

EXCELLENCE (Exceeds std)	SUCCESS (Meets std)	NEEDS IMPROVEMENT (Some) (Much)
☐	☐	☐ ☐

PART V · OVERALL PERFORMANCE AND POTENTIAL

a. RATER. Overall potential for promotion and/ or service in positions of greater responsibility.

AMONG THE BEST	FULLY CAPABLE	MARGINAL
☐	☐	☐

e. SENIOR RATER BULLET COMMENTS

b. RATER. List 3 positions in which the rated NCO could best serve the Army at his/her current or next higher grade.

_____

_____

_____

c. SENIOR RATER. Overall performance

☐☐ ■ ■ ■

1 2 3   4   5

Successful   Fair   Poor

d. SENIOR RATER. Overall potential for promotion and/or service in positions of greater responsibility.

☐☐ ■ ■ ■

1 2 3   4   5

Superior   Fair   Poor

NCO Evaluation Report (continued).

Commander's Inquiry

When a commander learns that a report made by a subordinate or a member of a subordinate command may have been illegal or unjust or may have violated the provisions of AR 623-205, he or she must investigate. The commander may not, however, direct that a report be changed or use command influence to alter an honest evaluation.

When the commander's inquiry finds that an error, a violation of the regulation, or some wrongdoing has occurred, the report is returned to the reviewer along with the investigation results. The commander then recommends to the rating officials that the report be corrected to account for matters revealed in the investigation. This recommendation is done with regard for the restrictions on command authority and influence mentioned above.

When a report has been corrected under the circumstances mentioned above, it is forwarded with no reference to action taken by the commander.

Rater Qualifications and Responsibilities

With few exceptions, the rater must be the first-line supervisor of the rated soldier for a minimum of three months and senior to the rated soldier either by grade or by date of rank. Members of other U.S. military services who meet these qualifications may also be raters.

Commanders may appoint U.S. civilian raters GS-6 and above when a first-line military supervisor is not available and when the civilian supervisor is in the best position to accurately evaluate the soldier's performance. The civilian rater must be officially designated on a published rating scheme established by the local commander. Members of the allied forces are not authorized to be raters.

Raters must counsel the rated soldier and assess his or her performance, using all reasonable means to do so, then prepare a fair, correct report.

Without a doubt, you will find NCOER counseling of good soldiers a pleasant experience. Counseling bad soldiers is a bad experience, yet you must face up to it if you are to be a good leader.

Keep a record of counseling sessions with problem soldiers, making notes of dates and matters discussed. If you have to give such persons bad NCOERs they may react vigorously, so you must have your facts in order. One or two sessions should be sufficient to straighten the problem performer out, but if not, you must be ready to back up your ratings.

Senior Rater Qualifications and Responsibilities

The senior rater must be in the direct line of supervision of the rated soldier for a minimum period of three months and senior to the rater in grade or date of rank.

Members of other U.S. military services who meet these qualifications may be senior raters, and civilians may be appointed as senior raters providing they are the supervisors in the best position to evaluate the soldier's performance and their appointments are published in a rating scheme established by the local commander. Members of allied forces are not authorized to be senior raters. A senior rater is not required when the rater is a general officer or equivalent.

The senior rater must become familiar with the rated soldier's performance and prepare a fair and correct report. Like the rater, the senior rater evaluates the rated NCO, but he or she focuses on potential, oversees the performance evaluations, and serves as a mentor. Since the senior rater's evaluation directly impacts the NCO's performance and professional development, it must reflect the entire rating period and not an isolated incident.

The senior rater must also do the following: prepare a fair and correct report to evaluate the NCO's performance, professionalism, and potential; date and sign part IIb of the NCOER; obtain the rated NCO's signature in part IIc; ensure that bullet comments are fully justified in part IVb–f; and ensure that "Do not meet minimum requirements" is entered in part Ve if the senior rater does not meet the minimum time requirement.

DA Pamphlet 623-205 states, "The better you know the rated NCO, the better you will do your duty as senior rater. Check early to see that the rater is counseling and has a checklist for each rated NCO. This will be a matter of command and inspection interest. When it's time to rate, make sure the rater's bullets follow the rules. Also see that excellence ratings in Part IV are fully justified."

Reviewer Qualifications and Responsibilities

The reviewer must be a commissioned or warrant officer, command sergeant major, or sergeant major in the direct line of supervision and senior in grade or date of rank to both the rater and the senior rater. There is no minimum time period requirement for reviewer qualification.

Commanders may appoint officers of other U.S. military services as reviewers when the grade and line-of-supervision requirements listed above are met and when either the rater or senior rater is a uniformed Army official.

In cases in which both the rater and the senior rater are other than uniformed Army rating officials, and no uniformed Army reviewer is available, the report is reviewed by an officer in the rated soldier's military personnel office.

Commanders may appoint U.S. civilians GS-6 and above or other civilian pay grades when the grade and line-of-supervision requirements are met and either the rater or senior rater is a uniformed Army official.

Members of allied forces are not authorized to be reviewers, and a reviewer is not required when the rater or the senior rater is a general officer or equivalent.

The reviewer ensures that the proper rater and senior rater complete the report, examines the evaluations, and resolves discrepancies and inconsistencies. The reviewer also ensures that the provisions for change-of-rater and relief-for-cause reports are complied with.

The reviewer ensures, too, that required comments have been made to explain low ratings on the NCOER and that allegations of injustice or illegality are resolved or brought to the attention of the commander. The reviewer is responsible for forwarding the report to the military personnel office.

Responsibilities of Commanders

Commanders ensure that official rating schemes are published, by name or duty position, and are posted in the unit so that each soldier knows his or her rater, senior rater, and reviewer.

Commanders are also responsible for ensuring the following:
• Each rating official is fully qualified and knows whom he or she is responsible to rate.
• Reports are prepared by the designated individuals.

- Rating officials give timely counseling.
- Each rated soldier is provided a copy of his or her completed evaluation report.
- Soldiers receive assistance in preparing and submitting appeals.
- Reports are prepared properly and submitted in time to reach the U.S. Army Enlisted Records and Evaluation Center (EREC) not later than 60 days after the ending month of the report.

Responsibilities of the Military Personnel Office

The Military Personnel Office (MILPO) initiates the report and forwards it to the rated soldier's commander for proper control. Returned reports are reviewed at the MILPO for completeness and administrative accuracy. The MILPO makes copies of the report and forwards one to the rated soldier and one to the EREC, and assists soldiers who appeal.

Appeals

The NCOER appeals system exists to ensure fairness, protect Army interests, and prevent unjustified attacks on the integrity or judgment of rating officials.

The burden of proof rests with the soldier making an appeal. Once NCOERs are filed in the soldier's official military personnel file (OMPF), they are presumed to be administratively correct, to have been prepared by the proper officials, and to represent the considered opinions and impartial judgments of rating officials.

The allegation of error or injustice does not constitute proof. Clear and convincing evidence must be submitted to cause alteration, replacement, or withdrawal of a report in the OMPF. The decision to appeal should not be made lightly. Frequently, sound evidence may be difficult to obtain, and in most cases, the appellant may be unable to analyze his or her own case objectively.

Normally, appeals are originated by the rated soldier, but in cases in which an appeal is originated by someone other than the rated soldier, it is not processed unless the rated soldier has been notified in person or in writing (by certified mail) and given the opportunity to submit statements pertaining to the case. Rating officials who claim "second thoughts" about ratings previously made have no grounds for submitting an appeal on behalf of the rated soldier.

Appeals alleging bias, prejudice, unjust ratings, or any matter other than administrative error will be adjudicated by the Army Enlisted Special Review Board. The board's determination is final.

To be considered, appeals must be received at EREC within five years of the date of the rated soldier's authentication or the MILPO's certification, if the soldier refused to sign the report. Appeals that do not meet this time restriction may be submitted to the Army Board for Correction of Military Records, in accordance with AR 15-185. Once the decision has been made to appeal an evaluation report, the following steps should be taken:

- Start by reading chapter 4, AR 623-205, "Appeals."
- Write down clearly and specifically what will be appealed and why it should be.
- Identify what evidence should be obtained to substantiate the appeal.
- Determine what evidence can be obtained.
- Obtain the evidence. If statements from persons are necessary, make sure they clearly identify their roles at the time of the contested report and ensure that the statements make specific, not general, comments. Seek statements from senior per-

sonnel who have specific knowledge of the facts; avoid statements from subordinates or persons whose knowledge of the facts may be limited. Obtain sworn statements, if possible.

- Documentary evidence, if not original, should be in certified true copies.
- Prepare the appeal in military letter format.

THE QUALITATIVE MANAGEMENT PROGRAM

In the fall of 1993, in an ALARACT (All Army Activities) message, senior Army personnel officials expressed their need to dispel myths circulating in the ranks about the Qualitative Management Program (QMP). The QMP was established in 1971, with the intended purpose of barring nonproductive NCOs from further service in the Army. The program's objectives have not changed. NCOs who cannot or will not meet minimum standards of service, or who exhibit moral or ethical misconduct, or who have not demonstrated the potential for continued service, are legitimate targets of the QMP. That is it. Officials screening NCO records at QMP boards do not engage in "witch hunts" to meet Army force reduction goals.

Board members are told that the program is *qualitative*, not *quantitative*. No minimum quotas or select goals are pre-established. QMP is not a force reduction tool, nor should it be used as such.

From 1988 to 1993, less than 2.5 percent of the NCO corps was identified for selection under the QMP, despite an accelerated need to reduce the size of the Army during that period. This statistic has remained relatively consistent. Board recommendations have also been consistent, reflecting chain of command recommendations in 95 percent of the cases.

QMP boards look at the whole record of a soldier being considered for elimination from the ranks. They are therefore able to spot downward or cyclical performance trends based on a greater period of time and more information than is available to NCOER raters and senior raters in the field.

The QMP is based on the premise that reenlistment is a privilege for those whose performance, conduct, attitude, and potential for advancement meet Army standards. The QMP also accomplishes the following:

- Improves the quality of the career enlisted force.
- Selectively retains the best qualified soldiers.
- Denies reenlistments to nonprogressive and nonproductive soldiers.
- Encourages soldiers to maintain their eligibility for further service.

The program is an effective way to rid the NCO corps of soldiers who do not measure up to Army standards. It is applied equally to all personnel, especially in the screening subprogram, which is conducted periodically for all sergeants through command sergeants major. The only soldiers who have anything to fear from the QMP are the poor performers.

Qualitative Retention Subprogram

The Qualitative Retention Subprogram consists of the use of reenlistment ineligibility points for each grade. Based on years of service, the reenlistment ineligibility point is the *maximum number of years of active federal service authorized for a soldier in a specific grade*.

Rank	Total Active Service
SPC, CPL	8 years
SGT	13 years
SGT (P)	15 years
SSG	20 years
SSG (P)	20 years
SFC	20 years
SFC (P)	24 years
1SG, MSG	24 years
CSM, SGM	30 years

Specialists, corporals, and sergeants who are on a local order of merit promotion list will be considered for reenlistment under the criteria of the rank to which they will be promoted. Staff sergeants, sergeants first class, and first and master sergeants selected for promotion by Headquarters, Department of the Army, may voluntarily continue on active duty if they are not beyond the reenlistment ineligibility point for the grade to which they will be promoted. Those who are beyond the point for the grade to which they will be promoted will not be considered for extension.

NCOs who are in DA-announced primary zones of consideration for promotion and who have reached or are beyond the reenlistment point may be voluntarily extended beyond their expiration term of service. Those with more than 20 years' service who have not received a waiver to reenlist and who were not selected will be retired by the third month after the promotion list is published.

Soldiers who apply for retirement before the announced zone of consideration will not be considered for promotion.

Extensions apply only to soldiers affected by the qualitative retention. They do not apply to those who have a DA bar to reenlistment imposed by qualitative screening.

Qualitative Screening Subprogram

The screening subprogram applies to enlisted members who are sergeants or above. It does not apply to members who have completed 28 years of active federal service or to command sergeants major, regardless of time in service. Selection for elimination under this program results in a DA-imposed bar to reenlistment.

Records are screened as follows:

For sergeant major	By DA Command Sergeants Major Selection Board
For staff sergeant, sergeant first class, master sergeant, first sergeant	HQDA promotion selection boards
For sergeant	Local selection boards

The appropriate DA selection boards review the performance portion of the OMPF maintained at EREC. From the OMPF, the board evaluates past performance and estimates potential to determine whether continued service is warranted.

Bars to reenlistment for those identified by the selection boards and approved by the Deputy Chief of Staff for Personnel (DCSPER) are imposed as directed by Commanding General, Total Army Personnel Command (TAPC).

Soldiers selected for a bar are informed by letter. Copies of documents in the individual's OMPF that contributed to the board's decision are attached as an enclosure to the letter. These documents are privileged information and must be treated with the utmost discretion.

Letters are forwarded through the chain of command to the individual's commander (lieutenant colonel and above). *They are not delivered to soldiers who have retirement applications approved or pending.*

The individual's commander (lieutenant colonel and above) may, within seven days after receipt of the notification letter, request withdrawal of the bar if it was improperly imposed or based on material error in the soldier's OMPF when reviewed by the board. A commander's request to withdraw the bar must provide specific information to refute the board's action.

The individual's commander must interview the soldier and give him or her the letter, enclosures, and endorsement. He must also ensure that the soldier understands the impact of the bar and available options. The commander must also ensure that the soldier completes DA Form 4941-R, *Statement of Option,* within seven days of receipt and returns it through the chain of command to TAPC.

A soldier may appeal. An appeal must arrive at TAPC not later than 12 months after the date of the bar letter. The soldier must understand that this appeal is the only one he or she may submit, although this does not preclude the commander's submitting an appeal on the soldier's behalf.

The appeal should address the basis for the bar and actions taken by the soldier to improve his or her performance to overcome noted deficiencies. Documents that demonstrate improved performance or the resolution of a deficiency (MILPO-authorized NCOER, award orders, revocation of a court-martial, removal of disciplinary data, and SDT results) should be attached to the appeal.

If the appeal is denied, the soldier's commander must reevaluate the soldier to determine whether there has been a demonstrated marked improvement in performance and potential.

For a soldier who has less than 18 months remaining until ETS at the date of the bar and who was not granted an extension to provide for the 18 months, no reevaluation is required. If the commander desires to reevaluate the soldier, an extension for the amount of time originally required to allow the 18-month period may be granted. For a soldier who has more than 18 months remaining until ETS on the date of the bar or for a soldier who was granted an extension to provide for the 18 months, the commander must reevaluate the soldier not less than 90 days before ETS.

Staff sergeants cannot be extended past 20 years. A soldier who has completed 18 or more years' service on the effective date of the DA bar letter may be extended to reach retirement eligibility.

The Command Sergeant Major Retention Program
The CSM Retention Program establishes procedures whereby outstanding command sergeants major may be retained beyond 30 years of active service. The program provides the Army the benefit of their long years of experience, expertise, and continued outstanding service.

STATEMENT OF OPTION

For use of this form, see AR 601-280, the proponent agency is DCSPER.

DATA REQUIRED BY THE PRIVACY ACT OF 1974

AUTHORITY: Title 5 USC Section 301

PRINCIPAL PURPOSE: To determine and select option after bar to reenlistment.

ROUTINE USES; Information is needed to ensure that soldier's option statement is properly identified with his records.

DISCLOSURE; Disclosure is voluntary, however, failure to furnish information could adversely affect soldier .

THRU: *(Include ZIP Code)*

TO: Commander
US Total Army Personnel Agency
ATTN: DAPC-PDT-SA
2461 Eisenhower Avenue
Alexandria, VA 22331-0400

DATE:

I WAS NOTIFIED OF MY DA BAR TO REENLISTMENT UNDER THE QUALITATIVE MANAGEMENT PROGRAM (AR 601-280) on
_____ . I HAVE CAREFULLY READ, HAVE BEEN COUNSELED, AND UNDERSTAND THE OPTIONS OPEN TO
ME AS A RESULT OF THE DA BAR TO REENLISTMENT. I HAVE CHOSEN THE FOLLOWING OPTION AS INDICATED BY MY
INITIALS AT THE BOX MARKED BELOW:

1. ☐ _____ I will submit an appeal. I understand this appeal must be submitted not later than 90 days after the date of notification.
If my appeal is not received by DA 4 months after the date of the bar or the appeal is denied, HQDA will automatically change this
option to option 2. Additionally, I understand that I can request an extension of service in order to process my appeal *(for a maximum of
9 months of service from the date of the bar letter)* as a separate action, provided the extension does not pass my Reenlistment
Ineligibility Point.

2. ☐ _____ I intend to complete my remaining term of enlistment and will take no further action. I understand that I will be
processed for separation *(IAW AR 635-200)* 60 days after the date of notification and that I may be separated prior to my current ETS. I
understand I can change to option 4 or 5 at a later date.

3. ☐ _____ Under the provision of paragraph 16-5, AR 635-200, I request to be discharged on_____
(Requested discharge date must be NLT 6 months from the date option is signed). I understand that recoupment of unearned
portions of Enlistment Bonus (EB)/Selective Reenlistment Bonus (SRB) is required. I also understand that once separated I will not be
permitted to reenlist at a later day. If this request is approved, it may not be revoked. *(This option form will be forwarded to the
discharge authority for approval/disapproval of this request.)*

4. ☐ _____ I intend to request immediate retirement, *(only those persons eligible to retire may choose this option, see AR
635-200.)* I understand my request for retirement must be submitted within 14 days of completion of the option statement for
a retirement date not later than 12 months from date of submission.

5. ☐ _____ I had at least 18 years of active Federal service at the date of the DA bar to reenlistment letter and will retire upon at-
training retirement eligibility *(20 years AFS).* If necessary, I will request to extend for _____ months, as a separate action, to achieve
20 years AFS and will retire no later than the last day of the month in which I attain retirement eligibility.

PRINTED/TYPED NAME AND RANK   SSN   ETS

SIGNATURE   DATE

ON _____ I PRESENTED THE DA BAR TO REENLISTMENT, EXPLAINED THE AVAILABLE OPTIONS, AND

COUNSELED THE SOLDIER ON HIS/HER RIGHTS UNDER AR 601-280 AND AR 635-200. AS THE COMMANDER, I HAVE

CHOSEN THE FOLLOWING OPTION AS INDICATED BY MY INITIALS AT THE BOX MARKED BELOW:

1. ☐ _____ I will submit an appeal based on my determination that the soldier has overcome the deficiencies cited by the
Selection Board or has so significantly improved his/her performance as to warrant reconsideration of the board's decision. I understand
this appeal must be submitted within 90 days of the date I presented the DA Bar.

2. ☐ _____ This soldier has been assigned to my command for less than 120 days; he/she was assigned on_____ .
I will submit a supplemental DA Form 4941-R indicating my decision on my options NLT_____ *(NLT 120 days from date of
assignment).*

3. ☐ _____ I will not submit an appeal. Action will be taken per AR 601-280 and AR 635-200 as necessary based on the
soldier's selected option *(above).*

PRINTED/TYPED NAME , RANK AND BRANCH OF
COMMANDER PRESENTING THE BAR   SIGNATURE   DATE

DA FORM 4941-R, MAY 88   EDITION OF NOV 87 IS OBSOLETE

Command sergeants major who wish to be retained beyond 30 years of service must submit a request for retention during their 28th year of service. During the 29th year of service, a request may be reconsidered if the applicant submits a new one. They may be retained up to 35 years' active service or to age 55, whichever is first.

The selection board consists of five members, one of whom is the Sergeant Major of the Army. The board president is a major general. Volunteering does not automatically ensure selection. Retention beyond 30 years is not a reward for past performance.

10

Promotion and Reduction

Soldiers are recommended for promotion only after they develop the skills, knowledge, and abilities to perform the duties and assume the responsibility of the next higher grade. Generally, if soldiers do well in their present grades, they will work well in the next higher grades.

The Army promotion system has the following objectives:

- Fill authorized enlisted spaces with qualified soldiers.
- Provide for career progression and rank that is in line with potential.
- Recognize the best-qualified soldier to attract and retain the highest-caliber soldier for a career in the Army.
- Preclude promoting the solder who is not productive or not best qualified.
- Provide an equitable system for all soldiers.

By using standard promotion scoring forms with predetermined promotion point factors, corporals, specialists, and sergeants can measure how well they qualify for promotion. They can set goals to increase their promotion potential. Staff sergeants, sergeants first class, first sergeants, and master sergeants can judge their qualifications when compared to other soldiers in their MOS. The Army promotes soldiers who are qualified and who will accept Armywide assignments.

The commanders below may promote, subject to authority and responsibility by higher commanders:

- *SPC and below.* Unit commanders may advance or promote assigned soldiers to PV2, PFC, and SPC.
- *SGT and SSG.* Field-grade commanders lieutenant colonel or higher may promote soldiers attached or assigned or on TDY to their command or installation.
- *SFC and above.* Headquarters, Department of the Army.
- *Hospitalized soldiers.* Commanders of medical facilities may promote hospitalized soldiers to SSG and below.
- *Students.* Commandants and commanders of training installations and activities.
- *Posthumous promotion.* Headquarters, Department of the Army.

ADVANCEMENT TO PRIVATE E-2 AND PRIVATE FIRST CLASS

Active Army personnel are advanced to the rank of private E-2 when they have completed six months of active federal service, unless it is stopped by the commander. ARNG and USAR personnel on initial active-duty training are advanced to private E-2 when they complete six months of service from the day of entry, unless it is stopped by the commander. To recognize outstanding performance, local commanders may advance limited numbers of soldiers to private E-2 who have at least four but less than six months' active service. *Advancement to private first class is not mandatory.* Under normal conditions, unit commanders may advance soldiers who qualify with twelve months' time in service and four months' time in grade.

To recognize outstanding performance, unit commanders may advance soldiers who qualify. Those who otherwise qualify must have a minimum of six months in service and two months' time in grade (which may be waived).

CRITERIA FOR PROMOTION TO SPECIALIST OR CORPORAL

Normally, commanders may advance to specialist or corporal soldiers who meet the following qualifications:

- Twenty-four months in service.
- Six months' time in grade, waiverable to three months.
- Security clearance appropriate for the MOS in which promoted; advancement may be based on granting an interim security clearance.

To recognize outstanding performance, commanders may advance soldiers on an accelerated basis, providing advancements do not cause more than 20 percent of the total number of assigned specialists and corporals to have less than 24 months' time in service, and providing soldiers meet the following qualifications:

- Twelve months in service.
- Three months' time in grade.
- Security clearance required for the MOS in which advanced; may be based on an interim clearance.

Unused waivers that are computed at unit level (not consolidated) may be returned to higher command for redistribution, providing that computation of the higher command's strength will allow additional promotions. For example, suppose that four companies in a battalion have ten promotion authorizations but use only eight. Computation of battalion strength indicates twelve promotions would have been authorized if consolidated. Thus the two unused authorizations may be redistributed.

Commanders with zero waiver authorizations may promote any soldier with 18 or more months' time in grade. Commanders may use all waiver authorizations to promote soldiers with 18 or more months' time in grade. In such cases, any remaining soldier with 18 or more months' time in grade also may be promoted.

PROMOTION TO SERGEANT AND STAFF SERGEANT

Promotion to sergeant and staff sergeant is made based on promotion point cutoff scores. Headquarters, Department of the Army, determines needs by grade and MOS. Based on this need, promotion point cutoff scores for primary and secondary zone promotions are announced.

One of a drill sergeant's duties is to inspect and instruct soldiers.

The promotion authority may waive no more than two of the requirements for soldiers who are otherwise highly qualified.

NCOs and commanders control or have influence over the points a soldier can attain for promotion. To begin with, NCOs are responsible for the points granted by the promotion board—200 maximum. NCOs are responsible for taking soldiers through NCOES—more points. If a soldier performs his or her duties in an outstanding manner, the good NCO leader may recommend him or her for the Army Achievement Medal or an Army Commendation Medal—another 15 or 20 points. Of the 200 points that can be given by the commander for the soldier's duty performance, the commander must rely heavily on the recommendations of NCOs. Finally, it is NCOs who teach soldiers how to shoot and how to stay in physical shape; if they have done their jobs well, the soldier could get another 100 points for military training.

So out of a possible maximum 800 points a soldier can earn for promotion, NCOs have a direct influence on more than 500 of them. A good NCO's influence is even more far reaching when he or she encourages a subordinate to pursue civilian correspondence and extension courses.

Effective July 1, 1994, NCOs began competing for promotion to staff sergeant on an 800-point scale.

Cutoff Scores

When a soldier's number of promotion points is known, many wonder why he or she cannot be promoted immediately if the cutoff is low enough. In the first place, soldiers may be selected for promotion three months before they have the required time in service.

Second, reports from the field reflecting the number of soldiers on promotion lists, their number of points, and their zones and MOSs arrive at HQDA about the middle of the month following the month the soldier appeared before the promotion board.

At this point, MOS and grade vacancies are computed. The total number of promotions for a particular grade (regardless of MOS) is determined by comparing the number of personnel projected to be in that grade against the number allowed in the Army budget for the month in which promotions are to be made. This projection includes losses, those promoted in and out of the grade, and reductions. Available promotions are distributed to MOSs based on the percentage of fill.

Promotions go to those MOSs with the greatest need first. Secondary zone (waiver) promotions are limited, so they go to MOSs with the greatest need after the primary zone (no waiver) promotions are distributed. At this time—which is one to two months after the soldier appears before the promotion board—the soldier's number of promotion points comes into the process. For example, if vacancies and budget permit the promotion of 100 soldiers from the primary zone of a particular MOS, a promotion cutoff score is established by going down the scores until the 100 limit is reached. That is, if the top 100 sergeants in an MOS have 716 or more points, the cutoff score would be 716. If the top 100 have 796 or more, the cutoff would be 796. If a cutoff for a particular MOS is high, that means that the available promotions went to soldiers in MOSs with a lower percentage to fill.

Time in Service and Time in Grade Requirements

The time in grade and time in service requirements for promotion to sergeant and staff sergeant are as follows:

SSG	10 months as SGT	(PZ) 84 months
		(SZ) 48 months
SGT	8 months as SPC or CPL	(PZ) 36 months
		(SZ) 18 months

Time in service may be waived for promotion in the secondary zone only. Soldiers being considered for promotion to sergeant and staff sergeant must appear for a selection board.

Soldiers may compete for promotion only in their career progression MOS. They must be fully qualified in the MOS in which recommended for promotion consideration. The commander's recommendation affirms that the soldier is qualified in his or her career progression MOS at the next higher grade. The goal of the personnel management system is that the soldier demonstrate qualifications for the next higher grade before competing for promotion.

Soldiers must be in the pay grade next below that of the promoted rank (no waiver granted), they must be physically qualified to perform duties of the MOS and grade to which promoted, and they must have appropriate security clearance or favorable security investigation required by the MOS in which promoted.

Educational requirements for promotion are completion of eighth grade or GED equivalent or higher education for promotion to sergeant; high school diploma, GED equivalent, or associate's degree or higher degree for promotion to staff sergeant.

School Requirements
To become a sergeant or staff sergeant, you must have completed the Primary Leadership Development Course or the Basic NCO Course, respectively.

Service-Remaining Obligations
The service-remaining obligation is three months for promotion to sergeant and twelve months for promotion to staff sergeant. Waivers are not granted. Service-remaining obligation is generally computed from the first day of the authorized month of promotion.

THE PAPERWORK
Promotion Packets
The promotion packet of a soldier who is on the recommended list is kept in the action-pending section of his military personnel records jacket until he or she is promoted. These documents are then given to the soldier. The counseling and promotion board documents of those who do not attain recommended list status are filed by the promotion authority for two years and then destroyed.

Recommended List
After completion of all promotion actions during the month, a recommended list is published. It lists all soldiers of the organization who have been selected but not yet promoted. Names are listed by grade and zone in ascending MOS and descending promotion point score order.

Soldiers are promoted from the current recommended list by MOS. Promotions are made on the first calendar day of the month in which they are authorized. Promotion orders may be published with future effective dates.

Soldiers are eligible for promotion on the first day of the third month following date of selection: A soldier is recommended in January 1996; he becomes eligible for promotion on April 1, 1996.

A soldier's name on the secondary zone list for promotion to sergeant is transferred to the primary zone list on the first day of the month in which he completes 33 months of active service. He becomes eligible for promotion in the primary zone on the first day of the month in which he completed 36 months' active service.

A soldier's name on the secondary zone list for promotion to staff sergeant is transferred to the primary zone on the first day of the month in which he completes 81 months of active service. He becomes eligible for promotion in the primary zone on the first day of the month in which he completes 84 months of active service.

Reevaluation
A soldier on the current recommended list for three months may ask to be reevaluated at that time and each three months thereafter if he or she is still promotable. A

soldier reevaluated is not immediately eligible for promotion based on his new score. He will continue to be eligible for promotion based on the promotion point score he held immediately before reevaluation. Eligibility under the old score continues until the reevaluated score becomes effective. The new score becomes effective three months from the date of reevaluation because of the three-month reporting time.

After the request for reevaluation is approved, the soldier appears before the organization's next regularly scheduled promotion board. His promotion list status is then based on the number of points he attains. If he remains on the list, his original selection date is adjusted to the date the promotion authority approves the board report. This gives the soldier a chance to improve his total score. He also runs the risk of lowering his standing if he makes a poor showing before the board.

Loss of recommended list status through reevaluation does not, however, preclude promotion consideration by future boards. Such consideration is not a vested right. Those being considered to regain recommended list status are subject to the provisions of chapter 7, AR 600-200, and the recommendations of their commanders.

Removals

Soldiers may be removed from promotions lists for the following reasons:

• Failure to qualify, for cause, for the security clearance required for the MOS in which recommended. Those who fail to qualify for a security clearance through no adverse reason are reclassified and remain on the list in the new MOS.
• Failure to reenlist or extend to meet a service-remaining obligation.
• Enstatement of a bar to reenlistment.
• Reclassification from an MOS because of inefficiency or misconduct.
• Erroneous listing due to not meeting the criteria for promotion.
• Enrollment in the weight control program.
• Failure to pass reclassification training.
• Reduction in grade after being placed on the recommended list.

A removal board is convened when required to determine whether a soldier should be removed from a recommended list. The board will be constituted as for promotion boards. The soldier being considered for removal has certain rights:

• He may appear before the board.
• He may challenge any member of the board for cause.
• He may request an available witness whose testimony is pertinent to his case.
• He may elect to remain silent, to make an unsworn statement, to make a sworn statement, or to be verbally examined by the board.
• He may question any witness appearing before the board.
• He may present written affidavits and depositions of witnesses.

Failure on the part of a soldier to exercise these rights is not a bar to the board proceedings or its findings and recommendations. The promotion authority is the final approval or disapproval authority on the board's recommendations. This action is final.

A soldier removed from a list and later exonerated is reinstated to the current local recommended list as soon as possible but not more than 10 days after being completely exonerated.

Recomputation of Promotion Points

A soldier with valid recommended list status for promotion to sergeant or staff sergeant as of the end of the month before the scheduled recomputation has his promotion points recomputed during that time. Promotion points are recomputed twice yearly without local promotion board action.

Commanders must ensure that all scores recomputed are completed by the end of the required month so that they will be reported in the following month's report of enlisted personnel eligible for promotion. If scores are not recomputed during the scheduled month for a valid reason (such as in-transit status), they are recomputed at the earliest possible date. This recomputed score is shown on the current recommended list as of the scheduled recomputation month. New scores become effective three months from the day of the scheduled recomputation month.

Recomputations are limited to items 1 through 7, DA Form 3355. Adjustment of Board Points (item 8) applies to soldiers who request reevaluation.

Points awarded are determined from the soldier's records as they were before the board proceedings were approved. The promotion authority or the MILPO may correct all known errors before the report of the board proceedings is approved. Other than to correct computation errors, no changes are made in the promotion point standings after the board proceedings are approved unless the promotion authority concludes that the soldier was considered in error or was granted more administrative points than he was entitled to. In such cases, the soldier is suspended from the promotion list.

ASSIGNMENTS AND HOW THEY AFFECT PROMOTIONS

Personnel on Temporary Duty

Commanders must ensure that soldiers are considered for promotion before they are placed on temporary duty, in isolated areas, or on special duty or assignment. Promotion authorities must ensure that they are kept informed of duty performance of soldiers on temporary duty.

Reassignment before Promotion

When a soldier is processing for transfer, the promotion packet and a copy of the current recommended list must be sealed in an envelope and filed in the action-pending section of the soldier's MPRJ. The gaining promotion authority should then put the soldier's name on his current recommended list on the reporting date as stated in the orders.

Newly assigned soldiers who are on a recommended list from a previous command are added to the current recommended list of the gaining command effective on the reporting date stated in reassignment orders.

No soldier who is on a recommended list should depart a unit (or be permitted to depart) until his or her promotion packet has been prepared and its presence in the MPRJ has been verified.

Reclassification of PMOS

A soldier on a recommended list who is voluntarily or involuntarily reclassified for reasons other than inefficiency or misconduct may compete against the announced DA promotion cutoff scores in the newly awarded MOS and be promoted in the new PMOS on the first day of the month following reclassification, if eligible.

SELECTION AND PROMOTION TO SENIOR NCO RANKS

Soldiers who are eligible for senior-grade promotions are given the opportunity to review their promotion packets well in advance of the promotion board's convening. Because the board uses your records to determine whether you will be selected, your review must be thorough.

At no cost, you may obtain copies of your Official Military Personnel File (OMPF) microfiche by writing to Commander, U.S. Army Enlisted Records and Evaluation Center, ATTN: PCRE-RF-I, Fort Benjamin Harrison, IN 46249. Be sure to include your Social Security number and sign your request. The OMPF consists of the *P-fiche* and the *S-fiche*. The P-fiche contains *performance* and commendatory and disciplinary data; the S-fiche contains *service* computation data (active-duty, promotion, separation, and other documents and administrative data).

Review these documents, particularly the P-fiche, very carefully. Be sure all documents on the fiche pertain to you. The board should catch discrepancies, but look and correct them at once.

You should also verify NCO Education System codes through your local personnel service center. All staff sergeants and sergeants first class in a zone of consideration should make sure the correct codes are posted on DA Form 2A, *Personnel Qualification Record*, Part 1, and DA Form 2-1, *PQR*, Part 2. The codes are as follows: "2" to denote Primary Leadership Development Course graduation, "W" for Basic NCO Course graduation, "T" for Advanced NCO Course selection or "S" for graduation, and "F" for Sergeant Major Course selection or "A" for graduation. Graduation from the First Sergeant Course, denoted by a "K," is not an NCOES requirement.

Be certain that any commendatory information not on file in your OMPF is provided to your MILPO at the time you screen your promotion jacket.

Make sure your official military photograph is current, especially if there has been a change in your physical appearance since the last one was taken. Your record gives a promotion board one view of the kind of soldier you are, but your photo shows board members what you look like in uniform. An outdated photo or none at all will count against you.

Although your local MILPO is required to inform you when a new official DA full-length photograph is required, it is your responsibility to have it taken and to ensure it meets the standards of AR 670-1, *Wear and Appearance of Army Uniforms and Insignia*, and AR 672-5-1, *Military Awards*.

The Total Army Personnel Command requires NCOs to update official photos every five years. New staff sergeants and command sergeants major are required to get an official photo taken within 60 days of pinning on their rank.

Eligibility

Eligibility for promotion to sergeant first class and above is based on date of rank. In addition, for first sergeant or master sergeant and above, cumulative enlisted service is also required.

The criteria for the primary and secondary zones of consideration for each grade are announced by Headquarters, Department of the Army, before each board. Soldiers may not decline consideration. The following general criteria must be met before the board convenes to qualify a soldier for inclusion in a zone of consideration:

•   Meet the announced date or rank requirements and other criteria prescribed by HQDA.

- Have the required cumulative enlisted service creditable in computing basic pay for promotion to first sergeant or master sergeant and above.
- Be on active duty on the convening date of the selection board.
- Have a high school diploma or GED equivalent or an associate's or higher degree.
- Not be barred from or denied reenlistment.

School Requirements
Promotion to sergeant first class requires completion of the Advanced NCO Course (ANCOC). Promotion to master sergeant, sergeant major, and command sergeant major, however, remain the same: ANCOC, none, and the Sergeant Major Course, respectively.

Selection Boards
Selection boards consist of five members, including both officers and senior NCOs. The president of each board is a general officer.

Soldiers do not appear in person before a selection board. No written communications from third parties, including a soldier's chain of command or supervisor, are authorized.

A soldier within an announced primary zone may write the president of the board inviting attention to any matter he or she feels is important in considering his or her records. Letters may not contain any information on the character, conduct, or motives of any person or criticism of any other person. Such letters must be received before the convening date.

Security Requirements
For promotion to sergeant first class, a soldier must have the security clearance required for the MOS in which promoted. For first sergeant or master sergeant and above, the soldier must have a favorable National Agency Check (NAC) completed or have a final secret security clearance or higher.

Selections
Selections are based on impartial consideration of all eligible soldiers in the announced zone. Boards select the best qualified in each career management field. They recommend a specified number of soldiers by MOS from the zones of consideration who are best qualified to meet the needs of the Army. The total number that may be selected in each MOS is the projected number the Army needs to maintain its authorized by-grade strength at any given time.

Soldiers who are not selected for promotion are not provided specific reasons for their not having been selected. Board members do not record reasons, nor do they give any reasons for selecting or not selecting a soldier. Selections are based on relative qualifications and the projected need in each career management field.

Acceptance
Unless a soldier declines promotion, it is accepted as of the effective date of the announcing order. Letters of declination must be sent through command channels to the MILPO not later than 30 days after the effective date of the promotion given in

the orders. Soldiers who decline promotion will be considered by the next regularly constituted board, providing they are otherwise eligible.

Soldiers promoted to sergeant first class and above incur a two-year service obligation. This obligation begins from the effective date of the promotion before voluntary nondisability retirement.

Frocking

When a soldier is frocked, he or she assumes the insignia of a higher grade so that his or her title is commensurate with the duty position, although no pay or allowances are authorized in the higher grade. Sergeants first class (promotable) to first sergeants, master sergeants (promotable), and command sergeants major (designate) may be frocked.

Enlisted Standby Advisory Board (STAB)

This board considers the following records:

• From a primary and secondary zone not reviewed by a regular board.

• From a primary zone that were not properly constituted because of a major material error when reviewed by a regular board. The Deputy Chief of Staff for Personnel or designee will approve cases for referral to a STAB upon declaring invalid, in whole or in part, an adverse NCO Evaluation Report or academic evaluation report that was reviewed by a promotion board, providing that with the absence of this report, or portions thereof, there is a reasonable chance the soldier would have been recommended for promotion. An error is major when, had it not existed, the soldier would clearly have been more competitive and his or her qualifications appear to have been increased to equal that of others who were selected.

• Of those recommended soldiers on whom derogatory information has developed that may warrant removal from a recommended list.

Only soldiers who were not selected from a primary zone of consideration will be reconsidered for promotion. Soldiers who were considered in a secondary zone are not reconsidered.

Removal from a Recommended List

Commanders may recommend that a soldier's name be removed from a DA recommended list at any time. The recommendation for the removal must be fully documented and justified. HQDA makes the final decision on the removal based on the results and recommendation of the DA Standby Enlisted Advisory Board.

Removal may be recommended for a number of reasons, including the following:

• Failure to make progress in the weight-control program.

• As a result of reprimand, admonition, censure, and other nonpunitive measures, including for substandard duty performance over a period of time.

• For misconduct.

Before forwarding a recommendation for removal, the initiator must send it in writing to the soldier. All documents must be included. The soldier must be allowed to respond to the proposed action and may submit a rebuttal within 15 days after receipt of the written notice. The commander initiating the removal may extend this time only for unusual circumstances beyond the soldier's control. A soldier who elects not to rebut must send a signed statement saying that he or she has reviewed the proposed action and elects not to submit a rebuttal.

Removal from a DA promotion recommended list has far-reaching, long-lasting effects on the soldier. The probability for subsequent selection for promotion is extremely unlikely.

REDUCTIONS IN GRADE
The commanders below may administratively reduce the grade of assigned soldiers:
- Specialist or corporal and below—company, troop, battery, and separate detachment commanders.
- Sergeant and staff sergeant—field-grade commanders of any organization authorized a lieutenant colonel or higher-grade commander. For separate detachments, companies, or battalions, reduction authority is the next senior headquarters within the chain of command authorized a lieutenant colonel or higher-grade commander.
- Sergeant first class and above—commanders or organizations authorized a colonel or higher grade commander. For separate detachments, companies, or battalions, reduction authority is the next senior headquarters within the chain of command authorized a colonel or higher-grade commander.

Erroneous Enlistment Grades
Soldiers in higher grades than authorized upon enlistment or reenlistment in the Regular Army or Army Reserve will be reduced to the one to which they are entitled. Authorized grades are prescribed in AR 601-210, AR 140-11, or AR 140-158.

Misconduct
For reductions imposed by court-martial, see the Manual for Courts-Martial. Sergeants first class and above cannot be reduced under the provision of Article 15, UCMJ.

Inefficiency
Inefficiency is defined as "demonstration of characteristics which show that the person cannot perform the duties and responsibilities of the grade and MOS" (AR 600-200). It may include any act or conduct that shows a lack of abilities and qualities required and expected of a person of that grade and experience. Commanders may consider misconduct, including conviction by civil court, as bearing on efficiency.

A soldier may be reduced under the authority of chapter 8, AR 600-200, for long-standing unpaid personal debts that he or she has not made a reasonable attempt to pay.

An assigned soldier who has served in the same unit for at least 90 days may be reduced one grade for inefficiency. The commander starting the reduction action will document the soldier's inefficiency. The documents should establish a pattern of inefficiency rather than identify a specific incident.

The commander reducing a soldier will inform him or her, in writing, of the action contemplated and the reasons. The soldier must acknowledge receipt of the letter, by endorsement, and may submit any pertinent matters in rebuttal. Sergeants and above may request to appear before a reduction board. If appearance is declined, it must be done in writing and will be considered as acceptance of the reduction action. A reduction board, when required, must be convened within 30 days after the individual is notified in writing.

Reduction Boards
When required, reduction boards are convened to determine whether an enlisted soldier's grade should be reduced. This convening authority must ensure that the following conditions exist:
• The board consists of officers and enlisted personnel of mature judgment and senior in grade to the person being considered for reduction.
• For inefficiency cases, at least one member must be thoroughly familiar with the soldier's specialty.
• The board must consist of three unbiased voting members.
• The board has an officer or senior enlisted member (or both) of the same sex as the soldier being considered for reduction.
• The composition of the board represents the ethnic population of soldiers under its jurisdiction.
• No soldier with direct knowledge of the case is appointed to the board.

A soldier who is to appear before the board will be given at least 15 working days' written notice before the date of the hearing so that the soldier or his counsel has time to prepare the case.

The convening authority may approve or disapprove any portion of the recommendation of the board, but his action cannot increase the severity of the board's recommendation. If he approves a recommended reduction, he may direct it. When the board recommends a reduction and the convening authority approves it, the soldier will be reduced without regard to any action taken to appeal the reduction.

The soldier has the following rights:
• He may decline, in writing, to appear before the board.
• He may have a military counsel of his own choosing, if reasonably available, or he may employ a civilian counsel at his own expense, or both.
• He may appear in person, with or without counsel, at all open proceedings of the board.
• If the soldier appears before the board without counsel, the president must counsel him on the action being contemplated, the effect of such action on his future in the Army, and his right to request counsel.
• He may challenge (dismiss) any member of the board for cause.
• He may request any reasonably available witness whose testimony he believes to be pertinent to his case. When requested, he must tell the nature of the information the witness will provide.
• He may submit to the board written affidavits and depositions of witnesses who are unable to appear before the board.
• He may employ the provisions of Article 31, UCMJ (prohibition against compulsory self-incrimination), or submit himself to an examination by the board.
• He or his counsel may question any witness appearing before the board.

Failure of the soldier to exercise his rights is not a bar to the board proceedings or its findings and recommendations.

Appeals
Appeals from reduction for misconduct are governed by Article 15, UCMJ; paragraph 135, MC: and AR 27-10.

Appeals based on reduction for failure to complete training will not be accepted.

Appeals from staff sergeants and below based on reduction for inefficiency or conviction by civil court are allowed. They must be submitted in writing within 30 workdays from the date of reduction. The officer having general court-martial jurisdiction, or the next higher authority, may approve, disapprove, or change the reduction if he determines that the reduction was without sufficient basis, should be changed, or was proper. His action is final.

Written appeals from sergeants first class and above based on reduction for inefficiency or conviction by civil court must also be submitted within 30 days of the date of reduction. A copy of all correspondence and the appeal are furnished the authority next above the officer who reduced the soldier. This officer, if a general, will take final action on the appeal. If not reviewed at the appellate level by a general officer, the file is then sent to the first general officer in the chain of command next above the officer who acted on the appeal for final review and action. This authority personally reviews the file, including action taken on the appeal, and makes final corrections where indicated.

Other Reasons for Reductions

When a separation authority determines that a soldier is to be discharged from the service under other than honorable conditions, he will be reduced to the lowest enlisted grade. Board action is not required for such actions. Also, soldiers appointed to a higher grade on entering or while attending a service or civilian school and who fail to complete the course successfully may be reduced.

Restoration to Former Grades

Grade restoration may result from setting aside, mitigation, or suspension of nonjudicial punishment; when a court-martial sentence is set aside or disapproved; when a conviction by a civil court is reversed; or when officers taking final appeal or review action after reduction direct that the soldier be restored to his former grade or any intermediate grade, on determining that reduction was without sufficient basis.

Records Check

All enlisted soldiers must keep tabs on their official records. Soldiers can check their official records at any time because of the new push-button phone service at the Enlisted Records and Evaluation Center, Fort Benjamin Harrison, Indiana. This interactive voice response system allows callers to check on NCO Evaluation Reports, official photographs, security clearance, and other important information. Any soldier who has a push-button touch-tone phone can use the system. When a caller dials DSN 699-3714 or commercial (315) 542-3714, a computer-generated voice welcomes the callers and asks for a Social Security number. Once the number is accepted, the caller is offered several types of information. This system is especially helpful to staff sergeants and senior NCOs who need to check their records before a promotion board or school selection board convenes. It is effective, efficient, and quick.

11

Personal Affairs

The higher one goes up the flagpole, the more the tail hangs out for all to see.
—GEN Creighton W. Abrams

Busy NCOs often allow their personal needs to pile up under more pressing professional matters. Doing so can be costly to you, and especially to your loved ones.

Consider, for example, that neglecting to get life insurance *and* a last will and testament can cause surviving family members to get left out in the cold, financially and otherwise. Consider, too, that medical bills for unforeseen illnesses and injuries can devastate your financial future. What can you do about portions of major bills disallowed by CHAMPUS or the Dependent's Dental Plan? Do you really understand your family's medical and dental benefits and how and under what circumstances CHAMPUS supplements are strongly recommended?

Suppose you're the kind of NCO who takes pride in hitting the ground running when assigned to a new job. What happens, for example, when you go to work in a new job in Europe or elsewhere overseas and your spouse and children remain behind in local quarters? Do your family members have what they need to achieve a decent quality of life and standard of living in their new environment? Where can they turn for help when associated problems arise?

What if, for some reason beyond your control and ability to rectify, your end-of-month leave and earnings statement reads "No pay due" and you must pay rent and meet other living expenses? Who can help fully or partially defray necessary payments to landlords, banks, and other creditors until your pay is sorted out?

Are your personal affairs in order? To what extent? Do you keep records? Where are they? Who else knows where your vital records are kept? Does your spouse and other next of kin know important account numbers and first and supplemental points of contact?

You must make the effort to consider and take charge of your personal affairs. It is your responsibility to plan for your personal needs and those of your family. Commanders, sergeants major, first sergeants, and other leaders frown on the NCO who is unable or unwilling to ensure that he or she is fully deployable. Deployability includes personal readiness.

ARMY COMMUNITY SERVICES (ACS)
The ACS is an official Department of the Army organization established to provide

information, aid, guidance, and referral services to military personnel and their families. ACS activities are monitored by the Army Adjutant General.

The ACS provides a wide variety of services, including the following:
- Referrals for handicapped dependents.
- Family counseling services.
- Financial planning services
- Lending services to provide bedding, linens, and housewares to military families until they can get settled at a new post.
- Volunteer services providing transportation to dependents when required.
- Child abuse information and referral.
- An emergency food locker from which needy families may draw supplies.

ARMY EMERGENCY RELIEF (AER)
The Army Emergency Relief operates as a part of the Army Community Services. AER provides badly needed financial assistance to soldiers and their dependents. A local AER officer can authorize interest-free cash loans. Large loans must be approved by Headquarters, AER.

AER loans may be approved for the following purposes:
- Defray living expenses because of nonreceipt of military pay.
- Provide money to help defray emergency travel expenses.
- Help pay rents, security deposits, and utilities.
- Help pay "essential POV expenses."
- Pay funeral expenses above and beyond those allowed by the government.
- Pay grants to the widows and orphans of deceased soldiers, in some cases.
- Provide cash for food when it is not available from the ACS food locker.
- Provide money to replace lost funds.

Soldiers must apply for AER loans through their unit commanders by filling out DA Form 1103, *Application for AER Financial Assistance*. The soldier must document his or her expenses or financial situation, and an allotment must be executed before the AER will disburse any money.

Each year, AER disburses millions of dollars to help soldiers and their families. The only source for these funds is cash donations by Army members solicited annually during Armywide fund-raising drives.

THE ARMY FAMILY ACTION PLAN
Today, more than half the active Army force is married. In the past few years, the Army has come to realize a greater responsibility to families. A new philosophy was specified by former Army Chief of Staff, GEN John Wickham, Jr., on August 15, 1983:

A partnership exists between the Army and Army families. The Army's unique missions, concept of service and lifestyle of its members all affect the nature of this partnership. Towards the goal of building a strong partnership, the Army remains committed to assuring adequate support to families in order to promote wellness, to develop a sense of community, and to strengthen the mutually reinforcing bonds between the Army and its families.

So was born the Army Family Action Plan (AFAP). The plan includes four major themes: relocation, medical, family support and role identity, and education and youth. The specific areas range from development of videos for overseas orientation programs, developing family-member support groups at installations and units, and attempting to correct medical staff shortages, to providing English-as-a-second-language instruction for family members whose native language is other than English. As an NCO, regardless of whether you now have a family or plan to have one someday, your understanding and full support of the Army Family Action Plan is essential to its success.

Following are brief definitions of the critical elements of the plan's philosophy. Their applications are much more far-reaching than to just the Army Family Action Plan itself—they are essential ingredients to the cohesion that makes the Army work.

Partnership. Partnership has to exist between the Army as an institution and the individuals who are part of it: soldiers, civilians, and family members. Partnership is a cohesion of the Army and family members based on mutual understanding of the mission and commitment to one another. It is a reciprocal relationship, based on moral and ethical responsibilities and statutory and regulatory requirements. Partnership between its members makes the Army an institution, not just a job or a work place.

Wellness. Wellness is the concern for developing those strengths, skills, aptitudes, and attitudes that contribute to the wholeness and health in body, mind, and spirit. Wellness is achieved by concentrating now, and in the future, on what is working well and by drawing on the characteristics of the Army's many healthy families, and transmitting those characteristics to the people who need assistance.

Sense of community. This is the center of the partnership, with all members offered the challenge and opportunity to work together for the common good. It means each member of the Army community has a special responsibility to make the institution a better place in which to live and work.

Partnership, wellness, sense of community—all are important to military community residents and officials. The following are a few of the many examples that illustrate the value of the AFAP:

• Quality child care is a top priority to the increasing number of spouses who work. AFAP initiatives bring about increased appropriated fund support for child care, fees for child care based on family income, better trained and higher paid caregivers and more of them, parent advisory boards, and an ongoing study of the demand for child care.

• Since relocation assistance and sponsorship are paramount, AFAP requests increased allowances for transportation of household goods, especially for junior enlisted soldiers. An automated relocation assistance system provides housing and other relocation information about areas in the United States and abroad.

• Because of the AFAP, Reservists may shop in commissaries during a specified number of days during the year.

Since the first AFAP conference was held in 1983, many laws have been passed or amended to resolve more than 100 quality of life issues affecting the Army family.

LEGAL ASSISTANCE

A legal assistance officer will advise you on such matters as a will, power of attorney, divorce and separation actions, estates, tax problems, and other civil matters. The legal assistance officer can also provide you a very useful "legal check-up," which is designed to identify any potential legal problems that you may have.

This officer is not normally permitted to represent you in civil court or to give you advice in matters of a criminal nature. Neither may he or she advise you about court-martial investigations or charges (a military counsel appointed by the judge advocate will assist you in such cases). If your problem requires the services of a civilian lawyer, the legal assistance officer can refer you, through cooperating bar associations, to civilian legal advisors or legal aid bureaus.

LIFE INSURANCE

It is beyond the scope of this book to discuss all the things to look for when you are shopping for life insurance. What kind of policy to get and how much insurance you may need depends strictly upon your individual or family situation. You are particularly insurable if you are still relatively young and you have school-age children who depend upon you. *Shop around.* There are numerous good individual and group insurance plans available; there are some pretty bad ones available as well (and plenty of unscrupulous insurance agents willing to take your money from you).

While you are on active duty you have Servicemen's Group Life Insurance (SGLI), which offers coverages up to a maximum of $200,000, for very low premiums. The maximum you will pay per month is $18, and that entitles you to $200,000 worth of coverage. And when you leave the service, your SGLI is convertible to Veterans Group Life Insurance (VGLI).

MEDICAL INSURANCE

Army health care beneficiaries—you and your family—should take a long-term view toward medical and dental health. Eat foods that contribute to a longer life. Exercise regularly for the same reason. Rest properly. Brush and floss after meals. Get periodic physical and dental examinations. Follow the advice of doctors, dentists, and other Army health and medical care providers. Stay healthy to limit the effects of illness or disease. Beware of unsafe acts and unsafe conditions to avoid injury. When a person is ill or injured, *nothing* matters more than recovery.

When an active-duty soldier becomes sick or gets hurt, the Army direct-care medical system provides care at no cost. In fact, AR 40-3, *Medical, Dental and Veterinary Care*, prohibits active-duty soldiers, including active-duty Reserve Component soldiers, from seeking and obtaining medical and dental care from civilian sources without prior authorization from the local Army medical treatment facility commander. So, while soldiers are on active duty, they do not need medical and dental insurance. But Army family members do—and have it provided by the Civilian Health and Medical Program of the Uniformed Services (CHAMPUS) and the Delta Dental Plan, which is offered through CHAMPUS.

CHAMPUS

Under CHAMPUS, soldiers' families have one of the best health plans anywhere. The program shares most of the costs of care from civilian hospitals and doctors when family members cannot get care through a military hospital or clinic. CHAMPUS is intended to supplement your spouse's and children's benefits at military medical facilities, but it does not duplicate benefits, and it recognizes different categories of eligible persons, for whom available benefits and costs vary. Some dependents are not eligible for CHAMPUS, such as parents, parents-in-law, and most other persons eligible for Medicare hospitalization insurance.

CHAMPUS is not free. Active-duty beneficiaries must pay part of their medical costs, as well as for care CHAMPUS does not cover. And CHAMPUS pays only for *medically necessary* care and services. Also, you or your care provider must file claims before CHAMPUS will pay its share of the bills, generally 80 percent of the CHAMPUS-allowed amount. You pay the other 20 percent, plus a deductible amounting to $150 per year for individual dependents or $300 a year for families. Army retirees are also covered by the program, but CHAMPUS pays 75 percent and the beneficiary pays the other 25 percent of allowed charges plus disallowed charges and the applicable deductible.

An upper limit (known as a "catastrophic cap") is placed on CHAMPUS-covered medical bills in any fiscal year. The limit that an active-duty family will have to pay is $1,000; the limit for all other CHAMPUS-eligible families (retirees) is $10,000, which makes the program significantly more beneficial to active-duty members than to retirees.

Whether you are on active duty or retired, it is especially important to use your benefits only when you really need them. Try to use military facilities (and Department of Veterans Affairs hospitals in the case of retirees) whenever possible. Doing so will save money for you and the federal government.

See your local CHAMPUS health benefits advisor (HBA) at the nearest military hospital or clinic to obtain the most current copy of the *CHAMPUS Handbook*. It explains how to enroll your family in CHAMPUS, who and what are covered by the program, what is not covered, where to get care, and how much you should expect inpatient and outpatient care to cost. The handbook discusses the purpose of non-availability statements—to inform CHAMPUS that needed care is not available at the local military medical facility—and how to file or appeal a claim.

If an eligible family member is admitted to a hospital, CHAMPUS coverage depends on the facts of the circumstance. If, for example, an ambulance is used, CHAMPUS will determine whether the circumstance was an emergency. If it was, CHAMPUS will pay its co-share percentage of allowable costs. If it was not an emergency, CHAMPUS may refuse to pay costs and the patient (the sponsor, you) may be liable for the entire bill.

If a family member needs outpatient care, determine if the care is available at the nearest military medical facility. If it is, make an appointment. If it is not, get a referral and seek care from a civilian provider. Complete a CHAMPUS Claim Form, DD Form 2520 (available from your HBA), and give it to the care provider. In an emergency, seek care and complete the claim form afterward. If the care provider accepts CHAMPUS, he or she files the claim with CHAMPUS, which pays its percentage of allowable charges to the provider. The provider then bills you for the remaining co-share amount plus any charges for care not covered by CHAMPUS. It pays to get the *CHAMPUS Handbook* and read about what is and is not normally covered.

If a doctor does not participate in the program, he or she will still send the medical bill to CHAMPUS. The patient (patient's sponsor) attaches his or her copy of the bill to a claim form and sends it to CHAMPUS, which will pay the patient the allowed amount. The patient must then add to the allowed amount received his or her co-share amount plus charges for care not allowed, and send the total amount for the bill to the care provider. In other words, it is less bureaucratic hassle to get care from participating doctors and other medical professionals.

Civilian care providers waste no time billing beneficiaries, while CHAMPUS lags in providing benefit co-share payments. Typically, over the course of four months the beneficiary normally receives monthly bills from civilian care providers. The language used in the bills tends to grow more threatening over time and can result, commonly around the 120-day mark, in notification that the bill is being turned over to a collection agency.

The response to the threats should be "Nuts!" (borrowing from one famous Army holdout). Organize bills as they come in. Keep them filed separately by provider—ambulance service, doctor, radiologist, and so forth—in chronological order. Visit your HBA when you have all providers' initial bills and no later than every 60 days thereafter so that the advisor may prod the system along. HBAs effectively represent you by serving as liaisons between civilian care providers and CHAMPUS; they expertly prod CHAMPUS to pay while prompting care providers to wait for payment. If a care provider is on your back, take relative bills, letters, conversation records, and CHAMPUS Explanation of Benefits statements to your HBA and say, "Help, please."

When checking the status of a claim, you or your spouse can speed things up by providing the following information to your HBA:

- Patient's full name.
- Sponsor's full name, rank, branch of service, and status (active, Reserve, retired).
- Sponsor's Social Security number.
- Sponsor's and patient's addresses and phone numbers.
- Name and address of the care provider (usually on the bill).
- Date(s) of care and nature of care.

CHAMPUS Supplements

If your dependents receive medical care outside the military system and you do not have any supplemental insurance to help pay your co-share, you can face major expenses. Even though CHAMPUS pays a generous share of the cost of civilian medical bills, your share can be substantial, according to the Department of Defense Office of Civilian Health and Medical Program of the Uniformed Services (OCHAMPUS, Aurora, CO 80045-6900).

CHAMPUS supplemental insurance policies are sponsored by various private and nonprofit associations and groups to reimburse beneficiaries for the co-share amounts they must pay after CHAMPUS pays the government's share of the cost. Before you buy any supplement, carefully consider which plan best suits your individual needs. Each supplemental policy has its own rules concerning acceptance for preexisting conditions, eligibility requirements for the family, deductibles, mental health limitations, long-term illness, well-baby care, handicapped care, filing limitations, conversion to Medicare, widow's or widower's benefits, allowed payments for inpatient charges, and rules concerning allowable charges.

Get answers to the following questions—draft a "Q & A" checklist—to accelerate toward a good CHAMPUS supplement purchasing decision:

- Must you meet a deductible before the plan begins paying?
- Is there a maximum limit on benefits?
- Is there a preexisting condition clause? Or, is there a waiting period before the policy will pay for preexisting conditions?

- Will the plan cover amounts beyond what CHAMPUS allows?
- Does the plan pay for services that are not covered by CHAMPUS?
- Does the plan specifically not cover other conditions?
- Must certain kinds of care be approved before getting the care?
- Is inpatient care covered? Outpatient care? Long-term care?
- Will the plan pay the CHAMPUS outpatient deductible?
- Will the plan pay the patient's cost-share amount (under the CHAMPUS diagnosis-related group payment system)?
- Does the plan convert to a Medicare supplement? If so, must it be in force as a CHAMPUS supplement for any specified length of time before conversion?
- Will the plan cover you overseas?
- How will the plan require premium payments? Monthly? Quarterly? Annually?
- Will premium payments be increased? Under what conditions?
- Does the plan offer rates based on military status (active, retired), or on an age scale? What is the scale?
- What are the membership fees, if any, when you join the organization that sponsors the plan?
- Does the plan cover the servicemember when he or she retires?
- Does coverage continue for surviving spouses at no charge?
- What are the time limitations, if any, for claim filing?
- Does the plan have different rates for nonsmokers and smokers?

Retirees who have a health-care plan that pays before CHAMPUS should ask whether they need a CHAMPUS supplement if, between them, the employer's plan and CHAMPUS will pay most or all of their civilian medical bills.

CHAMPUS Supplement Providers

Increasing medical costs and limits built into CHAMPUS drive the need for CHAMPUS supplemental insurance coverage. NCOs on active duty must decide based on their personal circumstances whether they need supplemental insurance. Army parents may need supplemental coverage. Retirees, especially, are strongly encouraged to research available supplemental policies and elect coverage under a plan that best fits their needs.

The following CHAMPUS supplement contacts have been compiled from a list provided by the Department of Defense and an independent list researched by the revisor. The list excludes plans that don't cover NCOs or are aimed at members of other branches of the armed forces. Reputable plans are underwritten by reputable insurance companies. Be sure to inquire about underwriting before making a purchasing decision.

American Military Association
Retirees Association
Fort Snelling Station
P. O. Box 76
Minneapolis, MN 55440-0076
(800) 562-4076

American Military
AMRA Group Insurance Plan
P. O. Box 2510
Rockville, MD 20852-0510
(800) 638-2610 or (301) 816-0045

American Military Society
P. O. Box 50282
Washington, DC 20004-0282
(800) 843-2043

Armed Forces Benefit Association
AFDBSI
909 N. Washington St
Alexandria, VA 22314
(800) 776-2264

Armed Forces Benefit Services, Inc.
AFBA Bldg.,
909 N. Washington St.
Alexandria, VA 22314-1556
(703) 549-4455

Army Aviation Association of America
Membership Services, Inc.
304 Vincent Pl.
McLean, VA 22101
(800) 394-4000

Association of Personal Affairs
P. O. Box 3357
Austin, TX 78764-9969
(800) 451-9143

Association of the U.S. Army
Kirke-Van Orsdel, Inc.
400 Locust St., 8th Floor
Des Moines, IA 50306
(800) 247-7988

Enlisted Association of the
    National Guard
NGAUS Insurance Plans
P. O. Box 907
Minneapolis, MN 55440-0907
(800) 441-2590

Military Benefit Association
108 N. Center St.
P. O. Box 549
Vienna, VA 22183-0549
(800) 336-0100

Military Order of the Purple Heart
Membership Services, Inc.
1304 Vincent Pl.
McLean, VA 22101
(800) 394-4000

Military Order of the World Wars
Membership Services, Inc.
1304 Vincent Pl.
McLean, VA 22101
(800) 394-4000

Mutual of Omaha Insurance Co.
Mutual of Omaha Plaza
Omaha, NE 68175
(800) 228-7100

National Association for
    Uniformed Services
P. O. Box 96987
Washington, DC 20090-6987
(800) 854-6287

National Defense Transportation
    Association
Membership Services, Inc.
1304 Vincent Pl.
McLean, VA 22101
(800) 394-4000

National Guard Association
    of the United States
NGAUS Insurance Plans
P. O. Box 907
Minneapolis, MN 55440-9863
(800) 328-3323

Non Commissioned Officers
   Association
NCOA Membership Services
P. O. Box 105636
Atlanta, GA 30348-5636
(800) 662-2620

Retired Association for the
   Uniformed Services
RAUS Group Insurance
P. O. Box 2510
Rockville, MD 20852-0510
(800) 638-2610 or (301) 816-0045

The Retired Enlisted Association
P. O. Box 50584
Washington, DC 20091-0584
(800) 843-2043

The Uniformed Services Association
Membership Services, Inc.
1304 Vincent Pl.
McLean, VA 22101
(800) 421-1470

United Services Life Insurance Co.
4601 Fairfax Dr.
P. O. Box 3700
Arlington, VA 22203
(800) 424-2300

Credit Union Group Insurance
P. O. Box 2510
Rockville, MD 20852-0510
(800) 638-2610 or (301) 816-0045

You may also get more information from the following commercial insurance carriers who underwrite and administer various CHAMPUS supplements: Reliance Insurance Co., Association and Society Insurance Corp., Academy Life Insurance Co., Lincoln National Life Insurance Co., Hartford Life Insurance Co., Pioneer Life Insurance Co., Monumental Life Insurance Co., Continental Casualty Co., and Allianz Life Insurance Co.

DENTAL INSURANCE

Just as you are covered under the Army direct-care system for medical purposes, so are you covered for dental care. And, just as CHAMPUS covers your eligible family members, the Dependent Dental Plan (DDP*DELTA, known as Delta Dental) covers CHAMPUS-eligible family members for dental care. Delta Dental is offered by the Office of Civilian Health and Medical Program of the Uniformed Services. The plan provides broad dental coverage for family members. Some services are covered at 100 percent; others are covered at 80, 60, or 50 percent; and some are not covered at all. Covered services are limited by special rules and conditions described in the DDP*DELTA booklet *Evidence of Coverage: Uniformed Services Active Duty Dependents Dental Plan,* available at your local Army dental activity or HBA office.

The annual maximum—the total amount that DDP*DELTA will pay—for covered dental procedures other than orthodontics is $1,000 for each patient per contract year, which normally runs from August 1 to July 31. The lifetime maximum for orthodontic treatment is $1,200 for each patient. Even if your dentist recommends needed types of care, DDP*DELTA may not pay for some or any of the cost of that care. If you are unsure whether your plan covers a particular service, see your local HBA or contact the DDP*DELTA Customer Service Center: *west of the Mississippi*—DDP*DELTA, P. O. Box 269023, Sacramento, CA 95826-9023, phone (916) 381-9369 7 A.M. to 5 P.M. Pacific time; *east of the Mississippi*—DDP*DELTA, P. O. Box

9086, Farmington Hills, MI, 48333-9086, phone (313) 489-2240 7:30 A.M. to 5 P.M. eastern time. Louisiana is considered west of the Mississippi. Michigan residents should call (810) 489-2240.

You and your dentist are encouraged to submit a predetermination request for more complicated treatments. The request procedure is covered on page 50 of the DDP*DELTA booklet. A predetermination is a nonbinding written estimate of how much DDP*DELTA will cover for a particular service.

See dentists who participate in the plan to save money, time, and paperwork. Your local HBA can tell you if your current dentist is a participant, or "Delta dentist."

Delta dentists have agreed not to charge more than Delta-approved fees and will submit claim forms for you. Non-Delta dentists will bill you for their normal charges, which may be higher than the Delta-allowed amount. You pay the dentist yourself, then file a claim for reimbursement from DDP*DELTA

Unlike the CHAMPUS health and medical program, the DDP*DELTA does cost the sponsor a monthly premium. As of August 1994, the monthly premium for single coverage was $10 and the monthly premium for family coverage was $20—very inexpensive compared with similar civilian policies. Part of the total monthly premium is paid by the government; the balance is paid by the military sponsor ($10 or $20) through payroll deductions. Annotations on your end-of-month leave and earnings statement will reflect premium deductions beginning one month after your single dependent or family is enrolled.

Visit your local Army personnel office, update or verify dependent information in the Defense Enrollment Eligibility Reporting System (DEERS), and complete DD Form 2494 to enroll your family members. Certain enrollment restrictions apply and are covered in detail in the DDP*DELTA booklet. Coverage will begin on the first day of the month following the month in which the sponsor's payroll deduction begins. Coverage benefits end on the last day of the month for which a premium has been paid.

YOUR WILL
The importance of having a will cannot be overemphasized. You may not consider that you "own" very much, but not having a will could cause many legal complications after your death. If you were to die without a will—*intestate*—your estate would be distributed according to the descent and distribution laws of your state of legal residence, or in the case of real property located in another state, the laws of that state.

If you are married, both you and your spouse should have wills, even if each will makes the same distribution of property and assets. It is particularly important to have a will if you have minor children so that their interests can be protected through a guardianship of your choice in the event both you and your spouse die.

Once you have made your will, review it periodically to keep it up to date. As circumstances change, you may want to update it to be sure that it still expresses your desires about the distribution of your property and assets.

Keep your will in a safe place. The safest place to keep it (and other important papers) is in a safe-deposit box at your bank. It is not a bad idea to send a copy of your will together with a statement as to the location of the original to the principal beneficiary or the person named in the will as the executor.

PERSONAL AFFAIRS RECORD

The simplest way to keep your survivors informed about arrangements you have made for them is to prepare a record of your personal affairs. As a minimum, be sure that they know the location of the following:

- Your birth certificate and those of all members of your immediate family.
- Your marriage certificate.
- Divorce papers or previous spouse's death certificate, if applicable.
- Your life insurance policies.

If you put the original of your will and other key documents in a safe-deposit box, be sure that your spouse or executor has access to it. If you die and no one has access to the box, a court order must be obtained to open it.

A personal affairs record is a necessity for the married soldier because it serves as a vital source of information for his or her family.

A personal affairs record can be detailed, but make sure it includes at least the following:

- Insurance policy numbers and their amounts. Include automobile and home-owner's policies.
- Previous years' tax records.
- Copies of titles and bills of sale.
- Information on bank accounts.
- A list of all pay allotments.
- Information regarding any veterans benefits to which you may be entitled.

If you are married, be sure someone in your family knows how to pay your household bills, when they are due, and where to find them.

MILITARY RECORDS

Keep a file of all records about your military service. Keep copies of orders, discharge certificate, awards, citations, letters of appreciation and commendation, medical and dental records, Leave and Earnings Statements, and other information about your military history, even old NCOERs. Information is frequently needed throughout your active service career and afterward, when you apply for certain benefits.

Emergency Data

Your DD Form 93, *Record of Emergency Data,* must be accurate and up to date at all times. This record tells your MILPO where your next of kin can be located immediately. It gives the name of the person you want to receive your pay if you are missing in action as well as other information of benefit to your dependents.

POWER OF ATTORNEY

A power of attorney is a legal document by which you give another person the power to act as your agent, either for some particular purpose or for the transaction of your business in general.

In the wrong hands, a power of attorney can ruin you because the agent who holds such a power has, within the limits granted by it, full authority to deal with your property without consulting you. *Grant it only to someone you can trust* and then only when you must.

	YOUR CHAIN OF COMMAND	PERSONNEL NCO OR OFFICER	RE-ENLISTMENT NCO	JUDGE ADVOCATE	INSPECTOR GENERAL	FINANCE OFFICER	CHAPLAIN	HOUSING OFFICER	TRANSPORTATION OFFICER	AMERICAN RED CROSS	ARMY COMMUNITY SERVICES	ARMY EMERGENCY RELIEF	EDUCATION OFFICER/ADVISOR
APPEALS	1	2		2	2		2						
ASSIGNMENT, REASSIGNMENT, MOS & PROFICIENCY PAY	1	1				2							
REENLISTMENT	1		1										
PERSONNEL MATTERS: PROMOTION, REDUCTION, DISCHARGE, RETIREMENT	1	1	2	2									
VETERANS' BENEFITS													
COMPLAINTS (REQUESTS FOR ASSISTANCE)	1	2	2	2	2	2	2	2	2	2	2	2	
DEBTS AND CIVILIAN CREDITORS	1	1		2		2	2				2		
DEPENDENTS' SCHOOLS	1	1									2		
FAMILY AND RELIGIOUS AFFAIRS	1	2					1			2	2		
TRAVEL OF DEPENDENTS, SHIPMENT OF POV AND HOUSEHOLD GOODS	1	2				2			1		2		
MEDICAL SERVICE (INDIVIDUAL & DEPENDENTS)	1	1											
PAY, ALLOWANCES AND INCENTIVE PAY	1	2				1							
LEAVES AND PASSES	1	2											
INSURANCE, ALL TYPES (SGLI & COMMERCIAL)	1	1				2							
LEGAL ASSISTANCE, INCLUDING U.S. AND FOREIGN LAW, WILLS AND POWERS OF ATTORNEY	1			1									
MILITARY EDUCATION	1	2	2										
NON-MILITARY EDUCATION	1	2											2
PX, COMMISSARY, QM SALES STORE	1				2								
GOVERNMENT QUARTERS, OFF POST HOUSING	1	2						1					
REGISTRATION/OPERATION OF PRIVATELY OWNED VEHICLE (POV), REGISTRATION OF FIREARMS	1												
ENTRY INTO USA, PASSPORT, VISA, NATURALIZATION, IMMIGRATION, BIRTH CERTIFICATE (Children born in foreign country)	1	2		1							2		
HOME CONDITIONS AND EMERGENCY LEAVE	1	2					2			2	2	2	
EMERGENCY FINANCIAL ASSISTANCE	1	2					1			2	2	2	
POSTAL SERVICE	1												
DRUG AND ALCOHOL REHABILITATION PROGRAM	1						2				1		

Guide for obtaining information and assistance. This chart shows some of the staff officers and support agencies who can help soldiers with advice and assistance in their personal affairs. In all cases, personnel should first contact the right person in their chain of command for guidance: immediate supervisors, squad leaders, first sergeants, or unit commanders. Number one (1) above indicates primary or key contacts; number two (2) indicates other contacts, as applicable. *Courtesy* SOLDIERS *magazine*

You may never need a power of attorney, or if you do need one, it may only be required to perform certain acts and no others—a limited or *special* power of attorney. Always consult a legal assistance officer or a lawyer before assigning a power of attorney, and cancel it as soon as it is no longer required.

BANK ACCOUNTS

If you are married, you and your spouse should decide who is going to keep the accounts. Make them joint accounts so that if anything happens to you, your family will have ready access to funds.

Current regulations require soldiers to have guaranteed direct deposit to a financial institution. With a guaranteed direct deposit from the U.S. Army Finance Center, you do not have to bother with anything but picking up your leave and earnings statement on payday.

DECIDING WHERE TO LIVE

Military families often must rent local housing while waiting for government quarters to become available. If you find yourself in that situation, you might want to consider renting an apartment on a month-by-month basis. Should you sign a lease for a specified period of time and then have to break it because a set of quarters unexpectedly becomes available, you have to forfeit your deposit (usually an amount equal to a month's rent).

Renting an apartment gives single soldiers a degree of independence and privacy not available in the barracks, and for this reason, many soldiers want to move off post.

Whether a single soldier can move off post depends on the following:

• Your post commander's policy. It is also up to the commanding officer of your unit. Some commanders are liberal in granting this privilege; it depends upon your unit's mission. Commanders of headquarters units can be more liberal than those of tactical or combat support units.

• The amount and quality of troop housing available. Some small, specialized units have trouble finding adequate troop housing, especially at overcrowded installations in metropolitan areas. Where sufficient troop housing is available, however, commanders normally fill the billets up first before allowing lower-ranking single personnel to move off post.

• Nonabuse of the privilege. Your commander will revoke permission to live off post as soon as you start coming to work late, running up debts, or causing disturbances among the local population.

Be sure that you can afford to live off post. Your military pay combined with your housing and substance allowances may be enough, depending on the geographical area, but just enough and no more. If supporting yourself in an apartment leaves you flat broke at the end of the month, you are better off living in the barracks.

Some soldiers find it a good idea to team up with two or three friends and rent a place by splitting all the costs. This is an excellent idea if your companions can be trusted to pay their share, take care of the communal areas, and respect your privacy and personal property.

PERSONAL PROPERTY

Joint ownership of property can have certain advantages in establishing an automatic and known passage of ownership upon the death of one owner and can also have certain disadvantages. Inquire into federal and state laws regarding ownership of family property, and take actions that put your estate in the most favorable ownership positions.

In the event of your death, your immediate personal effects will be forwarded at government expense to the person entitled to their custody. This does not give the recipient legal title to them, but they should be retained for disposition under the law.

If you own real estate in your name and it is not paid for, show on your personal affairs record whether there is a mortgage or a deed of trust against it, along with the name of the person or organization to whom you are indebted. Also include information about property taxes and insurance.

Transfer of automobile ownership is sometimes complicated because of varying state laws. Remember that joint titling may make you or your spouse subject to personal property taxes—active-duty personnel are generally exempt from payment of personal property taxes, so adding your spouse's name to an automobile title can cost you a lot of money.

INCOME TAXES

Military pay in general is subject to income tax. You do not pay tax on subsistence, quarters, and uniform allowances. Dislocation allowance, however, is taxable.

Any nonmilitary earnings, including the pay received while employed during off-duty hours and the income of any of your dependents, are taxable. Military pay is excluded from federal income tax for service in any area that the president of the United States designates by executive order to be a combat zone.

The Soldiers' and Sailors' Civil Relief Act assures that a state in which a soldier is stationed but is not the member's legal residence cannot tax service pay. Legal residence is established at enlistment or thereafter when a soldier executes DD Form 2058, *State of Legal Residence Certificate*.

The following states do not withhold income tax from the pay of military personnel: Alaska, Florida, Nevada, New Hampshire, South Dakota, Tennessee, Texas, Washington, and Wyoming. Soldiers claiming legal residence in foreign countries or U.S. territories are also exempt from paying state income taxes. Appendix K, "State Tax Withholding," to AR 37-104-3 contains specific information relative to each state for which withholding tax applies.

PERSONAL CONDUCT

NCOs should be above reproach at all times. This does not mean that a slip automatically spells disaster. Keep this in mind when your subordinates err.

Borrowing and Lending

Neither a borrower, nor a lender be;
For loan oft loses both itself and friend,
And borrowing dulls the edge of husbandry.
                                        —William Shakespeare

Never lend money to other soldiers for interest. Be careful about lending money to *anyone* based only on a verbal agreement, no matter how much is involved. Of course, if a friend or coworker asks for a small sum occasionally, to tide him over on a heavy date or to buy lunch, give it to him if you can afford to. But never telegraph through the outfit that you are an "easy touch." If you do, every freeloader in the unit will hit you up for small loans, which they will seldom repay. Young soldiers are particularly vulnerable to this sort of thing. Guard against it yourself and advise your subordinates to do the same. Be alert for soldiers who are habitual borrowers. They're heading for trouble, and if they are your subordinates, soon their trouble will be yours.

If a friend is really in trouble and you can help with a loan, then what are friends for? But have him back it up by signing a promissory note. This note is merely insurance against the unexpected, not an indication of distrust; his note will enable you to claim any unpaid debt against his estate, should he die. If your friend cannot pay you back all at once, be sure to give him receipts for each payment he does make. This will help you both later on if there is any disagreement.

Gambling

NCOs should *never* gamble with subordinates, no matter what the circumstances. Gambling can be as addictive and as ruinous to some people as alcohol and drugs are to others. When you acquire financial responsibility for other people—your family— they must always come first. Don't allow what can be an innocent and pleasant pastime to develop into a compulsion that will wreck your family. Never allow sharks—card, pool, loan, or otherwise—to operate in your unit.

Adultery

Adultery does occur and is not restricted to any particular rank. The best advice you can receive in regard to this subject and the best you can give someone else about it is this: *Don't do it.*

At some time in your career, though, the temptation to err will be strong, especially where alcohol and sex are readily available, the idle hours are long, and diversions are few. Precisely how a person deals with this problem depends on the individual. Keep up an active correspondence with your spouse. Go easy on the booze. Concentrate on your military duty, and cultivate your hobbies.

Should you succumb, you will have to live with your indiscretion. Repeated unfaithfulness becomes general knowledge in a small, tightly knit military community. Your soldiers will lose respect for you. Your superiors will give you frosty looks, and eventually someone in the chain of command will tell you to straighten up, or else. Adultery hurts everyone—you, your partner, family, friends. But adultery is particularly hard on the innocent parties and especially children.

A single person who enters into an adulterous relationship with a married man or woman is not much better off than the married person who is unfaithful. The single person's career (and life) can be as easily ruined by adultery as that of a married person. Adultery is punishable under the UCMJ.

Lying

Society would crumble if it were not for the accepted social lie. We all know that nobody wants to listen to someone else's personal problems. And nobody in his right mind tells everyone just exactly what he thinks of them. Military life is no different from civilian life in this regard.

Never lie to cover up mistakes, however, whether yours or those of your subordinates. Lying to a superior is wrong. Once a superior loses faith in you because of a lie discovered, no matter how small that lie may be, you may never be able to recover that confidence. And once you get away with a lie, it sometimes becomes necessary to tell more and more of them to cover up the initial one, until you create a tissue of lies that sooner or later will tear and expose the truth.

Indebtedness

The good NCO pays off debts. Keep tight control of your budget. Do not allow yourself to fall behind on credit payments. This will require restraint and self-denial at times. A letter of indebtedness from a creditor will harm your career as well as damage your reputation in the business world and make it harder for you to get credit when you really need it.

Our whole economy operates on indebtedness, and most of us are in debt for something: homes, cars, credit card services, and so on. You will, from time to time, counsel your soldiers on their indebtedness. Help them to learn to budget and overcome a vicious cycle.

Self-Perception

Sergeants have never been exactly humble. Captain Francis Grose "advised" the sergeants of the British Army of 1782: "Into whatever company you are admitted, you must be careful to impress everyone with an idea of your own consequence, and to make people believe that the sergeants are the only useful and intelligent men in the corps." Captain Grose was actually satirizing the attitude he found prevalent among some of the British NCOs of his day. Captain Grose's sergeants were in the habit of inflating their egos and boosting their sense of self-importance by bragging about how indispensable they were. These men, and those who think like them today, are right, but for the wrong reasons.

NCOs have always been important. In units in which the NCOs are highly motivated, mission oriented, and supportive of one another, things *click*. In units in which the NCOs are interested only in themselves, officers' careers get ruined, young soldiers quit the Army in disgust, and things go *clunk*. May you always serve in units that click, but should you have the misfortune to be assigned to one in which the clunk, *turn things around*. Don't wait for the officers to catch on, clue them in. As for your fellow NCOs, tell them, *follow me!* Rise to the occasion and do what has to be done. Do not try to find ways to get out of doing things. Do not look back. Get the job done. Never let there be any mistake that you are the finest.

12

Contemporary Issues

Moderation in temper is always a virtue, but moderation in principle is always a vice.   —Thomas Paine, 1792

American patriot Thomas Paine's "moderation in principle" can be interpreted to mean lowering standards. Do not! Instead, set and achieve high personal conduct and behavior standards and try your best to maintain them. Encourage your subordinates—*teach them how*—to conduct and behave themselves in a professional manner. Excellent conduct and performance are trademark personality traits of the professional NCO and will make a difference when hard advice must be given and difficult decisions must be made.

PROFESSIONAL ETHICS
Of the fourteen general principles of ethical government conduct, the one listed first is so placed for a reason—"Public service is a public trust, requiring [soldiers] to place loyalty to the Constitution, the laws, and ethical principles above private gain"— which goes to the heart of selfless and ethical service. Developing, achieving, maintaining, and teaching high ethical standards is NCO business.

In the January 1994 issue of *Army* magazine, letters-to-the-editor writers said the following about ethics:
- "Every day is a training day in the Army, ethics included."
- "No matter how professional an officer or NCO considers himself or herself to be, there is always room for improvement. Ethics is one area to which we have merely given lip service."
- "To me, character starts within a man's mind. Either he will compromise on small principles which he thinks no one will notice, or he will not." (Attributed by the letter writer to a midshipman's quote in *Time* magazine more than 50 years ago.)

Noncommissioned leaders and supervisors frequently face ethical problems that, if not handled properly, can damage or in some cases destroy unit cohesion, credibility, discipline, and effectiveness. You must therefore persuade your soldiers to do what is right, or exercise your authority to enforce conduct and behavior standards. And you must always set the example.

No Middle Ground
Nothing says more and *nothing* says less about an NCO than the way he or she acts or

behaves on and off duty. The honorable corporal, for example, is not the one whose conduct is exemplary on duty but despicable off duty, when he or she mentally or physically abuses family members. A reliable sergeant is not the one who accomplishes a key task, then later falsely reports sick-in-quarters because of a hangover. An honest staff sergeant is not the one whose NCO Evaluation Report reflects support for the Army Equal Opportunity Program but who secretly is a bigot, racist, or sexist.

The trustworthy platoon sergeant is not the one who stays focused on the commander's intent in battle but later distorts command philosophy during a media interview. A good first sergeant is not the one who deftly manages most company matters but downplays a subordinate's personal problem until the soldier goes AWOL. And the most conscientious command sergeant major is not the one who is always present during field training but habitually fails to enforce the Army's strict environmental preservation and pollution control policies.

The Professional Army Ethic
Fortunately, most NCOs do not fit into the portraits illustrated above; instead, they try to live the four-part Professional Army Ethic:
* Loyalty.
* Duty.
* Selfless service.
* Integrity.

Some NCOs are aware of the Ethics in Government Act of 1978. Most NCOs have attended periodic Common Military Training based on the Department of Defense *Joint Ethics Regulation*. And all NCOs who attend NCO Education System courses have been informed about AR 600-50, *Standards of Conduct*. Basically, the law and regulations address proper and improper ways to accept gifts, handle financial matters, seek part-time employment, use position or rank, raise funds, teach, speak in public, and write for compensation. The law also impels soldiers to always act with integrity, to use Army property and soldiers for government business only, to never use official position for personal gain, and to never coerce a soldier to help pay for a gift to a superior. These are easy requirements to meet, really, when you look at larger ethical issues.

When faced with an ethical matter, tackle it with the following reasoning process: Identify the problem; consider legal standards and national, Army, and individual values; and make a decision. FM 22-100, *Military Leadership*, explains the process. The manual also states, "The ethical development of self and subordinates is a key component of leader development. . . . Leaders must make a personal commitment to the Professional Army Ethic and strive to develop this commitment throughout the force."

NCOs may also turn to Training Circular 22-6, *The Army Noncommissioned Officer Guide*, which makes this point: "If the NCO is the 'backbone' of the Army, then the Professional Army Ethic is the 'heart' of the NCO Corps, and from that heart springs our pride."

When reported and put under command or public scrutiny, an NCO with a problem of the sort depicted above—or of the more serious type illustrated below—embarrasses and discredits the Army. And more importantly, a soldier who has or causes ethical problems distracts his or her leaders from mission accomplishment.

The Cost of Unethical Conduct

Suppose a heinously unethical act committed by a soldier made national news at a critical time for the Army, such as when the force was staging for battle a few short years ago in Southwest Asia. A resulting cry of "Foul!" from the public could have turned U.S. national support against the Army when it was most needed. Fortunately, the public remained squarely behind the military. Relatively few United States–led coalition casualties were suffered in the Persian Gulf War, while Iraqi military forces were severely punished. Kuwait was liberated and its oil fields were recovered, repaired, and protected—vast oil resources in Saudi Arabia suffered no damage—and thus U.S. and international vital interest in the region was preserved.

Now consider the profoundly negative national and international peace movement reactions to the My Lai massacre in South Vietnam during 1968. The unethical, criminal conduct of a single troop leader accelerated the loss of public support for the war effort, which resulted in a withdrawal policy that conceded defeat and capped an all-for-nothing human toll of horrendous proportion. The act also embarrassed and severely damaged the credibility and morale of the majority of U.S. soldiers who served with honor and distinction.

Combined, the numbers of Americans and Vietnamese killed, wounded, orphaned, displaced, relocated, captured, and missing totaled nearly 17.8 *million* soldiers and civilians, according to *Funk & Wagnalls New Encyclopedia*. In effect, the 58,000 American soldiers who died in the war, the 153,000 wounded, those still missing, and the thousands of veterans suffering today because of service-related illness are among the victims of a U.S. effort defeated by soured public sentiment. Certainly, the My Lai atrocity also factored into the animosity many citizens felt toward the U.S. military through the early 1970s.

NCOs must uphold and enforce ethical behavior and conduct standards to retain the trust and confidence of superior officers, including commissioned troop leaders who may face extremely hard ethical decisions on a future battlefield. The effort on your part, at your level, will help enable the Army to maintain the unwavering support of the nation.

Domestic Ethics

The best NCOs help fellow soldiers make ethically correct decisions; they also treat their families with respect, wholeheartedly support the Army Equal Opportunity Program, and avoid substance abuse like it was the bubonic plague. Noncommissioned professionals remain objective and uphold their binding oath or affirmation to support superior officers who must administer controversial personnel (homosexuality) and health (AIDS) policies.

NCOs, if they must, may lead with the full legal force of general military or delegated command authority under the provisions of AR 600-20, *Army Command Policy*. The finest NCOs rarely need to lean on regulations, however. Instead, they instinctively do what is right, for the right reasons, when necessary, no matter how hard doing so may be. Excellent NCOs earn their stripes every day.

THE ENVIRONMENT

In his 1992 primer for NCO environmental awareness, SGM Dan Hubbard of the Sergeants Major Academy addressed legal obligations and a vision statement for Army environmental strategy. His vision is this: "The Army will be a national leader in environmental and natural resource stewardship for present and future generations as an integral part of our mission." Every NCO should share the sergeant major's vision.

The NCO's Role in Environmental Stewardship (document number 62-122-416-N3) was published to be used in NCO Education System and functional courses taught at Fort Bliss, Texas. But NCOs throughout the Army can benefit from it. In it Hubbard said, "The senior leadership of our country has set in motion new laws governing our environment and the way we as soldiers train. As early as October 1991, the Training and Doctrine Command (TRADOC) established an environmental ethic that stated TRADOC's commitment to protecting our national heritage. We as NCOs are responsible for both enforcing the laws and regulations and instilling a sense of urgency and need in our subordinates."

Routine use of Army training areas causes soil erosion, gullying, and streambed sedimentation; decreases water quality; and destroys forested areas and ground-cover vegetation. Such destruction creates unsafe conditions, diminishes tactical advantage, hits the installation budget through fines and cleanup operations, and causes training downtime because of accidents, investigations, and repairs.

SOLDIERS magazine published the telephone numbers any soldier may use to call the Army Environmental Information Response Line. NCOs may use the hotline to ask questions or discuss environmental problems. The numbers are as follows:

- In the United States, (800) 872-3845.
- From overseas, (410) 671-1699; or DSN 584-1699.

The hotline's cost is tiny compared with the Army's investment of millions of dollars each year to preserve training areas in the United States and overseas.

Safety is among the many good reasons for the environmental investment. In the mid-1980s, one soldier drowned when the M-2 Bradley fighting vehicle he was driving slid into a sinkhole caused by environmental damage. By 1986, Army engineers addressed training-related environmental problems by constructing check dams and water retention basins to prevent runoff. Today, preservation and conservation are hot topics among senior commanders.

In another *SOLDIERS* magazine article, Bill Nicholls of the U.S. Army Europe Environmental Office said, "I don't feel we've deliberately abused the environment anywhere we've been. I think we've been a good neighbor. Every single soldier has a contribution to make and an obligation to observe environmental policy, both as a citizen of the world, and as a member of his nation's forces."

NCOs should know, obey, and enforce environmental protection and conservation policies. At a minimum, abide by the following rules:

- Avoid maneuver damage and report observed damage as soon as possible.
- Do not dig, cut down or "dismember" trees, or otherwise alter the environment unless you have approval from proper military authority (usually your commanding officer).
- Do not contaminate the soil or water with petroleum, oil, or lubricants (POL). Report POL leaks or spills immediately to your chain of command.
- Do not burn or bury garbage, refuse, or rubbish.
- Do not use tracers during training, set off pyrotechnics, or allow open flames in areas likely to catch fire.
- Obey posted environmental signs.
- Include environmental preservation in training plans.

The National Environmental Policy Act (NEPA) and the Federal Facilities Compliance Act (FFCA) are two overarching federal laws established to protect the environment and conserve natural resources. NEPA requires all federal agencies to consider environmental effects when planning and making decisions. AR 600-2, *Environmental Effects of Army Actions*, contains Army procedures for implementing NEPA. The FFCA authorizes regulatory agencies to impose fines on federal agencies that violate the Resource Conservation and Recovery Act. The FFCA may subject Army installations to fines and penalties of up to $25,000 for *each* violation.

FM 25-101, *Battle Focused Training*, states that leaders must protect resources, including land used for training. Soldiers must understand that protecting the environment is as central to the training objective as safety and mission accomplishment.

MILITARY AND THE MEDIA

When the media were excluded from covering Operation Urgent Fury on the island of Grenada in October 1983, military-media relations got so bad that a federal commission was formed to study and recommend solutions to the problem. Since that time, Army Public Affairs officials throughout the Army have worked to better educate commanders about press relations.

NCOs have a role to play in teaching soldiers about the media. If your soldiers see unescorted members of the press—newspaper, magazine, radio, or television reporters and crew members—they should inform their chain of command. This point is stressed during Media on the Battlefield exercises at the Joint Readiness Training Center (JRTC) at Fort Polk, Louisiana, and the National Training Center (NTC) at Fort Irwin, California.

Bona fide members of the press provide a service to the nation. Still, commanders often shun coverage because mission security and soldiers' lives come before immediately meeting the military's Constitutional obligation to account for its actions. The military-media relationship continues to be marked by a contest of wills regarding the "right to know" versus "operational security" (OPSEC).

Animosity between the military and the media does a disservice to both and the nation. For years, annual national polls have shown that citizens rate the military at the top of lists of the most credible of all vital national institutions. The press nevertheless is entitled under the First Amendment to investigate military activities and report news to the nation.

Thousands of soldiers participating in JRTC and NTC exercises are taught to say *nothing* to the media unless doing so is approved by escorting Army Public Affairs officials *and* the chain of command. When approval is granted, soldiers must guard against making comments about troop strength, position, direction, condition, tactics, strategy, or other factors an enemy may use to gain an advantage. Giving operational information will result in OPSEC leaks—the kind that compromise the mission and get units destroyed.

Some influential media members indignantly say the military is overly protective. It is indeed, because hostile enemy agent handlers use a low-tech/high-tech process called "content analysis" to piece together big tactical and strategic pictures from bits of information provided by soldiers to the media. U.S. intelligence services do the same thing. So do competing businesses and industries.

Professional media representatives—the majority of the credentialed U.S. press corps—understand and respect the Army's need to maintain security. Reporters willingly (sometimes grudgingly) comply with preestablished ground rules in an operational area. Occasionally, a reporter will try to circumvent proper military authority to get the story. Doing so can get the reporter and soldiers killed or captured.

In the spring 1991 issue of NCO Journal, MSG Ron Hatcher of Army Public Affairs said, "Advances in communications technology and the nature of low- and mid-intensity conflict make it such that any soldier can be approached by members of the news media during combat. Sergeants should train their soldiers so they know how to respond to questions without detracting from the mission or violating OPSEC." Hatcher said NCOs may use the "Five Knows" to train soldiers:
- Know the role and purpose of the American press, who do a job vital to democracy by keeping the public, your loved ones, and other soldiers informed.
- Know who you are talking to by *verifying* that media members in your area are escorted by an Army Public Affairs officer or NCO, or are registered by the corps or division public affairs office. Verify registration through command or staff channels.
- Know who will hear you, that whatever you say could be in the hands of the enemy within minutes because of modern press technology, which is not secure.
- Know your rights; it is your choice whether to speak to reporters—unless your leaders have decided that doing so would interfere with or jeopardize the mission.
- Know your limits; that is, do not talk about anything above your level, and do not speculate or repeat rumors. Remember that your comments represent your personal opinions and knowledge, not necessarily the views of your unit or the Army.

For more information about media training, contact your servicing Army Public Affairs Office.

ABSENCE WITHOUT LEAVE AND DESERTION
FM 22-101, *Leadership Counseling,* and AR 630-10, which among several topics covers absence without leave (AWOL), should each contain specific information about AWOL prevention—but they do not. FM 22-101 does not include in its "situations" section an AWOL scenario. In fact, no mention of AWOL is made in the counseling field manual. AR 630-10 merely lists after-the-fact policy and procedural matters. Neither addresses the steps leaders should take to *prevent* unauthorized absence.

FM 22-101 does give readers a lot of good advice about counseling soldiers with problems, but it does not specifically address the AWOL issue. Leaders need to know that they should use the same preventive measures that work well in other situations: Stay tuned to your soldiers' needs and problems, conduct regular professional and personal counseling, and ensure needs are met and problems resolved. "An ounce of prevention . . .

". . . is worth a pound of cure." After a soldier goes AWOL the unit leaders must store the soldier's personal belongings and turn in organizational issue items. Leaders change the soldier's status on unit manning documents and the duty roster, report the matter to higher authority, conduct an immediate inquiry to determine the soldier's location, notify the provost marshal (within 48 hours), and mail a notification letter to next of kin (on the 10th day). All of these steps are described in DA Pamphlet 600-8, *Management and Administrative Procedures.* The official next-of-kin letter is in AR 630-10 and communicates the following:

Dear Kinfolk,

I regret to inform you that PFC Kinfolk, Jr., has been absent without leave from this unit since such 'n' such date. Junior's absence could result in a trial by court-martial with loss of pay and allowances, which could mean his dependents would lose all rights to receive allotments, medical care, commissary and post exchange privileges, and other military benefits. Continued absence could also result in confinement or dismissal with other than honorable or bad conduct discharge.

If you know where Junior is, please urge him to return immediately to military control at the nearest military installation in order to avoid serious consequences or prolonged unauthorized absence.

Rest assured that he will be given a fair hearing and the opportunity to present any information on his behalf.

Sincerely,

The Commander

On the 31st day of a soldier's absence the unit commander drops the member from the unit rolls (DFR). If considered a "special category" absentee, the soldier may be dropped sooner. A special category soldier is one with access to top secret information during the last 12 months or current assignment to a special mission unit, according to AR 630-10, which also covers defection to another country. When placed into a DFR status, the former member is declared a deserter or defector.

When the soldier is dropped, the unit commander prepares a charge sheet, DD Form 458, for desertion (or defection) and any other military infractions under the UCMJ. Next, the commander prepares DD Form 553, *Warrant for Apprehension*. These two documents, along with a DA Form 4187, *Personnel Action Request* (entering the soldier into DFR status), constitute a deserter packet. The packet is necessary for a warrant to be entered into the FBI National Crime Information Center for apprehension.

If the soldier returns to military control prior to submission of the DFR packet, the soldier will be carried only as AWOL and remain assigned to the unit. DFR packets submitted after a soldier has returned to the unit could put the commander and the Army at risk of erroneous arrest and lawsuits. So follow proper reporting procedures to the letter.

If your commander is unsure about what to do in a particular case, the Army Deserter Information Point (ADIP) operates a 24-hour information line at DSN 699-3711, or commercial (317) 542-3711. The ADIP is located at Fort Benjamin Harrison, Indiana, which is closing not later than 1997. Contact your local provost marshal for the new number when Fort Harrison closes.

FAMILY ADVOCACY PROGRAM

It is said that when a person dies, the two most important things left behind are work and children. The saying should list children first. A soldier's children—and spouse—should be the most important people in his or her life. If they are not, it may be time for the soldier to reconsider priorities. Nothing about service, no family issue at home or in quarters, and no external pressure or stress can justify abusive treatment of loved ones.

It is wrong to verbally abuse (curse, defame, intimidate, belittle, embarrass, malign), or inflict physical pain (slap, hit, punch, kick, or otherwise harm), or neglect (omit necessary care for) the people who rely on you for their support, welfare, and safety—and who probably love you very much. Deal with the problems leading to the abuse. Do not vent frustration on family members. Cool off. Regroup your emotions. Refocus your attitude. Ask for forgiveness, and show loved ones that they come first. If you cannot, or if you have tried to avoid an abusive nature but failed, then call the local Army Family Advocacy Office to get help. If you supervise an abusive soldier or know someone else who is an abuser, follow the guidance in this section.

Public Law 135 provides that any individual who has reason to believe that a child is a victim of either child abuse or neglect shall make a report to the Child Protection Service. Failure to make such a report is a Class B misdemeanor. The penalty for a Class B offense is 180 days in jail and/or a fine of up to $1,000. There is no confidentiality between husband and wife or between physician and patient in reporting of child abuse. By law, it must be reported.

Here are national statistics provided by the Family Advocacy Program that relate the scope and serious nature of domestic violence:

* It occurs among every race and ethnic group, and at every socioeconomic level.
* Ninety percent of abusers are not mentally ill; they do need to learn new ways of dealing with conflict and how to reduce their need to control.
* Once it has happened, domestic violence tends to occur again and get more severe.
* There are about 200,000 reported cases of child abuse per year.
* About 800,000 cases of child neglect are reported each year.
* Child sexual abuse and molestation cases total 60,000 per year.
* Cases of child emotional abuse are unestimated.
* Most police who die in the line of duty are killed answering domestic violence calls.
* One fourth of all murders occur within the family—most between spouses.
* Spouse abuse occurs in up to six out of every ten American marriages.

Child and spouse abuse are extremely sensitive matters. Commanding generals at installations throughout the Army take a grim view of abusive soldiers.

Remember the fictitious corporal early in this chapter who performed well on the job but abused family members? What do you think a commanding officer would do about the matter? Forget consideration for job performance; the corporal would likely receive formal counseling up the chain of command, swift and just punishment if the circumstance warranted it, and command referral to officials of the Army Family Advocacy Program.

If a soldier's dependent reports abuse to you, it is your duty to immediately report the matter to your chain of command. Your superiors, acting within command channels, may take it upon themselves to investigate the allegation. If they do, advise them to promptly inform Family Advocacy officials to comply with Public Law 135. If you know that the abuse victims need protection, you should also advise that the military police or local civilian authorities be informed.

Abuse is a significant contemporary issue in the military, according to the May 16, 1994, issue of *Washington Times,* which said, "Spousal abuse in U.S. military families is occurring at double the civilian rate and every week someone dies at the hands of a relative in uniform, *Time* magazine reported yesterday." According to the Washington, D.C., newspaper, the national magazine cited a confidential Army survey that indicated abuse rose quickly, from nearly 28,000 instances reported in military families in 1986 to more than 46,000 cases in 1993—*a 60 percent increase during the period that connoted abuse in one of every three Army families.* The survey results stunned senior Army officials.

Army Times covered the story in June 1994 and reported that, of the 55,000 soldiers surveyed, nearly a third of the males acknowledged engaging in either minor or severe violence, including kicking, biting, punching, choking, or threatening with a weapon. The combined figures were higher, 40 percent, for female soldiers. The newspaper also reported potential causes of abuse, such as pressures and stresses associated with downsizing, transitions, and base closings. These factors may contribute to abuse but are not responsible for it. People are.

It is important to stress to an abusive soldier that most reported incidents of abuse or neglect lead to treatment and assistance, not to prosecution. Family Advocacy officials will work to preserve and protect the family unit. Program officials can verify whether a soldier is an abuser, then treat and rehabilitate both the abuser and the victims. A soldier's participation in the program is not intended to harm a military career; it is designed to be supportive and offer needed assistance. If abuse continues, however, officials may make recommendations regarding criminal or administrative actions. In cases where violence continues and when persons refuse to cooperate, command involvement must be initiated.

ALCOHOL AND DRUG ABUSE
As an NCO, you will at some time in your service encounter soldiers who depend on or abuse alcohol and other drugs. A drug is defined as "any substance which by its chemical nature alters structure or function in the living organism" (AR 600-85). This definition includes alcohol, glue, and aerosols, among many others. The harm and misery done to soldiers by substance abuse are incalculable.

Alcohol Abuse
AR 600-85 states that "the use of alcohol is legal [provided the consumer is of legal age] and [generally] socially acceptable, but it should not become the purpose or focus of any military social activity. Abuse or excessive use of alcohol will not be condoned or accepted as part of any military tradition, ceremony, or event."

It is your business to take action when the welfare of your troops is jeopardized. Document symptoms of abuse, seek professional advice from the local Community Counseling office, and inform your chain of command.

Drug Abuse
AR 600-85 is clear that drug abuse in the NCO corps is unacceptable: Abusers "have violated the special trust and confidence that the Army has placed in them." An NCO who is caught buying, selling, distributing, or using illegal drugs will be punished and separated from the Army.

Urinalysis testing is commonplace and random. If an NCO prescreens positive for substance abuse, the sample will be verified by a supporting forensic laboratory. A verified drug user may face the consequence of a court-martial and penalties including confinement, loss of all pay and allowances, and a less than honorable (e.g., bad conduct or dishonorable) discharge. Junior enlisted soldiers who abuse drugs may face the same consequences, but more often receive nonjudicial punishment (an Article 15), including loss of pay, reduction, and the stigma of reduction attached to their official records.

A few years ago, one bird colonel looked across his desk at a specialist who had been positively identified as a drug abuser. After announcing punishment in the field grade Article 15 proceeding (loss of pay, reduction to private E-2, and 45 days each of restriction and extra duty), the colonel—serious as death—said, "In Vietnam, I remember a soldier who took drugs. He almost got us killed because he was high. You remind me of him. I want that rank off your collar as soon as you leave my office." The message: No drugs tolerated in America's Army. Comply and enforce compliance.

Prevention and Control

The Alcohol and Drug Abuse Prevention and Control Program (ADAPCP) is an Army tool NCOs may use to counter the problem. The ADAPCP is a command program in which alcohol and other drug abuse and all related activities are addressed. Local ADAPCP clinical directors work for local medical treatment facility commanders. Program objectives are as follows:

- Prevent abuse.
- Identify abusers.
- Restore rehabilitated soldiers to duty or separate failures from service.
- Provide evaluation, research, and substance abuse education.
- Sustain the program.

You can help, too, by educating your soldiers. Motivate any abuser to recognize the advantages of self-referral. Otherwise, it is your responsibility to ensure that identified abusers receive command referral to the program. Abusers who do not cooperate and who are not rehabilitated will be separated.

The summer 1993 issue of NCO Journal advised supervisors to monitor and document job performance; confront an abuser (using counseling techniques); define the solution, which is tied directly to performance; then continue to monitor and document job performance, and make a referral decision. The Journal states that, "Having documented the return of old behaviors, you must confront the soldier. If you suspect a substance abuse problem, make an appointment for the soldier at the local Community Counseling Center. Tell the soldier he or she will keep the appointment or suffer the consequences (documented during previous counseling). Document acceptance or refusal of an evaluation or treatment. Most soldiers in this position will comply."

Several years ago, the Army introduced a stricter policy about substance abuse that basically says "zero tolerance." Treatment issues in the ADAPCP do not affect command administrative or disciplinary decisions made in the best interest of the Army, meaning entry of a soldier into a treatment plan in no way prevents separation processing.

ADAPCP and Efficiency Reports

A soldier's participation in the ADAPCP is not normally mentioned in an NCO Evaluation Report, but raters may make note of incidents of alcohol or drug abuse not derived from ADAPCP records. Once a soldier has been identified in a report as having a substance abuse problem, his or her voluntary entry into the ADAPCP or successful rehabilitation may be mentioned in subsequent reports.

AIDS

The devastating effects of Acquired Immune Deficiency Syndrome (AIDS) continue to be felt in the U.S. military community as well as throughout the nation and world. The illness is now spreading fastest in Asia, especially through prostitutes. It has already taken a huge toll on the continent of Africa and elsewhere in developing Third World regions. World Health Organization officials expect the fatal disease to spread fastest among populations least prepared to understand, avoid, and prevent its spread.

Soldiers who test positive for Human Immunodeficiency Virus-1 (HIV-1), the infection leading to AIDS, are prohibited as a matter of changed policy from being assigned to Table of Organization and Equipment (TOE) or Modified TOE units. To protect confidentiality, HIV-infected soldiers already in MTOE units will not be reassigned unless they have been in the unit for three years. Those who become infected after assignment will be permitted to complete three-year tours unless they request reassignments.

Another policy change allows HIV-positive soldiers to be assigned to units outside the continental United States, but only to Alaska, Hawaii, and Puerto Rico. And another change enables HIV-infected soldiers to reclassify and retrain in new specialties, provided the schooling does not exceed 20 weeks.

Mandatory testing and HIV prevention awareness are being emphasized Army-wide. You must teach your soldiers—and implore them to teach their families—to understand how to avoid and prevent the spread of the disease. Do not allow immature soldiers to make light of the issue. Doing so downplays the important role of HIV-AIDS awareness and could result in avoidable infections, prolonged illness, and death.

Military readiness, medical, and personnel policies associated with HIV-AIDS look to protect the Army's ability both to fulfill its Constitutional role and to confidentially identify, evaluate, and provide an appropriate level of care for infected members. Since November 1993, soldiers referred to Walter Reed Army Medical Center (WRAMC) for semiannual HIV staging evaluations have been managed as outpatients rather than inpatients. This policy reflects the evolving standards of practice at military hospitals and the need to maximize the efficiency of medical resources, according to an official WRAMC command memorandum distributed to all commanding generals in October 1993.

SOLDIERS magazine ran two stories about AIDS in July 1994, one about the human impact, the other about the implications of lifestyle decisions. The first story includes a somber photograph of an infected former Army wife with her eyes cast down. Resting on her breast is a portrait of her child. The little boy in the portrait looks alert and is wearing a long-sleeved white shirt, vest, and bow tie. The child's mother made this heartbreaking comment: "I'm dying of AIDS. But what hurts most is . . . I have to live with the fact that I killed my boy." She reportedly contracted HIV through unprotected sex and passed it to her son at birth. If you or your soldiers are considering starting a family, think about the lives you may bring into the world.

The other story in SOLDIERS looks at AIDS from the perspective of a young soldier who "has seen people throw their good judgment out the window and engage in behavior that puts them at risk for contracting HIV." The story plugs the value of using latex condoms to prevent disease transmission. Condoms are free through unit supply systems. One brand name has a national stock number. Condoms are also available at Army health clinics. Don't be too proud to get a supply for your soldiers. Since young males generally tend to be shy about asking for protection, put the condoms in a discreet, accessible location, make your soldiers aware of it, and keep it stocked.

According to the U.S. Center for Disease Control, HIV infection is spreading fastest among heterosexuals. "In the Army community alone, 860 current and former soldiers, civilian employees, and family members have died, and more than 3,500 from the same group are infected," *SOLDIERS* reported in July 1994. The mortality and infection figures will only go up. Do not let your soldiers down. Push AIDS awareness and education.

For more information, request from the Association of the United States Army a copy of its Institute of Land Warfare Paper No. 6, titled *AIDS and Its Impact on Medical Readiness*. Its author, Dr. (COL) Edmund C. Tramont, imparts information worth knowing. For example, the doctor says, "Acute diseases involving three organs of the body have most often affected military operations: the gastrointestinal tract, blood, and the genital tract, [that is], diarrhea, malaria, and gonorrhea, etc. HIV-1, the cause of AIDS, infects two of these organ systems. *HIV is a fatal sexually transmitted disease that contaminates blood!* As such, its impact on medical readiness is broad and far-reaching."

RACIAL PREJUDICE

The June 13, 1994, *Early Bird* news compilation from the Pentagon carried a page-one European *Stars and Stripes* story dated the previous day that included this headline: "Bias in Army Alive, NAACP Official Says." A few years earlier, *SOLDIERS* magazine published a story that indicated bias against minorities was "alive and well" outside the Army, too. Inside or outside of the service, racial prejudice and discrimination tear at the fabric of U.S. society. Since NCOs are in the soldier team building business, they should know that racism in all of its ugly forms has no place in the Army—it destroys soldier teams.

In a 1994 Associated Press story carried across the nation in subscriber newspapers, retired GEN Colin Powell addressed how black soldiers should look at the issue. He said, "African Americans have come too far, and have too far yet to go to make a detour into the swamp of hatred. . . . There is utter foolishness . . . there is evil, there is danger in the message of hatred." Soldiers of all races should understand the meaning of the general's message. Powell, who served with acclaimed distinction in the Army, commonly called on soldiers to maintain an attitude of tolerance. Tolerance will help, and so will viewing racism for what it is—a serious threat to individual rights and unit cohesion.

AR 600-20, *Army Command Policy*, is the starting point to learn about the Army Equal Opportunity (EO) Program. Commanders are responsible for everything their command does or fails to do. Commanders often turn to their first sergeants to provide advice and assistance on EO matters. The Army EO goal is to formulate, direct, and sustain a comprehensive effort to ensure fair treatment of all soldiers. NCO leaders must develop, establish, and maintain a climate of discipline through the implementation of an effective EO program. The policy of the Army is to provide equal opportunity and treatment for soldiers and their families without regard to race, color, religion, gender, or national origin, and to provide an environment free of sexual harassment both on and off post. Enough said. Enforce the policy.

SEXUAL HARASSMENT

Sexual harassment is a form of sex discrimination that involves unwelcome sexual advances, requests for sexual favors, or other verbal or physical conduct of a sexual nature. It can occur almost anywhere and violates acceptable standards of integrity and impartiality required of all Army personnel. Sexual harassment also interferes with mission accomplishment and unit cohesion. Such behavior by soldiers or Army civilians should not be tolerated.

An act of sexual harassment occurs in the following circumstances:

- Submission to or rejection of such conduct is made either explicitly or implicitly a term or condition of a person's job, pay, or career.
- Submission to or rejection of such conduct by a person is used as a basis for career or employment decisions affecting that person.
- Such conduct interferes with an individual's performance or creates an intimidating, hostile, or offensive environment.

Sexual harassment can include verbal abuse, profanity, off-color jokes, sexual comments, threats, barking, growling, oinking, or whistling at passersby to indicate a perception of their physical appearance. It also includes nonverbal abuse such as leering, ogling (giving a person the "once over"), blowing kisses, licking lips, winking, leaving sexually suggestive notes, and displaying sexist cartoons and pictures. Unwanted physical contact such as touching, patting, hugging, pinching, grabbing, cornering, kissing, blocking a passageway, and back and neck rubs may also constitute sexual harassment. The last two types of contact, assault and rape, are clearly criminal offenses as well.

The policy may make it seem as if it exceeds what is necessary to ensure that members treat one another with dignity and respect. It does, because sexual harassment continues to occur in all segments of society. Do your part to help reduce the problem, because like other EO matters, sexual harassment violates individual rights and damages unit cohesion. If you have any questions, contact your local Equal Opportunity NCO.

HOMOSEXUALITY

In March 1994, Headquarters, Department of the Army distributed an official message whose subject was Homosexual Conduct Policy. The remainder of this section is taken from the message, which became effective in February 1994.

The message implements Title 10 United States Code Section 654 and provides supplemental guidance for the Department of Defense homosexual conduct policy. As such, it constitutes changes to AR 600-20, *Army Command Policy*. The Department of Defense has stated that the suitability of persons to serve in the Army is based on their conduct and their ability to meet required standards of duty performance and discipline.

Definitions:

- *Bisexual.* A person who engages in, attempts to engage in, has a propensity to engage in, or intends to engage in homosexual and heterosexual acts.
- *Commander.* A commissioned or warrant officer who, by virtue of rank and assignment, exercises primary command authority over a military organization or prescribed territorial area that under pertinent official directives is recognized as "command."

- *Homosexual.* A person, regardless of sex, who engages in, attempts to engage in, has a propensity to engage in, or intends to engage in homosexual acts.
- *Sexual orientation.* An abstract sexual preference for persons of a particular sex, as distinct from a propensity or intent to engage in sexual acts.
- *Propensity.* Propensity to engage in homosexual acts means more than an abstract preference or desire to engage in homosexual acts; it indicates a likelihood that a person engages or will engage in homosexual acts.
- *Homosexual conduct.* "Homosexual conduct" is a homosexual act, a statement by a soldier that demonstrates a propensity or intent to engage in homosexual acts, or a homosexual marriage or attempted marriage.

A "homosexual act" means any bodily contact, actively undertaken or passively permitted, between members of the same sex for the purpose of satisfying sexual desires and any bodily contact (for example, hand-holding, slow dancing, or kissing) that a reasonable person would understand to demonstrate a propensity or intent to engage in such an act.

A "statement by a person that he or she is a homosexual or bisexual or words to that effect" means language or behavior that a reasonable person would believe was intended to convey the statement that a person engages in, attempts to engage in, has a propensity to engage in, or intends to engage in homosexual acts. This may include statements such as "I am a homosexual," "I am gay," "I am a lesbian," "I have a homosexual orientation," and the like.

A "homosexual marriage or attempted marriage" is when a person has married or attempted to marry a person known to be of the same biological sex (as evidenced by the external anatomy of the person involved).

Separation Policy
Homosexual conduct is grounds for separation from the Army.

Only a soldier's commander is authorized to initiate fact-finding inquiries involving homosexual conduct. A commander may initiate a fact-finding inquiry only when he or she has received credible information that there is a basis for discharge. Commanders are responsible for ensuring that inquiries are conducted properly and that no abuse of authority occurs.

A fact-finding inquiry may be conducted by the commander personally or by a person he or she appoints. It may consist of an examination of the information reported or a more extensive investigation as necessary. The inquiry should gather all credible information that directly relates to the grounds for possible separation. Inquiries shall be limited to the actual circumstances directly relevant to the specific allegations.

If a commander has credible evidence of possible criminal conduct, he or she shall follow the procedures in the *Manual for Courts-Martial*, ARs 27-10 and 195-2.

A commander will initiate an inquiry only if he or she has credible information that there is a basis for discharge. Credible information exists when the information, considering its source and the surrounding circumstances, supports a reasonable belief that a soldier engaged in homosexual conduct. It requires a determination based on articulable facts, not just a belief or suspicion.

A basis for discharge exists if the soldier has engaged in a homosexual act, the soldier has said that he or she is a homosexual or bisexual, or the soldier has made some other statement that indicates a propensity or intent to engage in homosexual acts or the soldier has married or attempted to marry a person of the same sex. Credible information exists, for example, when a reliable person states that he or she observed or heard a soldier engaging in homosexual acts, or saying that he or she is a homosexual or bisexual or is married to a member of the same sex. Credible information also exists when a reliable person states that he or she heard, observed, or discovered a soldier make a spoken or written statement that a reasonable person would believe was intended to convey the fact that he or she engages in, attempts to engage in, or has the propensity or intent to engage in homosexual acts.

Additionally, credible information exists when a reliable person states that he or she observed behavior that amounts to a nonverbal statement by a soldier that he or she is a homosexual or bisexual—that is, behavior that a reasonable person would believe intended to convey the statement that the soldier engages in, attempts to engage in, or has the propensity or intent to engage in homosexual acts. Commanders or appointed inquiry officers shall not ask, and soldiers shall not be required to reveal, whether a soldier is a heterosexual, a homosexual, or a bisexual. However, upon receipt of credible information of homosexual conduct, commanders or appointed inquiry officials may ask soldiers if they engaged in such conduct. The soldier should first be advised of the DOD policy on homosexual conduct and rights under [the] UCMJ. The prohibition against homosexual conduct is a long-standing element of military law that continues to be necessary in the unique circumstances of military service.

The Armed Forces must maintain personnel policies that exclude persons whose presence would create an unacceptable risk to the armed forces' high standards of morale, good order, discipline, and unit cohesion that are the essence of military capability. The presence in the armed forces of persons who demonstrate a propensity or intent to engage in homosexual acts would create an unacceptable risk to the high standards of morale, good order, discipline, and unit cohesion that are the essence of military capability.

13

Military Justice

A fact of military life is that, despite the availability of information on the subject and the effort of commanders to keep their soldiers informed, many individuals simply do not know very much about the military justice system. Specific provisions pertaining to administration of the military justice system are in the *Manual for Courts-Martial* and AR 27-10, *Military Justice*. It is the noncommissioned officer's business to know nonjudicial punishment thoroughly—as thoroughly as any commander—and, inasmuch as it is the noncommissioned officers who first become aware of the offenses referred to commanders for punishment, it would be very good to consider that "prevention is the best cure."

NONJUDICIAL PUNISHMENT

Article 15 of the Uniform Code of Military Justice (UCMJ) provides commanding officers the authority and procedures to impose disciplinary punishments for minor offenses without a court-martial. Such punishments may be in addition to or in lieu of admonition or reprimand. Unless the accused is embarked on a vessel, Article 15 punishment may not be imposed if the accused demands trial by court-martial.

Article 15 punishments are less severe than court-martial punishments. *Unlike a special or general court-martial, Article 15 is not considered a federal conviction for a criminal offense*. Article 15 is intended to provide a swift, efficient, and relatively easy method for punishing those committing minor offenses, maintaining discipline, and deterring future offenses. Under Article 15, commanders have a wide latitude of punishments that may be imposed ranging from oral reprimand to reduction in pay grades, fines, restriction, extra duty, or a combination of these. Article 15 is the most likely contact NCOs will have with the military justice system.

It is a mistake to disregard the effect of an Article 15 on a soldier's career. The original copy of DA Form 2617, *Record of Proceedings under Article 15, UCMJ*, may be filed in the official military personnel file performance portion of the permanent record. Records of Article 15 punishments can be used in a wide variety of personnel decisions and can lead to an involuntary administrative discharge.

Article 15 is not a legal process. Legal rules of evidence do not apply, and providing defense counsel at the hearing is not mandatory. Nevertheless, the accused does have protection against arbitrary use of Article 15. In addition to the right to demand trial in lieu of Article 15 punishment, the accused has the right to consult with counsel to decide whether to accept the punishment; if the accused accepts Article 15 and considers the punishment too harsh, he or she may appeal it. Other rights include the right to remain silent, to fully present his or her case in the presence of the imposing commander, to call witnesses, to present evidence, to be accomplished by a spokesperson, to request an open hearing, and to examine available evidence.

Persons Subject to Nonjudicial Punishment

Punishment may be imposed under Article 15 by a commanding officer upon commissioned and warrant officers and enlisted military personnel, except that punishment may not be imposed under Article 15 upon cadets of the United States Military Academy.

Nonjudicial punishment may not be imposed on an individual by a commanding officer after the person ceases to be of his command. The commander who has instituted the proceedings may, in the case of such a change in status, forward the record of proceedings to the gaining commander for appropriate disposition.

Purposes of Nonjudicial Punishment

Nonjudicial punishment may be imposed in appropriate cases for the following purposes:

- Correct, educate, and reform offenders who have shown that they cannot benefit by less stringent measures.
- Preserve, in appropriate cases, an offender's record of service from unnecessary stigmatization by record of court-martial conviction.
- Further military efficiency by disposing of minor offenses in a manner requiring less time and personnel than trial by court-martial.

Generally, the term *minor offenses* includes misconduct not involving any greater degree of criminality than is involved in the average offense tried by summary court-martial.

Nonpunitive measures usually deal with misconduct resulting from simple neglect, forgetfulness, laziness, inattention to instructions, sloppy habits, immaturity, difficulty in adjusting to disciplined military life, and similar deficiencies. These measures are primarily tools for teaching proper standards of conduct and performance and do not constitute punishment. Included are denial of pass or other privileges, counseling, administrative reduction in grade, extra training, bar to reenlistment, and MOS reclassification. Certain commanders have the authority, apart from any under Article 15, to reduce enlisted persons administratively for inefficiency or other reasons. Nonpunitive measures and nonjudicial punishment should not be confused.

A written admonition or reprimand should contain a statement indicating that it has been imposed merely as an administrative measure and *not* as punishment under Article 15. On the other hand, admonitions and reprimands that are imposed as punishment under Article 15 should be clearly stated to have been imposed as punishment under that article.

Commanding officers also have the authority to impose restraints or restrictions upon a soldier for administrative purposes, such as to ensure the soldier's presence within the command. This authority exists apart from the authority to impose restriction as nonjudicial punishment. These nonpunitive measures may also include, subject to any applicable regulation, administrative withholding of privileges.

Extra training or instruction is one of the most effective nonpunitive measures available to a commander. It is used when a soldier's duty performance has been substandard or deficient. For example, a soldier who fails to maintain proper attire may be required to attend classes on the wearing of the uniform and stand inspection until the deficiency is corrected.

MAXIMUM PUNISHMENTS FOR ENLISTED MEMBERS UNDER ARTICLE 15*

Note: The maximum punishment imposable by any commander under Summarized Procedures cannot exceed extra duty for 15 days, restriction for 14 days, oral reprimand, or any combination thereof.

Punishment	Imposed by Company-Grade Officers	Imposed by Field-Grade or General Officers
Admonition/Reprimand and	Yes	Yes
Extra Duties[1] and	14 days	45 days
Restriction or	14 days	60 days
Correctional Custody[2] (PVT1 to PFC) or	7 days	30 days
Restricted Diet Confinement (PVT1 to PFC attached or embarked on a vessel) and	3 days	3 days
Reduction: (PVT 1 to SPC or CPL) (SGT and SSG) and	One grade	One grade or more One grade in peacetime[3]
Forfeiture[4]	7 days' pay	Half of one month's pay for 2 months

---

[1]Combinations of extra duties and restriction cannot exceed the maximum allowed for extra duty.

[2]Subject to limitations imposed by superior authority and presence of adequate facilities. If punishment includes reduction to private first class or below, reduction must be unsuspended.

[3]Only if imposed by a field-grade commander of a unit authorized a commander who is a lieutenant colonel or higher.

[4]Amount of forfeiture is computed at the reduced grade, even if suspended, if reduction is part of punishment.

Summarized Proceedings

If, after a preliminary inquiry, a commander determines that the punishment for an offense should not exceed extra duty or restriction for 14 days, oral reprimand or admonition, or any combination of these punishments, then Summarized Proceedings under Article 15 may be used. The record of these proceedings is made on DA Form 2627-1. Generally, Summarized Proceedings are conducted as they are for more serious cases prosecuted under nonjudicial punishment except that the individual normally is allowed 24 hours to decide whether to demand trial by court-martial and to gather matters in defense, extenuation, and/or mitigation. Because of the limited nature of the punishments imposed under these proceedings, the soldier has *no right* to consult with legally qualified counsel nor the right to a spokesperson.

Nature of Punishments

Nonjudicial punishments include the following actions:
- *Admonition and reprimand.* An admonition or reprimand may be imposed in lieu of or combined with Article 15 punishments.
- *Restriction.* The severity of this type of restraint is dependent upon its duration and geographical limits specified when punishment is imposed. A soldier undergoing restriction may be required to report to a designated place at specified times if it is considered reasonably necessary to ensure that the punishment is being properly executed.
- *Extra duties.* This form involves the performance of duties in addition to those normally assigned to the person undergoing the punishment. Extra duties may include fatigue duties. In general, extra duties may not be assigned a specialist or corporal or above that would demean his or her position as a noncommissioned officer or specialist.
- *Reduction in grade.* This form involves these considerations:

    —Promotion authority. The grade from which a soldier is reduced must be within the promotion authority of the imposing commander or the officer to whom authority to punish under Article 15 has been delegated.

    —Lateral appointments or reductions of corporal to specialist are not authorized. An NCO may be reduced to a lower pay grade provided the lower grade is authorized in his or her primary MOS.

    —Date of rank. When a soldier is reduced in grade as a result of unsuspended reduction, the date of rank in the grade to which reduced is the date the punishment of reduction was imposed.

    —Entitlement to pay. When a soldier is restored to a higher pay grade because of a suspension or when a reduction is mitigated to a forfeiture, entitlement to pay at the higher grade is effective on the date of the suspension or mitigation.

    —Senior noncommissioned officers. Sergeants first class and above may not be reduced under the authority of Article 15.
- *Forfeiture of pay.* Pay refers to basic pay of the individual plus any foreign duty pay. Forfeitures imposed by a company-grade commander may not be applied for more than one month, while those imposed by a field-grade commander may not be applied for more than two months. The maximum forfeiture of pay to which a soldier is subject during a given month, because of one or more actions under Article 15, is one half of his pay per month. Article 15 forfeitures cannot deprive a soldier of more than two thirds of his or her pay per month.

FORFEITURES OF PAY AUTHORIZED UNDER ARTICLE 15

Maximum monthly authorized forfeitures of pay under Article 15, UCMJ, may be computed using the applicable formula below:

1. Upon enlisted persons:

$$\frac{(\text{monthly basic pay}^{1,2} + \text{foreign pay}^{1,3})}{2} = \text{maximum forfeiture per month if imposed by major or above}$$

$$\frac{(\text{monthly basic pay}^{1,2} + \text{foreign pay}^{1,3}) \times 7}{30} = \text{maximum forfeiture if imposed by captain or below}$$

2. Upon commissioned and warrant officers when imposed by an officer with general court-martial jurisdiction or by a general officer in command:

$$\frac{(\text{monthly basic pay}^{2})}{2} = \text{maximum authorized forfeiture per month}$$

---

[1] Amount of forfeiture is computed at the reduced grade, even if suspended, if reduction is part of the punishment imposed.
[2] At the time punishment is imposed.
[3] If applicable.

Combination and Apportionment

No two or more punishments involving deprivation of liberty may be combined in the same nonjudicial punishment to run either consecutively or concurrently, but other punishments may be combined. Restriction and extra duty may be combined in any manner to run for a period not in excess of the maximum duration imposable for extra duty by the imposing commander.

Suspension, Mitigation, Remission, and Setting Aside

Suspension. The purpose of suspending punishment is to grant a deserving soldier a probational period during which the individual may show that he or she deserves a remission of the suspended portion of his or her nonjudicial punishment. If, because of further misconduct within this period, it is determined that remission of the suspended punishment is not warranted, the suspension may be vacated and the suspended portion of the punishment executed.

Remission. Remission can cancel any portion of the *unexecuted* punishment. Remission is appropriate under the same circumstances as mitigation.

Setting Aside and Restoration. Under this action, the punishment or any part or amount thereof, whether *executed* or *unexecuted*, is set aside, and any property, privileges, or rights affected by the portion of the punishment set aside are restored. The basis for this action is ordinarily a determination that, under all the circumstances of the case, the punishment has resulted in a clear injustice.

Notification and Explanation of Rights

The imposing commander must ensure that the soldier is notified of the intention to dispose of the matter under Article 15. The imposing commander may delegate notification authority to another officer, warrant officer, or NCO (sergeant first class and above), providing that person outranks the person being notified. If an NCO is selected, that person should normally be the unit first sergeant or another NCO who is the senior enlisted person in the command in which the accused is serving.

The soldier must be given a "reasonable time" to consult with counsel, including time off from duty, if necessary, to decide whether to demand trial. The amount of time granted is normally 48 hours.

Before deciding to demand trial, the accused is not entitled to be informed of the type or amount of punishment he or she will receive if nonjudicial punishment is imposed. The imposing commander will inform the soldier of the maximum punishment allowable under Article 15 and the maximum allowable for the offense if the case proceeds to a trial by court-martial and conviction for the offense.

Right to Demand Trial

The demand for trial may be made at any time before imposition of punishment. The soldier will be told that if trial is demanded, it could be by summary, special, or general court-martial. The soldier will also be told that he or she may object to trial by summary court-martial and that at a special or general court-martial he or she would be entitled to be represented by qualified military counsel or by civilian counsel obtained at the soldeir's expense.

Appeals

Only one appeal is permitted under Article 15 proceedings. An appeal not made within a "reasonable time" may be rejected as untimely by the superior authority. The definition of what constitutes a "reasonable time" varies according to the situation. Generally, an appeal, including all documentary matters, submitted more than five calendar days (including weekends and holidays) after punishment is imposed will be presumed to be untimely. If, at the time of imposition of punishment, the soldier indicates a desire not to appeal, the superior authority may reject a subsequent election to appeal, even if it is made within the five-day period.

Appeals are made on DA Form 2627 or DA Form 2627-1 and forwarded through the imposing commander or successor-in-command to the superior authority. The superior must act on the appeal unless otherwise directed by competent authority. A soldier is not required to state the reasons for the appeal, but he or she may present evidence or arguments proving innocence or why the sentence should be mitigated or suspended. Unless an appeal is voluntarily withdrawn, it must be forwarded to the appropriate superior authority. A timely appeal does not terminate because a soldier is discharged from the service but will be processed to completion.

Announcement of Punishment

The punishment may be announced at the next unit formation after punishment is imposed or, if appealed, after the decision. It also may be posted on the unit bulletin board. The purpose of announcing the results is to avert the perception of unfairness of punishment and to deter similar misconduct by others.

Records of Punishment

DA Forms 2627 are prepared in an original and five copies. What happens to those copies, especially the original, is of the utmost importance to soldiers who receive punishment under nonjudicial proceedings.

Original. For enlisted soldiers, the original copy is forwarded to the U.S. Army Enlisted Records and Evaluation Center, Fort Benjamin Harrison, Indiana. The decision on where in the punished soldier's official military personnel file (OMPF) this copy will be placed is determined by the imposing commander at the time punishment is imposed and is final. The imposing commander will decide if it is to be filed in the performance fiche or the restricted fiche of the individual's OMPF.

Copy one. For those Articles 15 filed in the performance fiche of the OMPF, copy one is placed into the permanent section of the military personnel records jacket (MPRJ) unless the original is transferred from the performance to the restricted fiche, at which time it is destroyed. Otherwise, it is kept in the unit personnel files and destroyed two years from the date of punishment or on the soldier's transfer, whichever occurs first. Copies two through four are used variously as prescribed by AR 27-10, depending on whether forfeiture of pay is involved and whether the punished soldier appeals. Copy five is given to the individual.

Transfer or Removal of Records

Staff sergeants and above and commissioned and warrant officers may request the transfer of a record of nonjudicial punishment from the performance to the restricted fiche of their OMPF. To support such a request, the individual must submit substantive evidence that the purpose of the Article 15 has been served and that transfer of the record is in the best interests of the Army. The request must be made in writing to the Department of the Army Suitability Evaluation Board: President, DA Suitability Evaluation Board, HQDA (DAPE-MPC-E), Washington, DC 20310.

Soldiers may also apply to the Army Board for Correction of Military Records (ABCMR) for the correction of military records by the Secretary of the Army. AR 15-185, *Army Board for Correction of Military Records*, contains policies and procedures for making such applications.

COURTS-MARTIAL

Courts-martial are the agencies through which Army magistrates try personnel accused of violations of the punitive articles of the Uniform Code of Military Justice. These are Articles 77 through 134 of the UCMJ and are designed to provide punishment of three broad groups of crimes and offenses:

• Crimes common to both the military and civilian law, such as murder, rape, arson, burglary, larceny, sodomy, and frauds against the United States.

• Crimes and offenses peculiar to the military services, such as desertion, disobedience, misbehavior before the enemy, and sleeping on post.

• General offenses that are prosecuted under Article 134, the General Article, which covers "all disorders and neglects to the prejudice of good order and discipline in the armed forces, all conduct of a nature to bring discredit upon the armed forces, and crimes and offenses not capital."

During peacetime, courts-martial may impose sentences ranging from simple forfeiture of pay to confinement and forfeiture of all pay and allowances and death. (See appendix 12, MCM, for the Maximum Punishment Chart.) During time of war, a general court-martial may impose any penalty authorized by law, including death.

Composition of Courts-Martial

General courts-martial consist of a military judge and not fewer than five members or of a military judge alone. *Special courts-martial* consist of not fewer than three members or, if so detailed, a military judge and not less than three members or a military judge alone. *Summary courts-martial* consist of one commissioned officer.

Any commissioned officer on active duty with the armed forces is eligible to serve on courts-martial. Any warrant officer on active duty with the armed forces is eligible to serve on general and special courts-martial for the trial of any person other than a commissioned officer. Any enlisted person on active duty with the armed forces who is not a member of the same unit as the accused is eligible to serve on general and special courts-martial for the trial of any enlisted person who has personally requested in writing before assembly that enlisted members serve on the court.

Convening Authorities

General courts-martial may be convened by the president of the United States; the Secretary of the Army; the commander of a territorial department, army group, army, army corps, division, separate brigade, or corresponding unit; or any other commander designated by the Secretary of the Army or empowered by the president to convene such courts-martial. It is unlawful for any commander who is an accuser to convene a general court-martial for the trial of the person so accused.

Special courts-martial may be convened by any person who may convene a general court-martial or the commanding officer of a district, garrison, fort, camp, station, or other place where members of the Army are on duty.

Summary courts-martial may be convened by any person who may also convene a general or special court-martial and the commander of a detached company or other detachment of the Army, and any other officer empowered by the Secretary of the Army to convene such a court-martial. When only one commissioned officer is present with a command or detachment, that officer is the summary court-martial authority of that command or detachment and hears and determines all summary court cases.

Challenges

The military judge and members of a general or special court-martial may be challenged by the accused or the trial counsel for cause stated to the court. The military judge, or, if none, the court, determines the relevancy and validity of challenges for cause. Challenges by the trial counsel are ordinarily presented and decided before those by the accused are offered.

Each accused and the trial counsel is entitled to one preemptory challenge, meaning the accused may challenge any member of the court to sit on his trial without offering any reasons for the challenge.

Appeals

At the close of a trial or soon thereafter, if the accused is found guilty, the defense counsel should prepare a recommendation for clemency setting forth any matters as to clemency he or she desires to have considered by the members of the court of the reviewing authority. If the accused is convicted, the defense counsel advises him or her of appellate rights.

The Court of Military Review. The Judge Advocate General refers to a court of military review the record in every case of trial by court-martial in which the sentence, as approved, extends to death, dishonorable or bad-conduct discharge, or confinement for one year or more.

In a case referred to it, the court of military review may act only with respect to the findings and sentence as approved by the convening authority. If the court sets aside the findings and sentence, it may, except where the setting aside is based on lack of sufficient evidence, order a rehearing. If it sets aside the findings and sentence and does not order a rehearing, it orders that the charges be dismissed.

The Court of Military Appeals. The U.S. Court of Military Appeals, established under Article I of the Constitution, reviews the record in all the following cases:
- Those in which the sentence, as affirmed by a court of military review, extends to death.
- Those reviewed by a court of military review that the Judge Advocate General orders sent to the Court of Military Appeals for review.
- Those reviewed by a court of military review in which the Court of Military Appeals has granted a review. Reviewed cases may be forwarded to the U.S. Supreme Court.

Remission and Suspension of Sentences

The Secretary of the Army or his designated representative may remit or suspend any amount of the unexecuted part of any sentence, including all uncollected forfeitures other than a sentence approved by the president. The Secretary of the Army may, for cause, substitute an administrative form of discharge for a discharge or dismissal executed in accordance with the sentence of a court-martial. The convening authority may suspend the execution of any sentence, except a death sentence.

Effective Dates of Sentences

Whenever a sentence includes a forfeiture of pay or allowances in addition to confinement, the forfeiture applies to pay or allowances becoming due on or after the date of the sentence is approved by the convening authority.

Confinement included in a sentence begins to run from the date of sentencing by the court-martial. Reductions are effective on the date the sentence is approved. All other sentences of courts-martial are effective on the date ordered executed.

Who May Prefer Charges

Charges are initiated by anyone bringing to the attention of the military authorities information concerning an offense suspected to have been committed by a person subject to the UCMJ. This information may be received from anyone, whether subject to the UCMJ or not.

Action by Immediate Commander

Upon receipt of information that an offense has been committed, the commander exercising immediate jurisdiction over the accused under Article 15, UCMJ, must make a preliminary inquiry into the charges in order to permit an intelligent disposition of them.

Based on the outcome of the preliminary inquiry, a commander may decide that all or some of the charges do not warrant further action, and those charges may be dismissed. The commander may also decide, based upon the preliminary investigation, that the offenses committed warrant punishment under Article 15, UCMJ, or he or she may refer more serious charges to higher authority for trial by courts-martial.

Preparation of Charge Sheets

Rule 307 and appendix 4, MCM, contain specific instructions on the preparation of charge sheets, together with specimen forms for charges and specifications under the punitive articles of the Uniform Code of Military Justice. If you're not a legal clerk, it's important to get help from your JAG officer.

NCO Responsibilities

If you should be appointed to serve on a general or special court-martial as a member of the court, your duties and responsibilities will be very carefully explained to you before the court convenes and as the trial proceeds. If a soldier should seek your advice regarding what he or she should do in the event charges are brought against the individual, *advise the person concerned to seek assistance from an officer of the Judge Advocate General's Corps.*

Unless you are a legal clerk, your acquaintance with the military justice system will probably be only a superficial one. Your closest contact with the military justice system will come through your commander's exercise of judicial authority under Article 15 of the UCMJ, and you should be intimately familiar with every aspect of that part of the system. But you are neither an expert in military law nor a lawyer, and you should never take upon yourself the duties of counsel.

The *Manual for Courts-Martial* is an important text that every soldier should know well enough to understand what it contains and how to use it to answer questions on the military justice system. Do not, however, use that acquaintance to practice law.

Sources
AR 27-10, *Military Justice,* 1989.
FM 27-1, *Legal Guide for Commanders,* 1987.
FM 27-14, *Legal Guide for Soldiers,* 1986.
Manual for Courts-Martial, 1984.
The Servicemember's Legal Guide, 2nd Edition, by Lt. Col. Jonathan P. Tomes, U.S. Army, Stackpole Books: Harrisburg, PA, 1992.

14

Uniforms, Insignia, and Personal Appearance

WEARING THE UNIFORM

Your Army uniform is the outward evidence of your profession, your standing in that profession, and a prime indicator of the degree of respect with which you regard your service to the United States of America and the Army. The condition of your uniform and the way you wear it are also a reflection of your own self-respect.

One of the basic responsibilities of every NCO is to know the composition of the Army uniforms and how to wear them properly. This is not to say that a good NCO will fly into a huff every time he or she spots a soldier whose personal appearance is less than recruiting-poster sharp, but no NCO should tolerate negligence when it comes to good grooming or ignorance when it comes to wearing the Army uniform.

There are soldiers—some of whom are relatively high-ranking—who pay little attention to their uniforms and personal appearance. Good NCOs will not let this fact bother them, but as in all other things, they will overcome these bad examples by setting the proper example themselves.

Classification of Service and Utility Field Uniforms

Class A Service Uniform. *For men:* consists of the Army green AG 489 coat and trousers, a short- or long-sleeved AG 415 shirt, a black four-in-hand tie (tied in a slip knot with the ends left hanging), and other accessories. *For women:* consists of the appropriate Army green coat/jacket and skirt or slacks of the Army green uniform, Army classic uniform, and the Army green pantsuit; a short- or long-sleeved AG 415 shirt; a black necktab; and other authorized accessories. The Army green maternity uniform (slacks or skirt) is also a Class A service uniform when the tunic is worn. The necktab will be worn with both the short- and long-sleeved maternity shirts when the tunic is worn.

Class B Service Uniform. *For men:* consists of the same as for the Class A except the service coat is *not* worn. The black tie is required when wearing the long-sleeved AG 415 shirt and is optional with the short-sleeved shirt. *For women:* consists of the same as for the Class A except the service coat/jacket and the maternity tunic are *not* worn. The black necktab is required when wearing the long-sleeved AG 415 shirt and the long-sleeved maternity shirt. It is optional with the short-sleeved version of both shirts. The AG 489 skirt and jacket and the dress and jacket uniforms are classified as Class B service uniforms.

The following items are authorized for wear on Class B uniforms: marksmanship, identification, and foreign badges; regimental and infantry distinctive insignia; airborne background trimming; and service aiguillettes. Regimental insignia may be worn above the right breast pocket, but distinctive unit insignia will not be worn on the epaulets. In addition, sew-on insignia, badges, patches of any type, and the combat leader's identification (green tabs) will not be worn. Ranger and Special Forces metal tab replicas, however, may be worn as group 4 special skill badges in the same way they are worn on the dress blue coat.

Although this change in policy gives soldiers the option of what they will wear on green shirts, commanders may require wear of awards and decorations for parades, reviews, inspections, funerals, and ceremonial or social events.

Class C Uniforms. These are utility, field, and other organizational uniforms, such as hospital duty and food service uniforms.

Occasions When the Uniform Is Required to Be Worn

The Army uniform is worn by all personnel when on duty unless Headquarters, Department of the Army (HQDA), has authorized the wearing of civilian clothes. The following general rules apply:

A soldier prepares for a field exercise with the help of an NCO.

- Installation commanders may prescribe the uniforms to be worn in formations; duty uniforms are generally prescribed by local commanders or heads of agencies, activities, or installations.
- The wearing of combinations of uniform items not prescribed in AR 670-1 is prohibited.
- Uniform items changed in design or material may continue to be worn until wear-out date or unless specifically prohibited by Headquarters, Department of the Army.

Occasions When the Uniform May Not Be Worn

The wearing of the Army uniform is prohibited for all Army personnel under the following circumstances:
- In connection with the promotion of any political interests or when engaged in off-duty civilian employment.
- Except as authorized by competent authority, when participating in public speeches, interviews, picket lines, marches, rallies, or public demonstrations.
- When wearing the uniform would bring discredit upon the Army.
- When specifically prohibited by Army regulations.

Wearing of Headgear

The Army uniform is not complete unless the proper form of hat or cap is worn with it. Headgear is worn when outdoors.

Female personnel are not required to wear headgear when wearing the Army white or blue uniform to an evening social event. The appropriate headgear is, however, worn when wearing these uniforms on all other occasions.

Headgear is not required to be worn only if it would interfere with the safe operation of military vehicles. The wearing of military headgear is not required when in privately owned or commercial vehicles.

Uniform Appearance

The word "uniform" as used in this context means "conforming to the same standard or rule." Although absolute uniformity of appearance by all soldiers at all times cannot reasonably be expected as long as armies are composed of so many various individuals, soldiers, when in uniform, should project a military image that leaves no doubt that they live by a common standard.

One important rule of uniformity is that, when worn, items of the uniform should be kept buttoned, zippered, and snapped, metallic devices (such as collar brass insignia) should be kept in proper luster, and shoes should be cleaned and shined.

Lapels and sleeves of coats and jackets for both male and female personnel should be roll pressed (without creasing). The AG 489 dress and jacket uniform and all skirts should also be without creases.

Trousers, slacks, and sleeves of shirts, blouses, and dresses other than the AG 489 dress should be creased.

Care and Maintenance of the Uniform

All solid brass items (belt buckles, belt-buckle tips, collar brass insignia) should be maintained in a high state of luster at all times. These items come coated with a lacquer, and if their surfaces are kept protected and gently rubbed clean with a soft clean cloth, they will keep their shine for a long time. But when the lacquer coating becomes scratched, dirt begins to accumulate in the scratches, and the item can be kept shined only by completely removing the lacquer surface. The safest and most reliable method for removing the coating from brass items is to use Brasso polish applied with thumb and forefinger or a cloth.

Spit-shining does make shoes, boots, and equipment look sharp, but it dries out the leather.

Replace heels on shoes and boots after wear of $^7/_{16}$ of an inch or more.

Pay attention to the removal of stains from your clothing.

Never press dirty clothing, and be careful when you do press clothing that the iron is not too hot. Use a damp cloth between the iron and the fabric when pressing wool items, dampen the surface of cotton clothing before applying the iron, and observe the various fabric settings on the iron when pressing synthetic fabric.

Frequent cleaning of uniform items will increase their longevity and maintain the neat soldierly appearance that the uniform is designed to project. Rotating items of clothing, such as shoes and boots, will contribute to their longer life.

Many soldiers, as an economy measure, make minor repairs to their clothing themselves. The best advice to soldiers who want to look sharp is to have their insignia sewn on by a tailor and save money in some other way.

Fitting of Uniforms

Uniform items purchased in the Quartermaster Clothing Sales Store are fitted (or should be fitted) before they are taken off the premises. Personnel who purchase uniform items through the post exchange or from commercial sources should pay close attention to the proper fit of the items before wearing them. And some soldiers will gain or lose weight and, from laziness or excessive frugality, continue to wear improperly fitting uniform items.

An NCO should be able to tell at a glance whether a soldier (male or female) is wearing a properly fitted uniform. Fitting instructions and alterations of uniforms are made in accordance with AR 700-84 and TM 10-227, *Fitting of Army Uniforms and Footwear*.

The Clothing Allowance System

Clothing allowances are provided so that each soldier may maintain the initial clothing issue. Monthly clothing allowances provide for the cost of replacement and purchase of new items or the purchase of additional clothing items, not cleaning, laundering, and pressing. The basic allowance begins on the soldier's 181st day of active duty and is paid each month for the remainder of the first three-year period. The standard allowance begins the day after the soldier completes 36 months on active duty. The clothing allowance accrues monthly and is paid annually during the month of the soldier's basic active service date.

UNIFORMS
Temperate and Hot Weather Battle Dress

This uniform is authorized for year-round on-duty wear by all personnel when prescribed by the commander.

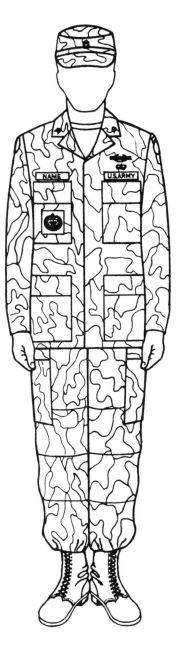

Temperate and hot weather BDU.

Maternity Work Uniform

This uniform is authorized for year-round on-duty wear by pregnant soldiers. It is not intended as a travel uniform, but it may be worn in transit between the individual's quarters and duty station.

Desert Battle Dress Uniform

The DBDU may be worn only when prescribed by the commander. The wear of the DBDU at public functions other than homecoming parades and activities directly related to the celebration of the return of soldiers from an operational area is not authorized without an exception from the major command.

Cold Weather Uniform

The OG 108 cold weather uniform is designed for year-round wear by all personnel when issued as organizational clothing and prescribed by the commander. It is not authorized for travel or for wear off military installations except in transit. Components of this uniform may be worn with utility and other organization uniforms as part of a cold weather ensemble when issued and prescribed by the commander.

Hospital Duty Uniform (Male)

This year-round duty uniform for all male soldiers in the Army Medical Specialist Corps and those in medical, dental, or veterinary MOSs is worn in medical healthcare facilities as prescribed by the medical commander. The commander may authorize the wear of this uniform in a civilian community when in support of civilian activities.

Hospital Duty and Maternity Uniform

This authorized year-round uniform is worn by Medical Specialist Corps personnel and enlisted women with medical, dental, or veterinary MOSs.

Flight Uniform

This uniform is authorized for year-round wear when on duty in a flying or standby-awaiting-flight status. Commanders may direct exceptions to wear policy.

Combat Vehicle Crewman Uniform

The CVC is a year-round duty uniform for combat vehicle crewmen when on duty or as directed by the commander. This uniform is not for travel.

Army Green Service Uniform (Male)

This uniform (Class A) and authorized variations (class B) may be worn by all male personnel when on duty, off duty, or during travel. These uniforms are also acceptable for informal social functions after retreat, unless other uniforms are prescribed by the host.

Army Green Classic Service Uniform (Female)

This uniform is authorized for year-round wear by all female soldiers. The guidelines for wear are similar to those for male soldiers wearing the Army green service uniform.

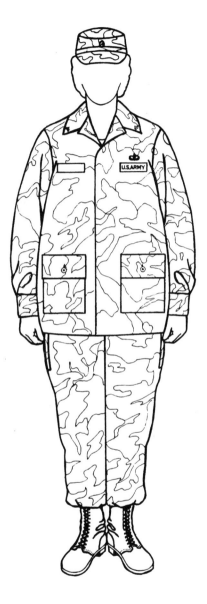

Maternity work uniform.

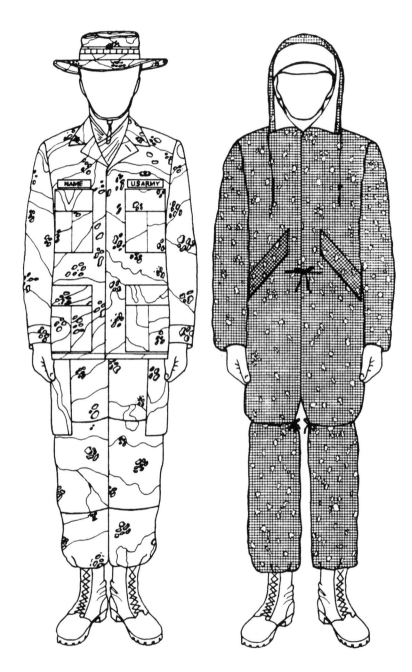

Desert BDU, daytime *(left)* and nighttime patterns.

CAMOUFLAGE CAP — Straight on head so that cap band creates a straight line around the head parallel to the ground. (subdued insignia of grade ONLY and centered from top to bottom, right to left)

UNDERSHIRT — Army Brown is authorized.

SHOULDER SLEEVE INSIGNIA — Current Organization — ½" down from shoulder seam and centered. (subdued only)

'US ARMY' DISTINGUISHING INSIGNIA — Centered immediately above and parallel to top edge of pocket.

BLACK BOOTS — Clean and shined at all times (no patent leather).

SOCKS — ONLY Olive Green, shade 408, is authorized for wear with combat or organizational boots.

BLACK BUCKLE & BLACK TIPPED BELT ONLY COMBINATION AUTHORIZED.

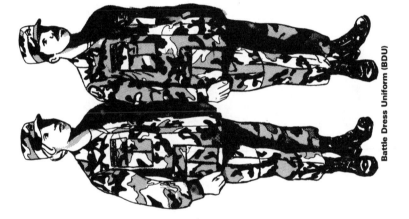

Battle Dress Uniform (BDU)

HAIR — Neatly groomed and will not present an extreme, ragged, or unkempt appearance. Hair will not extend below bottom edge of collar, nor be cut to appear unfeminine. Styles will not interfere with the proper wearing of military headgear.

INSIGNIA OF GRADE — Subdued pin-on, or sew-on, will be centered on each collar bisecting the collar 1" from the point.

SHOULDER SLEEVE INSIGNIA — FORMER WARTIME ORGANIZATION — ½" down from shoulder seam and centered (subdued only).

INSIGNIA NAMETAPE — Centered, immediately above and parallel to top of pocket.

Hospital duty uniform, male *(left)*, and female dress and pantsuit.

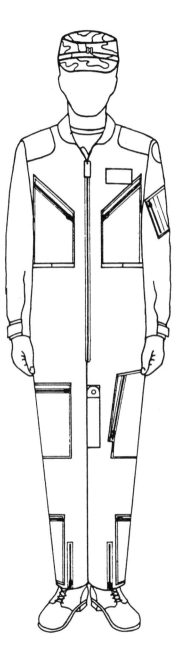

Flight uniform.

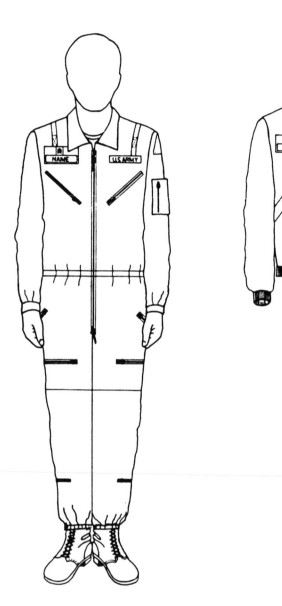

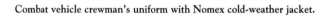

Combat vehicle crewman's uniform with Nomex cold-weather jacket.

A SOLDIER'S HAIR, SIDEBURNS, AND MUSTACHE ARE TO BE KEPT IN A NEAT MANNER AT ALL TIMES. (see AR 670-1 for guidelines.)

INSIGNIA OF BRANCH—Approximately 1" above notch and centered on collar with the center-line of the insignia bisecting the notch and parallel to the inside edge of the collar.

DISTINCTIVE UNIT INSIGNIA (crest)—Centered between outside edge of button and shoulder seam.

SPECIAL SKILL BADGE—¼" above ribbons.

SHOULDER SLEEVE INSIGNIA (Current Organization Patch)—½" down from shoulder seam and centered.

SERVICE RIBBONS—⅛" above pocket with or without ⅛" space between rows and will be worn from wearer's right to left in order of precedence.

INSIGNIA OF GRADE (Stripes)—centered halfway between shoulder seam and elbow and centered on sleeve.

MARKSMANSHIP BADGE—centered between top of button hole and top of pocket.

IDENTIFICATION BADGE—centered on pocket between bottom of flap and bottom of pocket.

SERVICE STRIPES (Hash Marks)—4" above bottom of sleeve and centered on the left sleeve (stripes run diagonally).

TROUSERS—will reach top of instep (may have a slight break in front), and cut diagonally to midpoint between top of heel and top of shoe at the rear.

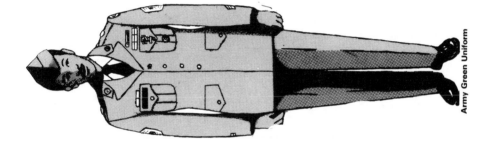

Army Green Uniform

GARRISON CAP—Worn with front vertical crease of cap centered on forehead in a straight line with nose. Cap will be slightly tilted to the right, but will not touch ear.

BLACK FOUR-IN-HAND TIE

US INSIGNIA—Approximately 1" above notch and centered on collar with centerline of insignia bisecting the notch and parallel to the inside edge of the lapel.

SHOULDER SLEEVE INSIGNIA/FORMER WARTIME ORGANIZATION—½" down from shoulder seam and centered.

UNIT AWARD EMBLEM—centered ⅛" above pocket.

NAMEPLATE—on flap of pocket centered between top of button and top of pocket.

INSIGNIA OF GRADE—same as other side.

OVERSEA BARS (Hershey Bars)—4" above and parallel to the bottom of the right sleeve and centered.

IDENTIFICATION TAGS (Dog Tags)—Worn when engaged in field training, when traveling in aircraft, and when outside CONUS.

BELT—1¼" black web or woven elastic web with a black or brass tip. The tip will pass through the buckle to the wearer's left; the brass tip only will extend beyond the buckle.

BUCKLE—1¾" x 2¼" oval shaped, plain-faced, solid brass.

BERET – Worn tilted slightly to back of head with insignia centered on the forehead and not forward of forehead hairline (insignia will be placed ¾" from bottom edge of Beret front, parallel to floor and centered on eyelet).

US INSIGNIA – Bottom of disk centered approximately ⅝" up from notch with center line of insignia parallel to inside edge of lapel.

SHOULDER SLEEVE INSIGNIA – FORMER WARTIME ORGANIZATION – ½" down from shoulder seam and centered.

UNIT AWARD EMBLEM – Centered with bottom edge ⅛" above top of nameplate.

INSIGNIA OF GRADE (STRIPES) – Centered halfway between shoulder seam and elbow and centered on sleeve.

NAMEPLATE – Centered 1-2" above top edge of top button.

OVERSEA SERVICE BARS (Hershey Bars) – 4" above and parallel to the bottom of the right sleeve and centered.

SKIRT – Not more than 1" above or 2" below crease in back of knee.

STOCKINGS – Unpatterned/non-pastel materials of sheer or semi-sheer, with or without seams.

PUMPS – Black Service, untrimmed, closed toe heel, heel 1" to 3" and sole thickness ½" max.

IDENTIFICATION TAGS (Dog Tags) – Worn when engaged in field training, when traveling in aircraft, and when outside CONUS.

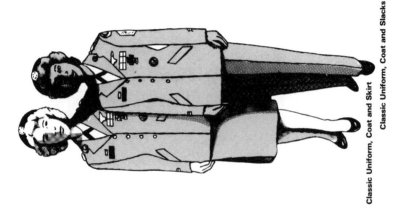

Classic Uniform, Coat and Skirt

Classic Uniform, Coat and Slacks

INSIGNIA OF BRANCH – Same as US Insignia.

DISTINCTIVE UNIT INSIGNIA (Crest) – Centered between outside of button and shoulder seam.

SPECIAL SKILL BADGE – ¼" above ribbons.

SHOULDER SLEEVE INSIGNIA (current organization) – ½" down from shoulder seam and centered.

SERVICE RIBBONS – Centered with bottom line positioned parallel to bottom edge of nameplate.

MARKSMANSHIP BADGE – Centered parallel to top edge of top button ¼" below service ribbons. (Slight adjustment to conform to individual figure differences authorized.)

IDENTIFICATION BADGE – Centered with top edge of badge parallel to top edge of third button from top.

SERVICE STRIPES (Hash marks) – 4" above bottom of the left sleeve and centered (stripes run diagonally).

SOCKS – Optional plain black cotton or cotton nylon may be worn with black oxford shoes or Jodhpur boots, when worn with slacks.

SHOES – Black Oxford leather (nonpatent) with maximum of 3 eyelets, closed toe and heel (heel no higher than 2").

JEWELRY: EARRINGS – Screw-on or post-type on optional basis with service, dress, and mess uniforms only. NECKLACE: A purely religious medal on a chain is authorized as long as neither is exposed. A WRIST WATCH AND NOT MORE THAN TWO RINGS ARE AUTHORIZED.

Green Maternity Service Uniform

This uniform is authorized for year-round wear by pregnant soldiers when on or off duty or during travel. This uniform and its variations (Class B) may be worn for formal and informal social functions after Retreat. Appropriate civilian maternity attire may be worn in lieu of this uniform for social functions.

Army Blue Uniform (Male)

This uniform is authorized for optional wear by enlisted personnel. Although primarily a uniform for social functions of a general or official nature before or after Retreat, it may be worn on duty if prescribed by the commander.

Army Blue Uniform (Female)

The guidelines for wear are similar to those for the blue uniform authorized for male soldiers.

Other Uniforms Authorized

- Army white uniform for both male and female soldiers.
- Food service uniform, including a maternity uniform.
- Army blue mess uniform.
- Army white mess uniform.

PERSONAL APPEARANCE

A vital ingredient of the Army's strength and military effectiveness is the pride and self-discipline that soldiers bring to their service. It is the responsibility of noncommissioned officers to assure that the military personnel under their supervision present a neat and soldierly appearance. It is the duty of each individual soldier to take pride in his or her appearance always.

Standards for Male Personnel

Many hairstyles are acceptable in the Army. So long as a soldier's hair is kept in a neat manner, the acceptability of the style should be judged solely by the criteria set forth in AR 670-1.

A soldier's face should be clean shaven, except that Army regulations do permit mustaches. If you decide to grow a mustache, keep it neatly trimmed and tidy. No portion should be permitted to cover the upper lip line or extend beyond the crease of the upper and lower lips. Handlebar mustaches, goatees, and beards are not authorized. Where beard growth is prescribed by appropriate medical authority, as is sometimes necessary in the treatment of different types of skin disorders, the length required for medical treatment should be specified: "A neatly trimmed beard is authorized. The length will not exceed $1/4$ inch," for example. If you should have such a soldier under your authority, follow his medical progress closely and be sure he keeps his exemption slip handy at all times when in uniform.

Standards for Female Personnel

The principle that soldiers should always maintain a neat and well-groomed personal appearance applies equally to men and to women, though the specific grooming standard for each reflects the traditional differences in appearance between the sexes.

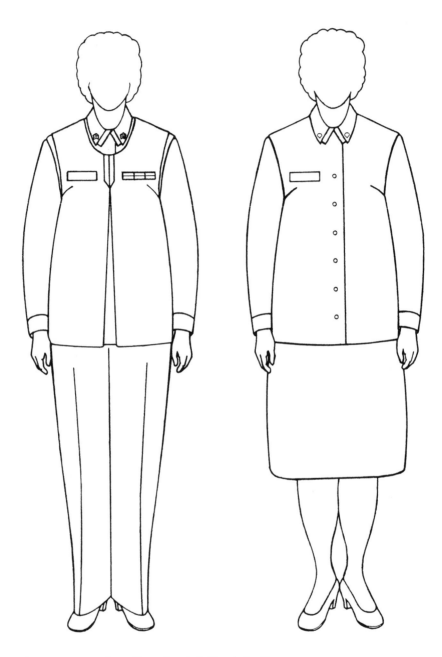

Army green maternity uniform, class A *(left)* and class B.

Army blue uniform with service cap.

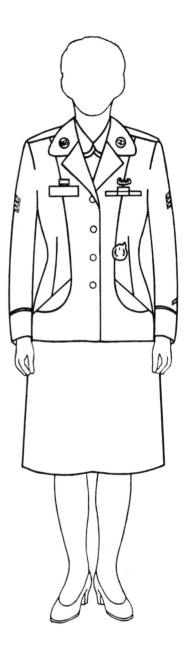

Army blue uniform with service cap.

Hair will be neatly groomed. The length and/or bulk of the hair should not be excessive or present a ragged, unkempt, or extreme appearance. Hairstyles will not interfere with the proper wearing of military headgear or protective masks.

Cosmetics shall be applied conservatively and in good taste.

Wearing of Civilian Jewelry

The wearing of a personal wristwatch, identification wrist bracelet, and not more than two rings is authorized with the Army uniform as long as they are not prohibited for safety reasons and the style is conservative and in good taste. The wearing of a purely religious medal on a chain around the neck is authorized, provided that neither the medal nor the chain is exposed.

No jewelry, watch chains, or similar civilian items, including pens or pencils, should be allowed to appear exposed on the uniform. Exceptions are that a conservative tie tack or tie clasp may be worn with the black four-in-hand necktie, and a pen or pencil may appear exposed on the hospital duty and food service uniforms.

Female soldiers may wear screw-on or post-type earrings with the service, dress, or mess uniforms. Earrings may not be worn with Class C utility uniforms (utility, field, or organization, including hospital duty and food service uniforms). Earrings will be small in diameter, 6 millimeters or $1/4$ inch; gold, silver, or white pearl; unadorned; and spherical. When worn, they will fit snugly against the ear and will be worn as a matched pair with only one in each earlobe.

Wearing of Civilian Clothing

Civilian clothing is authorized for wear when off duty unless the wear is prohibited by the installation commander within CONUS or the major command overseas. When on duty in civilian clothes, soldiers will conform to the appearance standards of AR 670-1, unless specifically authorized for mission requirements.

Security Badges

Security identification badges are worn in restricted areas as prescribed by local commanders. They are usually laminated plastic identification badges worn suspended from clips. They should never be worn outside the secure area for which they authorize an individual access. To prevent the possibility of losing them, some personnel suspend them from a chain worn around the neck and, when in public, under their outer garments.

DISTINCTIVE UNIFORM ITEMS

The following uniform items are distinctive and should not be sold to or worn by unauthorized personnel: all Army headgear, badges, decorations, service medals, awards, tabs, service ribbons, and appurtenances, insignia of any design or color that have been adopted by the Department of the Army.

Headgear

The following items of headgear are authorized for Army personnel:

Item	Female Version*
Beret, black (Ranger)	Beret, black, service
Beret, green (Special Forces)	

Item	*Female Version**
Beret, maroon (Airborne)	
Cap, cold weather (AG 344)	
Cap, cold weather, utility	
Cap, food handler's, white, paper	
Cap, garrison, green (AG 489)	Cap, garrison (AG 489)
Cap, hot weather	
Cap, service, green	Hat, service, green
Cap, service, white	Hat, service, white
Hat, camouflage, desert	
Hat, drill sergeant	

Service Stripes

Service stripes are diagonal chevrons worn on the left sleeve of the prescribed uniform coat that signify length of service. One stripe is authorized for each 3 years of active federal service, active Reserve service, or combination thereof. Service need not have been continuous, and a tenth stripe is authorized after 29 $^1/_2$ years.

Overseas Service Bars

Overseas service bars are gold lace, gold bullion, or gold color rayon bars, $^3/_{16}$ inch wide and 1 $^5/_{16}$ inch long on an olive green background that forms a $^3/_{32}$-inch border around the bar, for male personnel. Female personnel wear a bar $^1/_8$ inch wide and $^7/_8$ inch long on an olive green background that forms a $^1/_{16}$-inch border around the bar.

The overseas service bar is worn centered on the outside bottom half of the right sleeve of the Army green uniform coat for male personnel and the Army green and Army green pantsuit uniform coats for female personnel.

Shoulder Sleeve Insignia—Current Organization

Full-color shoulder sleeve insignia of an individual's current organization are worn centered on the left sleeve $^1/_2$ inch below the top of the shoulder seam on Army green coats for all personnel and the Army green pantsuit jacket for all female personnel.

Shoulder Sleeve Insignia—Former Wartime Service

At an individual's option, the shoulder sleeve insignia representing wartime service in a former organization may be worn on the right sleeve of all Army green uniform coats for all personnel and on the Army green pantsuit jacket for female personnel; a subdued version only may be worn on the field and work uniform coats and shirts.

Combat Leader's Identification

The Combat Leader's Identification insignia is a green cloth loop, 1 $^5/_8$ inches wide, worn in the middle of both shoulder loops of the Army green and cold weather coats. Personnel cease to wear them when reassigned from a command position or from an organization where these insignia are authorized to be worn.

---

*These are distinctively female items. Other items of headgear listed may be worn by female soldiers, as prescribed in AR 670-1.

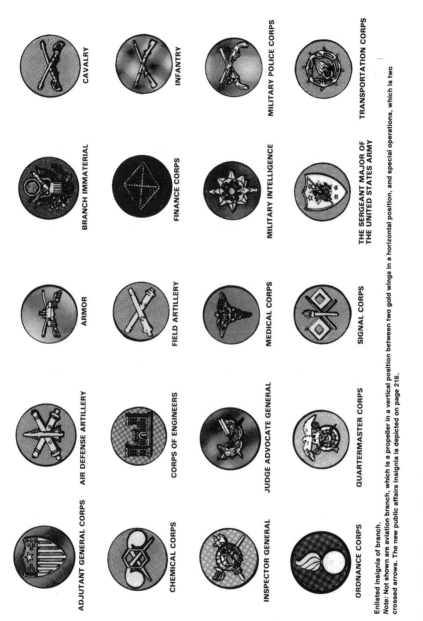

CAVALRY

INFANTRY

MILITARY POLICE CORPS

TRANSPORTATION CORPS

BRANCH IMMATERIAL

FINANCE CORPS

MILITARY INTELLIGENCE

THE SERGEANT MAJOR OF THE UNITED STATES ARMY

ARMOR

FIELD ARTILLERY

MEDICAL CORPS

SIGNAL CORPS

AIR DEFENSE ARTILLERY

CORPS OF ENGINEERS

JUDGE ADVOCATE GENERAL

QUARTERMASTER CORPS

ADJUTANT GENERAL CORPS

CHEMICAL CORPS

INSPECTOR GENERAL

ORDNANCE CORPS

Enlisted insignia of branch.
Note: Not shown are aviation branch, which is a propeller in a vertical position between two gold wings in a horizontal position, and special operations, which is two crossed arrows. The new public affairs insignia is depicted on page 216.

Selected enlisted insignia of branch.

The specific leaders in units authorized to wear the Combat Leader's Identification insignia are these: commanders, deputy commanders' platoon leaders, command sergeants major, first sergeants, platoon sergeants, section leaders (when designated in TOE), squad leaders and tank commanders, and rifle squad fire team leaders.

DISTINCTIVE UNIT INSIGNIA AND HERALDIC ITEMS

Distinctive unit insignia are made of metal or metal and enamel and are usually based on elements of the design of the coat of arms or historic badge approved for a specific unit. Sometimes erroneously referred to as "unit crests," distinctive unit insignia are subject to the approval of the Institute of Heraldry, U.S. Army, and, like shoulder sleeve insignia, are authorized for wear on the uniform as a means of promoting esprit de corps.

When authorized, these insignia are worn by all assigned personnel of an organization, except general officers. A complete set of insignia consists of three pieces: one for each shoulder loop and one for headgear (garrison, utility, cold weather caps, or berets).

Regimental distinctive unit insignia are worn by all personnel affiliated with a regiment. The "crest" of the affiliated regiment is worn centered and $1/8$ inch above the pocket seam or $1/2$ inch above unit and foreign awards, if worn, on the Army green, white, and blue uniforms. The DUI worn on the shoulder loops of the Army green, white, and blue (enlisted men only) coats and jackets is always the unit of assignment. If assigned and affiliated to the same regiment, then all three crests are the same.

Distinctive Items—Infantry

Infantry personnel are authorized to wear the following distinctive items:
• A shoulder cord of infantry blue formed by a series of interlocking square knots around a center cord. The cord is worn on the right shoulder of the Army green, blue, and white uniform coats and shirts, passed under the arm and through the shoulder loop and secured to the button on the shoulder loop.
• An insignia disc, branch, and "U.S.," of infantry blue plastic, $1 1/4$ inches in diameter. The disc is worn by enlisted personnel of the infantry, secured beneath the branch of the service and the U.S. insignia, with a $1/8$-inch border around the insignia. It is authorized to be worn on the Army green, blue, and white uniforms.
• An insignia disc, service cap, of infantry blue plastic, $1 3/4$ inches in diameter. This disc is worn secured beneath the insignia on the service cap. Criteria for wear are the same as those for the insignia disc.

Distinctive Items—Other than Infantry

Organizational Flash. This shield-shaped embroidered patch with a semicircular bottom approximately $2 1/4$ inches long and $1 7/8$ inches wide is worn centered on the stiffener of the beret by personnel authorized to wear one of the organizational berets (Ranger, Special Forces, and airborne).

Airborne Background Trimming. Background trimming is authorized for wear with the parachutist or air assault badge. When authorized, such background will be worn by all personnel of an airborne-designated organization who have been awarded one of the parachute badges or by personnel in an organization designated air assault who have been awarded the air assault badge.

ARMY INSIGNIA OF RANK

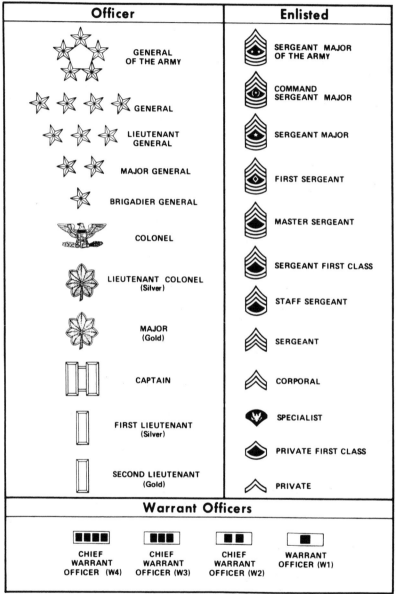

Officer | Enlisted

Officer

- GENERAL OF THE ARMY
- GENERAL
- LIEUTENANT GENERAL
- MAJOR GENERAL
- BRIGADIER GENERAL
- COLONEL
- LIEUTENANT COLONEL (Silver)
- MAJOR (Gold)
- CAPTAIN
- FIRST LIEUTENANT (Silver)
- SECOND LIEUTENANT (Gold)

Enlisted

- SERGEANT MAJOR OF THE ARMY
- COMMAND SERGEANT MAJOR
- SERGEANT MAJOR
- FIRST SERGEANT
- MASTER SERGEANT
- SERGEANT FIRST CLASS
- STAFF SERGEANT
- SERGEANT
- CORPORAL
- SPECIALIST
- PRIVATE FIRST CLASS
- PRIVATE

Warrant Officers

CHIEF WARRANT OFFICER (W4)

CHIEF WARRANT OFFICER (W3)

CHIEF WARRANT OFFICER (W2)

WARRANT OFFICER (W1)

Airborne Insignia. This white parachute and glider in a blue disk with a red border, approximately 2 $1/4$ inches in diameter, is worn by all personnel on jump status or by parachute-qualified personnel in special nonairborne duty (recruiting personnel or instructors). Enlisted personnel wear the insignia designed with the glider facing forward when it is worn centered on the left curtain of the garrison cap, 1 inch from the front crease.

Collar Brass Insignia

Collar brass insignia consist of "U.S." insignia and insignia of branch mounted on a 1-inch-diameter disc of gold-colored metal worn on the prescribed uniform in a prescribed manner.

Male personnel wear these approximately 1 inch above the notch centered on the collar with the center line of the insignia parallel to the inside edge of the lapel on the Army green, white, and blue uniform coats.

Female personnel wear the bottom of the insignia disc so that it is placed approximately 1 inch above the notch centered on the collar with the center line of the insignia bisecting the notch and parallel to the inside edge of the lapel of the Army green pantsuit jacket, and green, blue, and white uniform coats. On the green classic uniform coat, they are centered on the collar approximately $5/8$ inch up from the notch, with the center line of the insignia parallel to the inside edge of the lapel.

Enlisted Insignia of Rank

Enlisted insignia of rank come in three basic types: sew-on, pin-on, and shoulder mark type. The cloth sew-on sleeve insignia come in full-color; the metal pin-on collar insignia are either subdued metal or polished brass. Noncommissioned officers, privates first class, and privates E-2 are identified by a system of chevrons and/or arcs. Privates E-1 have no insignia or rank. The Army specialist grade is identified by a spread-eagle device.

Sources

Romana Danysh and John K. Manon, *Army Lineage Series. Infantry. Part 1: Regular Army*, Government Printing Office: Washington, DC, 1972, pp. 123–24.

AR 670-1, *Uniform and Insignia.*

AR 672-5-1, *Military Awards.*

AR 700-84, *Issue and Sale of Personal Clothing.*

FM 21-15, *Care and Use of Individual Clothing and Equipment.*

15

Awards and Decorations

The Army's awards and decorations program provides tangible recognition for acts of valor, exceptional service or achievement, special skills or qualifications, and acts of heroism not involving actual combat. It is the responsibility of any soldier having personal knowledge of an act, an achievement, or a service believed to warrant the award of a decoration to submit a formal recommendation for consideration.

Under this criteria, it is possible that a private may recommend a captain for a decoration, but usually the system works the other way. As an NCO, you must be alert for service or acts that warrant special recognition. The only consideration that should be used is this one: *Does the person's act or service warrant a decoration?*

CRITERIA

Award recommendations must be factual and specific, and they must clearly demonstrate that the person being recommended deserves recognition. If your narrative does not support award of a decoration—if you use clichés and gobbledygook in place of straightforward and factual prose narrative writing—your recommendation likely will be disapproved.

TIME LIMITATION

Awards for meritorious service should be anticipated, and your recommendation should be submitted far enough in advance to ensure that the award is ready in time to be presented to the individual before his or her departure.

Another reason for acting quickly is that the closer you are to the act or service for which an individual is being recommended, the fresher the details will be in your memory. In any event, each recommendation for an award of a military decoration must be entered into military channels within two years of the act, achievement, or service to be honored. No recommendation except the Purple Heart is awarded more than three years after the act or period of service to be honored (with the exception of lost recommendations or those circumstances covered in paragraph 1-30, AR 672-5-1). If a soldier under your supervision deserved an award recommendation, let him or her know about it. If the recommendation is not approved, at least the soldier will know you tried and will respect you for it.

PRECEDENCE

Decorations, the Good Conduct Medal, and service medals are ranked in the following order of precedence when worn or displayed:

> U.S. military decorations
> U.S. unit awards
> U.S. nonmilitary decorations
> Good Conduct Medal
> Army Reserve Components Achievement Medal
> U.S. service medals and training ribbons
> U.S. Merchant Marine awards
> Foreign military decorations
> Foreign unit awards
> Non–U.S. service awards

U.S. military decorations, the Good Conduct Medal, and U.S. service medals are ranked in the following order of precedence when worn or displayed:

> Medal of Honor
> Distinguished Service Cross
> Defense Distinguished Service Medal
> Distinguished Service Medal
> Silver Star
> Defense Superior Service Medal
> Legion of Merit
> Distinguished Flying Cross
> Soldier's Medal
> Bronze Star Medal
> Purple Heart
> Defense Meritorious Service Medal
> Meritorious Service Medal
> Air Medal
> Joint Service Commendation Medal
> Army Commendation Medal
> Joint Service Achievement Medal
> Army Achievement Medal
> Prisoner of War Medal
> Good Conduct Medal
> Army Reserve Components Achievement Medal

U.S. unit awards:

> Presidential Unit Citation
> Valorous Unit Award
> Joint Meritorious Unit Award
> Meritorious Unit Commendation
> Army Superior Unit Award

U.S. service medals:

> Army of Occupation Medal
> National Defense Service Medal

Antarctica Service Medal
Armed Forces Expeditionary Medal
Vietnam Service Medal
Southwest Asia Service Medal
Humanitarian Service Medal
Military Outstanding Volunteer Service Medal
Armed Forces Reserve Medal
NCO Professional Development Ribbon
Army Service Ribbon
Overseas Service Ribbon
Army Reserve Components Overseas Training Ribbon

Non–U.S. service medals:
United Nations Medal
Multinational Force and Observers Medal
Republic of Vietnam Campaign Medal
Kuwait Liberation Medal

WEARING OF MEDALS AND RIBBONS

All individual U.S. decorations and service medals (full-size medals, miniature medals, and ribbons) are worn above the left breast pocket or centered on the left side of the coat or jacket of the prescribed uniform (with the exception of the Medal of Honor, which may be worn suspended around the neck). Decorations are worn with the highest displayed above and to the wearer's right of the others.

RIBBONS REPRESENTING
DECORATIONS AND SERVICE MEDALS

		1		
2	3	4	5	
6	7	8	9	
10	11	12	13	
14	15	16	17	
18	19	20	21	

1. Medal of Honor
2. Distinguished Service Cross
3. Distinguished Service Medal
4. Silver Star
5. Legion of Merit
6. Distinguished Flying Cross
7. Soldiers Medal
8. Bronze Star Medal
9. Purple Heart
10. Meritorious Service Medal
11. Air Medal
12. Army Commendation Medal
13. Army Achievement Medal
14. Good Conduct Medal
15. National Defense Service Medal
16. Armed Forces Expeditionary Medal
17. Vietnam Service Medal
18. Southwest Asia Service Medal
19. NCO Professional Development
20. Army Service Ribbon
21. Overseas Service Ribbon

Full-size decorations and service medals are worn on the Army blue, white, and green uniform when worn for social functions. They are worn in order of precedence from the wearer's right to left, in one or more lines, without overlapping within a line, with one-eighth-inch space between lines. No line will contain fewer medals than the one above it. The Medal of Honor is worn with the neckband ribbon around the neck, outside the shirt collar and inside the coat collar, with the medal hanging over the necktie.

Miniature decorations and service medals are authorized for wear on the mess and evening mess uniforms only. They may be worn side by side or overlapped, but the overlap will not exceed 50 percent and will be equal for all. There are no miniature medals authorized for either the Medal of Honor or the Legion of Merit.

Service ribbons are worn in the order of precedence from the wearer's right to left in one or more lines either without a space between rows or with a one-eighth-inch space. No row should contain more than four service ribbons. Male personnel are authorized to wear them on the Army green, white, and blue uniforms; female personnel may wear them on the AG 489 skirt and jacket, AG 489 dress and jacket, Army green pantsuit, and Army green, classic, white, and blue uniforms.

Retired personnel and former soldiers may wear either full-size or miniature medals on appropriate civilian clothing on Veterans Day, Memorial Day, and Armed Forces Day, and at formal occasions of ceremony and social functions of a military nature.

Unauthorized Wearing of Decorations and Badges

Federal law prescribes stiff penalties for the unauthorized wearing of U.S. decorations, badges, appurtenances, and unit awards:

> Whoever knowingly wears . . . any decoration or medal authorized by Congress for the Armed Forces of the United States or any of the service medals or badges awarded to the members of such forces, or the ribbon, button, or rosette of any such badge, decoration or medal, or any colorable imitation thereof, except when authorized under regulations made pursuant to law, shall be fined not more than $250 or imprisoned not more than six months, or both.
>
> —62 Stat. 732, 25 June 1948, as amended 18 U.S.C. 704

The U.S. Code (18 U.S.C. 703) further prescribes:

> Whoever, within the jurisdiction of the United States, with intent to deceive or mislead, wears any naval, military, police, or other official uniform, decoration, or regalia of any foreign state, nation, or government with which the United States is at peace, or anything so nearly resembling the same as to be calculated to deceive, shall be fined not more than $250 or imprisoned not more than six months or both.

The Medal of Honor (MOH)

The Army and Air Force version of the Medal of Honor is the highest award for the risk of life "above and beyond the call of duty" involving actual conflict with an enemy; the Navy version can and has been awarded to noncombatants in peacetime, and Congress has similarly awarded special Medals to honor individual exploits during peacetime.

The Medal of Honor is designed in the form of a five-pointed star, made of silver and heavily electroplated in gold. In the center of the star appears the head of Minerva—the Roman goddess whose name is associated with wisdom and righteousness in war—surrounded by the words "United States of America." An open laurel wreath, enameled in green, encircles the star, and the oak leaves at the bases of the prongs of the star are likewise enameled. The Medal is suspended by a blue silk ribbon, spangled with 13 white stars (representing the 13 original states), and attached to an eagle supported by a horizontal bar upon which is engraved the word "Valor."

The reverse of the Medal is plain so that the name of the recipient may be engraved thereon; the reverse of the bar is stamped "The Congress to."

On 21 December 1861, President Lincoln approved the Medal of Honor for enlisted men of the Navy and Marine Corps; a similar medal was established for the Army on 12 July 1862, further amended by legislation enacted on 3 March 1863 to include officers and making the provisions retroactive to the beginning of the war. The first Army Medals were awarded on 25 March 1863. The Medal of Honor is awarded only to U.S. citizens, and only one Medal may be awarded to any one individual. The Army Medal may be awarded only to military personnel on active federal service.

An awards parade at Fort Monroe, Virginia.

Distinguished Service Cross (DSC)

Established by legislation on 9 July 1918 (as amended 25 July 1963), the Distinguished Service Cross evolved from the Certificate of Merit of 1847. The DSC is the second highest decoration for valor in war and is bestowed to recognize extraordinary heroism in connection with military operations in time of war. Unlike the Medal of Honor, however, the DSC may be awarded for heroism involving several acts over a short period of time that need not have been performed in actual conflict with an enemy but must have involved extraordinary risk of life. Successive awards are denoted by oak-leaf clusters.

Defense Distinguished Service Medal (DDSM)

Established by Executive Order 11545, 9 July 1970, the DDSM is awarded to any military officer who, while assigned to joint staffs and other joint activities of the Department of Defense, distinguishes himself by exceptionally meritorious service in a position of unique and great responsibility. It is not awarded for a period of service for which a Distinguished Service Medal or similar decoration is awarded. Subsequent awards are denoted by oak-leaf clusters.

Distinguished Service Medal (DSM)

Established by an act of Congress of 9 July 1918, the DSM is awarded to any person who, while serving in any capacity with the U.S. Army, has distinguished himself by exceptionally meritorious service in a duty of great responsibility. Awards may be made to persons other than members of the armed forces of the United States for wartime services only and then only under exceptional circumstances with the approval of the president. Successive awards are denoted by oak-leaf clusters.

Silver Star (SS)

Established by an act of Congress of 9 July 1918 (as amended by an act of 25 July 1963), the Silver Star is the third-ranking U.S. decoration for heroism in wartime.

When first established, the SS was worn in the form of a small silver star, three sixteenths inch in diameter, upon the respective service medal and ribbon to indicate each separate citation for gallantry in action earned during the campaign for which the service medal was authorized. These stars were known as "citation stars."

The current version of the SS is gilt bronze in the shape of a star one and a quarter inches across. On the obverse is a laurel wreath, within which is a silver star three sixteenths inch in diameter; on the reverse are inscribed the words "For Gallantry in Action." The SS may be awarded by any commander who has the authority to award the DSC, and the SS, like the DSC, may be awarded for acts of heroism that take place over a period of time. Successive awards are denoted by oak-leaf clusters.

Defense Superior Service Medal (DSSM)

Established by Executive Order 11904, 6 February 1976, the DSSM may be awarded to U.S. personnel who give superior meritorious service in a position of significant responsibility. It is not awarded to any individual for a period of service for which a Legion of Merit or similar decoration is awarded. Successive awards are denoted by oak-leaf clusters.

DECORATIONS, SERVICE MEDALS, AND BADGES

U.S. ARMY AND DEPARTMENT OF DEFENSE
MILITARY DECORATIONS

Medal of Honor (Army)

**Distinguished Service
Cross (Army)**

**Defense Distinguished
Service Medal**

**Distinguished Service
Medal (Army)**

Silver Star

**Defense Superior
Service Medal**

Legion of Merit

**Distinguished Flying
Cross**

**Soldier's Medal
(Army)**

Bronze Star Medal

Purple Heart

**Defense
Meritorious Service
Medal**

**Meritorious Service
Medal**

Air Medal

Joint Service Commendation Medal

Army Commendation Medal

Joint Service Achievement Medal

Army Achievement Medal

OTHER U.S. ARMY AWARDS

Prisoner of War
Medal

Good Conduct
Medal (Army)

Army Reserve
Components
Achievement
Medal

PRE-VIETNAM U.S. MILITARY SERVICE MEDALS

World War II
Victory Medal

Korean
Service Medal

U.S. ARMY AND DEPARTMENT OF DEFENSE
UNIT AWARDS

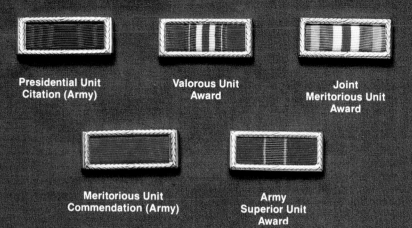

**Presidential Unit
Citation (Army)**

**Valorous Unit
Award**

**Joint
Meritorious Unit
Award**

**Meritorious Unit
Commendation (Army)**

**Army
Superior Unit
Award**

U.S. MILITARY SERVICE MEDALS AND RIBBONS

**National Defense
Service Medal**

**Antarctica
Service Medal**

**Armed Forces
Expeditionary
Medal**

**Vietnam
Service Medal**

**Southwest Asia
Service Medal**

**Humanitarian
Service Medal**

**Military
Outstanding
Volunteer
Service Medal**

**Armed Forces
Reserve Medal**

U.S. ARMY SERVICE AND TRAINING RIBBONS

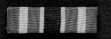

**NCO
Professional Development
Ribbon**

**Army
Service Ribbon**

**Overseas
Service Ribbon
(Army)**

**Army Reserve Components
Overseas Training Ribbon**

NON-U.S. SERVICE MEDALS

**United Nations
Medal**

**Multinational
Force Observers
Medal**

**Republic of
Vietnam
Campaign Medal**

**Kuwait
Liberation Medal**

U.S. ARMY BADGES AND TABS

Combat and Special Skill Badges

**Combat Infantryman Badge
1st Award**

**Combat Medical Badge
1st Award**

**Combat Infantryman Badge
2nd Award**

**Combat Medical Badge
2nd Award**

**Combat Infantryman Badge
3rd Award**

**Combat Medical Badge
3rd Award**

Expert Infantryman Badge

Expert Field Medical Badge

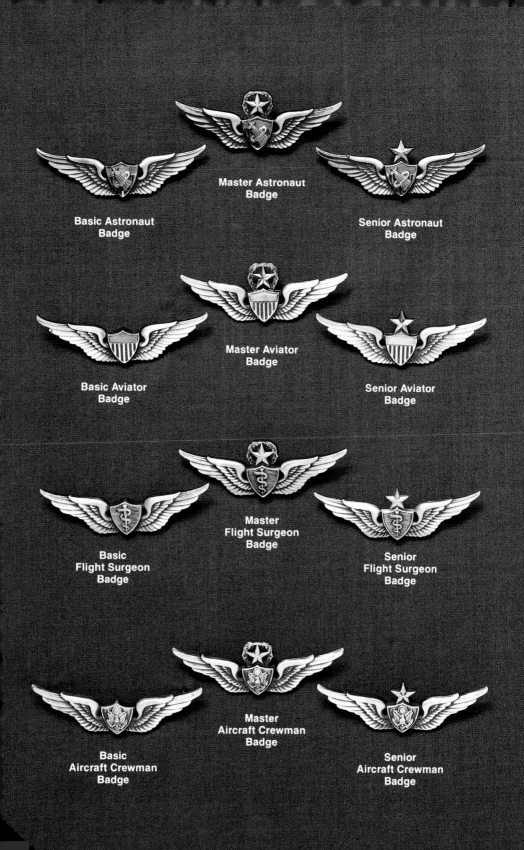

Master Astronaut
Badge

Basic Astronaut
Badge

Senior Astronaut
Badge

Master Aviator
Badge

Basic Aviator
Badge

Senior Aviator
Badge

Master
Flight Surgeon
Badge

Basic
Flight Surgeon
Badge

Senior
Flight Surgeon
Badge

Master
Aircraft Crewman
Badge

Basic
Aircraft Crewman
Badge

Senior
Aircraft Crewman
Badge

**Master Parachutist
Badge**

**Basic Parachutist
Badge**

**Senior Parachutist
Badge**

**Combat Parachutist
Badge (1 Jump)**

**Combat Parachutist
Badge (2 Jumps)**

**Combat Parachutist
Badge (3 Jumps)**

**Combat Parachutist
Badge (4 Jumps)**

**Combat Parachutist
Badge (5 Jumps)**

Air Assault Badge

Glider Badge

Pathfinder Badge

Special Forces Tab
(Metal Replica)

Ranger Tab
(Metal Replica)

Salvage Diver
Badge

Second Class Diver
Badge

First Class Diver
Badge

Master Diver
Badge

Scuba Diver
Badge

Master Explosive
Ordnance Disposal Badge

Basic Explosive
Ordnance Disposal Badge

Senior Explosive
Ordnance Disposal Badge

**Nuclear Reactor Operator
Badge (Basic)**

**Nuclear Reactor Operator
Badge (Second Class)**

**Nuclear Reactor Operator
Badge (First Class)**

**Nuclear Reactor Operator
Badge (Shift Supervisor)**

**Parachute Rigger
Badge**

**Driver and Mechanic
Badge**

Marksmanship Badges

Marksman

Sharpshooter

Expert

Identification Badges

Presidential Service

Vice-Presidential Service

Secretary of Defense

Joint Chiefs of Staff

Army Staff

Guard,
Tomb of the Unknown Soldier

Drill Sergeant

U.S. Army Recruiter
(Active Army)

U.S. Army Recruiter
(Army National Guard)

U.S. Army Recruiter
(U.S. Army Reserve)

Legion of Merit (LM)

Established by an act of Congress of 20 July 1942, the LM is awarded to any member of the armed forces of the United States or a friendly foreign country who distinguishes himself by outstanding meritorious conduct in the performance of outstanding services. Successive awards are denoted by oak-leaf clusters.

Distinguished Flying Cross (DFC)

Established by an act of Congress of 2 July 1926, the DFC may be awarded, in war or peace, to U.S. military personnel who distinguish themselves by heroism or extraordinary achievement while participating in aerial flight. Such awards are made only to recognize single acts of heroism or extraordinary achievement that are not sustained operational activities against an armed enemy. An act of heroism must be evidenced by voluntary action above and beyond the call of duty. Achievement awards must have resulted in an accomplishment so exceptional and outstanding as to clearly set the individual apart from other persons in similar circumstances. Awards to foreign personnel serving with the U.S. armed forces may be made only in connection with actual wartime operations. Successive awards are denoted by oak-leaf clusters.

Soldier's Medal (SM)

Established by an act of Congress of 2 July 1926, the SM is awarded to U.S. and foreign military personnel in recognition of heroism not involving actual conflict with an enemy. The performance must have involved personal hazard or danger and voluntary risk of life of approximately the same degree as that required for award of the Distinguished Flying Cross, but awards of the SM are not made solely on the basis of having saved a life. Subsequent awards of this decoration are denoted by oak-leaf clusters.

Bronze Star Medal (BSM)

Originally established by Executive Order 9419 of 4 February 1944 (superseded by Executive Order 11046 of 26 August 1962), the BSM can be awarded to U.S. and foreign personnel, both military and civilian, for acts that display heroism, meritorious achievement, or service performed in connection with military operations against an armed force. A bronze V device is worn to denote awards for heroism, and successive awards are denoted by oak-leaf clusters.

Purple Heart (PH)

Originally established by GEN George Washington on 7 August 1782, the Purple Heart is the oldest U.S. military decoration. The PH is awarded in the name of the president to any member of the armed forces or any civilian of the United States who, while serving under competent authority in any capacity with one of the U.S. armed services after 5 April 1917, has been wounded or killed or who has died or may die after being wounded.

A "wound" is defined as any injury (not necessarily one that breaks the skin) caused by an outside force or agent. Multiple injuries suffered at the same moment from the same agent are considered as one wound. Specific examples of injuries that would be authorized the award of the PH are those incurred while making a parachute landing from an aircraft that had been brought down by enemy fire or injuries received as the result of a vehicle accident caused by enemy fire (paragraph 2-19b, AR 672-5-1).

The modern version of the medal bears the profile of George Washington and is engraved with the words "For Military Merit" on the reverse. Subsequent awards of the PH are denoted by oak-leaf clusters.

Defense Meritorious Service Medal (DMSM)

Established by Executive Order 12019 of 3 November 1977, the DMSM is awarded in the name of the Secretary of Defense to any member of the armed forces who, while serving in any joint activity of the Department of Defense on or after 3 November 1977 and for a period of 60 days or more, demonstrates incontestably exceptional service or achievement of a magnitude that clearly places him above his or her peers. Subsequent awards of the DMSM are denoted by oak-leaf clusters.

Meritorious Service Medal (MSM)

Established by Executive Order 1144.8 on 16 January 1969, the MSM is awarded to any member of the armed forces of the United States who, while serving in a non-combat area after 16 January 1969, has distinguished himself by outstanding meritorious achievement or service. The achievement or service must have been comparable to that required for the Legion of Merit but in a position of lesser, though considerable, responsibility. This decoration is the equivalent of the Bronze Star Medal for recognition of outstanding meritorious noncombat achievement or service and takes precedence with, but after, the BSM when both are worn on the uniform. This decoration is not awarded to foreign personnel. Subsequent awards are denoted by oak-leaf clusters.

Air Medal (AM)

Established by Executive Order 9242-A, 11 September 1942, the AM is awarded to any person who, while serving in any capacity in or with the Army, shall have distinguished himself by meritorious achievement while participating in aerial flight. Awards may be made in recognition of single acts of merit or heroism or for meritorious service. A system of denoting successive awards of the medal was devised using bronze arabic numerals instead of oak-leaf clusters. Therefore, an individual holding 15 awards of the AM wears the numeral "14" on the suspension ribbon and service ribbon.

Joint Service Commendation Medal (JSCM)

Established by Department of Defense Directive 1348.14, 17 May 1967, the JSCM is awarded to any member of the armed forces who distinguishes himself by meritorious achievement or service while serving in any joint assignment. Awards made for acts or services involving direct participation in combat operations on or after 25 June 1963 may be denoted by the bronze V device. Subsequent awards of the JSCM are denoted by oak-leaf clusters.

Army Commendation Medal (ARCOM)

Established by War Department Circular 377, 18 December 1943 (amended in DA General Orders 10, 1960), the ARCOM is awarded to any member of the armed forces who distinguishes himself by heroism, meritorious achievement, or meritorious service. The ARCOM may also be awarded to a member of the armed forces of a friendly foreign nation who distinguishes himself by an act of heroism, extraordinary achievement, or meritorious service that has been of mutual benefit to a friendly nation and the United States. Awards of the ARCOM may be made for acts of valor performed under circumstances described above that are of lesser degree than those required for award of the Bronze Star Medal and may include acts that involve aerial flight. Awards may also be made for noncombat acts of heroism that do not meet the requirements for award of the Soldier's Medal. This decoration is primarily awarded to company-grade officers, warrant officers, and enlisted personnel.

Joint Service Achievement Medal (JSAM)
The Joint Service Achievement Medal is awarded to any member of the armed forces of the United States, below the grade of full colonel, who distinguishes himself or herself by meritorious achievement or service while serving in any joint activity after 3 August 1983. Military personnel on temporary duty to a joint activity for at least 60 days are also eligible.

The required achievement or service, while of lesser degree than that required for award of the Joint Service Commendation Medal, must have been accomplished with distinction. Subsequent awards are designated by oak-leaf clusters.

Army Achievement Medal (AAM)
The Army Achievement Medal is awarded to any member of the armed forces of the United States, or to any member of the armed forces of a friendly foreign nation, who, while serving in any capacity with the Army in a noncombat area on or after 1 August 1981, distinguishes himself by meritorious service or achievement of a lesser degree than that required for award of the Army Commendation Medal. Subsequent awards are designated by oak-leaf clusters.

Prisoner of War Medal (POWM)
This award is authorized for all U.S. military personnel who were taken prisoner of war after 6 April 1917 during an armed conflict and who served honorably during the period of captivity.

Good Conduct Medal (GCM)
Established by Executive Order 8809, War Department Bulletin 17, 1941, and amended in 1943 (Executive Order 9323, War Department Bulletin 6, 1943) and 1953 (Executive Order 10444, Department of the Army Bulletin 4, 1953), the GCM is awarded to enlisted personnel for exemplary behavior, efficiency, and fidelity to active federal military service. Generally, the qualifying period is three years of continuous active service completed on or after 26 August 1940. Exceptions are for those who are separated from the service by reason of physical disability incurred in the line of duty, who died or were killed before completing one year of service, or who separated after more than one year but less than three years (draftees). Those exceptions apply only to the first award.

Isolated examples of nonjudicial punishment are not necessarily automatically disqualifying but must be considered on the basis of the soldier's whole record; consideration as to the nature of the infraction, the circumstances under which it occurred, and when it occurred must be duly weighed by the individual's commander. Conviction by court-martial terminates a period of qualifying service; a new period begins following the completion of the sentence imposed by court-martial.

Successive awards of the GCM are identified by clasps, or bars one eighth by one and three eighths inches, or bronze, silver, or gold, with loops (also called knots) that indicate each period of service for which the medal is authorized. The first award is the actual medal itself. Successive awards are indicated with clasps with loops.

Army Reserve Components Achievement Medal

Established by DA General Orders 30, 1971, this medal may be awarded upon recommendation of the unit commander for four years of honest and faithful service on or after 3 March 1972. Service must have been consecutive, in the grade of colonel or below, and in accordance with the standards of conduct, courage, and duty required by law and customs of the service of an active-duty member of the same grade. The reverse of this medal is struck in two designs for award to personnel whose service has been primarily in the Army Reserve or primarily in the National Guard.

U.S. ARMY AND DEPARTMENT OF DEFENSE UNIT AWARDS

Unit awards are authorized in recognition of group heroism or meritorious service, usually during a war, as a means of promoting esprit de corps. They are of the following categories: unit decorations, infantry and medical streamers, campaign streamers, war service streamers, and campaign silver bands.

U.S. unit decorations, in order of precedence listed in this section, have been established to recognize outstanding heroism or exceptionally meritorious conduct in the performance of outstanding services. These awards may be worn permanently by those who served with the unit during the cited period. The Presidential Unit Citation (Army), the Valorous Unit Award, the Meritorious Unit Commendation, and the Army Superior Unit Award may be worn temporarily by those serving with the unit subsequent to the cited period.

Presidential Unit Citation

The Presidential Unit Citation is awarded to units of the armed forces of the United States and cobelligerent nations for extraordinary heroism in action against an armed enemy occurring on or after 7 December 1941. The unit must display such gallantry, determination, and esprit de corps in accomplishing its mission under extremely difficult and hazardous conditions as to set it apart from and above other units participating in the same campaign. The degree of heroism required is the same as that which would warrant award of a Distinguished Service Cross to an individual. The Presidential Unit Emblem (Army) is a blue ribbon set in a gold-colored metal frame of laurel leaves.

Valorous Unit Award

Criteria for the Valorous Unit Award are the same as those for the Presidential Unit Citation except that the degree of valor required is that which would merit award of the Silver Star to an individual. The emblem is a scarlet ribbon with the Silver Star color design superimposed in the center, set in a gold-colored metal frame with laurel leaves.

Joint Meritorious Unit Award

The Joint Meritorious Unit Award is awarded to Joint Activities of the DOD for meritorious achievement or service, superior to that normally expected, during combat with an armed enemy of the United States, during a declared national emergency, or under extraordinary circumstances that involve the national interest.

Meritorious Unit Commendation

The Meritorious Unit Commendation is awarded for at least six months of exceptionally meritorious conduct in support of military operations to service and support units of the armed forces of the United States and cobelligerent nations. The degree of achievement is that which would merit the award of the Legion of Merit to an individual. The emblem is a scarlet ribbon set in a gold-colored metal frame with laurel leaves.

Army Superior Unit Award

The Army Superior Unit Award is given for outstanding meritorious performance of a difficult and challenging mission under extraordinary circumstances by a unit during peacetime. The emblem is a scarlet ribbon with a vertical green stripe in the center, on each side of which is a narrow yellow stripe, set in a gold-colored metal frame with laurel leaves.

SERVICE MEDALS

Service or campaign medals denote honorable performance of military duty within specified limited dates in specified geographical areas. With the exception of the Humanitarian Service Medal, the Armed Forces Reserve Medal, the Army Reserve Component Achievement Medal, the Army Service Ribbon, and the NCO Professional Development Ribbon, they are awarded only for active federal military service.

Service medals are worn in order by the date when the person became eligible for the award, not by the date of entry in the records or the date upon which the award was established. Foreign military service medals are worn following authorized U.S. decorations. Not more than one service medal is awarded for service involving identical or overlapping periods of time, except that each of the following groups of service medals may be awarded to an individual provided he or she meets the criteria prescribed by chapter 4, AR 672-5-1. For information concerning the criteria for the award of any service medal not listed below, see chapter 4, AR 672-5-1.

Army of Occupation Medal

Established by the War Department General Orders 32, 1946, this medal is awarded for service for 30 consecutive days at a normal post of duty with the Army of Occupation of Berlin.

This medal was previously authorized for post–World War II occupation duty in Germany, Austria, Italy, Japan, and Korea (see paragraph 4-24, AR 672-5-1). Berlin service does not authorize the wearing of a clasp on either the service medal or the service ribbon.

National Defense Service Medal

This medal is awarded for honorable active service for any period from 27 June 1950 to 27 July 1954 or for the period from 1 January 1961 to 14 August 1974. The NDSM was again authorized for wear by those who served honorably during the Persian Gulf hostilities. Subsequent award of the NDSM is denoted by a bronze service star.

Antarctica Service Medal

This medal is awarded to any member of the armed forces who meets one of the following criteria:
• Is a member of a direct support or exploratory operation in Antarctica.
• Participates in or has participated in a foreign Antarctic expedition in coordination with a U.S. expedition while under the sponsorship and approval of a U.S. government authority.
• Participates in flights as a member of the crew of an aircraft flying to or from the Antarctic continent in support of operations there.
• Serves aboard a U.S. ship operating south of latitude 60 degrees south in support of U.S. programs in Antarctica.

Effective 1 June 1973, minimum time limits for the award are 30 days' duty at sea or ashore south of latitude 60 degrees south. Flight crews of aircraft providing logistics support from outside the Antarctica area receive one-day credit for flights in and out during any 24-hour period. Days need not be consecutive.

Personnel who remain on the Antarctic continent during the winter months are eligible to wear a clasp with the words "Wintered Over" on the suspension ribbon of the medal and disc, five sixteenths inch in diameter, with an outline of the Antarctic continent inscribed thereon fastened to the bar ribbon. These appurtenances are awarded in bronze for the first winter, gold for the second, and silver for personnel who "winter over" three or more times. Not more than one clasp or disc is worn on the ribbon, and no person is authorized to receive more than one award of the medal.

Armed Forces Expeditionary Medal

Established by Executive Order 10977, dated 4 December 1961 (Department of the Army Bulletin 1, 1962), this medal is authorized for U.S. military operations, U.S. operations in direct support of the United Nations, and U.S. operations of assistance for friendly foreign nations.

Operations are defined as military actions or the carrying out of strategic, tactical, service, training, or administrative military missions and the process of carrying on combat, including movement, supply, attack, defense, and maneuvers needed to gain the objectives of any battle or campaign.

Designated areas and dates of service for eligibility are in AR 672-5-1. Subsequent awards of this medal are denoted by bronze service stars.

Vietnam Service Medal

The Vietnam Service Medal is awarded to all members of the armed forces who served in Vietnam and contiguous waters or airspace there after 3 July 1965 and through 28 March 1973. Members of the armed forces in Thailand, Laos, or Cambodia or the airspace thereover who during the same period served in direct support of operations in Vietnam are also eligible. See AR 672-5-1 for authorized campaigns and dates.

Personnel who qualified for the Armed Forces Expeditionary Medal for reason of service in Vietnam between 1 July 1958 and 3 July 1965 (inclusive) may be awarded the Vietnam Service Medal in lieu of the Armed Forces Expeditionary Medal upon request to the individual's unit personnel officer. If such a request is made and granted, the individual automatically loses entitlement to the Armed Forces Expeditionary Medal for any period of Vietnam service.

One bronze service star (or a combination of bronze and silver stars, as applicable) may be worn on the suspension ribbon and bar representing this medal.

Southwest Asia Service Medal

Established by executive order on 13 March 1991, the Southwest Asia Service Medal (SWASM) is awarded to U.S. military personnel who have served in the Persian Gulf area since 2 August 1990. Subsequent awards of the SWASM are denoted by service stars affixed to the medal.

Humanitarian Service Medal

Established by Executive Order 12019, 3 November 1977, and implemented by DOD Directive 1348.5, 23 June 1977, the Humanitarian Service Medal is authorized to be awarded to any armed forces personnel who directly participated in a Department of Defense–approved humanitarian act or operation, except when a by-name eligibility list is published.

No more than one award of this medal may be made for the same act or operation. Subsequent awards are designated by bronze numerals. Operations for which award of the Humanitarian Service Medal have thus far been approved are listed in appendix B, AR 672-5-1.

Military Outstanding Volunteer Service Medal

Receipt goes to members of the armed forces of the United States who subsequent to 31 December 1992 perform outstanding volunteer community service of a sustained, direct, and consequential nature. To be eligible, an individual's service must (1) be to the civilian community, including the military family community; (2) be significant in nature and produce tangible results; (3) reflect favorably on the military service and the Department of Defense; and (4) be of a sustained and direct nature.

The MOVSM is intended to recognize exceptional community support over time and not a single act or achievement. Further, it is intended to honor direct support of community activities. The medal was established by Executive Order 12830 dated 9 January 1993.

Armed Forces Reserve Medal

Honorable and satisfactory service is required in one or more of the Reserve components of the armed forces for a period of 10 years, not necessarily consecutive, provided such service was performed within a period of 12 consecutive years. Periods of service as a member of a Regular component are excluded from consideration.

Required also is earning a minimum of 50 retirement points per year (AR 135-180). Individuals are advised to consult the unit instructor of their organization as to individual eligibility.

One 10-year device is authorized to be worn on the suspension and service ribbon to denote service for each 10-year period in addition to and under the same conditions as prescribed for the award of the medal. It is a bronze hourglass with a five-sixteenths-inch Roman numeral X superimposed.

NCO Professional Development Ribbon

Established by the Secretary of the Army 10 April 1981 and effective 1 August 1981, the NCO Professional Development Ribbon is awarded to members of the U.S. Army, Army National Guard, and Army Reserve for successful completion of designated NCO professional development courses. The ribbon is awarded for four levels of professional development:
- Primary—Primary Leadership Development Course (PLDC).
- Basic—Basic NCO Course (BNCOC).
- Advanced—Advanced NCO Course (ANCOC).
- U.S. Army Sergeants Major Academy.

Army Service Ribbon

Established by the Secretary of the Army on 10 April 1981 and effective 1 August 1981, the Army Service Ribbon is awarded to members of the U.S. Army, Army National Guard, and Army Reserve who have successfully completed initial entry training. Enlisted persons are eligible upon completion of initial MOS-producing courses. For those enlisted persons assigned an MOS based on civilian or other-service acquired skills, it is awarded after four months of honorable active service.

Overseas Service Ribbon

Established by the Secretary of the Army on 10 April 1981 and effective 1 August 1981, the Overseas Service Ribbon is awarded to all members of the U.S. Army, Army National Guard, and Army Reserve credited with a normal overseas tour completed in accordance with AR 614-30. A soldier who has overseas service credited by another armed service is also eligible for this ribbon. The ribbon is not authorized for completion of an overseas tour of duty for which a service medal has been authorized.

Army Reserve Components Overseas Training Ribbon

Established by the Secretary of the Army on 11 July 1984, the ribbon is awarded to members of the U.S. Army Reserve components for successful completion of annual training or active-duty training for a period of not less than 10 days on foreign soil.

NON–U.S. SERVICE MEDALS

United Nations Medal

This medal may be awarded to personnel who have been in the service of the United Nations for a period of not less than six months with one of the units designated in AR 672-5-1.

Multinational Force and Observers Medal

To qualify for this medal, a soldier must have served with the Multinational Force

Observers at least 90 days after 3 August 1981. Subsequent awards for each completed six-month tour are indicated by an appropriate numeral, starting with numeral "1."

Republic of Vietnam Campaign Medal

Authorized for acceptance by Department of Defense instructions 1348.17, 31 January 1974, by members of the armed forces who meet the following criteria:

• Have served in the Republic of Vietnam for six months during the period 1 March 1961 to 28 March 1973, inclusive.

• Have served outside the geographical limits of the Republic of Vietnam and contributed direct combat support to the Republic of Vietnam Armed Forces for six months. Such persons must meet the criteria established for the Armed Forces Expeditionary Medal (Vietnam) or the Vietnam Service Medal during the period of service required to qualify for the Republic of Vietnam Campaign Medal.

• Have served under the conditions listed above for less than six months and have been wounded by hostile forces, captured (but later escaped, rescued, or released), or killed in action or otherwise in the line of duty.

Personnel assigned to the Republic of Vietnam on 28 January 1973 must have served a minimum of 60 days in the Republic of Vietnam as of that date or completed a minimum of 60 days' service during the period of 29 January 1973 to 28 March 1973, inclusive. Claims of eligibility for award of this medal for periods of service before 1 March 1961 or after 28 March 1973 must be forwarded to the Secretary of Defense for approval.

Kuwait Liberation Medal

To qualify for the Kuwait Liberation Medal, PERSCOM has stated, members must have served or flown into the Persian Gulf war zone between 17 January 1991, the start of the air war, and 28 February 1991, when offensive operations ended. The war zone includes Kuwait, Saudi Arabia, Oman, Bahrain, Qatar, the United Arab Emirates, the Persian Gulf, the Gulf of Oman, the Gulf of Aden, and part of the Arabian Sea.

U.S. ARMY BADGES AND TABS

Badges and tabs are appurtenances of the uniform. In the eyes of their wearers, several badges have a significance equal to or greater than all but the highest decorations. There is no established precedence with badges as there is with decorations and service medals or ribbons. The badges are of three types: combat and special skill badges, marksmanship badges and tabs, and identification badges. Badges are awarded in recognition of attaining a high standard of proficiency in certain military skills. Subdued combat and special skill badges and the Ranger and Special Forces tabs are authorized on field uniforms.

Combat and Special Skill Badges

The following badges are awarded to denote excellence in performance of duties under hazardous conditions and circumstances of extraordinary hardship as well as for special qualifications and successful completion of prescribed courses of training. (See AR 672-5-1 for details.)

Combat Infantryman Badges. Awarded to infantry personnel in the grade of colonel or below who, after 6 December 1941, satisfactorily perform duty while assigned or attached as a member of an infantry brigade, regiment, or smaller unit during any period such unit is engaged in active ground combat. Members of attached Ranger companies are also eligible.

Expert Infantryman Badge. Awarded to infantry personnel of the active Army, ARNG, and USAR who satisfactorily complete prescribed proficiency tests.

Combat Medical Badges. Awarded to members of the Army Medical Department, the Naval Medical Department, or the Air Force Medical Service in the grade of colonel (Navy captain) or below who have satisfactorily performed medical duties while assigned or attached to a medical detachment of an infantry unit meeting the requirements for the combat infantryman badge.

Expert Field Medical Badge. Awarded to Army Medical Service personnel who satisfactorily complete prescribed proficiency tests.

Stars for Combat Infantryman and Combat Medical Badges. The second and succeeding awards of the Combat Infantryman and the Combat Medical Badges, made to recognize participation and qualification in additional declared wars, are indicated by the addition of stars to the basic badges.

Army Astronaut Badges. The Army Astronaut Badge has been added to the authorized special skill badges, but the requirements for award of this badge are not stated in the regulations. These badges are awarded in three degrees: basic, senior, and master.

Army Aviation Badges. There are nine badges relating to Army aviation—three each for Army aviators, flight surgeons, and aircraft crewmen—in the degrees of basic, senior, and master.

The Master Army Aviator Badge, the Senior Army Aviator Badge, and the Army Aviator Badge are awarded upon satisfactory completion of prescribed training and proficiency tests as outlined in AR 600-105.

The Master Aircraft Crewman Badge, the Senior Aircraft Crewman Badge, and the Aircraft Crewman Badge are authorized for award to enlisted personnel who meet the prescribed requirements. (See AR 672-5-1.)

Glider Badge. No longer awarded, but still authorized for wear by individuals who were previously awarded the badge.

Parachutist Badges. To be awarded the Master Parachutist Badge, an individual must meet the following criteria: have participated in 65 jumps, 25 with combat equipment, 4 at night, and 5 mass tactical jumps; have graduated as jumpmaster or served as jumpmaster on 1 or more combat jumps or on 33 noncombat jumps; have been rated excellent in character and efficiency; and have served on jump status for not less than 36 months.

For the Senior Parachutist Badge, an individual must meet the following criteria: have been rated excellent in character and efficiency with participation in 30 jumps, including 15 jumps made with combat equipment, 2 night jumps, and 2 mass tactical jumps; have graduated from a jumpmaster course or served as jumpmaster on one or more combat jumps or 15 noncombat jumps; and have served on jump status for not less than 24 months.

The Parachutist Badge is awarded for satisfactory completion of the course given by the Airborne Department of the Infantry School or while assigned or attached to an airborne unit or for participation in at least one combat jump.

Combat Parachutist Badges. Participation in a combat parachute jump entitles the individual to wear a bronze star, or stars, affixed to the Parachutist Badge.

Pathfinder Badge. Awarded upon successful completion of the Pathfinder course conducted at the Infantry School.

Air Assault Badge. Awarded to personnel who have satisfactorily completed either the Training and Doctrine Command (TRADOC) prescribed training course or the standard air assault course while assigned or attached to the 101st Air Assault Division since 1 April 1974.

Ranger Tab. Awarded to any person who successfully completes a Ranger course conducted by the Infantry School. *

Special Forces Tab. Awarded to any person who successfully completes the Special Forces Qualification Course conducted by the Special Forces School of the Special Warfare Center. This tab also may be awarded for former wartime service. See AR 672-5-1 for details.*

Diver Badges. Awarded after satisfactory completion of prescribed proficiency tests (AR 611-75). Five badges are authorized for enlisted personnel.

Driver and Mechanic Badge. Awarded only to enlisted personnel to denote a high degree of skill in the operation and maintenance of motor vehicles.

Explosive Ordnance Disposal Badges. There are three badges under this heading, any of which may be awarded to soldiers: Master Explosive Ordnance Disposal Badge, Senior Explosive Ordnance Disposal Badge, and Explosive Ordnance Disposal Badge. They are awarded to individuals assigned to duties involving the removal and disposition of explosive ammunition under hazardous conditions.

Nuclear Reactor Operator Badges. The Shift Supervisor Badge, the Operator First Class Badge, and the Operator Basic Badge were awarded upon completing the Nuclear Power Plant Operators Course or equivalent training and after operating nuclear power plants for specific periods. These badges are no longer awarded but are still authorized for wear by individuals to whom they were previously awarded.

Parachute Rigger Badge. Awarded to any individual who successfully completes the Parachute Rigger Course conducted by the U.S. Army Quartermaster School and who holds a Parachute Rigger MOS or skill identifier.

Physical Fitness Training Badge. This badge is awarded to soldiers who obtain a minimum score of 290 on the Army Physical Fitness Test (APFT) and who meet the weight control requirements of AR 600-9.

Marksmanship Badges and Tabs

These badges and tabs include basic marksmanship qualification badges, excellence in competition badges, distinguished designation badges, the United States Distinguished International Shooter Badge, and the President's Hundred Tab.

Only members of the armed forces of the United States and civilian citizens of the United States are eligible for these qualification badges. Qualification badges for marksmanship are of three types: basic qualification, excellence in competition, and distinguished designation. Basic qualification badges (including Expert, Sharpshooter, and Marksman Badges) are awarded to those individuals who attain the qualification score prescribed in the appropriate field manual for the weapon concerned. Excellence in Competition Badges are awarded to individuals in recognition of an eminent degree of achievement in firing the rifle or pistol. Distinguished Designation Badges

---

*Note: Highly qualified soldiers who have earned both the Ranger and the Special Forces tabs are authorized to wear both, according to a recent DA change.

are awarded to individuals in recognition of a preeminent degree of achievement in target practice firing with the military service rifle or pistol.

The Distinguished International Shooter Badge is awarded to military or civilian personnel in recognition of an outstanding degree of achievement in international competition.

A President's Hundred Tab is awarded each person who qualifies among the top 100 contestants in the President's Match held annually at the National Rifle Matches.

Identification Badges

Identification badges are worn to signify special duties.

Presidential Service Identification Badge. The Presidential Service Certificate and the Presidential Service Badge were established by Executive Order 11174, 1 September 1964.

The Presidential Service Certificate is awarded in the name of the president of the United States as public evidence of deserved honor and distinction to members of the armed forces who have been assigned duty in the White House for at least one year after 20 January 1961. It is awarded to Army members by the Secretary of the Army upon recommendation of the military aide to the president.

The Presidential Service Badge is issued to members of the armed forces who have been awarded the Presidential Service Certificate. Once this badge is awarded, it may be worn as a permanent part of the uniform.

Vice-Presidential Service Identification Badge. The Vice-Presidential Service Badge was established by Executive Order 11544, 8 July 1970. It may be awarded upon recommendation of the military assistant to the vice president and may be worn as a permanent part of the uniform.

Secretary of Defense Identification Badge. Military personnel who have been assigned to duty and have served not less than one year after 13 January 1961 in the Office of the Secretary of Defense are eligible for this badge. Once awarded, it may be worn as a permanent part of the uniform. It also is authorized for temporary wear by personnel assigned to specified offices of the Secretary of Defense.

Joint Chiefs of Staff Identification Badge. This badge may be awarded to military personnel who have been assigned to duty and who have served not less than one year after 16 January 1961 in a position of responsibility under the direct cognizance of the Joint Chiefs of Staff. Once awarded, the badge may be worn as a permanent part of the uniform.

Army Staff Identification Badge. This badge has been awarded by the Army since 1920 and is the oldest of the five types of identification badges now authorized for officers. It was instituted to give a permanent means of identification to those commissioned officers who had been selected for duty on the War Department General Staff, with recommendation for award based upon performance of duty. It has been continued under the present departmental organization.

Between 30 September 1979 and 28 May 1985, the badge could also be awarded to the Sergeant Major of the Army and to other senior NCOs (SGM E-9) assigned to duty with the same staff units. Effective 28 May 1985, qualifying service must be on the Army General Staff or assigned to the Office of the Secretary of the Army. Once awarded, this badge may be worn as a permanent part of the uniform.

Guard, Tomb of the Unknown Soldier Identification Badge. (See AR 672-5-1.)
Army ROTC Nurse Cadet Program Identification Badge. (See AR 672-5-1.)
Drill Sergeant Identification Badge. (See AR 672-5-1.)
U.S. Army Recruiter Identification Badge. (See AR 672-5-1.)
Army National Guard Recruiter Identification Badge. (See AR 672-5-1.)
U.S. Army Reserve Recruiter Identification Badge. (See AR 672-5-1.)
Career Counselor Badge. (See AR 672-5-1.)

APPURTENANCES

Appurtenances are devices affixed to service or suspension ribbons or worn in place of medals or ribbons. They are worn to denote additional awards, participation in a specific event, or other distinguished characteristics of the award.

Service Ribbons

Service ribbons are identical to the suspension ribbons of the medals they represent and are mounted on bars equipped with attaching devices; they are issued for wear in place of medals. The service ribbon for the Medal of Honor is the same color as the neck band, showing five stars in the form of a letter M.

Miniature Medals

Miniature replicas of all medals except the Medal of Honor and the Legion of Merit in the Degrees of Chief Commander and Commander are authorized for wear on specified uniforms in lieu of the issued medals. Miniatures of decorations are issued only to foreign nationals and with the award of the Distinguished Service Medal to U.S. personnel (award elements issued by the Secretary of Defense include miniature medals).

Oak-Leaf Cluster

A bronze or silver twig of four oak leaves with three acorns on the stem, thirteen thirty-seconds inch long for the suspension ribbon and five sixteenths inch long for the service ribbon, is issued in lieu of a decoration for second or succeeding awards of decorations (other than the Air Medal) and service medals. A silver oak-leaf cluster is issued to be worn in lieu of five bronze clusters. Five one-sixteenth-inch oak-leaf clusters, joined together in series of two, three, and four clusters, are authorized for optional purchase and wear on service ribbons.

Numerals

Arabic numerals three thirteenths inch high are issued in lieu of a medal or ribbon for second and succeeding awards of the Air Medal, the Humanitarian Service Medal, the Multinational Force and Observers Medal, the Army Reserve Components Overseas Training Ribbon, and the Overseas Service Ribbon. The numeral worn on the NCO Professional Development Ribbon denotes the highest completed level of NCO development. The numerals are worn centered on the suspension ribbon of the medal or the ribbon bar.

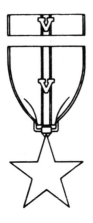

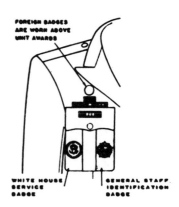

Wearing of appurtenances on medals and ribbons.

V Device

The V Device is a bronze letter V, one fourth inch high with serifs at the top of the members (that is, the little strokes at the tops of the arms of the V that look like little rectangles). The V Device denotes awards of a medal for heroism and may be awarded with the Bronze Star Medal, the Air Medal, the Joint Service Commendation Medal (when the award is for acts or services involving direct participation in combat operations), and the Army Commendation Medal.

Clasps

Clasps are authorized to be worn on the Good Conduct Medal, the Army of Occupation Medal, and the Antarctic Service Medal.

Service Stars

The service star is a bronze or silver five-pointed star three sixteenths inch in diameter. Three-sixteenths-inch service stars joined together in a series of two, three, and four stars are authorized for optional purchase and wear on service ribbons. Service stars, signifying participation in a combat campaign, are authorized for wear on the Armed Forces Expeditionary Medal and the Vietnam Service Medal. (Note: Bronze and silver stars are worn on U.S. Navy decorations in the same manner as oak-leaf clusters are worn on Army and Air Force decorations.)

Arrowhead

The arrowhead is a bronze replica of an Indian arrowhead, one fourth inch high. It denotes participation in a combat parachute jump, combat glider landing, or amphibious assault landing, while assigned or attached as a member of an organized force carrying out an assigned tactical mission. It is worn on the service and suspension ribbons of the Vietnam Service Medal and the Armed Forces Expeditionary Medal.

Lapel Buttons

Lapel buttons are authorized for wear on the *left* lapel of civilian clothing only. They are available for service ribbons and other decorations and badges. Included in this category are the Army Lapel Button, which is awarded to any soldier (except retirees) who completed nine months' honorable active federal service after 1 April 1984, and the U.S. Army Retired Lapel Button.

FOREIGN INDIVIDUAL AWARDS

Decorations received from a foreign government in recognition of active field service in connection with combat operations or for outstanding or unusually meritorious performance may be accepted and worn upon approval of the Department of the Army. Without this approval, they become the property of the United States and must be deposited with the Department of the Army for use or disposal.

Qualification and special skill badges may be accepted if awarded in recognition of meeting the criteria, as established by the awarding foreign government, for the specific award.

Foreign badges are authorized for wear only on service and dress uniforms. The German marksmanship award (*Schützenschur*) may be worn only by enlisted personnel, on the right side of the uniform with the upper portion attached under the center of the shoulder loop and the bottom portion attached under the lapel.

CERTIFICATES AND LETTERS

As a senior NCO, you may write and sign letters of appreciation and commendation for other enlisted personnel. Frequently, soldiers will ask for these accolades, but you should be constantly alert to any circumstances that may authorize a letter of appreciation or commendation for a deserving individual. When writing these letters, you should give them your best effort and put as much into composing them as you would into the writing of a recommendation for a decoration. An important responsibility is to see that your commander is aware of those deeds that deserve special recognition, and you should not be hesitant to recommend personnel for consideration. But do the commander a favor: Prepare a draft citation or letter and offer it along with your verbal recommendations. The CO may sign the final product, but if the person being recommended is one of your soldiers, you should write the original draft—you know your soldiers better than the commander does.

Certificates and letters may be nothing more than pats on the back. Nevertheless, they go a long way toward boosting the morale of most recipients, and their judicious use is a good way to recognize faithful and competent service.

Certificate of Achievement

Commanders may recognize periods of faithful service, acts, or achievements that do meet the standards required for decorations by issuing to individual military personnel a *Certificate of Achievement*, DA Form 2442.

Certificates of Achievement are awarded under local criteria and may be used for awarding the Good Conduct Medal, for participation in the Department of the Army Suggestion Program, or to recognize meritorious acts or service.

Letters of Commendation and Appreciation

Acts or services that do not meet the criteria for decorations or a Certificate of Achievement may be recognized by written expressions of commendation or appreciation. These letters are typed on letterhead stationery and do not contain formalized printing, seals, or other distinguishing features that depart from normal letter form.

16

Pay and Entitlements

The purpose of this chapter is to explain some basic facts about your Army pay and benefits and provide you a quick reference for questions that may come up in your day-to-day operations.

The soldier who enlists in the Army for the money is in the wrong business. Relatively substantial paychecks do not start coming until a soldier reaches the senior noncommissioned ranks with 20 to 26 years of service.

If pay and benefits were the only inducement to a military career, then we would have no Army. Soldiers reenlist because they like the Army, and when the Army no longer offers young people the challenges and adventure of military life, they will not stay.

PAY
Military pay consists of basic pay, special and incentive pay, and allowances. Pay is computed on the basis of a 30-day month, and soldiers may elect to be paid once a month (at the end of the month) or twice a month (on the 15th and the 30th of each month).

In order to change your pay option, contact your local finance and accounting office to execute DA Form 3685, *JUMPS—Army Pay Elections*. Which option you select depends upon how you budget your money. Some soldiers find that they can get along quite well with one lump-sum pay at the end of the month; others prefer to get paid twice a month. Read the pay elections form carefully before filling it out. Submit your options to the finance officer as early in the month as possible to give the finance center enough time to process your request so that your new option will be reflected during the *next* pay period.

Report discrepancies in your pay *immediately*. To do so, you must know what you are authorized.

Leave and Earnings Statement (LES)
The LES is a computerized monthly statement of account for each soldier paid under the Joint Service Software (JSS) system, which has replaced JUMPS. The LES shows all entitlements earned, collections affected, and payments made during the period

JUMPS - ARMY PAY ELECTIONS

For use of this form, see AR 37-104-3; the proponent agency is USAFAC

PRIVACY ACT OF 1974 (5 USC 552a)

AUTHORITY: Title 37 USC, Section 101.
PRINCIPLE PURPOSE: To provide the service member a means of electing the manner in which he/she desires to receive pay and allowances.
ROUTINE USES: To establish account of the MMPF. Although disclosure of this information is voluntary, if the member does not provide it, input will automatically be established to receive all pay at end of month by "Check for Cash."

HOW DO YOU WANT TO BE PAID?   **Please check one item.**

☐ ONCE A MONTH   ☐ TWICE A MONTH   ☐ TOTAL ACCRUAL
   (Complete A & B)   (Complete C & D)   (Read E)

A If you checked once a month, please check one item.

☐ ALL PAY END-OF-MONTH

☐ MID-MONTH PAY OF $ _____
(Not to exceed ½ of total)
ACCRUE BALANCE OF PAY (Read E)

☐ ACCRUE $ _____ EACH MONTH/
BALANCE OF PAY END-OF-MONTH
(Read E)

B Please check one method of payment.

☐ SURE PAY/DIRECT DEPOSIT
(Complete F)

☐ CHECK to address (Complete G)

☐ CHECK to me at my unit

☐ CASH

C If you checked twice a month, please check one item.

☐ ½ OF PAY MID-MONTH
BALANCE OF PAY END-OF-MONTH

☐ MID-MONTH PAY OF $ _____
(Specify amount, not to exceed ½ of total)
BALANCE OF PAY END-OF-MONTH

☐ ACCRUE $ _____ EACH MONTH
MID-MONTH PAY OF $ _____
(Not to exceed ½ of total)
BALANCE OF PAY END-OF-MONTH (Read E)

D Please check one method of payment for Mid-Month and one for End-Of-Month

(You can have only one check address)*

	MID-MONTH	END-OF-MONTH
CHECK to address (if SURE PAY/ DIRECT DEPOSIT, Complete F) (All other address checks complete G)	☐	☐
CHECK to me at my unit	☐	☐
CASH	☐	☐

*YOU <u>CAN</u> <u>NOT</u> COMPLETE BOTH BLOCK F and G.

E ALL AMOUNTS ACCRUED MAY BE WITHDRAWN AT ANY TIME UPON APPLICATION TO YOUR FINANCE OFFICER.

F Please read the back of this form carefully before completing this block.

☐ SF 1199A Attached

☐ SF 1199A on File
   in my PFR

☐ Other (complete lines
   1 thru 5 at right)

1. (Name of Financial Organization) _____

2. (Savings or Checking Account No.) _____

3. (Name of account holder) _____

4. (Street No., RR #, P.O. Box
of the Financial Organization) _____

5. (City, State, Country of the
Financial Organization) _____

G 1. (Name to be entered on check) _____

2. (Street No., RR #, P.O. BOX) _____

3. (City, State, Zip Code) _____

I HEREBY AUTHORIZE PAYMENT AS SPECIFIED ABOVE

_____   _____   _____
      (Signature)   (SSN)   (Date)

_____
(Printed Name & Organization)

DA FORM 3685, OCT 86   EDITION OF DEC 82 IS OBSOLETE covered by the statement. In addition, this statement provides the solder a complete record of transactions that affect his or her leave account for the period of the statement. It also serves as the official leave record.

Each finance and accounting office (FAO) exerts every effort to assure that delivery of the LES is accomplished no later than by pertinent end-of-month payday. The FAO delivers the LESs to the unit commander, who determines the best way to distribute them to the individuals concerned. In many units, though, personnel simply pick them up from their first sergeant or administrative office.

Study your LES very carefully. Should you discover any item you believe to be in error or should there be an entry recorded thereon that you do not understand, consult with your local finance office immediately. If, during a routine audit of your pay record, it should be discovered that you have been overpaid at some time in the past, the government will collect what is due.

Net Pay Advice

Under JSS a form called the Net Pay Advice (NPA) will be issued at midmonth. All Active Army soldiers will receive the NPA, even if they have not elected the midmonth pay option. The NPA will provide midmonth pay data for soldiers who have elected the midmonth pay option. It will provide administrative remarks for all soldiers, regardless of the pay option they have selected.

Collections of Erroneous Payments

Local payments in excess of earned entitlements that are less than two months old upon computer update are affected immediately. If these payments are two or more months old, collection action is delayed for two months to allow time for unit commanders to arrange for prorated collection, if necessary, before computer collection action is initiated.

When an error is discovered, the U.S. Army Finance and Accounting Center prepares an adjustment authorization and forwards the original to the individual's servicing finance and accounting office and suspends a copy for 60 days. A remark is then printed on the affected soldier's LES advising him to contact his servicing finance office. If at the end of 60 days the finance center has not received a rebuttal from the soldier's finance officer, collection action is taken under the statutory one-third rule. If the indebted soldier's ETS falls within 90 days of the date of the adjustment authorization, an accelerated deduction—two thirds of the affected soldier's pay per month—is automatically initiated. This is the maximum amount that may be deducted from a soldier's pay unless he or she specifically authorizes a higher amount.

Soldiers may appeal the validity of a debt, the amount, or the rate of payment. If an enlisted soldier's appeal is denied, the Chief of Personnel Operations, Department of the Army, may consider his case for remission or cancellation of the indebtedness.

The amount deducted for any period normally will not exceed an amount equal to two thirds of a soldier's pay, and monthly installments may be increased or decreased to reflect changes in pay.

Advance Payments

An advance of pay is authorized upon permanent change of station to provide a soldier funds for expenses, such as transportation, temporary storage of household goods, packing and shipping costs, and securing new living quarters. Advance payments are limited to no more than one month's advance pay of basic pay less deductions or, if warranted, not more than three months' basic pay less deductions at the old station, en route, or within 60 days after reporting to a new station.

Requests for advance pay from enlisted personnel in pay grades E-1 through E-4 must be approved by their commander, and this approval must be indicated in the *Pay Inquiry Form* (DA Form 2142) together with a statement that the circumstances in the individual's case warrant advancing the amount requested and that advancing a lesser amount would result in hardship to the soldier or his family.

The DA Form 2142 must also include a statement that the enlisted person will have at least enough time left to serve on his or her current enlistment to completely repay the advance. If six or twelve months are allowed for repayment, for instance, the statement must show that the soldier has at least that much time to serve on his or her current enlistment beginning with the first month following the month in which the advance is made.

The commander's approval for an advance of pay is not required for enlisted personnel in pay grades E-5 through E-9, but advances are not made to senior-grade personnel when it is apparent that the tour of duty (obligated service) will terminate before completion of the scheduled repayment of the advance.

Lump-Sum Payments

A lump-sum payment is made to pay bonuses and accrued leave paid on immediate reenlistments. These payments are made by cash or check through the use of a local payment. Lump-sum payments are always made in even dollar amounts. The maximum amount that may be paid is the gross amount of the enlistment minus the estimate of federal and, when applicable, state taxes. When the computation results in a new amount due in dollars and cents, the amount to be paid may either be the lesser full dollar amount or be rounded to the next higher dollar.

Basic Pay

Basic pay is established by law and is that pay a soldier receives, based on grade and length of service, exclusive of any special or incentive pay or allowances.

Reserve Drill Pay

Reserve drill pay, like basic pay, is established by law. And like basic pay, Reserve drill pay is pay a soldier receives based on grade and length of service. Unlike monthly basic pay, however, Reserve drill pay is computed and paid for the number of days' service rendered. It is comparable to basic pay.

Basic Allowance for Subsistence (BAS)

Upon entitlement to BAS (separate rations) a soldier's unit commander forwards to the finance officer a DA Form 4187, *Personnel Action* (see chapter 8, DA Pamphlet 600-8), in duplicate, showing the effective date and hour of entitlement to BAS. When a soldier ceases to be entitled to BAS, the unit commander forwards to the finance officer a DA Form 4187 showing date and hour of termination.

MONTHLY BASIC PAY (EFFECTIVE 1 JANUARY 1995)

Years of Service

Grade	Less than 2	2	3	4	6	8	10	12	14	16	18	20	22	24	26
O-10	6978.30	7223.70	7223.70	7223.70	7223.70	7501.20	7501.20	7916.70	7916.70	8482.80	8482.80	9051.00	9051.00	9051.00	9614.70
O-9	6184.50	6346.50	6481.80	6481.80	6481.80	6646.50	6646.50	6923.10	6923.10	7501.20	7501.20	7916.70	7916.70	7916.70	8482.80
O-8	5601.60	5769.60	5906.40	5906.40	5906.40	6346.50	6346.50	6646.50	6646.50	6923.10	7223.70	7501.20	7686.00	7686.00	7686.00
O-7	4654.50	4971.00	4971.00	4971.00	5193.90	5193.90	5494.80	5494.80	5769.60	6346.50	6783.00	6783.00	6783.00	6783.00	6783.00
O-6	3449.70	3790.20	4038.60	4038.60	4038.60	4038.60	4038.60	4038.60	4176.00	4836.30	5082.90	5193.90	5494.80	5680.80	5959.50
O-5	2759.10	3239.70	3463.80	3463.80	3463.80	3463.80	3568.50	3760.80	4012.80	4313.10	4560.00	4698.60	4862.70	4862.70	4862.70
O-4	2325.60	2832.00	3021.00	3021.00	3077.10	3212.70	3432.00	3624.90	3790.20	3956.70	4065.60	4065.60	4065.60	4065.60	4065.60
O-3	2161.20	2416.50	2583.30	2858.10	2994.90	3102.30	3270.30	3432.00	3516.30	3516.30	3516.30	3516.30	3516.30	3516.30	3516.30
O-2	1884.60	2058.00	2472.90	2556.00	2608.80	2608.80	2608.80	2608.80	2608.80	2608.80	2608.80	2608.80	2608.80	2608.80	2608.80
O-1	1636.20	1703.10	2058.00	2058.00	2058.00	2058.00	2058.00	2058.00	2058.00	2058.00	2058.00	2058.00	2058.00	2058.00	2058.00
Officers with more than 4 years' active duty as enlisted or warrant officer															
O-3E	0.00	0.00	0.00	0.00	2994.90	3102.30	3270.30	3432.00	3568.50	3568.50	3568.50	3568.50	3568.50	3568.50	3568.50
O-2E	0.00	0.00	0.00	2556.00	2608.80	2691.60	2832.00	2940.60	3021.00	3021.00	3021.00	3021.00	3021.00	3021.00	3021.00
O-1E	0.00	0.00	0.00	2058.00	2199.00	2280.00	2362.50	2444.40	2556.00	2556.00	2556.00	2556.00	2556.00	2556.00	2556.00
Warrant officers (for Army, Navy, and Marine Corps)															
W-5	0.00	0.00	0.00	0.00	0.00	0.00	0.00	0.00	0.00	0.00	0.00	3757.80	3900.30	4013.10	4182.00
W-4	2202.00	2362.50	2362.50	2416.50	2526.30	2637.60	2748.30	2940.60	3077.10	3185.10	3270.30	3375.90	3489.00	3597.60	3760.80
W-3	2001.30	2170.80	2170.80	2199.00	2224.50	2387.40	2526.30	2608.80	2691.60	2772.00	2858.70	2969.70	3077.10	3077.10	3185.10
W-2	1752.90	1896.30	1896.30	1951.50	2058.00	2170.80	2253.30	2335.80	2416.50	2501.40	2583.30	2664.60	2772.00	2772.00	2772.00
W-1	1460.10	1674.30	1674.30	1814.10	1896.30	1977.60	2058.00	2143.20	2224.50	2307.30	2387.40	2472.90	2472.90	2472.90	2472.90
Enlisted members															
E-9	0.00	0.00	0.00	0.00	0.00	0.00	2561.70	2619.00	2678.40	2739.90	2801.40	2855.70	3005.40	3122.40	3297.90
E-8	0.00	0.00	0.00	0.00	0.00	2148.00	2209.80	2268.00	2326.80	2388.30	2442.90	2502.90	2649.90	2768.10	2945.10
E-7	1499.70	1619.10	1678.80	1737.90	1797.00	1854.30	1913.70	1973.40	2062.50	2121.00	2179.80	2208.30	2356.50	2473.80	2649.90
E-6	1290.30	1406.40	1464.90	1527.30	1584.60	1641.60	1701.90	1789.50	1845.60	1905.30	1934.10	1934.10	1934.10	1934.10	1934.10
E-5	1132.20	1232.40	1292.40	1348.50	1437.30	1495.80	1554.90	1612.20	1641.60	1641.60	1641.60	1641.60	1641.60	1641.60	1641.60
E-4	1056.00	1115.40	1181.10	1272.00	1322.40	1322.40	1322.40	1322.40	1322.40	1322.40	1322.40	1322.40	1322.40	1322.40	1322.40
E-3	995.10	1049.70	1091.40	1134.60	1134.60	1134.60	1134.60	1134.60	1134.60	1134.60	1134.60	1134.60	1134.60	1134.60	1134.60
E-2	957.60	957.60	957.60	957.60	957.60	957.60	957.60	957.60	957.60	957.60	957.60	957.60	957.60	957.60	957.60
E-1	854.40	854.40	854.40	854.40	854.40	854.40	854.40	854.40	854.40	854.40	854.40	854.40	854.40	854.40	854.40

E-1 with less than 4 months—790.20

ONE-DAY RESERVE DRILL RATES (EFFECTIVE 1 JANUARY 1995)

Years of Service

Grade	Less than 2	2	3	4	6	8	10	12	14	16	18	20	22	24	26
Commissioned officers															
O-10	232.61	240.79	240.79	240.79	240.79	250.04	250.04	263.89	263.89	282.76	282.76	301.70	301.70	301.70	320.49
O-9	206.15	211.55	216.06	216.06	216.06	221.55	221.55	230.77	230.77	250.04	250.04	263.89	263.89	263.89	282.76
O-8	186.72	192.32	196.88	196.88	196.88	211.55	211.55	221.55	221.55	230.77	240.79	250.04	256.20	256.20	256.20
O-7	155.15	165.70	165.70	165.70	173.13	173.13	183.16	183.16	192.32	211.55	211.55	226.10	226.10	226.10	226.10
O-6	114.99	126.34	134.62	134.62	134.62	134.62	134.62	134.62	139.20	161.21	169.43	173.13	183.16	189.36	198.65
O-5	91.97	107.99	115.46	115.46	115.46	115.46	118.95	125.36	133.76	143.77	152.00	156.62	162.09	162.09	162.09
O-4	77.52	94.40	100.70	100.70	102.57	107.09	114.40	120.83	126.34	131.89	135.52	135.52	135.52	135.52	135.52
O-3	72.04	80.55	86.11	95.27	99.83	103.41	109.01	114.40	117.21	117.21	117.21	117.21	117.21	117.21	117.21
O-2	62.82	68.60	82.43	85.20	86.96	86.96	86.96	86.96	86.96	86.96	86.96	86.96	86.96	86.96	86.96
O-1	54.54	56.77	68.60	68.60	68.60	68.60	68.60	68.60	68.60	68.60	68.60	68.60	68.60	68.60	68.60
Commissioned officers with more than four years' active duty as an enlisted member or warrant officer															
O-3E	0.00	0.00	0.00	0.00	0.00	103.41	109.01	114.40	118.95	118.95	118.95	118.95	118.95	118.95	118.95
O-2E	0.00	0.00	0.00	85.20	86.96	89.72	94.40	98.02	100.70	100.70	100.70	100.70	100.70	100.70	100.70
O-1E	0.00	0.00	0.00	68.60	73.30	76.00	78.75	81.48	85.20	85.20	85.20	85.20	85.20	85.20	85.20
Warrant officers															
W-5	0.00	0.00	0.00	0.00	0.00	0.00	0.00	0.00	0.00	0.00	0.00	125.26	130.01	133.77	139.40
W-4	73.40	78.75	78.75	80.55	84.21	87.92	91.61	98.02	102.57	106.17	109.01	112.53	116.30	119.92	125.36
W-3	66.71	72.36	72.36	73.30	74.15	79.58	84.21	86.96	89.72	92.40	95.27	98.99	102.57	102.57	106.17
W-2	58.43	63.21	63.21	65.05	68.60	72.36	75.11	77.86	80.55	83.38	86.11	88.82	92.40	92.40	92.40
W-1	48.67	55.81	55.81	60.47	63.21	65.92	68.60	71.44	74.15	76.91	79.58	82.43	82.43	82.43	82.43
Enlisted members															
E-9	0.00	0.00	0.00	0.00	0.00	0.00	85.39	87.30	89.28	91.33	93.38	95.19	100.18	104.08	109.93
E-8	0.00	0.00	0.00	0.00	0.00	71.60	73.66	75.60	77.56	79.61	81.43	83.43	88.33	92.27	98.17
E-7	49.99	53.97	55.96	57.93	59.90	61.81	63.79	65.78	68.75	70.70	72.66	73.61	78.55	82.46	88.33
E-6	43.01	46.88	48.83	50.91	52.82	54.72	56.73	59.65	61.52	63.51	64.47	64.47	64.47	64.47	64.47
E-5	37.74	41.08	43.08	44.95	47.91	49.86	51.83	53.74	54.72	54.72	54.72	54.72	54.72	54.72	54.72
E-4	35.20	37.18	39.37	42.40	44.08	44.08	44.08	44.08	44.08	44.08	44.08	44.08	44.08	44.08	44.08
E-3	33.17	34.99	36.38	37.82	37.82	37.82	37.82	37.82	37.82	37.82	37.82	37.82	37.82	37.82	37.82
E-2	31.92	31.92	31.92	31.92	31.92	31.92	31.92	31.92	31.92	31.92	31.92	31.92	31.92	31.92	31.92
E-1	28.48	28.48	28.48	28.48	28.48	28.48	28.48	28.48	28.48	28.48	28.48	28.48	28.48	28.48	28.48

E-1 with less than 4 months—26.34

Officers receive $246.16 per month (FY 95). BAS rates for enlisted personnel are as follows:

	E-1 (less than 4 months)	All Other Enlisted
When on leave or authorized to mess separately	$6.44/day	$6.98/day
When rations in-kind are not available	7.26/day	7.87/day
When assigned to duty under emergency conditions where no messing facilities of the United States are available	9.63/day	10.42/day

Entitlement to BAS terminates automatically upon permanent change of station. Care should be taken during in-processing at a new duty station that entitlement is revalidated for personnel authorized separate rations.

Basic Allowance for Quarters (BAQ)

BAQ is paid at three different rates.
- Without dependents, full rate (paid to soldiers living off post).
- Without dependents, partial rate (paid to soldiers living in unit barracks).
- With dependents.

BAQ terminates for married personnel when they occupy government quarters or when dependency terminates. Dependency is verified by the local finance and accounting officer when the soldier submits DA Form 3298, *Authorization to Start and Stop BAQ Credit.* The documentary evidence that must be submitted to substantiate dependence includes the original or certified copy of a marriage certificate, the individual's signed statement (when called to active duty or active duty for training for 90 days or less), birth certificate, or a public church record of marriage issued over the signature of the custodian of the church or public records, and, if applicable, a divorce decree. Entitlements must be recertified upon permanent change of station.

	BAQ RATES (1995)		
Pay Grade	Without Dependents Full Rate	Partial Rate	With Dependents
E-9	454.80	18.60	599.40
E-8	417.60	15.30	552.60
E-7	356.40	12.00	513.00
E-6	322.80	9.90	474.30
E-5	297.60	8.70	426.30
E-4	258.90	8.10	370.80
E-3	254.10	7.80	345.00
E-2	206.40	7.20	328.50
E-1	183.90	6.90	328.50

Variable Housing Allowance (VHA)
The VHA was implemented to afford service personnel a tax-free amount of money for housing in addition to BAQ. The size of the allowance depends on the grade of the soldier and the size of his or her family. It is based on the typical housing costs for each rank in a certain area and biased toward meeting all the housing expenses for soldiers in high-cost areas.

Family Separation Allowance
Two separation allowances are payable to eligible personnel to help meet additional family expenses during periods of separation:
- FSA I is paid to a soldier who has dependents and is serving in an overseas location where dependents are not permitted and where government bachelor quarters are not available to help cover living expenses. The amount of this allowance is the same as the BAQ that a soldier *without* dependents would receive.
- FSA II is paid to soldiers with dependents and in any grade who are involuntarily separated from their families because of PCS to a station where dependents are not authorized or temporary duty for a continuous period of more than 30 days away from their permanent duty station.

Station Allowances
A list of areas where station allowances are authorized is in chapter 4, part 3, *DOD Pay Manual,* and chapter 4, part G, volume 1, *Joint Travel Regulations.* These allowances are paid to offset the high cost of living in certain geographical areas (overseas and in the United States). They consist of housing (HOUS) and cost of living (COLA) allowances. A temporary lodging allowance (TLA) and interim housing allowance (IHA) may also be paid in certain cases.

Clothing Maintenance Allowance
Clothing maintenance allowance is paid at two different rates:
- Basic, which covers replacement of unique military items that would normally require replacement during the first three years of service.
- Standard, which covers the replacement of unique military items after the first three years of service.

Female personnel are also authorized an initial cash allowance established by AR 700-84 for the purchase of undergarments, dress shoes, and stockings.

A soldier receives the clothing maintenance allowance annually, on the last day of the month in which the soldier's anniversary date of enlistment falls.

Civilian Clothing Allowance
When duty assignments require soldiers to wear civilian clothing, they receive lump-sum payments under the following circumstances:
- When both winter and summer civilian clothing ensembles are required.
- When either winter or summer ensembles are required.
- When in a TDY status from 16 to 30 days.
- When in a TDY status over 30 days.

Foreign Duty Pay

All enlisted personnel assigned to an area outside the contiguous 48 states and the District of Columbia where an "accompanied by dependents" tour of duty is not authorized have entitlement to foreign duty or "overseas pay." Chapter 6, part 1, DOD Pay Manual, lists the places where foreign pay is authorized.

Hostile Fire Pay (HFP)

Hostile fire pay is paid to soldiers permanently assigned to units performing duty in designated hostile-fire areas or to soldiers assigned to temporary duty in such areas. Hostile fire pay is authorized on a monthly basis or one-time basis, depending upon the soldier's period of exposure to enemy fire.

Diving Pay

To qualify for special pay for diving duty, a soldier must be a rated diver in accordance with AR 611-75 and be assigned to a TOE or TD position of MOS OOB or to a position that has been designated diving duty by the Assistant Chief of Staff for Force Development, Department of the Army.

Flight Pay

Flight pay is authorized for enlisted crew members.

Demolition Pay

A soldier is entitled to receive incentive pay for demolition duty for any month or portion of a month in which he or she was assigned and performed duty in a primary duty assignment.

Parachute Pay

Soldiers who have received a designation as a parachutist or parachute rigger or are undergoing training for such designations and who are required to engage in parachute jumping from an aircraft in aerial flight and actually perform the specified minimum jumps (see Table 2-3-3, DOD Entitlements Manual) are authorized parachute duty pay. An additional amount is authorized for parachutists who are assigned to positions requiring high altitude, low-opening (HALO) jump status.

Experimental Stress Pay

Experimental stress duty pay is authorized for all Army personnel who, on or after July 1, 1965, participate in thermal stress experiments or experimental pressure chamber duty.

Special Duty Assignment Pay

Special duty pay is authorized on a graduated scale for enlisted members in designated specialties who are required to perform extremely demanding duties or duties demanding an unusual degree of responsibility. Qualifying jobs include career counselor, recruiter, and drill sergeant.

Enlistment Bonus

The enlistment bonus is an enlistment incentive offered to those enlisting in the Regular Army for duty in a specific MOS. The objective of the bonus is to increase the number of enlistments in MOSs that are critical and have inadequate first-term manning levels. Section A, chapter 9, part 1 of the *DOD Pay Manual* gives basic conditions of entitlement, amount of the bonus, time of payment, and reduction and termination of the award.

Selective Reenlistment Bonus (SRB)

The SRB is a retention incentive paid to soldiers in certain selected MOSs who reenlist or voluntarily extend their enlistment for additional obligated service. The objective of the SRB is to increase the number of reenlistments or extensions in critical MOSs that do not have adequate retention levels to man the career force.

The SRB is established in three zones: Zone A consists of those reenlistments falling between 21 months and 6 years of active service; Zones B and C consist of those reenlistments or extensions of enlistments falling between 6 and 14 years of service.

Payments are based on multiples, not to exceed six, of a soldier's monthly basic pay at the time of discharge or release from active duty or the day before the beginning of extension, multiplied by years of additional obligated service.

The SRB is paid by installments. Up to 50 percent of the total bonus may be paid as the first installment, with the remaining portion paid in equal annual amounts over the remainder of the enlistment period.

A list of the MOSs designated for award of SRB and enlistment bonuses is in the DA Circular 611-series, *Announcement of Proficiency Pay/Selective Reenlistment Bonus/Enlistment Bonus/Comparable MOS for Bonus Recipients.* Periodic program changes are announced by Headquarters, Department of the Army.

Allotments

An allotment is a specified amount of money withheld from military pay, normally upon the soldier's authorization, for a specific purpose. Payment is made by government check and mailed to the payee.

Allotments are made by filling out DD Form 2558, *Authorization to Start, Stop, or Change an Allotment for Active Duty or Retired Personnel.* These forms are prepared by the individual's military personnel office, unit personnel office, or finance office, and by Army Emergency Relief and the American Red Cross. Preparation of allotment documents in the finance office, rather than in the personnel office, is intended to eliminate delays of one or more days. When there is a delay near the end of the processing month, the effective date of an allotment may be delayed a full month. Commanders may have DD Form 2558 prepared in the unit personnel office, if it will conserve time and assure that there will be no delays in transmission to the finance office.

Repayment of Army Emergency Relief Loans (AER). These allotments are authorized in multiples. AER allotments are established for a definite term of not less than three months (although this provision may be waived in certain cases).

AUTHORIZATION TO START, STOP OR CHANGE AN ALLOTMENT FOR ACTIVE DUTY OR RETIRED PERSONNEL	CONTROL NO.
	PREPARED BY

TO BE COMPLETED BY ALLOTTER

1. ALLOTTER'S NAME (Last, First, Middle Initial) (Print or type)	2. SOCIAL SECURITY NUMBER	3. GRADE (AD only)

4. ALLOTTER'S MAILING ADDRESS (Street or Box Number, City, State, Zip Code)	5. EFFECTIVE DATE (YYMM)	6. ALLOTMENT AMOUNT (Per Month) $

7. ALLOTTEE'S NAME (First, Middle Initial, Last)	8. ALLOTMENT ACTION

8. ALLOTMENT ACTION

a. START	b. STOP	c. CHANGE

9. CREDIT LINE (If applicable)

10. ALLOTMENT CLASS AUTHORIZED (X only one)

C	CHARITY / CFC (Note 2)
D	SUPPORT (Note 1)
F	CHARITY - EMERGENCY / ASSISTANCE FUND CONTRIBUTIONS
H	REPAYMENT OF HOME LOAN (Note 2)
I	INSURANCE
L	REPAY SERVICE ORGANIZATION (Red Cross, etc.)
N	PAY PREMIUMS ON USGLI OR NSLI TO VA (Note 2)
S	PAYMENT TO FINANCIAL ORGANIZATION / VEAP (Note 3)
T	LIQUIDATION OF DEBTS TO U.S. OR DELINQUENT STATE / LOCAL INCOME / EMPLOYMENT TAXES
X	LOCALLY PAID ALLOTMENT
	OTHER (Specify)

11. ALLOTTEE'S MAILING ADDRESS (Street or Box Number, City, State, Zip Code)

12. IF FOREIGN ADDRESS COMPLETE AS FOLLOWS (Province, Country)

13. REMARKS

14. ACCOUNT NUMBER / POLICY NUMBER

15. TOTAL CLASS L AMOUNT $	16. TOTAL CLASS T AMOUNT $

17. SIGNATURE OF ALLOTTER	18. DATE (YYMMDD)

NOTE 1. Must be different address than allotter. Each dependent allotment must have a different credit line. Only one support allotment per dependent is allowed.

NOTE 2. May not be started after retirement.

NOTE 3. May not be started or changed after retirement.

DD Form 2558, MAR 90

398/079

Combined Federal Campaign Contributions (CFC). This allotment is authorized to be in effect one at a time only. CFC allotments are made for a period of 12 months, beginning in January and ending in December. Military personnel who execute the *Payroll Withholding Authorization for Voluntary Charitable Contributions* (a Civil Service form) may do so in lieu of DA Form 1341.

Payment to a Dependent (SPT-V). This kind of allotment is authorized in multiples. This voluntary allotment is paid to a soldier's dependent without regard to whether the soldier is already receiving BAQ. In addition, *involuntary* SPT-V allotments can be administratively established. Normally, the amount of these allotments is not permitted to exceed 80 percent of a soldier's pay. Not more than one SPT-V allotment may be made to the same person.

Payment to a Financial Institution for Credit to a Member's Account (FININ). Only two of these allotments are authorized to be in effect at any one time. FININ allotments are for payment to a financial organization for credit to the allotter's savings, checking, or trust accounts. The FININ allotment may be established for an indefinite term and for any amount the soldier designates, provided he or she has sufficient pay to satisfy the deduction of the allotment.

Payment for Indebtedness to the United States (FED). FED allotments are for the purpose of payment of delinquent federal, state, and local taxes and/or indebtedness to the United States. A separate allotment is required for each debt or overpayment to be repaid.

Payment of Home Loans (HOME). Only one HOME allotment is authorized to be in effect at any one time. This allotment is authorized for repayment of loans for the purchase of a house, mobile home, or house trailer. A HOME allotment is established for an indefinite term and for any amount designated provided the soldier's pay credit is sufficient to satisfy the deduction of the allotment.

Payment of Commercial Life Insurance Premiums (INS). These allotments are authorized in multiples. INS allotments must be made payable to a commercial life insurance firm. INS allotments are not authorized for payment of insurance on the life of a soldier's spouse or children except under a family group contract or for health, accident, or hospitalization insurance. INS allotments are established for an indefinite period and in the amount of the monthly premium as indicated by the number on DA Form 1341.

Repayment of American Red Cross Loans (REDCR). REDCR allotments are authorized in multiples.

Servicemen's Group Life Insurance (SGLI). Maximum coverage is $200,000, with an automatic deduction of $16 per month for premiums, unless the soldier declines coverage or requests a reduced amount of coverage.

Educational Savings Allotment (EDSAV). This allotment is authorized to allow soldiers entering service after December 13, 1976 (except those who enlisted under the Delayed Entry Program before January 1, 1977) to participate in the Veterans Education Assistance Program (VEAP). Only one such allotment is authorized. The EDSAV allotment is established with no discontinuance date. The soldier may stop it at any time after one year of participation.

Class X Allotments. A Class X allotment is paid locally and is authorized in emergency circumstances when other classes of allotments are impracticable. This instance applies overseas only. Class X allotments may be ordered by a commander as a standby allotment when adequate provision for the financial support of a soldier's dependents has not been made.

BENEFITS AND ENTITLEMENTS
Government Quarters
Bachelor accommodations for enlisted personnel range from the fairly austere communal living conditions offered junior enlisted personnel in troop units to the small but private and well-appointed quarters offered senior NCOs in bachelor enlisted quarters (BEQ). During the course of an Army career, you will see them all if you do not marry at a young age.

Modern troop billets are dormitory-style facilities with central air conditioning and heating; two-, three-, or four-person rooms; recreational facilities; and convenience facilities. Less than a generation ago, the bulk of the Army's bachelor enlisted personnel were living in one- and two-story wooden World War II barracks that were hot in the summer, cold in the winter, a real effort to keep clean, and generally overcrowded—older soldiers remember very well living in large troop bays, double-bunked, with only a small wooden footlocker and a metal wall locker to use for the storage of their uniforms and personal clothing.

Family housing—where it is available—ranges in style from detached single-family housing to high-rise apartment-style buildings accommodating scores of families. In some cases, the quarters you are assigned will be in excellent condition and will require little maintenance to keep them that way; others will cause you constant maintenance headaches.

When reporting to some new duty stations, you will find pleasant family housing waiting for you; at other stations, you will have to wait weeks or even months to get any kind of quarters. In some areas, the waiting list for government housing is so long that you might find it necessary to buy or rent off the post. Your family housing officer will be of great assistance to you if you should decide to occupy off-post quarters. Each installation and each major overseas command has a different family housing situation.

Because of your rank, you may very well find yourself either the senior occupant of a multiple dwelling or responsible for a number of families in a stairwell of such a dwelling. These assignments are necessary, and you should consider them as part of your obligation as an NCO to the military community in which you live. You should discharge them with the same dedication and enthusiasm that you devote to your primary duties, but be prepared for many headaches, and expect that from time to time your patience will be severely tried.

Occupancy of family quarters carries the responsibility for doing "handyman work." The facilities engineer performs all maintenance and repairs other than those that are within the capabilities of the occupants. Emergency work or work beyond your individual capabilities can be obtained by making a service call or submitting a job order request to the installation repair and utilities office. Do not, however, expect the engineers to drop everything and run to your quarters, no matter how severe the emergency.

If you are fortunate enough to be assigned to a single-family dwelling, you will be expected to perform that type of self-help maintenance that is done by any prudent homeowner to conserve funds and preserve the premises, such as minor carpentry, maintenance of hardware (door hinges, etc.), touch-up and partial interior painting, caulking around doors and windows, repair of screens, repair of simple plumbing malfunctions (minor leaking, defective washers, simple drainage stoppages), and so forth. Accumulate a set of tools that you can use around the house or apartment for this minor maintenance work.

No matter where you live—family quarters or the barracks—you are expected to exercise individual initiative to preserve energy and utilities. Soldiers are among the most flagrant violators of good energy conservation, wasting water and electricity and fuel as if there were no tomorrow. Remind yourself and others to be conservation conscious.

Your quarters will be inspected by someone from the housing office before you are cleared to vacate your quarters. This inspection can be very rigorous. The specific details will be furnished to you by the housing officer. Some people prefer to hire a civilian contractor do to the work for them. You can avoid this unnecessary expense if you and your family take proper care of your quarters while you are living in them. For example, use rugs on the floors, keep the walls clean and in good repair, and keep your appliances clean.

Commissary and Post Exchange Services

The price you pay for a grocery item in the commissary is the same price the government pays for it: If an item is sold to the government for 85 cents, then that is its cost to you. Even the commissary surcharge and tipping do not add as much to the cost of an item as do the standard markups found on similar items in civilian retail outlets.

The commissary surcharge pays for operating supplies, equipment, utilities, facility alterations, and new construction.

Here are some tips that will help you to cut down on grocery expenses when commissary shopping:

• Avoid shopping as a team. Surprisingly, statistics show that families tend to spend nearly one fourth more when both wife and husband shop together.

• Never shop when you are hungry. You buy more when your resistance is low.

• Cut out and save manufacturers coupons that come to you through the mail, in newspapers, and in magazines. But do not buy something simply because you have a coupon for it. Use coupons to buy those items you planned to buy anyway.

• Do not assume that items prominently displayed are automatically on sale.

• Buy in large quantities if you can save by doing it.

• Avoid precut meat items. You can save by cutting things like chicken yourself. A roll of luncheon meat is cheaper than packages of individually sliced cuts.

• Avoid snack items—they are expensive—and substitute fruits and vegetables instead.

• Do comparison shopping. Get to know the prices for specific items in the commissary as opposed to the civilian marketplace. When the local drugstore or supermarket has a special sale, check it out. Sometimes you can buy certain items cheaper on sale than you can in the commissary.

The Post Exchange Service was designated the Army and Air Force Exchange Service (AAFES) in 1948. What originally began as an outlet "To supply troops at reasonable prices with articles of ordinary use . . . not supplied by the Government . . .

to afford them the means of rational recreation and amusement" has since become a multibillion-dollar enterprise that spans the globe. Many post exchange stores are actually department stores designed for family shoppers, although single soldiers can buy all the necessities of barracks life. Some stores even permit personnel in uniform to be waited on first during certain hours of the day, such as the lunch hour.

Several hundred military exchanges are operated throughout the world by the Department of Defense. (AAFES, headquartered in Dallas and headed by a general officer, operates outlets worldwide. At a minimum, AAFES customers save the state sales tax, which is not charged.

Identity Cards

Your DD Form 2A, *U.S. Armed Forces Identification Card* (green, active-duty), is possibly the most important military document you possess; DD Form 1173, *Uniformed Services Identification and Privilege Card*, is equally important to military dependents. These cards identify the bearers as persons who are entitled to the wide range of entitlements, privileges, and benefits authorized for military personnel and their dependents.

All ID cards are the property of the U.S. government. They are not transferable. The individual (or sponsor) to whom the card is issued must turn in cards in the following circumstances:

- Expiration of the card.
- Change in eligibility status (such as change in grade or rank and changes caused by disciplinary action, discharge, death, retirement, reenlistment, age, marriage, or release to inactive duty of the sponsor).
- Replacement by another card.
- Request from competent authority.
- Demand of the installation commander, verifying activity, or issuing activity.
- Recovery of a lost card after a replacement has been issued.
- Request by the installation commander for temporary safekeeping while an individual is taking part in recreation and gymnastic activities.
- Official placement of a sponsor in a deserter status.
- Change in the status of a sponsor if it terminates or modifies the right to any benefit for which the card may be used.

A lost ID card must be reported promptly to military law enforcement authorities or to ID card issuing authorities. DA Form 428, *Application for Identification Card*, or DD Form 1172, *Application for Uniformed Services Identification and Privilege Card*, is used for this purpose. The form also becomes the application for a new card, provided the individual continues to be eligible to receive it. DA Form 428 or DD Form 1172 must contain a statement of the circumstances of the loss, what was done to recover the card, and the card number, if known.

Any NCO who is performing his or her official duties may confiscate an ID card that is expired, mutilated, used fraudulently, or presented by a person not entitled to use it. Managers and employees of benefit and privilege activities may confiscate any expired or obviously altered ID card or document.

Military Identification Cards. DD Form 2A (green) is issued to the following:

- All military personnel on active duty for more than 30 days.

• Members of the Army National Guard and the U.S. Army Reserve serving on initial active duty for training or a special tour of active duty for training for more than 30 days.
• Cadets of the U.S. Military Academy.

Commissary Cards. Since 1 January 1990, National Guard and Reserve soldiers and their families have been required to present their Armed Forces Commissary Privilege cards to enter and shop in commissaries. They also must show their military or family member ID cards.

Dependent ID Cards. DD Form 1173 is used throughout the Department of Defense to identify persons, other than active-duty or retired military personnel, who are eligible for benefits and privileges offered by the armed forces.

Dependent ID cards are authorized for issue to lawful spouses; unremarried former spouses married to the member or former member for a period of at least 20 years, during which period the member or former member performed at least 20 years of service; children (adopted, legitimized, stepchildren, wards); parents (in special cases); and surviving spouses of active-duty or retired members. See AR 640-3 for specific details.

Generally, DD Forms 1173 are replaced for the same reasons that govern replacement of military ID cards.

To verify eligibility for issue of a dependent ID card, sponsors must be prepared to show marriage certificates, birth certificates, death certificates (in the case of unremarried widows or widowers), or any other documentation prescribed by AR 640-3 required to establish dependency.

Abuse of Privileges. All DD Forms 2, DD Forms 1173, and other authorized identification documents issued to Army members and their dependents may be confiscated and overstamped for abuse of privileges in Army facilities. Medical benefits, however, cannot be suspended for these reasons.

Abuse of privileges includes the following:
• Unauthorized resale of commodities bought in Army activities to unauthorized persons, whether or not to make a profit (customary personal gifts are permissible).
• Shoplifting.
• Unauthorized access to activities.
• Misuse of a privilege (such as allowing an unauthorized person to use an otherwise valid ID card to gain access to a facility).
• Issuing dishonored checks in Army facilities.

Penalties for abuse of privileges in an appropriated or nonappropriated fund facility are warning letter, temporary suspension of privileges, and indefinite suspension of privileges.

Leave

All members of the Army serving on active duty are entitled to leave with pay and allowances at the rate of two and a half calendar days each month of active duty or active duty for training, including the following:
• Members of the Army serving in active military service, including members of the Army National Guard and the Army Reserve serving on active duty for a period of 30 days or more.

• Members of the Army National Guard and Reserve who are serving on initial active duty for training or active duty for training for a period of 30 days or more and for which they are entitled to pay.
• Members of the Army National Guard who are serving on full-time training duty for a period of 30 days or more and for which they are entitled to pay.

The following circumstances do not qualify as periods of earned leave:
• AWOL.
• Confinement as a result of a sentence of court-martial; confinement for more than one day while awaiting court-martial (providing the court-martial results in a conviction).
• When in excess leave.
• Unauthorized absence as a result of detention by civil authorities.
• Absence due to misconduct.

The total accumulation of accrued leave (earned leave) at the end of a fiscal year (September 30) cannot exceed 60 days. Leave accumulated after that date is forfeited. The single exception to this policy applies to personnel who, after January 1, 1968, serve in a designated combat zone, who may accumulate up to 90 days' leave. Leave that begins in one fiscal year and is completed in another is apportioned to the fiscal year in which each portion falls.

Upon discharge and immediate reenlistment, separation at ETTS, or retirement, soldiers are authorized to settle their leave accounts for a lump-sum cash payment at the rate of one day of basic pay for each day of earned leave, up to 50 days. Public Law 94-212, 9 February 1976, limited to a maximum of 60 days' settlement for accrued leave during a military career.

The following types of leave are authorized:
• *Advance leave.* Leave granted before its actual accrual, based on a reasonable expectation that it will be earned by the soldier during the remaining period of active duty.
• *Annual leave.* Leave granted in execution of a command's leave program, chargeable to the soldier's leave account. Also called "ordinary leave," as distinguished from emergency leave and special leave.
• *Convalescent leave.* A period of authorized absence granted to soldiers under medical treatment that is prescribed for recuperation and convalescence for sickness or wounds. Also called "sick leave," convalescent leave is not chargeable.
• *Emergency leave.* Leave granted for a bona fide personal or family emergency requiring the soldier's presence. Emergency leave is chargeable.
• *Environmental and morale leave.* Leave granted in conjunction with an environmental and morale leave program established at overseas installations where adverse environmental conditions exist that offset the full benefit of annual leave programs. This leave is chargeable.
• *Excess leave.* This leave is in excess of accrued and/or advance leave, granted without pay and allowances.
• *Graduation leave.* A period of authorized absence granted, as a delay in reporting to the first permanent duty station, to graduates of the U.S. Military Academy who are appointed as commissioned officers. Not chargeable, providing it is taken within three months of graduation.

- *Leave awaiting orders.* This is an authorized absence, chargeable to accrued leave and in excess of maximum leave accrual, awaiting further orders and disposition in connection with disability separation proceedings under the provisions of AR 635-40.
- *Reenlistment leave.* This leave is granted to enlisted personnel as a result of reenlistment. May be either advance leave or leave accrued or a combination thereof; chargeable against the soldier's leave account.
- *Rest and recuperation—extensions of overseas tours.* This is a nonchargeable increment of R&R leave authorized enlisted soldiers in certain specialties who voluntarily extend their overseas tours. It is authorized in lieu of $50 per month special pay. The tour extension must be for a period of at least 12 months. Options under this program include nonchargeable leaves of 15 or 30 days.
- *Rest and recuperation leave (R&R).* This leave is granted in conjunction with rest and recuperation programs established in those areas designated for hostile fire pay, when operational military considerations preclude the full execution of ordinary annual leave programs. R&R leave is chargeable.
- *Special leave.* This is leave accrual that is authorized in excess of 60 days at the end of a fiscal year for soldiers assigned to hostile fire/imminent danger areas or certain deployable ships, mobile units, or other duty.
- *Terminal leave.* This leave is granted in connection with separation, including retirement, upon the request of the individual.

When possible, soldiers should be encouraged to take at least one annual leave period of about 14 consecutive days or longer (paragraph 203b, AR 630-5). Personnel who refuse to take leave when the opportunity is afforded them should be counseled and informed that such refusal may result in the loss of earned leave at a later date.

Leave is requested on part I, DA Form 31, *Request and Authority for Leave.* Requests for leave must be processed through the individual's immediate supervisor, although this step may be waived where supervisory approval or disapproval is inappropriate. This approval authority (generally, the soldier's commanding officer) ascertains that the individual has sufficient leave accrued to cover the entire period of absence requested.

Personnel should be physically present when DA Form 31 is authenticated and when commencing and terminating leave. Commanders may, at their discretion, authorize telephonic confirmation or departure and return.

Pass

A pass is an authorized absence not chargeable as leave, granted for short periods to provide respite from the working environment or for other specific reasons, at the end of which the soldier is actually at his or her place of duty or in the location from which he or she regularly commutes to work. This provision includes both regular and special passes.

Regular passes are granted to deserving military personnel for those periods when they are not required to be physically present with their unit for the performance of assigned duties. Normally, regular passes are valid only during specified off-duty hours, not more than 72 hours, except for public holiday weekends and holiday periods which, by discretion of the president, are extended to the commencement of working hours on the next working day.

Special passes are granted for periods of three or four days (72 to 95 hours) to deserving personnel on special occasions or in special circumstances for the following reasons: as special recognition for exceptional performance of duty, such as Soldier of the Month or Year; to attend spiritual retreats or to observe other major religious events; to alleviate personal problems incident to military service; to vote; or as compensatory time off for long or arduous duty away from home station or for duty in an isolated location where normal pass is inadequate.

Passes may not be issued to soldiers so that two or more are effective in succession or used in a series, through reissue immediately after return to duty.

Extension of a pass is authorized provided the total absence does not exceed 72 hours for a regular pass, 72 hours for a special three-day pass, and 96 hours for a special four-day pass. Special passes will not be extended by combination with public holiday periods or other off-duty hours in cases in which the combined total will exceed the maximum limits of a three-day or four-day pass. Extensions beyond the authorized maximum are chargeable to leave (paragraph 11-6, AR 630-5).

17

Assignments

There are two old Army sayings that every soldier knows by heart: "Never volunteer" and "There are only two good posts in the Army: the one you just left and the one you want to go to." Add to these "The grass is always greener on the other side of the fence" and "You can never go back," and you have some wisdom about the Army that some soldiers never learn. The Army sends soldiers where it needs them, and *everyone* must take his or her turn.

The professional soldier never endures an assignment alone. The Army really is a great big family that shares its mutual experiences—the good times and bad times.

PERSONNEL ACTION REQUEST

DA Form 4187, *Personnel Action Request*, gives soldiers a way to communicate to Pers-Com their personal choices for such things as assignments, schools, and special duty. This document is considered before making an assignment, but the needs of the Army always come first. Nevertheless, the request is given full consideration whenever possible. It is incumbent upon the individual soldier to check his or her field file (DA Form 2A and 2-1) approximately one month after submitting DA Form 4187 to ensure assignment requests are in the file.

THE ENLISTED PERSONNEL ASSIGNMENT SYSTEM

The primary goal of the Enlisted Personnel Assignment System is to satisfy the personnel requirements of the Army. The secondary goals are as follows:

- Equalize desirable and undesirable assignments by reassigning the most eligible soldier among those of similar MOSs and grade.
- Equalize the hardships of the military service.
- Meet the personal desires of the soldier.
- Assign each soldier so that he or she will have the greatest opportunities for professional development and promotion advancement.

Normally, the military personnel office (MILPO), in coordination with the unit, compares authorized and projected positions with current assigned strength and known or projected gains and losses to determine the requirements for assignments.

PERSONNEL ACTION

For use of this form, see DA PAM 600-8 and AR 680-1; the proponent agency is MILPERCEN.

DATA REQUIRED BY THE PRIVACY ACT

Authority: Title 5, section 3012; Title 10, U.S.C. E.O. 9397. Principal Purpose: Use by service member in accordance with DA Pamphlet 600-8 when requesting a personnel action on his/her own behalf *(Section III)*. Routine Uses: To initiate the processing of a personnel action being requested by the service member. Disclosure: Voluntary. Failure to provide Social Security Number may result in a delay or error in processing of the request for personnel action.

THRU: *(Include ZIP Code)*	TO: *(Include ZIP Code)*	FROM: *(Include ZIP Code)* COMMANDER

SECTION I - PERSONAL IDENTIFICATION

NAME *(Last, first, MI)*	GRADE OF RANK/PMOS *(Enl only)*	SOCIAL SECURITY NUMBER

SECTION II - DUTY STATUS CHANGE *(Proc 9-1, DA Pam 600-8)*

The above member's duty status is changed from _____

_____ to _____

_____ effective _____ hours, _____ 19 ____

SECTION III - REQUEST FOR PERSONNEL ACTION

I request the following action:

TYPE OF ACTION	Procedure	TYPE OF ACTION	Procedure
Service School *(Enl only)*		Reassignment Married Army Couples	
ROTC or Reserve Component Duty		Reclassification	
Volunteering For Oversea Service		Officer Candidate School	
Ranger Training		Asgmt of Pers with Exceptional Family Members	
Reasgmt Extreme Family Problems		Identification Card	
Exchange Reassignment *(Enl only)*		Identification Tags	
Airborne Training		Separate Rations	
Special Forces Training/Assignment		Leave - Excess/Advance/Outside CONUS	
On-the-Job Training *(Enl only)*		Change of Name/SSN/DOB	
Retesting in Army Personnel Tests		Other *(Specify)*	

SIGNATURE OF MEMBER *(When required)*	DATE

SECTION IV - REMARKS *(Applies to Sections II, III, and V) (Continue on separate sheet)*

SECTION V - CERTIFICATION/APPROVAL/DISAPPROVAL

I certify that the duty status change *(Section II)* or that the request for personnel action *(Section III)* contained herein -

☐ HAS BEEN VERIFIED   ☐ RECOMMEND APPROVAL   ☐ RECOMMEND DISAPPROVAL

☐ IS APPROVED   ☐ IS DISAPPROVED

COMMANDER/AUTHORIZED REPRESENTATIVE	SIGNATURE	DATE

DA FORM DEC 82 **4187**   EDITION OF FEB 81 WILL BE USED.   COPY 1

DA Form 4187 is the soldier's basic request form for any personnel action.

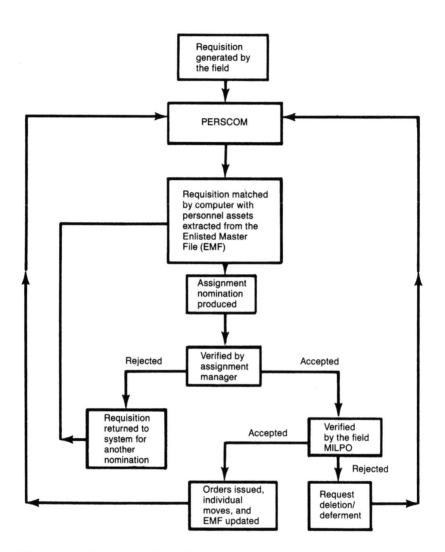

This flow chart illustrates the Enlisted Personnel Assignment System.

Requisitions are then prepared for these requirements and submitted to Commanding General, Total Army Personnel Command (PersCom) in Alexandria, Virginia. On receipt, PersCom edits and validates the requisitions. It is the responsibility of the requisitioning unit not to over- or underrequisition and to resolve any discrepancy before submitting the validated requisition for processing.

Soldiers become available to be assigned against these requisitions for a variety of reasons. Soldiers who enlist in the Army are available for assignment on completion of training and award of an MOS. Others are available when they have done one of the following:

- Volunteered for reassignment.
- Completed an overseas tour of duty.
- Completed schooling or training.
- Completed a stabilized tour of duty.
- Completed normal time on station in the continental United States for a given MOS ("turnaround time" varies by MOS).

The Centralized Assignment Procedure III (CAP III) System is used to assign all soldiers except those completing basic and advanced individual training. This automated nomination/assignment procedure compares the requirements recorded on requisitions against selected qualification factors for each soldier. Some of the major qualifications considered are grade, MOS and skill level, area of preference, and Special Qualification Identifier (SQI). Other qualifications considered are the expiration of term of service (ETS), the number of months since last PCS, the number of months since return from overseas, the soldier's availability month compared with requirement month on the requisition, and an Additional Skill Identifier (ASI). An ASI (expressed as the sixth and seventh characters of an MOS Code) identifies skills acquired through functional training or OJT in maintenance and operation of weapon or equipment systems or subsystems and other training not identified by MOS or SQI (see AR 611-201).

Each soldier is compared with each requisition and given a numeric score for every one for which he or she can be nominated. Once a soldier's record has been reviewed and awarded points for a qualitative match to each requisition, the system then selects that group of nominations that provides the best overall requisition fill in terms of quantity and quality. The assignment preferences of the individual and the requirements of the positions receive maximum consideration within the primary goal of filling all the Army's requirements. The nomination process has three basic goals:

- Each valid requisition must have at least one soldier nominated to it, provided sufficient soldiers are available for assignment in the requisition MOS and grade.
- Requisitions are filled by relative priority. When a shortage of soldiers exists, the shortage is shared proportionately by all requisitioning activities according to priority.
- A soldier is nominated to an assignment for which he or she is well qualified.

The CAP III produces nominations to match the requisition. These nominations are then passed to an assignment manager for verification. Based on a review of all available information, the assignment manager either accepts a soldier for the assignment or rejects all nominees and returns the requisition to the selection process for new nominations. If maintained by the Enlisted Personnel Management Directorate, PersCom, the career management individual files (CMIF) are also included in this review. A qualified individual may also be selected manually to match the requisition regardless of nomination by CAP III.

Assignment instructions are transmitted to both the losing and gaining commands or installations by the automated digital network (AUTODIN). The losing commander then verifies the assignment. This step is the key in the process. Because of delays in reporting and errors in the databases, the individuals selected may not qualify for the assignment. When assignment instructions are received by the losing commander's military personnel office, the soldier's qualifications and eligibility are verified. The MILPO interviews the soldier and reviews his or her records.

A young Signal Corps soldier wires a tactical antenna to support unit communications.

If the soldier is qualified and the assignment is in keeping with announced Department of the Army policy, the process is finished when the necessary orders for travel are issued. If the soldier does not qualify or cannot qualify in time to meet the requirement, a deletion or deferment request is submitted in accordance with AR 614-200.

Homebase and Advance Assignment Program (HAAP)

A soldier is given a *homebase assignment* when he or she is projected to return to his or her previous permanent duty station after completing a short tour. An *advance assignment* is given when a soldier is projected to be assigned to a duty station other than his or her previous permanent duty station after completing a short tour.

Eligible soldiers are given a homebase or an advance assignment when selected for a dependent-restricted short-tour area. The Homebase and Advance Assignment Program (HAAP) minimizes family dislocation and reduces the expenditure of PCS funds. Only active Army sergeants through the ranks of first sergeant and master sergeant who are assigned to dependent-restricted 12-month short-tour areas are affected. HAAP assignments are not furnished to sergeants major or first sergeants or master sergeants (promotable), except that consistent with the needs of the Army, the CSM/SGM Office, PersCom, honors individual preferences when issuing assignment instructions to personnel in these ranks returning to CONUS.

The following primary factors determine HAAP assignments:
- The needs of the Army.
- Professional development.
- Least-cost factors.
- Assignment choice.
- Regimental affiliation.

Requests for PCS or Deletion from Assignment

AR 614-200 establishes specific policies governing individual requests submitted by soldiers for a PCS or deletion from assignment instructions. A soldier may submit a request for any of the following reasons:
- *Extreme family problem that is temporary and can be resolved in one year.*
- *Extreme family problem that is not expected to be resolved in one year.*
- *Sole surviving son or daughter.* The sole surviving son or daughter of a family that has suffered the loss of the father, the mother, or one or more sons or daughters in the military service will not be required to serve in combat. Soldiers who become sole surviving sons or daughters after their enlistment may request discharge under AR 635-200. A soldier may waive entitlement to assignment limitations, whether entitlement was based on his or her own application or the request of his or her immediate family.
- *Assignment of married Army couples.* Army requirements and readiness goals are paramount when considering personnel for assignment. Married Army couples desiring joint assignment to establish common household (joint domicile) must request such assignment. The assignment desires of soldiers married to other soldiers are fully considered. There are two ways for married Army couples to apply for joint domicile assignment: (1) by applying on a one-time basis to be continually considered for worldwide joint assignments. Thereafter, when one member is being considered for reassignment, the other will automatically be considered for assignment to the same location or area. Or, (2) by applying for joint domicile assignments each time consid-

eration is desired. In this case, the spouse who has received assignment instructions must submit an application for joint domicile consideration.

- *Exchange assignments.* For mutual convenience, CONUS-assigned soldiers may request an exchange assignment with a soldier within CONUS; a soldier assigned overseas may request an exchange assignment with a soldier within his or her same overseas command.

DA Pam 600-8 contains detailed guidance for preparing and processing requests for an exchange assignment. The *Army Times* publishes lists of soldiers who desire to contact others to arrange for exchange assignments.

- *Assignment from duty requiring extensive TDY.* Soldiers assigned to duties requiring extensive travel or family separation may, on completing three years in that duty, request assignment. For this purpose, extensive travel/family separation is defined by AR 614-200 as "TDY away from the home station requiring travel or family separation for 4 or more days per week for not less than 22 weeks per year."

CAREER DEVELOPMENT PROGRAMS

A career development program is a system of intensive management of selected MOSs or career management fields (CMF). Career development programs are established to ensure that there are enough highly trained and experienced soldiers to fill positions that require unique or highly technical skills. To develop soldiers with the required proficiency, career fields within each program often require the following:

- Frequent movement from one job to another to gain required experience.
- An above average frequency of advanced training.
- Lengthy or frequent training periods.
- A combination of any of the above factors.

Unless otherwise stated in AR 614-200, volunteers for a career development program should submit applications on DA Form 4187, using DA Pam 600-8 for detailed application procedures. In applying for career programs and related training, applicants should consider the prerequisites listed in DA Pam 351-4 for the appropriate course of instruction.

Chapter 7, AR 614-200, contains the minimum requirements (subject to change) for each career program. Attaining the prerequisites does not automatically ensure entry into a career program. The appropriate career management branch selects the best qualified soldiers for a career program.

Waivers are not granted for remaining service requirements for formal training. Waivers for other eligibility requirements or selection standards are considered unless otherwise stated in AR 614-200. Waivers cannot be implied. Each must be specifically requested. In the application for entry into the program or training requested, the applicant must include the reason for the waiver.

Career development programs include the following:

- Intelligence Career Program.
- Noncommissioned Officer Logistics Program (NCOLP).
- Explosive Ordnance Disposal (EOD) Career Program.
- Technical Escort (TE) Career Program.
- Personnel Specialty Career Program (PSCP).
- Army Bandsman Career Program (ABCP).
- Enlisted Club Management Career Program.

Assignment to Specific Organizations and Duty Positions

AR 614-200 contains specific policies and procedures for nomination, evaluation, selection, and assignment of enlisted soldiers to the following:

- Presidential support activities.
- Drill Sergeant Program.
- Assignment as instructors at uniformed service schools.
- Assignment to international and overseas joint headquarters, U.S. Military Missions, Military Assistance Advisory Groups (MAAGs), and Joint U.S. Military Advisory Groups (JUSMAG).
- Assignment to certain organizations and agencies: Office of the Secretary of Defense and Office of the Joint Chiefs of Staff; U.S. Central Command; U.S. Readiness Command (USREDCOM) and Joint Deployment Agency; Defense Communications Agency; Defense Intelligence Agency; HQDA, PersCom, and HQ TRADOC; U.S. Military Academy, U.S. Army Command and General Staff College, and U.S. Army War College; U.S. Disciplinary Barracks; lst Battalion, 3rd Infantry (The Old Guard), Fort Myer, Virginia; U.S. Army Military District of Washington; U.S. Army Intelligence and Security Command; Office of the Assistant Chief of Staff for Intelligence; U.S. Army Correctional Activity; U.S. Army Courier Service; U.S. Army Service Center for the Armed Forces; U.S. Army Element, Armed Forces Police Department, Washington, D.C.; U.S. Army Criminal Investigation Command; and Defense Logistics Agency.
- Reserve Component or Reserve Officer Training Corps (ROTC) duty.
- Food inspection specialists.
- Selection and assignment of first sergeants.

Drill Sergeant Program

The Drill Sergeant Program is designed to allow highly motivated, well-qualified professionals to serve as cadre at the following:

- U.S. Army Training Centers (USATC).
- TRADOC training centers.
- U.S. Army Correction Activity, Fort Riley, Kansas.

To be eligible to enter the Drill Sergeant Program, all candidates must meet the following nonwaiverable prerequisites:

- Pass the Army Physical Fitness Test (APFT) shortly after arrival at the duty station (AR 600-9). Volunteers must have successfully passed the APFT within the last six months and must furnish a copy of their physical test score cards with their applications. Weight limits are prescribed in AR 600-9.
- Have no speech impairment.
- Display good military bearing.
- Have no record of emotional instability as determined by screening of health records.
- Be a high school graduate or possess the GED equivalent.
- Have demonstrated leadership ability during previous tours of duty.
- Have no record of disciplinary action or time lost during the current enlistment or in the last three years, whichever is longer.
- Have demonstrated the capability to perform in positions of increased responsibility as a senior NCO in the Army.

- Have been placed consistently in the upper half of his or her peer group as demonstrated by MOS evaluation.
- Not have received enlistment bonus or selective reenlistment bonus for current service obligation if PMOS is not among those authorized for drill sergeant positions.

Soldiers assigned to drill sergeant duty incur a 24-month obligation for drill sergeant duty after successful completion of Drill Sergeant School and a stabilized tour for 24 months with an option to extend an additional 6 to 12 months. The tour of duty for a drill sergeant does not exceed 36 months.

As an exception to AR 614-6, CG, PersCom, may grant a second PCS in the same fiscal year for personnel who volunteer for drill sergeant duties, fail to graduate from Drill Sergeant School, or are removed from the program, either voluntarily or involuntarily. Applications should be submitted through channels on a DA Form 4187.

Drill sergeants inspect a field training area. Fulfilling a drill sergeant assignment can be career enhancing and personally rewarding.

Selection and Assignment of First Sergeants

The soldier having acquired that degree of confidence of his officers as to be appointed first sergeant of the company, should consider the importance of his office; that the discipline of the company, the conduct of the men, their exactness in obeying orders, and the regularity of their manners, will in great measure depend on his vigilance.

—von Steuben, *Regulations for the Order*
of the Troops of the United States,
approved by Congress, 29 March 1779

Only the most highly qualified and motivated senior soldiers are selected and assigned to first sergeant positions. Moreover, first sergeant duty assignments must be career enriching and serve as professional development experience for soldiers in career management fields where first sergeant opportunities are available.

Sergeants first class and master sergeants are assigned as first sergeants based on outstanding qualities of leadership, dedication to duty, integrity and moral character, professionalism, MOS proficiency, appearance and military bearing, physical fitness, and proven performance or potential for the first sergeant position.

Soldiers who meet the above requirements and who complete the First Sergeant's Course are eligible for award of SQI M.

Attendance at the First Sergeant's Course at Fort Bliss, Texas, is mandatory for award of the SQI M.

OVERSEAS SERVICE

Many Americans work very hard all their lives, and then in their declining years, when they at last have the leisure and money to travel, they see the world. Soldiers not only see the world when they are young, but they also have the unique opportunity to live among foreign peoples for extended periods of time and learn about their cultures from firsthand experience.

There are two ways that you can approach your first overseas tour. You can go kicking and screaming and spend your time in some foreign country, isolated in the American community, never venturing very far outside the cocoon of familiar surroundings, counting the dreary days until you rotate, or you can approach foreign service as a thrilling adventure to be experienced to the fullest, and you can be a goodwill ambassador for the United States of America.

Running afoul of the law in a foreign country can be very dangerous. In countries where a Status of Forces Agreement (SOFA) exists between the United States government and the foreign government, soldiers may be tried for offenses under the laws of the country concerned.

Most major overseas commands operate orientation programs for newly arrived personnel in the command. These courses attempt to expose soldiers to the culture in which they will be living in order to lessen the effect of culture shock that some people experience the first time they encounter an alien society. When you receive overseas assignment instructions, it would be a very good idea for you and your spouse (if you have one) to study the language of the country to which you will be going. Some special assignments require extensive formal language training, but most Army installations do provide some language instruction for soldiers and their dependents who are bound overseas. Learning the rudiments of a foreign language can be fun, and speaking a foreign language is a very valuable skill to have once you arrive at your overseas duty station.

Standards of living overseas vary depending on the country. Germany's standard of living is very high, and your money will not go far there; other countries are beset with substantial economic problems, and the standards of living in those places can sometimes be so low that only the very rich can afford luxuries that are considered common in the United States, and you won't be able to afford them at local prices.

As with everything else, what you get out of your situation is what you make of it. And remember that your overseas tour will not last forever; sooner or later you must leave to come home. Emotional attachments are very hard to break off, so be warned if you establish any kind of relationship with a foreign man or woman. What usually starts as a casual, fun-filled lark, a pleasant way to pass the time, frequently develops into a serious involvement. If it is not consummated by marriage, its termination can be an emotional trauma that will be very painful for both of you. A sad commentary on this subject is the thousands of illegitimate children American servicemen have abandoned in various foreign countries over the years.

Policies
The chief consideration in selecting a soldier for service overseas is that a valid authorization exists for his or her military qualifications. Equitable distribution is made, within a given MOS and grade, of overseas duty assignments, considering both desirable and undesirable locations. All reasonable efforts are made to minimize periods of forced separations and any adverse effects of overseas service encountered by soldiers and their families.

Between overseas tours, with the exception of Hawaii, soldiers are assigned in their sustaining base for at least 12 months on station. Consistent with Army needs, soldiers are retained as long as possible in the continental United States. Among individuals who have previous overseas service, those with the earliest date of return from overseas normally will be selected first. Subject to personnel requirements to short-tour areas, soldiers who have completed a normal overseas service tour in a short-tour area will not be assigned to another short-tour area on their next overseas assignment.

Temporary Deferments
Because of the possible adverse effect on command operational readiness, granting of deferments for overseas service is strictly controlled and held to an absolute minimum. The needs of the service are the major determining factor in granting deferments.

Normally, once an application has been submitted, the soldier will be retained at the home station, pending a final decision. When a soldier requests deferment and it results in his or her having less remaining time in service than the length of the prescribed tour, the individual will continue on the overseas assignment. Unless he or she voluntarily reenlists or extends to be eligible to complete the prescribed tour, the individual must sign a counseling statement, which is a bar to reenlistment.

Applications are initiated by the individual concerned on DA Form 4187.

Deferments and Deletions
The following conditions normally warrant deferments:

- A recent severe psychotic episode involving a spouse or child after a soldier receives assignment instructions.
- The soldier's children are being made wards of the court or are being placed in an orphanage or a foster home because of family separation. This separation must be because of military service and not because of neglect or misconduct on the part of the soldier.
- Adoption cases in which the home study (deciding whether a child is to be placed) has been completed and a child is scheduled to be placed in the soldier's home within 90 days.
- Illness of a family member (see AR 614-30 for details).
- Terminal illness of a family member where death is anticipated within one year.
- The death of a soldier's spouse or child, after receipt of assignment instructions.
- Prolonged hospitalization of more than 90 days when the soldier's presence is deemed essential to resolve associated problems.
- Documented rape of the soldier's spouse or child within 90 days of the scheduled movement date, when the soldier's presence is deemed essential to resolve associated problems.
- Selection to attend the Basic or Advanced NCO Courses or OCS, where attendance will delay overseas travel more than 90 days.
- Enrollment in the Drug and Alcohol Abuse Residential Rehabilitation Treatment Program.
- Pregnancy or related complications exceeding 90 days.

Eligibility for Overseas Service
Personnel are assigned to short-tour overseas assignments according to the following priorities:
- Volunteers who have completed a minimum of 12 months' time on station or are not otherwise stabilized.
- Personnel with no previous overseas service.
- Personnel in CONUS who have not previously served in a short-tour area and whose last overseas assignment was a "with dependents" tour; those whose last overseas tour was a "with dependents" tour in a long-tour area and who previously served a short tour; those whose last overseas tour was in a short-tour area and who were in accompanied status; and those who have not previously served in a short-tour area and whose last assignment was an "all others" tour.
- Personnel in Hawaii after completion of a prescribed accompanied tour.
- Personnel in CONUS whose last overseas tour was in a short-tour area and who were in an unaccompanied area.
- Personnel in Hawaii after completion of a prescribed "all others" tour.

Personnel are assigned to long-tour overseas areas according to the following priorities:
- As in the first two conditions listed for short-tour overseas assignments.
- Personnel serving in CONUS whose last overseas tour was "with dependents" in a short-tour area.
- Personnel serving in CONUS whose last overseas tour was "all others" in a short-tour area; "all others" in a long-tour area; and "with dependents" in a long-tour area.

- Personnel in Hawaii after completion of a prescribed "with dependents" tour or an "all others" tour.

Curtailment of Tours

Overseas commanders may curtail overseas tours when military requirements so dictate. They may also disapprove curtailment requests.

When curtailments of more than 60 days are considered, commanders must recommend curtailments and request reassignment instructions from PersCom as early as possible but not later than 45 days before the departure date. Curtailing a tour must not cause an emergency requisition to fill the vacated position.

Overseas commanders may, at any time, curtail the tour of a soldier who has discredited or embarrassed or may discredit or embarrass the United States or jeopardize the commander's mission. They may also curtail tours when family members are moved to the United States because of criminal activity, a health problem, or death in the immediate family living with the sponsor. In exceptional cases, the commander may waive advance HQDA coordination and attach the soldier to the nearest personnel assistance point for issue of PCS orders. These exceptions are as follows: potential defectors, extreme personal hardship, and expeditious removal of a soldier in the best interests of the service (for example, when a soldier causes an embarrassment to the command in its relationship with a foreign government).

Pregnant soldiers are not curtailed from their overseas tour solely because of their pregnancy. If noncombatant evacuation is ordered, however, pregnant soldiers who have reached the seventh month of pregnancy will be curtailed and evacuated. Such a curtailment does not, however, preclude the solder being reassigned overseas again after completion of the pregnancy and discharge from inpatient status.

Extension of Tours

Acceptable members are encouraged to extend their overseas tours. Major overseas commanders may disapprove requests for extension. AR 614-30 lists rules and approval authorities for extensions of overseas tours.

Kinds of Overseas Tours

Personnel accompanied or joined by their dependents at government expense must have enough remaining service to serve the tour prescribed for those "with dependents."

Army personnel married to each other and serving in the same overseas area serve tours in accordance with AR 614-30. They must extend or reenlist, if necessary, to have enough time in service to serve the tour prescribed by the table before compliance with orders directing movement.

The "all others" tour is served by soldiers who meet the following criteria:

- Elect to serve overseas without dependents.
- Are serving in an area where dependents are not permitted.
- Do not have dependents (this rule does not apply in areas where personnel who have dependents must serve "with dependents" tours).
- Are divorced or legally separated and pay child support.

Tours normally will be the same for all personnel at the same station. Where there are personnel of more than one service, the service having the main interest (normally, the most personnel in the area) develops a recommended tour length that is coordinated with the other services. Tour length may vary within any given country or area, depending on the specific duty station. AR 614-30 lists overseas duty tours for military personnel.

RELOCATION ASSISTANCE
Sponsorship Program
The sponsorship program assists soldiers and their dependents in establishing themselves at a new duty station and guides soldiers while they adjust to their new work environment.

A "sponsor" is an individual designated by name at a gaining organization to assist incoming members and their families in making a smooth transition into the unit and community environment. The act of sponsorship is the guided integration of new soldiers into the unit and the community. This act includes the exchange of correspondence between the incoming soldier and a sponsor before the new soldier's arrival and assistance and orientation after arrival. Sponsors should be a grade equal to or higher than that of the incoming soldier; be the same sex, marital status, and MOS; be familiar with the surrounding area; and not have received assignment instructions.

Sponsors' duties are varied:
- Forward a welcoming letter to the incoming soldier. It should include the sponsor's duty address and telephone number and home address and home telephone number, as well, but this is not specifically required by the regulation.
- Try to provide information requested by incoming soldiers.
- Advise the incoming soldier that he or she will be met at the point of arrival in the area or at the aerial port of debarkation.
- Offer to assist in getting temporary housing (guest house or similar accommodations). The sponsor should contact the housing referral office for guidance and information. Sponsors are not required to contract for permanent or temporary housing, but if the sponsor desires to provide this service and the incoming soldier agrees, the sponsor should seek legal advice about the commitments and liabilities involved.
- Accompany the incoming soldier after his or her arrival in the unit while he or she goes through in-processing.
- Acquaint the incoming soldier with the surrounding area and facilities.
- Introduce the incoming soldier to his or her supervisors and immediate chain of command.

Gaining commanders are required to send incoming soldiers welcoming letters. Informality and information sharing are the primary goals of these letters. This letter also responds to any request for specific information appearing in item 42 of DA Form 4787. The welcoming letter and its enclosures should as a minimum contain the gaining unit's address and telephone number and the following information:
- The projected availability of government and economy housing, including when available, rent and utility costs, security deposit, and advance rent requirements.
- The location of the family housing referral office.
- Education facilities available for dependents in both the military and the civilian communities.
- The types of household goods that are essential, optional, or not required at an overseas location.
- The type of climate and recommended clothing.

- Local vehicle registration, safety, emission standards, and insurance requirements and, when available, typical insurance rates.
- The availability of military and civilian medical and dental care facilities.
- Community services and facilities that are available both on and off post.
- The host nation's culture, customs, and lifestyle.
- Local firearms laws and restrictions.
- Problems they might have when shipping pets to the overseas command.

Commanders are also responsible for ensuring that sponsors are provided enough time from their duties to help new soldiers and arranging transportation for sponsors to meet new members arriving with their dependents at the point of arrival and bring them back to the unit (overseas only).

The incoming soldier should answer the sponsor's letter immediately and do the following:

- Inform the sponsor of his or her time, date, and point of arrival (including flight numbers). Any changes to the itinerary should be reported to the sponsor immediately.
- Provide the sponsor a unit mailing address and telephone number (commercial or DSN).
- Inform the sponsor of the expected departure date from the losing duty stations.
- If desired, provide the sponsor with leave addresses and telephone numbers.

Orientation Program
Commanders and supervisors are responsible for conducting a thorough and timely orientation to start new arrivals off properly. These orientations should make the new soldier feel needed and wanted and instill in him or her the motivation to contribute to the unit's mission.

Transportation of Household Goods
Transportation of household goods at government expense is authorized for soldiers in accordance with the table below. For information on authorized weight limitations for other grades, see *Joint Federal Travel Regulations* (JFR).

PCS WEIGHT ALLOWANCE (POUNDS)

Pay Grade	With Dependents	Without Dependents
E-9	14,500	12,000
E-8	13,500	11,000
E-7	12,500	10,500
E-6	11,000	8,000
E-5	9,000	7,000
E-4 (over 2 years' service)	8,000	7,000
E-4 (2 years' service or less)	7,000	3,500
E-3	5,000	2,000
E-2, E-1	5,000	1,500

18

The Drawdown

During the evening of Columbus Day 1994, a solemn President Bill Clinton addressed the nation in a brief, live national broadcast from the Oval Office. Instead of marking the national holiday, however, the president spoke about two pressing military issues outside the United States and about deployed servicemembers. Clinton praised the U.S. forces deployed to support the reestablishment of democracy in Haiti, the poorest nation in the Western Hemisphere. He also made comments supporting other U.S. forces, including the mechanized 24th Infantry Division, which had again been rapidly deployed to deter Iraq's massed forces on the Iraq-Kuwait border.

Clinton hailed the liberating change that had occurred in Haiti thanks to the strength and professionalism of U.S. military forces, and he made it clear to Saddam Hussein that the Iraqi threat to Kuwait would be met with overwhelming lethal force, just as it was during the Gulf War. The president's words, which were carried to U.S. forces overseas on the Armed Forces Network, were meant both to bolster the morale of the uniformed men and women who were in harm's way and to serve notice to the world that the United States stands by its commitments to support democracy and defend vital national interests.

Ironically, the active ranks of the Army continued to be thinned in 1994 to accommodate shrinking military budgets and the paradigm shift described at the beginning of this *Guide*—even as the force was called upon to take on an increasingly active role in an unpredictable, unstable world. The completed and planned reductions in Active Army Component manpower are listed in *Army Budget Fiscal Year 1995: An Analysis*, published in May 1994 by the Association of the United States Army (AUSA). The document shows the following Active Component personnel strengths (in thousands):

- FY 93—572.
- FY 94—540.
- FY 95—510.
- FY 96—500.
- FY 97 through FY 99—495.

In FY 89 there were 770,000 members in the Active Component. The planned reductions through FY 99 represent the removal of more than one third (36 percent) of the Army's active forces. Reserve Component personnel strength is scheduled to drop from 686,000 to 575,000 and Army Civilian personnel strength from 294,000 to 269,000 during the same period, according to the AUSA. In the decade between 1989 and 1999 the Reserve Components will be reduced by more than one fourth (26 percent), and Army Civilian strength will be cut by one third (33 percent), according to the AUSA.

Using information provided by the AUSA and simple math, it is easy to compute the total numeric effect of the drawdown on the Army: a net loss of about three out of every ten members. Put another way, America's Army of 1999 will operate with about 70 percent of the personnel it had in 1989, and the deepest cuts will have come from the Active Component, the core of the war-fighting force. Senior leaders are working hard to offset the personnel reductions by an increase in the technological edge the Army has over hostile military forces.

The drawdown continues to be a distracting, frustrating experience for leaders throughout the ranks. Nevertheless, NCOs in uniform today understand better than ever the critical importance of leading from the front, of staying in top physical condition, and of remaining focused on their profession.

Recent events such as those in Haiti and the Middle East illustrate cold, hard facts about military service: The NCO must remain ready to deploy and operate in hostile environments. Further, NCOs have a special obligation to ensure the readiness of the soldiers they supervise, lead, and train. For these reasons, Army service standards remain at an all-time high. It is therefore quite important to heed Sergeant Major of the Army Richard Kidd's advice: "Stay in your lane." Stay focused on your purpose as an NCO and help your soldiers stay focused through the remainder of the drawdown period.

TOUGHER STANDARDS
Weight Control
In the early 1970s, too many NCOs were fat. One former sergeant in the 82nd Airborne Division was proud of being a lean member of the Airborne community. He recalled that paratroopers in 1974 would ridicule and prod fat soldiers who could not pull their weight. Overweight paratroopers could not keep up with infantry units when they moved out on monthly 12-mile and quarterly 25-mile road marches. Fat soldiers fell out of daily 3- and weekly 5-mile runs. Overly fat soldiers in the division's 325th Infantry were shunned and drummed off jump status, and thus out of the elite division. Call it a bias, but keep in mind that the Army did and still does discriminate when it comes to service standards.

As an NCO, should you tolerate a fat soldier? Should you allow yourself to become overweight? Obviously not, especially since AR 600-9, *The Army Weight Control Program*, mandates stringent weight and body fat standards.

Local Bar to Reenlistment
Soldiers who exceed the allowable weight for their height must be tape tested, in compliance with AR 600-9. Those who fail the tape test are counseled, entered into the Army Weight Control Program, and "flagged"—meaning that they may receive no favorable actions (no schooling, no promotions) until they meet the standards of the program. Soldiers who will not or cannot comply and who have no medical reason for failure to comply with the program will be barred from reenlisting and

processed for separation from service. Soldiers can be barred for other reasons as well, such as for misconduct.

NCOES Misconduct

Misconduct embarrasses the NCO corps. Misconduct at an NCO Education System (NCOES) course will result in administrative removal from the course and a bar to reenlistment. Any NCO who is found to be guilty of misconduct in an NCOES course can count on encountering a serious problem when he or she returns to home station. The commandant of the NCO academy where the misconduct occurred may sign a letter addressing the matter to the first general officer in the soldier's chain of command. Beyond the profoundly negative impact of an official reprimand from a commanding general, misconduct results in a negative *Army Evaluation Report* (AER), DA Form 1059, which is filed in the soldier's permanent Official Military Personnel File.

As an NCO, you must understand—and make your soldiers understand—the importance of NCOES to development and career. Do not take selection or attendance lightly. Do not look at attendance as "a break" from routine duties. Focus on the purpose of attendance at the Primary, Basic, or Advanced NCO Courses. Do not fall in with "party animals" who look at the mission of the local NCO academy with disdain. Study the course materials presented to you. Learn all you can about leadership and common tactical drills and other components of the program of instruction.

Keep this in mind: The "Exceeded Course Standards" block of the AER is restricted to the top 20 percent of each class—and there is no rule stating that academy cadre must check the block for any percent. Do your best, buckle down and succeed, and avoid any possibility of misconduct. Remember that the Army is always looking to retain and promote the best and to eliminate substandard soldiers.

The APFT

Graduates of the the Master Fitness Trainer Course know the purpose of the Army Physical Fitness Test (APFT). It is to measure a soldier's and a unit's ability to accomplish the tasks listed on the Mission Essential Task List. That is basically it. Chapter 3 discussed the APFT in detail. Here, you should know that failing two record APFTs will result in the initiation of a separation action. This standard is in place for good reasons, not the least of which is the critical importance of physical fitness to mission accomplishment.

Good NCOs take part in and lead daily PT sessions. Nothing will improve your credibility in front of your troops more than your unfailing participation in rigorous fitness training. Showing your younger soldiers that you can hack it physically will matter most when they must turn to you for leadership under tough field training exercise or operational conditions.

Drug and Alcohol Abuse

These issues, addressed in chapter 12, remain hot topics in troop units throughout the Army. It is not that drug and alcohol abuse are major problems in the Army today—they are not—but instances of abuse do still occur and signify to leaders the need to get involved and resolve such problems as soon as they surface. Substance abuse distracts leaders from other, more productive work and reflects unfavorably on the abuser.

Soldiers who use drugs and any who peddle drugs do not belong in the United States Army. A soldier who relies on alcohol to make it through the day or one who feels he or she must turn to some drug to get by or get high should have the personal courage to quit or to seek help from the local Alcohol and Drug Abuse Prevention and Control Program (ADAPCP) office.

While substance abuse and the drawdown are not directly related, it is a fact that abusers who fail rehabilitation are eliminated from service and thus "contribute" to the Army's mandated smaller end strength requirement. Nobody in authority in the Army wants any soldier to make such a contribution. Stay away from drugs and avoid alcohol abuse.

Qualitative Management Program

The Qualitative Management Program (QMP) was discussed in chapter 9. Soldiers identified for elimination from service under the terms of the QMP also "contribute" to reduced end strength requirements. To avoid this problem, remain competitive within your MOS and career field by meeting the requirements of your specialty. Attend NCOES training when selected. Get the civilian education recommended on your NCO Professional Development Career Map. Volunteer for functional, special, or additional skill identifier-producing courses. Do what is professionally necessary to be considered "among the best qualified" come time for promotion. If you are in a dead-end MOS, get out of it and into a critical MOS. Discuss career plans with the senior NCOs in your unit, especially your first sergeant or command sergeant major. Ask your NCO leaders to review your performance and personnel file and to offer recommendations—and heed their advice.

Promotions

This is number one: Look out for the soldiers you supervise. Prepare your junior enlisted troops for soldier and promotion boards. Guide any NCOs you supervise. Do the mandatory NCOER counseling and follow up. Your superiors will look favorably upon you if you are known for taking care of your soldiers.

Know and do your job, keep track of your accomplishments, and do not be shy about asking that they be included on your NCOER. Contact your branch sergeant major to find out what the current emphasis is in your MOS, and then make sure you meet the requirement, whatever it is.

Stay fit and trim, and make sure your Army green uniform fits perfectly. Ask senior NCOs to scrutinize your photo. If an error is spotted, retake your photograph. The extra effort it takes to ensure that your DA Full Length Photograph is first rate will pay dividends if it stands out when it is reviewed by centralized school and promotion selection boards. (See chapter 10 for more promotion details.)

Reenlistment and Retention

Stay Army! At least consider that the years you have invested in the Army are an investment in yourself as well. Why waste it? Make it tough on the drawdown bean counters at the Pentagon. Reenlist, and remain eligible for reenlistment. Pass the APFT. Meet the NCOES schooling requirement. Get your commander's recommendation. Qualify every year with your primary individual weapon. (Weapon qualification is not a tough requirement to meet if you are a tanker, for example, and you must fire Tank Table VIII each year. But you may have to work with your operations NCO to set up a range if you are in a combat service support unit that is not assigned weapons. Or, you may have to tag along with another unit on post that is going to the qualification range. The point: Get onto the range and stay current.)

Retention Control
It is a fact of modern military life that you must continue to move up, or eventually you must move out of the service. A soldier must continue to show potential or face the

Military police provide forward security during a Mobile Operations on Urban Terrain exercise.

inevitable retention control point (RCP), which varies by rank. The best way to avoid the RCP is to remain competitive, as described above. If you are a supervisor, inform your soldiers about the RCP for their ranks, and help them remain competitive as well.

Presently, the RCP is as follows:

- Promotable corporal or specialist—8 years.
- Promotable sergeant—15 years.
- Promotable staff sergeant—22 years.
- Sergeant first class—22 years.
- Promotable sergeant first class—24 years.
- Master sergeant—24 years.
- First sergeant—24 years

Selective Early Release Board (SERB)

The SERB is an end strength tool that is designed to pry senior NCOs from the service. Unfortunately, the individual has no control over whether a SERB is convened. But every senior NCO does have the opportunity to avoid being a SERB target. Suffice it to say that you must be highly competitive to remain at the top of the NCO corps. If you have done everything possible to be as competitive as possible, try harder. Got a bachelor's degree? Get a master's. Already graduated from the Sergeants Major Course? Seek attendance at high-level DOD or sister service courses. When was the last time you qualified with your individual weapon? What was your score on the last semiannual APFT? Have you served in many leadership positions? Do you need to lose weight and have your DA photo retaken? Take a hard, objective look at yourself and determine your level of competitiveness versus your peers'.

SEPARATION ENTITLEMENTS

If you or someone you know happens to be in a specialty that is affected by the Enlisted Voluntary Early Release Program, take an educated look at what is being offered. Consider the entire benefits package, not just the Special Separation Bonus (SSB) or Voluntary Separation Incentive (VSI) money. Ensure that you or your soldier who is affected gets the required counseling prior to separation. Help your soldier think through the decision process. Too many soldiers take the SSB "Cadillac Bonus" money and fail to consider investment or tax advantages of the VSI. The VSI pays less immediately but is worth far more over time.

In May 1994 the Total Army Personnel Command announced the specialties and ranks that would be affected by the 1995 drawdown effort. Thousands of soldiers were affected, including senior master sergeants in the Special Forces and young corporals who faced retention control points. Most of the affected soldiers were mid-career NCOs with 6 to 20 years' service. Many of these soldiers, like the soldiers affected in previous years, focused solely on getting their exit bonus and getting out. If a soldier is set financially and does not have to concern himself or herself with meeting future financial needs, then the SSB might be the way to go. If, however, a soldier is like the vast majority of people who must make ends meet on a monthly basis, the VSI is probably the more sensible exit bonus.

19

Transitions

SEPARATIONS

How and why a soldier is separated from the Army depends on many factors, according to AR 635-200, *Enlisted Personnel*. Separation policies in AR 635-200 promote readiness of the Army by providing an orderly means to accomplish the following:

- Ensure that the Army is served by individuals capable of meeting required standards of duty performance and discipline.
- Maintain standards of performance and conduct through characterization of service in a system that emphasizes the importance of honorable service.
- Achieve authorized force levels and grade distribution.
- Provide for the orderly administrative separation of soldiers in a variety of circumstances.

AR 635-200 "provides the authority for separation of soldiers upon expiration of term of service (ETS); the authority and general provisions governing the separation of soldiers before ETS to meet the needs of the Army and its soldiers; the procedures to implement laws and policies governing voluntary retirement of soldiers of the Army for length of service; and the criteria governing uncharacterized separations and the issuance of honorable, general, and under other than honorable conditions discharges."

The following selected entries are the authorized types of separations under the provisions of AR 635-200:

- *Chapter 4—Separation for Expiration of Service Obligation.* A soldier will be separated upon expiration of enlistment or fulfillment of service obligation.
- *Chapter 5—Separation for Convenience of the Government.* A Chapter 5 separation covers the following: involuntary separation due to parenthood; lack of jurisdiction as ordered by a U.S. court or judge thereof; aliens not lawfully admitted to the United States; personnel who did not meet procurement medical fitness standards; failure to qualify medically for flight training; personality disorders; concealment of arrest record; and failure to meet Army body composition and weight control standards.
- *Chapter 6—Separation Because of Dependency or Hardship.* Soldiers of the Active Army and the Reserve Components serving on active duty or active duty for training

may be discharged or released because of genuine dependency or hardship. Dependency exists when death or disability of a member of a soldier's (or spouse's) immediate family causes that member to rely upon the soldier for principal care or support. Hardship exists when in circumstances not involving death or disability of a member of the soldier's (or spouse's) immediate family, separation from the service will materially affect the care or support of the family by alleviating undue and genuine hardship.

- *Chapter 7—Defective Enlistments, Reenlistments, and Extensions.* This chapter provides the authority, criteria, and procedures for the separation of soldiers because of minority, erroneous enlistment, or extension of enlistment, defective enlistment agreement, and fraudulent entry.
- *Chapter 8—Separation of Enlisted Women for Pregnancy.* Chapter 8 provides authority for voluntary separation of enlisted women because of pregnancy. An enlisted woman who elects to remain on active duty when counseled may, if she is still pregnant, subsequently request separation. Conversely, an enlisted woman who requested separation in writing may subsequently request withdrawal of the separation request.
- *Chapter 9—Alcohol or Other Drug Abuse Rehabilitation Failure.* A soldier who is enrolled in the Alcohol and Drug Abuse Prevention and Control Program for substance abuse may be separated because of inability or refusal to participate in, cooperate in, or successfully complete such a program.
- *Chapter 10—Discharge for the Good of the Service.* A soldier who has committed an offense or offenses punishable by a bad conduct discharge or dishonorable discharge under the provisions of the Uniform Code of Military Justice and the *Manual for Courts Martial* may submit a request for discharge for the good of the service. The request does not prevent or suspend disciplinary proceedings. (See AR 635-200, pages 43–45 for details.)
- *Chapter 11—Entry Level Status Performance and Conduct.* This chapter provides guidance for the separation of personnel because of unsatisfactory performance or conduct (or both) while in entry-level status. It covers inability, lack of reasonable effort, or failure to adapt to the military environment.
- *Chapter 12—Retirement for Length of Service.* A soldier who has completed 20 years' active federal service and who has completed all required service obligations is eligible to retire. Upon retirement, the soldier is transferred to the U.S. Army Reserve Control Group (Retired) and remains in that status until active service time plus control group time equals 30 years, and then is placed on the retired list. A Regular Army soldier who has completed at least 30 years of active federal service will, upon request, be placed on the retired list.
- *Chapter 13—Separation for Unsatisfactory Performance.* A soldier may be separated per this chapter when unqualified for further military service because of unsatisfactory performance, under the following circumstances: (1) the soldier will not develop sufficiently, or (2) the seriousness of the circumstance is such that retention would have an adverse impact on military discipline, good order, and morale, and (3) it is likely that the soldier will be a disruptive influence, and (4) it is likely that the circumstances will continue to recur, and (5) the ability of the soldier to perform duties, including potential for advancement or leadership, is unlikely, and (6) the soldier meets retention medical standards.
- *Chapter 14—Separation for Misconduct.* This chapter establishes procedures for separating personnel for misconduct because of minor disciplinary infractions, a pat-

tern of misconduct, commission of a serious offense, conviction by civil authorities, desertion, and absence without leave. A discharge under other than honorable conditions is normally appropriate for a soldier discharged under this chapter.

• *Chapter 15—Separation for Homosexuality.* This chapter, which has undergone microscopic review during the last several years, remains in effect with changes based upon recent policy guidance. Homosexual conduct is grounds for separation from the Army. (See the section on homosexuality in chapter 12 for more information.)

DISCHARGES

For whatever reason, sooner or later each soldier must quit the service. In this section, we will consider the various types of discharges, the operation of the U.S. Army Transfer facilities, retirement, and veterans' rights.

Honorable Discharge

An honorable discharge is given when an individual is separated from the military service with honor. An honorable discharge cannot be denied to a person solely on the basis of convictions by courts-martial or actions under Article 15 of the Uniform Code of Military Justice. Denial must be based on patterns of misbehavior and not isolated instances. An honorable discharge may be awarded when disqualifying entries in an individual's service record are outweighed by subsequent honorable and faithful service over a greater period of time during the current period of service.

Unless otherwise ineligible, a member may receive an honorable discharge if he or she has, during the current enlistment or extensions thereof, received a personal decoration or is separated by reason of disability incurred in the line of duty.

General Discharge

A general discharge is issued to an individual whose character of service has been satisfactory but not sufficiently meritorious to warrant an honorable discharge. Such persons would have, for example, frequent punishments under Article 15 of the UCMJ or be classified as general troublemakers.

Other than Honorable Discharge

Discharges that fall within this category are given for reasons of misconduct, homosexuality, or security, or for the good of the service and are covered by AR 635-200. No person shall receive a discharge under other than honorable conditions unless afforded the right to present his or her case before an administrative discharge board with the advice of legal counsel.

Uncharacterized Separations

There are two types of uncharacterized separations, those given when a soldier is in entry-level status and those given because of void enlistments or inductions.

Bad Conduct or Dishonorable Discharge

A soldier will be given a bad conduct discharge pursuant only to an approved sentence of a general or special court-martial. A soldier will be given a dishonorable discharge pursuant only to an approved sentence of a general court-martial. The appellate reviews must be completed and the affirmed sentence ordered duly executed. Dishonorable and bad conduct discharges result in expulsion from the Army.

TRANSITION FACILITIES

U.S. Army transfer facilities provide an informal, quiet atmosphere centrally located at a post where personnel being separated may be processed within acceptable time limits. AR 635-10 prescribes that overseas returnees, except retirees, be separated on the first workday after their arrival at the separation transfer point, when possible. Personnel being released from active duty discharged before ETS or the period for which ordered to active duty are separated by the third workday after approved separation. All others are separated on their scheduled separation dates, except for those individuals who elect to be separated on the last workday before a weekend or a holiday.

Medical Examination

There is no statutory requirement for soldiers to undergo a medical exam incidental to separation. It is Army policy, however, to accomplish a medical examination if a soldier is active Army and retiring after 20 or more years of active duty, if a soldier is being discharged or released and requests a medical examination, if review of the soldier's health record by a physician or physician's assistant warrants an exam, or if an examination is required by AR 40-501, *Standards of Medical Fitness*.

Each soldier undergoing separation processing will have his or her medical records screened by a physician, regardless of whether a separation physical has been requested. As a responsible noncommissioned officer, advise your soldiers that a separation physical may be one of the most important medical examinations of their lives. Separation physicals end in a personal interview with a doctor. That interview is the proper time to bring up every single medical fact incident to military service. This interview substantiates service connection should a soldier, after discharge, request disability compensation from the Department of Veterans Affairs based on military service. Above all, each soldier being separated or retired from the service should make a copy of his or her medical and dental records and keep them after discharge.

Career and Alumni Program

The Army Career and Alumni Program (ACAP) is a transition and job assistance initiative located at military sites worldwide. Each ACAP site includes a transition assistance office (TAO) and a job assistance center (JAC), which are available for all Active and Reserve Component soldiers, Army civilians, and military and civilian family members. The TAO provides eligible clients with transition advice and serves as a focal point for problems. The JAC provides clients with job search training, individual assistance and counseling, and a referral service.

Transition Assistance. The TAO synchronizes current preservice transition services on an individual basis to help personnel leaving the Army and provides the following:

- First step in the transition process.
- Individual transition plans.
- Awareness of available resources.
- Defense Outplacement Referral System.
- Federal and public sector job information.

Ideally, the TAO staff likes to see you 180 days before your separation or retirement date, but if that is not possible you are eligible to be seen at the ACAP office until you are discharged from the Army.

Job Assistance. The JAC conducts individual, small-, and large-group workshops to accomplish the following:

- Target your second career.
- Prepare for interviews.
- Find hidden markets for your skills.
- Evaluate job offers.
- Build negotiating skills.
- Teach you to dress for success.
- Track job leads.
- Evaluate employment agencies, job fairs, and automated résumé services.
- Develop your résumé.
- Help with essential correspondence.

Like the TAO staff, the JAC staff encourages you to start the ACAP process 180 days prior to your discharge date.

Employment Network. The Army Employment Network (AEN) is an ACAP database that contains information from employers who are committed to considering Army personnel for employment. The AEN provides the company name, location of all branches of the company, total number of personnel hired annually, the types of positions for which a company hires, points of contact, and in some cases a listing of currently available positions.

The network is linked to regional, federal Office of Personnel Management computers that list federal jobs, and is also tied to the Department of Veterans Affairs, which with the ACAP conducts a combined three-day job training seminar, three-hour training session, and six-hour training workshop. Clients choose the seminar, session, or workshop, depending on their needs and available time. For more information about the ACAP, call toll-free in the continental United States (800) 445-2049. If you are stationed overseas, call DSN 221-0993. If you are an NCO, you should visit your local ACAP office and learn more about the program, then relate it to every soldier you supervise.

RETIREMENT

My sword I give to him that shall succeed me in my pilgrimage, and my courage and skill to him that can get it.   —John Bunyan

The important thing to remember is that, when a soldier puts the uniform into the closet for the last time, he or she does not have to stay in there with it. Those who do often do not last very long. You should begin early in your career to think of retirement not as a thing that comes near the end of active life, but the point of departure between the end of one exciting and fulfilling career and the beginning of another.

Making the Decision

Only you can make the decision to retire. If you are married, you will want to discuss the decision thoroughly with your spouse and family, but in the final analysis, it is you who must submit that application for retirement.

Read the literature on retirement procedures and veterans benefits so that when you arrive at the transfer point for discharge, you will already know what to expect. Do not wait for someone else to tell you what your rights and benefits are. If you are to be retired at a post that does not have a transfer activity, your processing will be done at the local military personnel office, and to an extent, you will be on your own there unless the personnel officer has people as experienced in processing retirements as the commander of a transfer activity.

Submission and Withdrawal of Retirement Applications

Any soldier who has completed 19 or more years' service may apply for retirement. The request must be made within 12 months of the requested retirement date, except that the retirement approval authority is authorized to set a minimum time for submission, which cannot be less than two months before the desired retirement date. Generally, to be eligible, all service obligations incurred as a result of schooling, promotion (unless a waiver is granted), and duty tours must be completed.

A retirement application cannot be withdrawn unless it is established that retaining the soldier concerned will be for the convenience or best interest of the government or will prevent an extreme hardship to either the soldier or his immediate family. The hardship must have been unforeseen at the time of the retirement application. Requests for withdrawal must be fully documented.

Terminal Leave

Deciding whether to take terminal leave may not be an easy decision. Whether to take it depends upon how much leave a soldier has accrued at the time of retirement, how much leave he or she may have previously cashed in for pay, and what plans the retiree may have for job-hunting activities, travel, or vacation.

Personnel taking terminal leave will be allowed to finish processing at the local transfer activity before departure on leave. On the day of retirement, a telephone call from the retiree, verifying his status and whereabouts, is all that is needed to finish outprocessing; the retiree's DD Form 214 will be sent via registered mail. Arrangements to pick up retired ID cards may be made at any military installation.

Allotments

Retirees are permitted to continue allotments that they had in effect while on active duty with few exceptions.

Requests to establish, discontinue, or change an authorized allotment after retirement may be submitted to Retired Pay Operations by letter over your signature. No specific form is required. Forms are provided, however, with USAFAC Pamphlet 20-194, *Retired Pay Information*, a copy of which should be forwarded to you by the Retired Pay Operations, U.S. Army Finance and Accounting Center, Indianapolis, Indiana.

Ceremonies

Each soldier who retires from the U.S. Army is authorized to participate in a retirement review in honor of the occasion. These reviews are generally held on the last day of the month, and all personnel retiring from the service on that day at any specific post or installation are honored at the same special formation. You will be given the option to accept or decline a ceremony during your preretirement processing.

CHAMPUS Entitlement
The spouses and children of retired service personnel continue to remain eligible for CHAMPUS benefits.

Checks
If you do not already have your active-duty paychecks going to a financial institution, consider doing so when you retire. The direct deposit system guarantees the deposit of your retirement check in the bank or credit union of your choice.

Discharge Certificates
Your DD Form 214, *Certificate of Release or Discharge from Active Duty,* is the most important of all the documents you will accumulate during your retirement processing; it is one of the most important documents you will ever receive during your military career. At the time of your retirement you will receive copies 1 (original) and 4 (carbon) of DD Form 214. *Be sure to make copies of these forms and protect the originals.* DO NOT LET THE ORIGINALS OUT OF YOUR POSSESSION.

Military Installation Privileges
Retired members, their dependents, and unmarried surviving spouses are authorized the use of various facilities on military installations when adequate facilities are available. This privilege includes commissary stores, post exchanges, clothing sales stores, laundry and dry-cleaning plants, military theaters, Army recreation services facilities, officer and NCO messes, and medical facilities.

Army regulations regarding exchange and commissary privileges for retired personnel apply overseas only to the extent agreed upon by the foreign governments concerned.

Mobilization Planning
All eligible retired Regular Army personnel are subject to recall to active duty during a time of national emergency.

At the announcement of mobilization, retired personnel will be ordered to active duty in their retired grade. Initially, current medical fitness retention standards will apply until such time as the Secretary of the Army directs the application of mobilization standards.

Pay
There are two ways of computing your retired pay:
- *Retired pay based on length of service:* basic monthly pay multiplied by 2.5 percent times years of active service; up to 75 percent of basic pay.
- *Retired pay based on disability:* basic monthly pay multiplied by the percentage of disability.

Your paycheck will be mailed to you (or to your bank). The Retired Pay Operations Office at Indianapolis will mail a computation form to you when your retired pay account is initially established.

Queries concerning retired pay should be submitted in writing to Commander, USAFAC, ATTN: Retired Pay Operations, Indianapolis, IN 46249. Telephone inquiries may be made by calling (800) 428-2290; Indiana residents call collect, (317) 542-2900.

Retired Personnel Records
Military personnel records for retired personnel (except general officers) are on file at the U.S. Army Reserve Components Personnel and Administrations Center, 9700 Page Boulevard, Saint Louis, MO 63132. All inquiries requesting information from these records should be addressed to the Commander of the USARCPAC and must include as a minimum your full name, grade, Army service number, and Social Security number.

You should, however, make copies of all the important documents in your military personnel file at some point before you retire.

If you should consider that an error or injustice has occurred and desire to request a review of your case by the Army Board for Correction of Military Records, you should apply in writing on DD Form 149, *Application for Correction of Military or Naval Record.* The application should be addressed to Army Board for Correction of Military Records, Department of the Army, Washington, DC 20310.

Survivor Benefit Program (SBP)
The SBP allows retired personnel to provide an annuity to certain designated survivors. Various amounts and types of coverage may be elected, with the maximum being 55 percent of the amount of a member's retired pay at the time of death. These persons may be the widows or widowers, dependent children, or other persons with an insurable interest in a retired soldier. A detailed description of the SBP is provided in AR 608-9.

Travel and Transportation Allowances
Retired Army personnel are authorized travel allowances from their last duty station to their home. Shipment and storage of household goods incident to retirement is authorized on a one-time basis, subject to weight limitations and other controls. Specific information relative to shipment and storage of household goods is contained in DA Pam 55-2, *Personal Property Shipping Information.*

Retired personnel are eligible for space-available travel, category 4, within the continental limits of the United States or DOD-owned or DOD-controlled aircraft. Dependents of retired personnel are not authorized space-available travel on military aircraft flying within the continental limits of the United States and therefore may not accompany retired members on such flights.

Department of Veterans Affairs (Disability) Compensation
If you believe that you have a condition that may entitle you to VA compensation, file your claim at the time of separation. If the VA, upon reviewing your medical records, finds that you do have grounds for seeking compensation, an appointment for a physical exam will be made for you at the Department of Veterans Affairs hospital closest to your retirement home. Your claim will be processed based upon the examination results.

You cannot receive both VA compensation for disability and an Army retirement check. Therefore, the amount of your VA disability is deducted from your regular retirement check (which is issued by the U.S. Army Finance Center). Your monthly income will remain the same, except that part will be paid by the Department of the Army and part by the VA.

Wearing the Uniform, Military Titles and Signatures, Awards, and Decorations

Wearing of the uniform by retired personnel is a privilege granted in recognition of faithful service to the country. Retired personnel may wear the uniform when such wear is considered appropriate.

Retired personnel wear the same uniform prescribed for active-duty personnel. Retired personnel not on active duty may wear the uniform with decorations and awards. Shoulder sleeve insignia are not authorized for wear on the uniform by retired personnel except that the solder sleeve insignia of a former wartime unit may be worn on the right shoulder.

All retired personnel not on active duty are permitted to use their military titles socially and in connection with commercial enterprise. Such military titles must never be used in any manner that may bring discredit to the Army or in connection with commercial enterprises when such use, with or without the intent to mislead, gives rise to any appearance of sponsorship, sanction, endorsement, or approval by the Department of the Army or the Department of Defense.

Retired personnel who have not received the awards to which they are entitled or who desire replacement of items previously issued that were lost, destroyed, or unfit for use without fault or neglect on their part may obtain them upon written application.

Requests should be addressed to the Commander, U.S. Army Reserve Components Personnel and Administration Center, 9700 Page Boulevard, Saint Louis, MO 63132. The application should include a statement or explanation of the circumstances surrounding the loss or nonissue of the items concerned. Replacements are made at cost. No money should be mailed for replacements until you are instructed to do so.

VETERANS' RIGHTS

The benefits discussed in this section are available to *all* veterans regardless of status. All VA benefits (with the exception of insurance and certain medical benefits) payable to veterans or their dependents require that the particular period of service upon which the entitlement is based be terminated under conditions other than dishonorable. Honorable and general discharges qualify the veteran as eligible for benefits. Dishonorable discharges and bad conduct discharges issued by general courts-martial are a bar to VA benefits. Other bad conduct discharges and discharges characterized as other than honorable may or may not qualify depending upon a special determination made by the VA, based on the facts of each case.

In order to prove your eligibility for VA benefits, you must remember to do these things:

- Keep a complete copy of your medical records.
- Protect your DD Form 214, *Discharge Certificate*.

Burial

Burial is available to any deceased veteran of wartime or peacetime service (other than for training) who was discharged under conditions other than dishonorable at all national cemeteries having available grave space, except Arlington Cemetery.

VETERANS BENEFITS TIMETABLE

You Have *(after separation from service)*	Benefits	Where to Apply
Time varies	**GI Education:** The VA will pay you while you complete high school, go to college, or learn a trade, either on the job or in an apprenticeship program. Vocational and educational counseling is available.	Any VA office
10 years	**Veterans Educational Assistance Program:** The VA will provide financial assistance for the education and training of eligible participants under the voluntary contributory education program. Vocational and educational counseling is available upon request.	Any VA office
12 years, although extensions are possible under certain conditions	**Vocational Rehabilitation:** As part of a rehabilitation program, the VA will pay for tuition, books, tools, or other expenses and provide a monthly living allowance. Employment assistance is also available to help a rehabilitated veteran get a job. A seriously disabled veteran may be provided services and assistance to increase independence in daily living.	Any VA office
No time limit	**GI Loans:** The VA will guarantee your loan for the purchase of a home, manufactured home, or condominium.	Any VA office
No time limit	**Disability Compensation:** The VA pays compensation for disabilities incurred or aggravated during military service.	Any VA office
1 year from date of mailing of notice of initial determination	**Appeal to Board of Veterans Appeals:** Appellate review will be initiated by a notice of disagreement and completed by a substantive appeal after a statement of the case has been furnished.	VA office or hospital making the initial determination
No time limit	**Medical Care:** The VA provides hospital care covering the full range of medical services. Outpatient treatment is available to all service-connected conditions, or non-service-connected conditions in certain cases. Alcohol and drug dependence treatment is available.	Any VA office
Time varies	**Burial Benefits:** The VA provides certain burial benefits, including interment in a national cemetery and partial reimbursement for burial expense.	VA national cemetery having grave space, any VA office
No time limit	**Readjustment Counseling:** General or psychological counseling is provided to assist in readjusting to civilian life.	Any Vet Center, VA office, or hospital
Within 90 days of separation	**One-Time Dental Treatment:** The VA provides one-time dental care for certain service-connected dental conditions.	Any VA office or hospital
No time limit	**Dental Treatment:** Treatment for veterans with dental disabilities resulting from combat wounds or service injuries and certain POWs and other service-connected disabled veterans.	Any VA office or hospital
1 year from date of notice of VA disability rating	**GI Insurance:** Low-cost life insurance (up to $10,000) is available for veterans with service-connected disabilities. Veterans who are totally disabled may apply for a waiver of premiums on these policies.	Any VA office
120 days or 1 year beyond with evidence of insurability; or up to 1 year if totally disabled	**Veterans Group Life Insurance:** SGLI may be converted to a 5-year non-renewable term policy. At the end of the 5-year term, VGLI may be converted to an individual policy with a participating insurance company.	Office of Servicemen's Group Life Insurance, 213 Washington St., Newark, NJ 07102, or any VA office
No time limit	**Employment:** Assistance is available in finding employment in private industry, in federal service, and in local or state employment service.	Local or state employment service, U.S. Office of Personnel Management, Labor Department, any VA office
Limited time	**Unemployment Compensation:** The amount of benefit and payment period vary among states. Apply after separation.	State employment service
90 days	**Reemployment:** Apply to your former employer for employment.	Employer
30 days	**Selective Service:** Male veterans born in 1960 or later years must register.	At any U.S. post office; overseas at any U.S. embassy or consulate

Eligible veterans' dependents may receive a headstone or grave marker without charge and shipped to a designated consignee. The cost of placing the marker in a private ceremony must be borne by the applicant. The VA may pay an amount not to exceed the average actual cost of a government headstone or marker as a partial reimbursement for the cost incurred by the person acquiring a nongovernment headstone or marker for placement in a cemetery other than a national cemetery.

Conversion of SGLI to VGLI

A servicemember has 120 days after separation to apply for Veterans Group Life Insurance (VGLI), with no exam requirements. Beyond the 120 days, a soldier has one year to apply, but there are then some exam requirements. During the 120 days after separation, the SGLI coverage continues without premiums.

After five years, the VGLI expires and is not renewable, but before it expires, it can be converted to an individual commercial policy at standard rates, without physical examination or other proof of good health. The Office of Servicemen's Group Life Conversion Notice and a list of participating insurance companies will be sent to you. Hundreds of companies participate in the conversion program.

Employment

Priority referral to job openings and training opportunities is given to eligible veterans, with preferential treatment for disabled veterans. Additionally, the job service assists veterans who are seeking employment by providing information about job marts, OJT and apprenticeship training opportunities, and so on in cooperation with VA regional offices and Veterans Outreach Centers.

Veterans may seek employment with the federal government and receive some breaks when applying for federal employment:

• A five-point preference is given to those who served during any war, in any campaign, in an expedition for which a campaign medal has been authorized, or for 180 consecutive days between January 31, 1955, and October 15, 1976.

• A 10-point preference is given to those who were awarded the Purple Heart, have a current service-connected disability, or are receiving compensation, disability retirement benefits, or pension from the VA.

• A veteran with a 30 percent or more disability may receive appointment without competitive examination with a right to be converted to career appointments and retention rights in reductions in force.

Education Benefits

See your Army Continuing Education Services (ACES) counselor for details on the GI Bill, the Veterans Education Assistance Program (VEAP), and other education benefit programs.

GI Loans

The purpose of VA GI loans is to buy a home; to buy a residential unit in certain condominium projects; to build a home; to repair, alter, or improve a home; to refinance an existing home loan; to buy a manufactured home (with or without a lot); to buy a lot for a manufactured home that you already own; to improve a home through installation of solar heating and/or cooling system or other weatherization improvements; to purchase and simultaneously improve a home with energy-conserving measures; to refinance an existing VA loan to reduce the interest rate; to refinance a manufactured home loan in order to acquire a lot; and to simultaneously purchase and improve a home. Eligibility requirements vary, based on period of service (except that all veterans, to be eligible, must have an other than dishonorable discharge certificate).

The loan terms are subject to negotiation between the veteran and the lender. The repayment period or maturity of GI home loans may be as long as 30 years and 32 days. Newly discharged veterans have certificates of eligibility mailed to their homes by the VA shortly after discharge. Other veterans may secure their certificates by sending VA Form 26-1880, *Request for Determination of Eligibility and Available Loan Guaranty Entitlement,* along with required supporting documents, to the VA regional office nearest them. Active-duty personnel may also take advantage of these loans.

One-Time Dental Treatment
In addition to dental conditions that qualify for treatment because of service connection, veterans are entitled to one-time dental treatment without review of service records to establish service connection. This treatment must be applied for within 90 days of separation. Do not fail to take advantage of this very important benefit. Contact the local VA office and you will be sent a copy of VA Form 10-10, *Application for Medical Benefits.*

Unemployment Compensation
The purpose of unemployment compensation for veterans is to provide income for a limited period of time to help them meet basic needs while searching for employment. The amount and duration of payments vary because they are governed by state laws. Benefits are paid from federal funds. Veterans should apply immediately after discharge at the nearest state employment service, *not* at the VA. A copy of DD Form 214 is needed to establish type of separation from the service.

VA Correspondence and Records
Keep a file of every paper the VA may send you. Your dealings with the VA will require patience and persistence; the degree of either required will depend to a large extent on how busy your local VA office is. Invariably, VA personnel are courteous, and they try to be helpful, but processing your claim may take months.

VA Medical Benefits
The Department of Veterans Affairs offers the whole spectrum of medical benefits to qualified veterans: alcohol treatment; blind aids and services; domiciliary care; drug treatment; hospitalization care for dependents or survivors; nursing home care; outpatient dental treatment; outpatient medical treatment; and prosthetic appliances.

Eligibility criteria for hospitalization gives top priority to veterans needing hospitalization because of injuries or disease incurred or aggravated in line of duty in active service. Veterans who are receiving compensation or who would be eligible to receive compensation (except for retirement pay) who need treatment for some ailment and connected with their service are admitted as beds are available. Under certain circumstances, veterans who were not discharged or retired for disability or who are not receiving compensation and who apply for treatment of a non-service-connected disability may be admitted to a VA hospital. Any veteran with a service-connected disability may receive VA outpatient medical treatment.

Vocational Rehabilitation

Generally, a veteran is eligible for vocational rehabilitation twelve years following discharge or release from active service. A four-year-extension is possible under certain circumstances, and further extensions may be granted for veterans who are seriously disabled when it is determined by the VA to be necessary because of disability and need for vocational rehabilitation.

Eligible disabled veterans may get training up to a total of four years or its equivalent in part-time or combination of part-time and full-time training.

Eligibility for this training is determined by the VA.

Sources
AR 612-10, *Reassignment Processing and Army Sponsorship (and Orientation) Program.*
AR 614-30, *Overseas Service.*
AR 635-10, *Processing Personnel for Separation.*
AR 635-200, *Separations Enlisted Personnel.*
DA Pam 600-5, *Handbook on Retirement Services.*
DA Pam 600-8, *Management and Administrative Procedures.*
VA FS 1S-1, *Federal Benefits for Veterans and Dependents.*

Index